INSANITY FAIR

INSANITY FAIR

by

DOUGLAS REED

JONATHAN CAPE
THIRTY BEDFORD SQUARE
LONDON

FIRST PUBLISHED 1938

JONATHAN CAPE LTD.   30 BEDFORD SQUARE, LONDON
AND 91 WELLINGTON STREET WEST, TORONTO

PRINTED IN GREAT BRITAIN IN THE CITY OF OXFORD
AT THE ALDEN PRESS
PAPER MADE BY JOHN DICKINSON & CO. LTD.
BOUND BY A. W. BAIN & CO. LTD.

CONTENTS

1	JOURNEY'S BEGINNING	7
2	THE WAR CALLED GREAT	24
3	GREEN AND PLEASANT LAND	48
4	PARISIAN ATTIC	53
5	NORTHCLIFFIAN EPISODE	57
6	MUSCLING IN	62
7	GERMAN JOURNEY	67
8	HINDENBURG ON THE RHINE	74
9	GERMAN FREEDOM	81
10	BRENDA MARY	102
11	GRAND OLD MAN	105
12	BRÜNING'S FALL	109
13	PAPEN APPEARS	114
14	HITLER'S VICTORY	117
15	REICHSTAG FIRE	130
16	SPIRIT OF POTSDAM	143
17	NO JEWS IS GOOD JEWS	151
18	MIDSUMMER NIGHTMARE	160
19	MECKLENBURG IDYLL	175
20	HINDENBURG GOES TO VALHALLA	177
21	GERMAN LEAVETAKING	181
22	YEARS THAT THE LOCUST	184
23	HITLER AND EDEN	188
24	MOSCOW EXCURSION	193
25	FEATS OF MEMORY	205
26	NEWSPAPER MEN	207
27	EDEN	211
28	ENGLISH APRIL	216
29	THREE JUST MEN	220
30	GENEVAN SHADOW SHOW	226
31	BOUND FOR DANUBIA	232
32	THE OTHER GERMANY	235
33	SERB SOLILOQUY	254

34	BORIS AND HIS BULGARS	270
35	GRECIAN DETOUR	280
36	GETTING THROUGH THE DARDANELLES	290
37	'TRUTH PREVAILS'	303
38	RUMANIAN RUMINATION	316
39	LITTLE ENTENTE	323
40	MAGYARLAND	328
41	WINDSOR INTERLUDE	334
42	GADARENE GALLOP	339
43	ENGLAND GROPING IN THE DARK	360
44	FIRST MAKE MAD	369
45	FADE OUT	379
	INDEX	381

NONE of the characters in this book is imaginary. They all exist, believe it or not.

None of the opinions expressed in this book commits any third party. They are mine, all mine, and nobody's but mine.

None of the material in this book has been published before, but I wrote a full-length book about the Reichstag Fire, which is briefly discussed in this volume, and it was published (*The Burning of the Reichstag*) by Messrs. Victor Gollancz.

Insanity Fair is to be published in the United States under the title *European Cavalcade*.

6

CHAPTER I

JOURNEY'S BEGINNING

My first glimpse of Insanity Fair was of uniforms and warlike preparations, a fitting introduction for a male of my generation. The jingle-jangle, clip-clop of horse artillery riding out of St. John's Wood barracks are the first sounds I remember hearing. I was being held up at an opposite window to watch the troops leave for South Africa; I think the arms that held me were those of a nurse, so that I must have been in better circumstances then than later. Nineteen years afterwards I leaned against the wall of a Flanders farmhouse, in a drizzling dusk, and watched horse artillerymen with streaming rubber cloaks drive their guns by. The war had finished that morning. The jingle-jangle, clip-clop took me back to the window in St. John's Wood.

The years between those two wars look to me, in retrospect, like a street in Westbourne Grove or some other Victorian suburb. One day like another, one house like another, a grey vista of ugliness and repression. Many Londoners who were born around 1900 must have similar memories. The Berliner has the woods and lakes waiting for him half an hour away. The Viennese carries with him through life the picture of his native hills golden in the sun or white with snow, of becandled Christmas trees in the windows, of priestly processions chanting their way to the Stefansdom with banners of red and gold. The Budapester has his Danube and does not need to be rich to know music, wine and song.

London was too big, you could not escape it. I bicycled furiously, at the week's end, in search of a green and pleasant land. Marble Arch, Maida Vale, Kilburn, Brondesbury, Cricklewood, Hendon, Edgware, Stanmore and other bosky names fell behind me, but when the time came to turn back the promised land still lay over the next horizon. I had found only a belt of pseudo-countryside, flowerless, dusty, with stunted trees. Wherever a green meadow or a shady wood offered a notice forbade me to approach it.

Of country pursuits little was to be seen. The countryfolk devoted their energies to stilling the tea-drinking mania of my compatriots. Every hut and hamlet bore the sign 'Teas'. Once I rode in search of the Thames, the chief river of my native land. After some hours I discovered it at Staines and spent a week's salary on the hire of a punt. This I propelled, until I tired, between a double row of notices offering me tea, forbidding me to land, and threatening me with prosecution. I came back believing that I had had a good day. The lot of a Londoner did not then seem to me insufferable. I knew nothing else. Long afterwards, when I saw other cities and countries, my gorge began to rise. Am I right now or was I right then? Anyway, when people speak longingly of their childhood and youth I feel superior to them, because my own were so dull that the present is infinitely preferable. I feel that I am living on an ascending, they on a descending scale of happiness. Those grey London years, before I sailed down Southampton Water bound for France, are like the wasteful blank pages that inexplicably begin most books.

For I am a Londoner. My father came from the West Country and my mother from Ireland, but I was born in St. John's Wood and spent nearly all my days before the war between Shoot Up Hill, a pleasant name, strangely bestowed before the Petrol Age, and St. Paul's. Only once, when I was very young, did we go to live at Southend, where the sea at stated times retires out of sight. On these vast mud flats I wandered, and saw with quaking heart a drowned man fished out of the sea. Here my infant sister fell face downward while paddling in the fringes of the sea, during one of its rare visitations, and my mother with piercing cries rushed in her heavy flounced skirts and petticoats to rescue her, and, scarlet-faced and shamed by so much commotion, I drove home with them in a brougham. Here my father told me how he had kicked

8

his top hat all the way down Queen Victoria Street on Mafeking Day and on Mafeking Night had transplanted a 'To Let' board from the garden of an empty house to the forecourt of the little church which we attended on Sundays.

I was certainly in better circumstances then, for I went to a school which now claims to rank among the public schools of England, and in England public schools draw their scholars from a narrow moneyed class. The head master habitually dressed like a Scottish dominie caricatured by *Punch*. With long hair and beard, a tam o'shanter, and a cloak streaming behind him, he stalked about the windy streets, a picture of stern and wild Scottish righteousness, and deeply impressed the matrons of Southend.

One morning he assembled the whole school in the main hall for an unknown purpose and, gaunt and terrifying, to my uneasy surprise called for 'Douglas Reed' to step forward. I was about nine years old. I stepped out and stood, the focus point of invisible dotted lines running from the curious eyes of a hundred schoolfellows. In a breathless silence the dominie spoke. I had in my possession a toy cannon; where had I got it? I had indeed a small toy cannon, worked by a spring, which I had found during playtime the day before behind a tree in the playground and had shown with much glee to other boys. I told him this. 'You lie,' said he. 'No, it's true,' I answered. 'You lie.' 'No, it's true.' 'You lie,' thundered the dominie, 'you took it from another boy's desk.' A figure of righteous wrath, he pointed a long bony finger at me, and shouted, 'Tell the truth, tell the truth!' The deity that punishes bad boys seemed to have taken earthly shape. I had an awful feeling of guilt. So holy a man could not be wrong. He roared louder, 'Did you take it from another boy's desk? Say yes!' 'Yes,' I said. I was thrashed before the school. I dared not tell my parents; they would never believe me, I thought. Some distrust of myself, which I only conquered many years later, dated from this time.

We came to London. I went to another school, in Kilburn.

9

This school was public, but not a public school. All might attend it. It was free, though for the benefit of those who strove after superiority it had a separate department where the scholars paid two shillings a week, and to this I belonged. Although we had a common playground and fell over each other's legs a great social gulf was fixed between the two-shilling boys and the free boys and we never mixed. The head master was an estimable man who habitually stood at the door through which we filed after playtime and at random picked a boy here and a boy there for a box on the ears that sounded like a pistol shot. To receive one of these unmerited buffets from the good Dr. Nairn counted on balance as a distinction. We never bore him malice and thought of him in after years with mild affection. If boys feel that a master is mean in his soul and hates them they loathe him but if their instinct tells them that he is ultimately a just man they respect him and don't give a hoot for his canings.

Stands St. Augustine's where it stood? Red brick Gothic in a grey Georgian world of Avenues and Terraces, that in their drooping lace curtains and coy aspidistras belie these fair and verdant names. Cross housewives and pinched servants toiling on their knees to give a transient whiteness to the sacred front steps, their behinds turned to the blue sky and the trees. All else could be ugly and dingy, the house could be dirty without and dark within, but the front steps had to be white and the woman who did not laboriously hearthstone them in the morning was a slattern and the butt for her neighbours' malice.

Is the 'recreation ground' with its sparse grass and tortured shrubs still there, and the bright yellow cake with bright pink icing, a slab even bigger than a man's hand for a penny?

One day I shall brave Edgware Road, Maida Vale and the Kilburn High Street and go and see if St. Augustine's, with other great British institutions, has survived a world war unchanged. I hardly know what I learned there. The curriculum was a simple one, meant for boys who were going to become clerks and shopkeepers and would not need to know very much.

Reading I hardly needed to learn, for it is an inborn passion; arithmetic I have never yet learned; history, although I then habitually gained top marks by reciting parrotwise pages of dates which I immediately afterwards forgot, I can only retain by seeing the places where things have happened; geography only came to me years later through travel. Classical education was none; and if any undeveloped talent for music, painting, or sculpture ever lurks in the boys who go to such schools it must, save in a case of genius, be efficiently nipped in the bud.

But when I was thirteen I left St. Augustine's and began to earn my living. One day I was a schoolboy, wearing the unsuitable clothes that were my penance for my parents' belief that we belonged to a superior class: the shopkeepers called these garments Eton Jackets and my derisive schoolmates called them bumfreezers. The next day, my fingers still tingling from Mr. Nairn's congratulatory parting handshake, I had begun to serve a term as office-boy to a publishing firm.

I continued to wear my only suit, the bumfreezer with the Fauntleroyan collar, for several months, until my employers made me the vehicle of a protest to my parents. Then I was bought a brown trouser suit the jacket of which, to my grief, was not slit at the back as were those of all the other men in my immediate circle whom I held to be really well dressed; why, I complained to myself, did my parents insist in making me conspicuous.

I was paid eleven shillings a week. Five years later, when I was eighteen, this had risen to eighteen shillings. When I was sixteen I obtained a post at thirty shillings a week, but my employers would not part with me without the full month's notice to which the law entitled them because they paid me my fourteen weekly shillings monthly, and my prospective new employer would not wait.

About eight in the morning I left the mass-produced street in Brondesbury, which looks like the Dionne quintuplets carried to infinity, where we lived, and by means of a circuitous railway journey with long walks at either end reached the Strand, where the publisher had his office. About seven-thirty in the evening I returned. Later I went and returned by bicycle, haring down Maida Vale and through Hyde Park, past posters that said 'Bleriot flies the Channel' or 'Sinking of the *Titanic*', and darting in and out of the traffic in emulation of the evening newspaper runners, those trick-cyclists of the streets in pre-war London.

My days I spent in typing letters, running messages, sticking on stamps, running up to the storerooms where the books were kept in brown paper packages on racks. The smell of those dust-covered shelves is with me now. I had an hour for lunch, but ten minutes was usually enough to eat a pork pie and then I retired with three sticks of chocolate cream to a window ledge on the top story of the publishing house, a vantage point among the chimney pots with a glimpse of the Strand where I was for a moment captain of my soul. All the contents of the dusty racks were at my disposal. I followed Napoleon to Moscow, Murat to Pozzo and Bernadotte to Sweden; I went with Scott to the South Pole, shared his despair at finding that Amundsen had got there first, and I went out into the snow with Oates; I sailed in the *Cutty Sark* and walked with Brummel along Haymarket, jibing at his fat friend; I was besieged in Ladysmith, but never lost my faith in Bobs, whom I had seen cutting down mutineers in India; I communed with Shakespeare, St. Francis of Assisi and Borrow; Anthony Hope took me to tea with Miss Dolly and I marvelled at their gift of idle repartee. Taking books at random from the shelves, my mind consumed a prodigious literary Irish Stew.

When the clock struck two I had to leave this brave world with its spacious horizon and climb down from my crow's nest to a nether world of endless boredom. The minutes trailed by on leaden feet until six o'clock. Opening letters, typing letters, closing letters, sticking stamps on letters. I loathed it and, continually reproached, I had an ineradicable feeling of guilt about myself. The manager had the same effect on me as the dominie at Southend, although he looked quite different, with his neatly brushed grey hair, his pince-nez, his striped trousers and morning coat. One day, opening the morning mail, I threw into the wastepaper basket an envelope containing a cheque. A summons to the presence, words of stern reproach that I could be so forgetful of all that had been done for me. I was fifteen. I fetched my overcoat and walked along Essex Street, under the archway, down the steps, through the passage where the blind man stands, to the Embankment. A cold November sun glinted on the Thames. I stopped to contemplate His Majesty's Ship *President*, that stationary barque where city clerks of a seafaring bent do physical jerks in the evenings as Naval Volunteers. How many generations of office boys have woven their dreams about the *President*, wished that it would suddenly leave its moorings and take them with it, far away to a world of spacious skies and sunny strands.

Then I went on, across Blackfriars Bridge, bound for Dover. The London Docks never occurred to me, so hamstrung is the mind of a London boy; he may work for years alongside the Thames at Blackfriars and never know where are the docks or how to get to them, never see the steamers white and gold but only dull barges trailing behind puffing tugs. Dover was the place for a boy who meant to run away to sea. Running away to sea was a brave, flashing jewel that I had long kept in a private casket at the back of my mind. But now that the moment had come I found that it was not easy. How did you run away to sea? I did not know. At last the word 'Dover' suggested itself. It had a salty tang; the Dover Road was a romantic place, a good approach to so great an undertaking, with a sinister inn where strange adventures, as I remembered from a breathless evening at the Lyceum, had befallen Henry Irving. At Dover would be ships.

So Dover it was. I knew that it lay vaguely somewhere southeast of London, so I tacked to port at the end of Blackfriars Bridge and set my course for Southwark and the Old Kent Road. I had but a few pence. A pawnbroker in a side street gave me three shillings for my overcoat. In brown suit, shiny starched collar and bowler hat I plodded on. Greenwich already reeked of the sea and boasted of Nelson; my spirits rose and I greeted Greenwich as one seafaring man greeting another. My feelings were mingled, of awe at what I had done, elation at finding myself bound for Dover when I should have been licking stamps, and trepidation about the future. At Crayford dusk and a drizzle began to fall together. At Dartford I found a Sailors' and Soldiers' Home and a pretty girl in charge of it, whose friendliness would have enchanted me a few years later but now embarrassed me when I only wanted to avoid notice. She gave me supper for a few pence, smoothed the sheet and thin coverlet on a plank bed that cost another sixpence, and in the morning sped me on my way with hot coffee and a quick hug with one arm. She asked no questions.

The Dover Road belied its promise. Coming through Rochester I asked a burly cheerful policeman where it was, and regretted this immediately when he asked me what I was about. My trousers were muddied half-way to the knee, the bowler hat was turning soft with the rain. The feeling of guilt that had always accompanied me since the incident of the toy cannon overwhelmed me and I went scarlet as I told him 'I'm on a walking tour'. 'In those clothes' he said ironically. Then he pointed the way, turned on his heel and without another word went on his business. I continued on mine. The Dover Road lay glistening and grey between muddy brown fields. I was cold and wet. In Maidstone I spent my last few pence on biscuits and chocolate. The daylight began to fail and I had to find somewhere to sleep. I passed through the town and on the farther side came to a row of half-built houses, the twins of those I had left behind me in Brondesbury. On the plank flooring of a doorless and windowless backroom I tried to sleep. I grew colder and colder and ached in every joint. I didn't sleep a wink. Shivering, thirsty and hungry, I got up when I thought dawn must be near and started off again for Canterbury. By the afternoon I had shot my bolt. Dover seemed far off and uncertain, night was again at hand: I had eaten hardly any-

thing that day and saw no prospect of finding a place to sleep.
I turned back. London had beaten me. I trudged back
through the night and the next day and came into London on
the next evening. I came through Poplar, with its crowded
Jewish streets and smelly naphtha flares, and here, one of the
meanest places in London, a grand Guardee officer came
striding towards and past me — scarlet and blue, tall bearskin
on his head, sword and gold braid. An unusual sight anywhere
in England, where officers in uniform are only seen in barracks
or in processions, but stranger still in dingy Poplar.

I forgot that I was hungry and cold and miserable and tasted
glory for a moment, as most boys do when they see a uniform.
I knew him. He was a Jew. Somewhere in Hampstead existed
at that time a thing called a cadet battalion — somehow I had
come to belong to it. Its members, embryonic week-end
soldiers, were boys under sixteen. They had rifles, red coats,
and even — sheer bliss — busbies. Mine were lying at home
now, as I came through Poplar. We had two Jewish officers,
both bespectacled, one very tall and thin, one short and plump.
I had met the tall and thin one, on his homeward way from
some parade. What stirred this martial enthusiasm in them?
England's need? The title of Lieutenant? The thought of a
uniform almost as grand as that of a Guards officer and pro-
curable cheaply from cousin Moss in Covent Garden? Who
knows. I knew many Jews later, in the war, and they were
neither better nor worse, braver nor less brave than the others.

I crept through the city, along Oxford Street and Edgware
Road, came to a Brondesbury deserted by all save marauding
cats, let myself in with my latchkey and was found dead asleep
the next morning by my father, who had spent some harassing
days. Next day the stamp-sticking began again. For a time I
was regarded with the respect due to a near-runaway and
reproofs became fewer. I still regret that I had not the
gumption to complete that adventure.

The routine of boredom was resumed. The same trivial
tasks presented themselves at the same times, like parts on a

moving belt in a factory. I lived for the evenings and Saturday afternoons — less for Sundays, which I had come to connect with compulsory church going, raindrops trickling down window panes, and the most mournful sound I know — that of a barrel-organ in a London suburban street.

But the evenings were different. I courted death by my bicycle dashes from the Strand to Brondesbury. I finished work at six, and by seven I reckoned to have reached home, swallowed a cup of tea, changed into flannels, and continued my journey to Willesden, where behind a gaunt black fence was a large field where many men played cricket. In the height of the summer, and failing rain, you could count on two hours of daylight and here, as long as a man could see the ball, I stood, for the most part vainly waiting for it to come to me. I had then an unquestioning and impressionable mind and had acquired a fervent belief in the paramountcy among sports of this grim game, which sometimes remains unfinished after three days of languid combat. To be critical about cricket was then to show yourself a heretic, but no methodical effort to produce good cricketers was ever made. Athletics were a closed book at the schools I went to, and in many of the Continental cities I have since come to know I have envied the unmoneyed young men their opportunities for developing their bodies and learning to run, jump and swim.

In the winter you went to the pictures or the Kilburn Empire. The pictures offered darkness and armchairs made in pairs, so that no dead upholstered arm intervened between yourself and the girl you took with you; you watched Mary Pickford go with the jerky movements of a robot to some romantic tryst and ate chocolates at $7\frac{1}{2}$d. a quarter-pound.

At the Kilburn Empire you booked a front seat in the circle at 1s. 3d., and set out soon after supper time, freshly washed and brushed, with a pleasurable feeling of anticipation to attend the second house. In the circle you were a gentleman; Ethiopia was hardly more remote or more unknown to you than the gallery. George Robey cocked a knowing eye and sang 'Swish'

while the well-bred among the audience told each other con-
fidentially that he was an Oxford man. Harry Champion hit
the bull's-eye of British humour by singing about boiled beef and
carrots. Charlie Chaplin as the drunken swell fell out of his
stage-box in the Mumming Birds' stage-on-a-stage sketch.

The audience applauded everything: I never remember dis-
approval. A Hebrew comedian, who caricatured the most
marked facial and other characteristics of the Jews, was en-
thusiastically received; so was the gentle and magnanimous
Jew in 'Only a Jew' who triumphed over his Gentile adversary
in a stupendous life-and-death struggle in which the two threw
lamps, chairs and practically everything else on the stage at
each other. Manly or patriotic sentiments, lustily sung, were
enough to gain applause that genius might often have envied.
A large man in a red shirt, riding breeches and sombrero, a
simple soul from the great open spaces, regularly brought down
the house by singing this verse:

> My father was a white man
> Who bore an honoured name,
> My mother was a paleface
> Whose life was without shame:
> I never will disgrace them,
> Temptation I'll defy,
> I'll always be a white man,
> A white man till I die-hie.

Another, a retired colonel who in retirement could not break
himself of the habit of wearing his regimental mess kit, came on
the stage accompanied by two ladies who from the circle passed
easily as his nieces and moved a 1912 audience, to whom King
George was practically unknown, almost to tears with this
refrain:

> 'God save the King!'
> Can't you hear them shouting,
> Can't you hear them shouting

As the King goes by
'God save the King!'
That's the song they sing.
'Long live the King!'
Is the nation's loving cry.

I liked it as much as any of them. I felt a better man afterwards.
When the war came, and I took the first opportunity to show my
khaki in a stall at the Kilburn Empire, I felt I had never heard
nobler sentiments than these, sung by a large blonde in a pink
dress:

We don't want to lose you
But we think you ought to go,
For your King and your Country
Both need you so.
We shall want you and miss you,
But with all our might and main
We shall hug you, squeeze you, kiss you,
When you come back again.

To which my same self ten years later would have answered
gently but firmly: 'Sez you.'

King Edward died and the tolling of bells in the early
morning, as I was dressing for the office, brought tears to my
father's eyes, although I had never deemed him to be deeply
patriotic. I watched the funeral. Down the Edgware Road
came the music of Chopin's funeral march, then slow-stepping
guardsmen and then, between the comic metal helmets of an
English county regiment, I saw the coffin go past, and the
kings follow it. King George, then little known, looking cold
and pinched; Kaiser Wilhelm, upright and self-conscious,
glancing or glaring about him; King Alfonso, with his pendulous Habsburg lower lip and slouched shoulders and his
cocked hat on the back of his head.

I stayed up all night to make sure of a front place on the
kerbstone in Whitehall for the Coronation and then was

driven away by the police just before the procession began, so that in the end I only got glimpses of it between masses of other people's heads by straining my tiptoes to the utmost. But I saw, for the first time, Edward Prince of Wales, pink and boyish in his coronation robes, with his brothers and sisters all crammed into the same lumbering gala coach.

Life was a gloomy corridor that began in Brondesbury and ended in the Strand and had no exits, only an occasional tiny window through which came a glimpse of a wider world. I did not grow much after I was thirteen; days spent in dark and stuffy storerooms and snatched meals of hamrolls and chocolate cream saw to that. At Easter and Whitsun I put metal clips round my trouser ankles and pedalled hard in search of quiet meadows, streams to bathe in, shady groves. I never found them, and innumerable boards warning me that I should be prosecuted if I trespassed made me feel guilty to look for them. Once a year I had a fortnight's holiday and sometimes went to Hove, which, like a lady who has married beneath herself, averts a shuddering face from her lusty plebeian spouse, Brighton. At Hove my grandfather, for some reason hidden from me, lived in a big house with many servants and a marvellous garden. Across the garden wall came the sharp clipped report of bat meeting ball, for here Sussex County had their home. With awe I heard that my father had once played for the Gentlemen of Sussex. A curtain was lifted, and I peeped for a moment into a finer and brighter world, as I did too when my mother, who set much store by such things, told me of a kinsman, so distant that he seemed enchanted, who had achieved a Jamaican judgeship and of another who as a Catholic Bishop had blessed the body of the Prince Imperial — that Prince who may or may not have had the blood of the Bonapartes in his veins, and was killed in the Zulu war.

I sometimes called on my grandfather, in awe and trepidation, for he was a daunting figure with his bald head and mutton chop whiskers. He was normally irritable, lived to be over eighty, and in his last years was furious when a doctor, telling him that these now were numbered, sought to console him with the remark 'After all, you've had a pretty good innings'. From that moment the sound of the cricket balls, coming over the garden wall, must have had a sinister ring for him. Like a local Dick Whittington he had been thrice mayor of Hove and he must have been a man of progressive mind, for I was proudly told that he was responsible for the bandstand on the front and even for the Hove lawns, a modest green carpet laid down in his time between the gaunt Georgian terraces and the knobbly beach. Some time before the war he died and my respect for him, the worthy representative of a long line of prosperous west-country lawyers, increased in death as I read in the 'Wills' column of the *Daily Mail* that he had left a large fortune. I showed the cutting with pride to my fellow office boys in the publishing house and my stock with them rose steeply. Such is the power of reflected glory, for not a penny of the many thousands trickled through to my family, far less to me, until twenty-five years later, when the death of an aunt brought a very modest legacy.

After five years a first modest bid for freedom was successful. In 1914 I became a junior clerk in Lloyds Bank. I earned nearly a pound a week and after a few months I was to have thirty shillings. I had begun to climb the social ladder, several rungs of which lay between office-boy and bank clerk. Vistas undreamed of opened to me. I could now aspire to play bank cricket, which meant a great field unshared by other teams, your name in obscure corners of the newspapers, a pavilion to change in and an exquisite though tormenting walk from the pavilion to the wicket, a blazer in mauve and green which had only the drawback of resembling too closely the colours vaunted by Mrs. Pankhurst and her suffragettes.

Still moving up the social ladder, I became a Saturday afternoon soldier as a private in the Artists' Rifles. This was one of those military formations, apparently peculiar to England, reserved to persons of superior social standing. I am still not sure how I came to get in, since the unwritten law was that the recruit should have a public school education, and the man without this advantage who found himself in a company of others from the public schools in pre-war England usually felt like one of Bateman's subjects, the Guardsman who dropped his rifle on parade, or something of that sort. The cult of the public school fetish was at its height and I had absorbed a real veneration for this superior class from reading this sort of statement: 'The British private soldier will follow a public school man into hell but not a ranker wallah.'

Later, in the war, I remember an officer of foreign extraction, who had acquired an English name at its outbreak, who was wont to expatiate on the merits of a public school upbringing with tears in his eyes. I do not think he liked me much, and thought he indicated the reason when one winter's day, while we were digging reserve trenches in France, he asked me pointedly before the others what school I had been to. And another time, when we were in billets in a bleak Flanders village, he called me aside and strongly reproved me for going about with a drummer. The bandsmen were hired men and proletarians.

However, my fellow Artists were good enough to me, and thankfully I went shooting and marching with them on Saturdays. Archduke Franz Ferdinand had been murdered at Serajevo and the summer was full of rumours of war. So the Artists were all agog when, on the first Saturday in August, they and all England's volunteer soldiers set out for their yearly fortnight's training in camp. I was nineteen and I hoped against hope that war would come as we detrained at Salisbury Plain. I had nothing against Germany. I had only known four Germans in my life. They lived at a boarding-house near my home in Brondesbury and on summer evenings in 1913 and 1914 they used to stand at the garden gate and talk with me and my friends of the war that was coming, of the way that Germany was going to pulverize England, of the secret things that Germany had in store for that great day. We neither took this talk seriously nor amiss nor gave it a second thought.

21

But now, as I sang 'Who were you with last night?' lustily with Artists, London Scots and others in a great marquee at Salisbury, I longed for war. It would mean that I should not have to go back to the bank, that this glorious fortnight would be indefinitely prolonged, that I should see foreign countries. Brought up on pictures of dying soldiers pressing the folds of a Union Jack to their lips and exclaiming 'England, my England', I had no idea what war meant. To me it spelt freedom.

The sun went down in a blaze of red that I shall never forget and as I lay trying to sleep on the unaccustomed ground the noise of a motor car broke the stillness of the night. It grew louder and louder, chugged into the camp, and stopped.

'War', I thought. It was. Next day we trained back to town, went home for a few hours to pay farewells and then set out again for mobilization and an unknown future. A soldier on active service, I turned out of the garden gate of the little house in Brondesbury, one of the thousands that stretch in endless facsimile in those streets. I never saw it again. I had packed my pack as foursquare as I could get it, and from one end of it hung and clattered an enamel mug which would not go in but was essential, as my instructions told me, to a campaigning soldier. My sister, a child of fifteen with her hair in two stiff plaits, came bareheaded with me as far as the corner. When I next saw her she was a married woman. At the hardware store there we parted and I turned down the Kilburn High Road for the last time.

The corridor had opened. I lay for a week on the hard boards of a schoolroom floor in St. Pancras and drilled in the asphalt playground; I toiled over Hampstead Heath and slept in alcoves at Lord's Cricket Ground built originally for the hungry relatives of Etonians and Harrovians; I stood guard at the Tower of London, and I rushed about fields at Bricket Wood at intervals falling on my stomach and dispatching with unerring aim hordes of imaginary Germans who offered themselves as targets at a distance not too near to be unpleasant nor too far to make marksmanship difficult. In the war no attacks of this kind were made; and I only once saw a German who gave me a chance of a potshot.

One October afternoon, as we were drilling in the fields, a motor cycle came up the lane at speed and stopped alongside. 'France', I thought. A few hours later I was handing a postcard for my parents to a man on South Kensington station in the few moments that our train stopped there.

That night I stood for the first time on a ship — my imagination afire. It was a cattleboat and I stood in the prow as it moved down Southampton Water. The night was dark, no lights were shown, the shore was a shapeless mass a little darker than the night itself. Suddenly a searchlight struck across the water, like a magician's wand, and turned the little steamer, with its dungy smell, into a dazzling white barque, filled with statuesque knightly figures that looked silently at the land they were leaving, some for the first, many for the last time. Then the white ship slipped through the beam and was lost in the darkness beyond.

CHAPTER 2

THE WAR CALLED GREAT

I GAZED with sleepy but eager eyes at the picture framed by the round metal rim of the porthole. The smooth and silent. sea; a city, soft and golden in a misty dawn; a jetty, with a lighthouse, and, indifferently watching our incoming ship, a solitary soldier in baggy red trousers, long-skirted coat and kepi. France. Boulogne. We bumped against the great wooden baulks, gangways slithered out, I felt the cobbles beneath my feet for the first time, and feasted insatiable eyes on the people and things I saw. Technically I had shared in the retreat from Mons and qualified for the Mons Star.

The Artists marched to an open place and there, self-conscious under the measuring gaze of the townsfolk, piled arms, a trying operation for inexpert spare-time soldiers; seldom are the tripods of rifles assembled without some of them suddenly crashing to pieces. Then we stood about and stood about. The officers walked up and down. Nothing happened. We had not breakfasted and were hungry. A fellow Londoner and myself sidled off to a grocer's shop a few yards away. We found that we had learnt French perfectly at school. 'Des sardines. Des biscuits. Du chocolat.' It was easy. Our pockets full we left the shop and found that the Artists had gone to the war. They had vanished. Our rifles and packs had vanished with them.

Now our French failed us. The townsfolk met the panic-stricken inquiries of two youths in khaki with tranquil incomprehension. We rushed through the streets at random. By the grace of God we came on the battalion tramping to the station. We fell into the ranks, struggled frenziedly like Laocoon with the serpentine coils of our webbing equipment, seized our rifles from cursing comrades. At the station, the crushing obloquy of the company commander fell upon us, already scarlet with heat and guilt. We were on active service now, he thundered.

Did we know what crime we had committed? Desertion on active service! Did we know the penalty for that?

Good God, we thought, is he going to have us shot before we have been half an hour in France? The horrors of war rose vividly before our eyes. Chastened we filed with the others into the cattletrucks that are made to carry forty men or ten horses, and these rumbled off slowly towards Flanders.

We marched and drilled in Flanders fields, the towers of Bailleul dominating our daily life, while a pom-pom spat futile puffs of white smoke at the first frail German aeroplanes, and these dropped their first futile jampot bombs that made little holes in ploughed fields. Twenty-two years later hundreds of Abyssinians and Spaniards and Chinese were being killed by a single bomb.

We slept in lofts and granaries and greenhouses, while eastward shell-fire grumbled intermittently through the night. We turned out sleepily for a rush to the front when it swelled to a continuous roar and went back to bed again when it dwindled.

We went up over the frozen Lys to Armentières and into the trenches, whose inhabitants, the survivors of the first British army that went to France, looked like bears in their shaggy goatskin coats. I slept soundly in a little dugout built mainly of ten-pound tins of corned beef. Hardly a shot disturbed the quiet. We came out, and in a chilly December dawn Pigeon Rust, the company sergeant-major, stripped to the skin in a Flanders courtyard and took a bath in a bucket of cold water.

One by one the Artists disappeared, to officer-depleted front line battalions. Men who had marched beside us one day vanished and we saw them the next with the star on their shoulders, or read their names under 'Officers killed' in the casualty lists. Drafts from home replenished the battalion strength, and we were withdrawn to St. Omer, British headquarters. Here we spat and polished, paraded in the Grand' Place each morning, and marched off in separate guards to give the approaches to the town that protection which its dignity as the seat of British headquarters demanded. I was a lance-corporal with one stripe, and no colonel ever led his battalion more proudly than I marched behind my three good men and true.

For many months we watched the roads, railways and canals entering the town. If a German regiment or a car full of German officers had tried to enter St. Omer we should have been ready for them, but none ever did, and if any German agents came to St. Omer they presumably used the great open spaces between the carefully guarded means of obvious approach. So diversions were rare in these long watches.

Once an elderly officer with a muffler concealing his tabs came out of the town for a stroll along the poplar-lined canal path, asked me what I did in civil life, and other things, and went his way without showing the requisite pass. I demanded it again, and his companion, a tall and handsome staff officer, turned back and said, 'Don't you know who that is? It's Sir John French'. This was Major Fitzgerald, who went down with Kitchener in the *Hampshire*.

Well, I thought, the Commander-in-Chief ought to be the first man to comply with orders. Yet I did not feel equal to arresting the Commander-in-Chief. So they went down the path under the poplars and a moment later another man, in a quasi-military uniform, came through the guard. This was the detective whose duty was to follow Sir John French, but whom Sir John French could not bear to see. He pursued his charge like a deer-stalker, stealing from poplar to poplar in his efforts to remain unseen. Soon afterwards this curious procession returned, saluted with presented arms by the entire guard.

Another figure came down the path under the poplars, running. A slight boyish figure with a pink face, thin putteed legs beneath guardee knickerbockers, jog, jog, jogging along the bridle path. For the second time I saw the Prince of Wales. With that excess of zeal which Talleyrand rightly deprecated, I turned out the guard and presented arms. The runner changed his trot to a walk and saluted, but an unfriendly look from the Royal eye, as I thought, travelled across the moss-covered sluice gates.

The elderly French reservists who shared the watch with us looked after him, shrugged incomprehending shoulders, and when their relief arrived related what they had seen with fluent gestures, caricaturing the action of the runner's legs and arms with movements that the baggy red trousers and shapeless blue coats made doubly grotesque.

Kitchener came, and Millerand, and I lay on a hillock under a blazing sun and watched as they inspected the Brigade of Guards, drawn up on a plateau above St. Omer. In the immobile phalanx of rigid men some detail jarred, like a missing rail in a fence, and my eye roved about until I found what it was: a Guards officer saluting with his left hand because his right arm was missing.

The eastward wind brought the grumble of the guns, and troops continuously passed through to the front; but I sunned myself on the terrace of the café in the Grand' Place, held Georgette's hand in the estaminet, and when I drew my occasional ten francs hired one of the boats in which the peasants brought the vegetables to markets, and propelled it with a spade-headed pole along rush-lined canals and waterways. With Baby Allen and Frank Reynolds I found an idyllic retreat, a patch of lush grass, rush screened, at a place where the water widened and was clear, and we bathed naked, scandalizing some peasant women who came by in a boat. They did not see another full summer, Allen, lively as a cricket, and Reynolds, a dreamer.

My turn came. I found myself, as the walnuts ripened, in a restful château, learning to be an officer. I learned to read the stars, to find my way by compass at night, to make a sketch-plan of the countryside, and other things that I was glad to know but found no use for in that war. As a promising pupil, I commanded my fellow cadets on a Cook's tour to the trenches, at Hooge. We came at an unhealthy moment. I shared a trench bay with a private of the Worcestershires, an old soldier, steady, grizzled, resigned. Wrapped in a blanket, I lay on the fire-step while heavy shelling rocked the trench, splashed

27

dirt in my face, grazed my nose with a tiny fragment of metal.

The old soldier told me not to be afraid. I was not, very much. I was still master of my nerves, and ready to lie there without flinching until a howitzer shell fell on me, although this would not have helped the British Empire. If you are young, in good health and have not been much bombarded, steadiness under fire is not difficult; but I admire those men, like my old soldier companion, who know what a bombardment is and does and still remain master of themselves.

In the next bay was a machine-gunner. He was at the end of his nerves and shivered as if with ague. He survived that night, at all events. And next evening I led my first command back to the quiet château. I was still dead asleep when the Commandant, who feared we had had heavy casualties in the liveliness at the front, cantered round for information; and again I suffered heavy rebuke. I always had an unfortunate talent for antagonizing senior officers.

At last I pinned the gold stars on my shoulders, buckled a leather belt around my rough private soldier's jacket, and, with Allen and Reynolds, found myself travelling by Pullman Car to London, surrounded by fellow officers whom my arm still itched to salute. We were second lieutenants in the Sherwood Foresters. What memories of Robin Hood led me to pick that name from the list of regiments? Anyway, I chose it, and the others followed suit. We belonged to that between-decks class which England had devised in her hour of need, and for which she simultaneously found the name of temporary gentlemen. 'Gentleman' and 'of independent means,' as Karl Silex remarked in his study of England through German eyes, are in England interchangeable terms. I had £50 to buy myself a uniform, more money than I had ever had, and I revelled in spending it. I lolled in a stall at the Hippodrome, the chorus girls tripped along a gangway built over the stalls, and I recognized in one a demure neighbour from Brondesbury. I became acquainted with a stage-door and she saw me off when the train for the front left Victoria.

At the head of our Nottinghamshire and Derbyshire miners Allen, Reynolds and I trudged along the muddy road from Poperinghe to Ypres, where the gaunt ruin of the Cloth Hall reared itself against grey Flanders skies. We went to the trenches; we stayed four days; we returned to billets. Trenches, billets, trenches, billets, all through the winter and spring of 1914 and 1915, and we never saw a German. Our men were undersized, bow-legged, dour, cynical, the underfed heirs of England's era of greatest prosperity, the slaves of Old King Coal; they had the hearts of lions, never showed emotion and would stand any hardship, but bitterness was deep within them, and why not?

I took them out into No Man's Land to repair barbed wire and as heavy shelling blew neighbouring trenches into the air they only remarked nonchalantly, 'Thank God we've got a navy'.

I took them on carrying parties and from the wings of the salient machine-gun bullets came hissing between us like flying snakes, one of them hitting the man before me in the thigh, so that he staggered off on one stiff leg exclaiming, 'Oh, oh, oh, oh, oh!' collapsed and was carried away. 'Worth a quid!' said Private Redfern calmly, looking after him. 'Worth ten', tranquilly answered Private Cooke.

I led them on a pitch dark night back from the trenches across shell-riddled ground calf-deep in mud and water, came to a ditch, felt gingerly with my foot and discovered a plank over which I safely passed, calling over my shoulder, 'Plank here, Sergeant Grundy'. Followed a loud splash in the darkness, floundering sounds, and the sergeant's voice urbanely remarking, 'It must have been a very thin 'un, sir'.

Tenderly, but without emotion, they watched round Private Redfern as he lay from dawn to dusk in a snowbound trench with a bullet hole between the eyes, moaning faintly.

With exclamations of shocked propriety, but otherwise unmoved, they regarded Private Hopkins of the Duke of Cornwall's, whose friends had forgotten to bury him. All that remained was head and shoulders, with outflung arms, and his feet, in their boots, near by. He was a good-looking lad, his eyes were open and calm, and the wind played with his hair as if he were alive. That he should be left like that scandalized the Foresters, and they quickly put him in a sandbag.

They made ribald jokes about Private Connolly, who having taken a large piece of shell in his behind plunged for cover into a flimsy makeshift shelter of corrugated iron, leaving only the seat of the trouble to protrude into the trench for attention by the stretcher-bearers.

I loved it. I loved the men and admired the officers. I loved the star on my shoulder, my revolver, my orderly, the officers' mess. No Germans bore down on me with bayonets, no heavy bombardment came my way in these nine months in the trenches. Bullets hit the man on my right and him on my left. Shrapnel burst almost in my ear, but not a drop of the rain of pellets touched me. A shell dropped beside me but politely did not explode.

These things are the small change of warfare. Charging into a curtain of machine-gun fire, standing still under a barrage: these are the real tests of a man's nerve, and I was spared them.

Still immature and romantic, the moments of fright were not yet enough to outweigh my delight in my commission, in the stupendous drama all about me. I gave little thought to the outcome of the war. It seemed likely to last a long while, and that suited me, as I pottered about the trenches in front of Ypres.

Once, peeping over the parapet, I actually saw a German. Perhaps his trench was fallen in or flooded. He calmly climbed out of it, walked a few yards silhouetted giant-like against the sky, and disappeared, just as I squeezed the trigger.

At night I went out into No Man's Land to inspect a two-man patrol and found them crouching behind a tree stump. They had just seen a German patrol stroll calmly past, they said. 'Why didn't you shoot them?' I asked. They were at a loss for an answer. Live and let live seemed to be their motto. Soldiers on both sides at that time, knowing that local exploits in that interminable muddy line of deadlocked armies could only be as the fleabite to the elephant, did not gratuitously annoy each other. This was remarked far, far back at Headquarters, and though it did not lead to any brilliant strategic scheme for a smashing break through, it possibly produced the multigraphed list of questions which junior officers in the front line were recommended to ask themselves, beginning with 'Am I offensive enough?'

Colonel Hobbs came plodding across the shell-pitted ground in the dusk to inspect the front line, an almost biblical figure with shepherdlike staff, long waterproof cape and steel helmet. His underlip was long and pendulous, his mouth open, his eyes were as empty of emotion under fire as at the head of the mess table, with the port at his left hand. He was a little deaf, and could only be startled when a shell, arriving unheard, burst close to him; that rippled the surface even of his self-mastery and made him jump.

He led us once up the Ypres road, through Flamertinghe, into which gigantic shells were falling from the great Austrian siege howitzers. It was like a walk to the electric chair. The concentrated gaze of six hundred Sherwood Foresters was fixed on Flamertinghe, visible from afar off, as the centipede that was the battalion drew near on leaden feet. The regular timing of the explosions showed that a 15-inch shell would fall while the battalion was passing through Flamertinghe. If it fell plumb on the battalion practically nothing would remain over. We could well have been halted until a shell fell and then passed through.

The colonel, erect and imperturbable, rode on as if going to the meet. Dotted lines from six hundred pairs of eyes led to the village ahead. The leading platoon, headed by myself, reached the village, entered, had nearly traversed it when an express train took wings and flew towards us. Nearly a ton of explosive-laden metal came rushing through the air. We marched on, outwardly unmoved. A loud earthquake happened near at hand, followed by a dead silence and then the patter-smack-crash of shell fragments, bricks, tiles and other debris deluging the battalion. Brickbats knocked off the colonel's helmet, sent his charger rearing and prancing, but he only cocked an eye over his shoulder and coldly surveyed a ragged battalion, most of which had in the last shattering moment ducked for cover. The cold, compelling glance was effective; quickly the broken ranks closed and resumed the march. The shell had fallen behind some houses. Only a few men had been killed, at the rear, where the stretcher-bearers were busy. We went on.

I sat with Crosbie in a dugout and secretly revered him. He had a dark, handsome, sensitive face, like a Gascon; young in years, but a veteran of the war. Outside in the trench our mess cook and our orderlies squatted and cooked the midday hash. One of those sudden shells arrived that explode simultaneously with the noise of their approach; whiz-bang. The dugout rocked. We ran out. One orderly had got a blighty — a wound not serious, but enough to take him to England — and he was going to England as fast as he could. We saw only his head, travelling rapidly along the zigzag trench leading to the rear. The cook, bleeding from several wounds, lay on his back, Crosbie gently telling him to lie still. Whiz-bang, whiz-bang, whiz-bang. In such a moment you are convinced that the next shell will explode in the same place as the last, but Crosbie was cool and detached. Whiz-bang, whiz-bang, whiz-bang. Three more, all around us, and then another three, and debris deluging down on us. At last the stretcher-bearers came and got the cook away, Crosbie went calmly back to the ramshackle dugout, I strolled to another part of the trench.

Spring came, and early summer, and we went back to Calais for a rest. After the quiet months the summer storm on the Somme was brewing, and we were to be fattened for the sacrifice. I lived for the day. I rode horseback along the sands and bathed in the sea. Seeking safety in numbers, we made the inevitable sight-seeing tour of the houses of pleasure. Rows of chemised ladies paraded before us for our inspection and postured before us in attitudes, enticing or coy. We bought them drinks, they sat on our knees, we gave them twenty francs and went in search of more exclusive company.

A fortnight, gloriously begun, less gloriously ended. Turning a reluctant back on the pleasures of Calais, I marched with the battalion through a ripening June-time countryside to Picardy. Golden fields and shady orchards called to us, but we tramped on and on, left-right, left-right, fifty minutes at a time and ten minutes' halt, while the gunfire grew louder in the distance and the fertile countryside gave way to a land trodden and ridden brown by swarming English armies assembling for the great offensive.

The Somme lay before us. The Somme. None of us then knew what that one word contained in blood and suffering. Many of us were sceptical; others itched to be at the enemy after long months of inactivity. The flower of British manhood remained there, mown down by an enemy still unreached, unseen. For weeks on end British divisions were flung head-on against prepared defensive positions of enormous strength. Snug in deep concrete dugouts the Germans waited till the barrage lifted, then came up and knocked the khaki skittles down with their machine-guns. After the slaughter the British armies had nibbled a small dent in the impregnable German line.

The 2nd Sherwoods went the way that all flesh went on the Somme. One morning they stood with thumping hearts, the Colonel, Baby Allen, Frank Reynolds and the others, looking at their synchronized wrist watches, and the men with their bayoneted rifles looking at them, and then they were up and away over the trench ladders, and the next moment they were no more.

But I was not with them. I was up above. Just before that day I was transferred to the Royal Flying Corps. I packed my valise, hiked backwards from the trenches, and while the drum-fire pulverized the tortured fields around the Somme I rode above the smoke and din in an aeroplane, map-marked the fall of shells and the position of troops, tapped messages on a wire-

C

less transmitter, and anxiously scanned the sky for the swooping Immelmann or Boelcke. I was an observer, and proudly wore the feathered O.

I had a grand life. Number Nine Squadron lay against a wood that sloped down to the Somme. We bathed in it, and in the great mess marquee ate abundantly of apricots and greengages. We paid flying visits to Amiens. I gazed in respectful awe at my new companions; Leman who had been schooled by the self-same dominie who thrashed me about the toy cannon, the lion-hearted South African Scaife and his Suffolk pilot Coller, the dour Macdonald in his neat tartan riding breeches, Hollinghurst who had left a thumb in Gallipoli, the wealthy Australian Bell and others, many soon to be killed. Only three years before I had stopped kicking a football about somewhere at Golders Green and gazed spellbound at the first aeroplane I had ever seen. I had longed to fly. Now I sat among flying men and was one of them. It was sheer bliss.

We flew BE2C's. The observer sat between the pilot and the engine, surrounded by struts and stays and cross-bracing wires. He had around him several metal pegs and was supposed in the heat of combat, while the machine dived and banked, to fight off the enemy by transferring his machine-gun from the one to the other and then firing through the small apertures left by the struts and wires. It was like fighting from an animated parrot's cage. I was never attacked by a German aeroplane in a BE2C. I was not meant to be killed in that war.

July passed, and August, and September came and brought rumours of mysterious new machines that were to be let loose against the enemy on September 15th. Tanks! I travelled daily overhead and watched British infantry wrest a few yards of trench here, a few yards there, round Ginchy, Guillemont and Falfemont Farm. Sometimes on summer evenings we cruised high up in a peaceful blue vault and looked down on fifty miles of front from Arras to Soissons. The guns would bark and counterbark angrily at each other, their innumerable flashes answering each other like heliographs and growing more

34

brilliant as the dusk neared, the noise of the bombardment making our aeroplane vibrate and the passage of shells through the air, which we sometimes saw, causing it violently to oscillate. Or we would fly in a morning mist, so thick that we could only see what lay straight beneath us, and we had to fly so low that we could almost see the features of the men in the trenches.

Such a morning was that of September 11th. We flew lower and lower, Hollinghurst with his thumbless hand on the joystick, I staring at the trenches until my eyes nearly started out of my head to see whether the troops at Guillemont had gained another yard or two of trench during the night. I think they were Guards. They had advanced a little and were trying to secure themselves in their newly won ground. Here an officer waved a white paper to me, and I made a dot on my trench map, there a green flare was lit, there a signal given with a pocket-torch, but from there came machine-gun fire. So we circled round and round, lower and lower, trying to plot the line to the last remnant of trench and shell-hole.

Afterwards I remembered hearing the shot that hit me. Not one of a thousand machine-gun bullets sprayed at random into the blue, but a lucky potshot. That German could not have done it again in a hundred years.

I was hit where you would expect to be hit if you were sitting down and being fired at from below. Nothing I had ever read or imagined about being wounded had prepared me for that terrific blow. I seemed to shoot out of the aeroplane and fall back again. Who did that, I thought, looking round vaguely for my assailant. Then I remembered that I was in an aeroplane, felt the blood streaming over my leg, and slumped into my seat. I heard Hollinghurst shouting 'Are you hit?' and nodded drowsily. 'Are you bad' he howled, above the noise of the engine, 'or can you wait until we get back to the aerodrome?' But I was not equal to more than a plain nod or shake. I wanted to go home immediately, without any argument. So I stayed still and he, like a sportsman, brought the machine down behind the trenches among barbed wire and shell-holes, at the risk of his own life, and at the cost of the aeroplane. I tumbled out somehow, and somebody gave me a cigarette that tasted like brown paper. Somebody else cut my leather coat off me. Twenty years later to a day I opened an old tin trunk in Vienna, found that coat with the bullet hole and the dried blood, had it patched and used it for driving about, and very useful it was, being lined with fleece, and in the depth of a Vienna winter an ordinary English overcoat leaves you cold. One morning when Brenda Mary was cold, going skating, I wrapped her in it, and she was beautifully warm.

Then I was bumped along in an ambulance, I lay on a stretcher in some clearing station, where a man shouted repeatedly, 'Oh my God, Oh my God!' and people with bullets in the guts and in the head and no arms and no legs were carried in and out without pause, and a cheery nurse, a grand girl, brought me a glass of milk and said breezily, 'Don't look so sorry for yourself'. If there were any justice in this world, I thought, she would be shot in the behind immediately. Then a train, where the major suddenly materialized and said 'Goodbye' to me; a long, long journey, and a big hospital with a fat surgeon, of whom I asked, 'Is it bad?' and he said, 'Well, it's not very nice'.

They cut me open, beginning where the bullet went in and going on, apparently, until hope failed, so that I must have looked like a large rumpsteak. Later, X-rays showed the bullet in my back, the tip just not touching the junction of the lowest rib and the spine. I woke up as they were pulling the packing out of the wound and shrieked like a banshee. I lay in bed, unable either to lie still or to move, and read the *Pickwick Papers* in fitful glimpses. What a book! I seemed to see the pages as through dark smoked glasses. I was at Rouen, and out of the mist around me my father suddenly materialized, thoughtfully sent over by the War Office to see me before I expired.

A hospital ship, and an elderly uniformed medico at Southampton who, without knowing what ailed me, looked at me rancorously and told his superior that I was fit to travel,

36

apparently wishing me to John O'Groats or further. Even lying helpless and half-conscious on my back I seem to inspire antagonism in some people. But his superior overruled him, I went to London, an ambulance took me to Regent's Park, where I was removed while two servant girls watched and one remarked, 'Doesn't he look sweet', and I entered the hospital, run by Colonel and Mrs. Hall-Walker, who later became Lord and Lady Wavertree, and most lavishly cared for hundreds of wounded officers during the war.

A clever Jewish surgeon deftly hanked the bullet out of my back, I hobbled about the West End and the front at Brighton for many months, spent the £250 which my wound cost England, and in July was back in France. Eighteen years afterwards that wound suddenly opened up one day in Vienna and a splinter of pelvis emerged.

'It's a darned reliable war, always there to go back to when you're broke,' remarked Hoppy Cleaver, a new acquaintance, three times wounded, decorated, who refused to take the war seriously at any time. Number Sixteen Squadron lay on an aerodrome in sight of the ruined pitheads of Lens. The major was Portal who by now must be a big noise in the Royal Air Force; his officers then deeply respected his coolness and gift of leadership. Men from all parts of the Empire and beyond gathered round the mess table.

We flew RE8's and the observer had a clear field of fire and a rotating machine-gun mount. They were slow machines. We pottered around the trenches observing the fall of shells or we ambled gingerly across and took photographs of the enemy lines. Our casualties during the autumn and winter were few.

The opposing armies stood like wrestlers locked in an iron stranglehold, swaying no more than a few feet this way or that. Northward, at Ypres, the history of the Somme was being repeated. In the mud of Passchendaele British divisions were flung prodigally, head on, against enormously strong positions. Plodding doggedly through a quagmire, they were mown down from the concrete machine-gun posts. 'At Passchendaele you've

37

got the choice of standing on a duckboard and being killed by a shell or getting off and being drowned,' said the British infantryman. Of what avail was gallantry without strategic inspiration? The two great British offensives on the Western front are dreary to recall. The strategic principle was that of battering your head against a wall. If Germany was to be starved out anyway, what was the purpose of this squandering of life? That offensives could be successful, even on the dead-locked Western front, the Germans proved.

In our quiet retreat west of Lens we had as little understanding for the greater picture of the war as village-folk in peace time have for great issues of international politics. Our vision was bounded by the few yards of trench and shell-hole that we patrolled. We were vaguely perturbed by the collapse of Russia, vaguely reassured by the intervention of America; operations in Italy, Salonika, Mesopotamia and elsewhere were Double Dutch.

Between flights we stood on our aerodrome and watched the war. On a lovely September evening a fast German chaser hopped unnoticed across our lines and bagged a British observation balloon tethered near by. It fell in a dissolving mass of crimson flame and black smoke. The German turned on the little white speck beneath him that was the parachute of the balloon pilot. Machine-gunning hard he dived on the helpless swinging figure, rose-coloured in the sun's last rays. If he had not paused for this he would have got away, but now, when he turned to go, two British chasers were on him. Three shining white machines, soaring, leaping, falling, charging, their tracer machine-gun bullets blazing a yellow trail, they rode about the darkening sky like knights jousting at each other with golden lances. They got the German down, landed near him, took him, only slightly hurt, to the nearest officers' mess and drank with him.

And once, in the full heat of the day, another German chaser sped across and destroyed five observation balloons tethered at intervals between our aerodrome and the line. The pilot of the first balloon jumped when he saw the German coming, the pilot of the second jumped when he saw the first go up in flames, the pilot of the third jumped when he saw the German machine-gunning the second, and so on. It was a valiant exploit, but it was like a Charlie Chaplin film to watch and, as nobody was going to be actually hurt, the audience on our aerodrome hooted with uncontrollable laughter. Chinese coolies working near at hand looked from us to the burning balloons with incomprehension written on their faces. Oriental passivity was not equal to this test; they were deeply perplexed men. One came running over to us and, pointing to the five holocausts, said with childish concern, 'Engliss ballon, Engliss ballon'. 'Yes', we said, still laughing, 'Engliss ballon, Engliss ballon'.

The winter came, and Christmas Day, and Eric Read, my Canadian near-namesake, and I toasted each other riotously in the mess. On Boxing Day we went up in pairs taking photographs, Douglas flying me in the first machine, Read flying his observer Donovan in the second. Slowly, fighting the wind, we drew over the lines until the pulverized pitheads of Lens lay beneath us, and the heavens seemed to crack asunder as a shell burst plumb between us. Not sure if I were still alive, I looked round and saw Read's machine fall over sideways in a slow, graceful curve. It looked like the practised art of a figure-skater; but it meant that Read was dead in his cockpit. He stiffened as he died and locked the rudder against the direction of his spin, so that his machine spiralled down slowly and crashed with a relatively light impact. Donovan, after falling 6000 feet with a dead pilot, stepped out of the wreck physically unscathed.

And Crompton and I went night-bombing, a first initiation in that art, on a dank and misty night. A hair on the head is little, a hair in the soup is much; the hairsbreadth by which our starboard wing-tip missed the dimly-seen squadron offices as we left the ground with engine all out was a great deal. Peering down the narrow funnel of relative visibility directly beneath us which was all that the mist-banks allowed us to see, we dumped our bombs when we thought we recognized an enemy landmark and turned with quaking hearts for home and a dreaded landing. Fumbling through the fog, we at last hit on the flares and Crompton throttled down to land. By this time I was the lucky survivor of several crashes due to misjudged landings. I thought we were going to overshoot the aerodrome, which we could scarcely see, and hit that squadron office. Inexcusably yielding to back-seat nerves I shouted to Crompton, 'You're going to overshoot', and so wrong was I that just then we hit the ground and overturned. The instinct of self-preservation was so strong that, though I was not belted in, I found myself, upside down, but still seated firmly on my seat, clinging on like grim death to everything I could lay hands on. Crompton lay tangled up in his belt, uttering North Country imprecations, and to get the pin out and release him was not easy with his weight bearing on it.

The Germans, skilful campaigners, quietly followed us home one night and dropped their needle-pointed, shrapnel bombs all round us, the landing flares making it easy for them. In the mess we precipitately abandoned hard-won whiskies and took a prostrate position on the floor, and the major's dog, Yace, left us at speed with a piece of bomb in the neck, to return a day or two later looking glum and embittered.

The Allies gradually won the mastery of the air. At home the Zeppelin and Gotha raids became fewer and in France our fighters brought the big German bombers down in increasing numbers of nights: one met its end over our aerodrome one starlit night, exploding like a box of fireworks. But on land the Germans were full of fight. The Russian collapse had freed masses of men and in March came the great offensive, when the Fifth British Army was rolled up and the German wave began once more to roll menacingly towards Paris.

Sixteen Squadron was sent into the air to a man and a machine. For the first time I saw something like war as the picture books show it. Instead of the lifeless lunar landscape of the trenches, masses of Germans moving forward in the open.

The air was so packed with aeroplanes that sardines in comparison seemed to be lolling in luxury. The cloud ceiling was low, about 2000 feet, and in that narrow space hundreds of machines swooped and zoomed, spitting fire at each other and at the troops below.

Nickel, my Toronto pilot, dived on German troops marching along a road, machine-gunning them furiously through the airscrew, and as he turned to regain height I continued with my gun. Black anti-aircraft shells burst on all sides; and the flaming onions, green incendiary projectiles that rose as if tied together on a string, came groping towards us. Aeroplanes flashed by on all sides, friend and foe almost impossible to distinguish.

We dropped our bombs on a German battery, zoomed cloudward, and my heart missed a beat, for immediately above us a German fighter dropped out of the clouds. He flew the same course, his landing wheels almost touching our top plane, the black crosses almost near enough for me to touch. Here at last was the enemy, after three and a half years of war. Frantically, in the rear cockpit of the swaying, bumping, racing aeroplane, I swung my machine-gun on its rotary mount and blazed away into the brown fabric above me. It fell over, just as Read's machine had fallen over, and dropped past us, showing its stomach like a dying fish, down and down, and crashed near the railway embankment at Achiet le Grand. For the first time, in my definite knowledge, I had inflicted some damage on the enemy. We went home, inspected the bullet holes in our aeroplane, and I had a little cross, with a date against it, painted on the barrel of my machine-gun.

St. George's Day, and the British Navy, with a flicker of Nelson, dashed across the Channel and sank a couple of cruisers in the mouth of Zeebrugge Harbour to bottle up the German submarines lying in the Bruges Canal. On that same morning Nickel and I went up on patrol and were climbing from the aerodrome, about 300 feet up, when I heard a crash. I saw nothing, but knew what had happened. We had collided with another aeroplane. I felt Nickel wrenching at broken

41

controls. I saw the sky and then the earth, and then the sky again, and the wing of the machine describing great arcs. I clung to my machine-gun mount like a drowning man. The crash seemed never to come, though the fall probably lasted no longer than a second.

Then it came, a terrific impact, and a bounce and rending wood and snapping wires and myself saying to myself, 'I'm still alive'.

Suddenly blazing petrol was everywhere and 800 rounds of machine-gun ammunition, stacked in drums around my head, exploded in staccato chorus. Bullets exploded like this do not travel, but I did not believe this as I fought to free myself from the coiling wires and wreckage; they were going off in my ear. The wires would not let me go, the rubber band that held my goggles fell away, burned through. Then suddenly I was rolling on the ground to put out my burning leather coat. I stood up and looked back at the holocaust. No sign of Nickel. I could not get within ten yards of it for the heat. I ran round, met Nickel running round to look for me. The machine-gun ammunition was still exploding. We beat a hasty retreat. A hundred yards away lay the other aeroplane.

A sergeant came running over the field, gave me a surprised look, and said, 'Oo sir, what 'ave you done to your face?' I put up my hand and fingered it. It felt funny.

It was. A few hours later it looked like a dog's dinner. The doctor put picric acid on it, and for weeks I was as yellow as a daffodil. It swelled like a football. It blistered, and the blisters peeled. Boils appeared between the blisters. My beard grew through both. Nickel and I travelled together to the base hospital. An imperturbable Australian was there, chatting about this and that while a doctor deeply probed a nasty wound in his shoulder. He happened to glance at us as our bandages were taken off. His treasured imperturbability failed him. Surprise came over his face and his mouth opened. Then he recovered himself, asked, 'What is it, boys, a touch of gas?' and resumed being a stoic.

My head swathed in bandages, with a single eye-slit, I wandered about London, from theatre to dance-club, and squandered the £200 which this damage to my face was worth to England. I expected to be disfigured for life, but the quick touch of picric acid possibly saved this. Such as it is, my face healed beautifully, I spent a June week in a Hampshire cottage lent me by a compassionate lady with a weakness for wounded officers, I sailed her dinghy up and down the Itchen, and in July I was back on the aerodrome with Sixteen Squadron.

I was weary of the war and dreaded the peace. I did not know what I should do when it came. But for the grace of God I should have become one of those men, captains all, who subsist for the rest of their lives on their war service: I saw many of them afterwards in Germany, where they actually succeeded in making themselves masters of the State. I had no qualifications, no talents, no influence. My parents lived almost in poverty. I had no public school education, and without it you feel like Little Tich among a crowd of Carneras, when you seek to muscle-in and make a place for yourself in England. The League of the Old School Tie, a solid phalanx, stands guard over the approaches to advancement and shoots strangers at sight. Few are those who get through, though the garrison usually suffers you once you are in. I had seen this bottle-neck system at work in the war itself. As Raymond Asquith wrote from the front: 'If you look at any list of honours it's always the same story. The Dukes are proved to be the bravest men of all, and after them the Marquesses.' Twenty years afterwards the same story was told in other words by Professor John Hilton of Cambridge University, when he said that the odds against a non-public schoolboy getting into one of the reserved stalls of life were one thousand to one; to get there, he said, you must have been to the right school and be entitled through life to wear the right school tie. In 1937 a distinguished churchman put the thing in a nutshell when he said, 'The first public school man was born in Nazareth, and his name was Jesus Christ; the second was his disciple, St. Paul.'

We flew about the pock-marked map that was the front, gnats biting vainly at an elephantine war. I flew with Solomon, painter, good pilot, courageous officer, Jew, and we had to delay to remedy a camera defect, so that when we crossed the line our companions had already taken their pictures and gone home, and we went over alone. On we crawled, a long way over enemy land, a lonely feeling when you are all alone, the air feels quite different on that side of the trenches, and I looked over the side and saw a pair of black crosses below us, climbing like lightning. Desperately I swung my machine-gun round and gave him a burst to starboard and another to port, as he passed beneath us. Then my gun jammed, and in another instant he was fast on our tail and stinging hard, swaying from side to side and giving us a burst each time he got us dead on his sights. The noise of a machine-gun fired point-blank is the loudest noise I know. I struggled frantically with my useless gun but the parts slipped about all over the cockpit. I curled myself up into a ball as he poured bullets into us and then quickly uncoiled myself at the thought that this might mean that one bullet would go through several things, whereas it might otherwise only make one hole. Cumbersomely Solomon heaved our heavy old RE8 from side to side, trying vainly to elude a foe as swift and sure as a swallow. I thought this martyrdom would never end, and felt sick; I had a mental vision of an observer I had seen lifted out of his cockpit on the aerodrome a little while before, his flying suit spangled with little stars of blood, so that he looked like St. Sebastian. How that German missed us I can't imagine; afterwards we found that he had shot all round us, like a knife thrower. At last, scarcely daring to believe my eyes, I saw him turn away, and looking round I saw the reason: we had reached the lines, and many of our own machines were about. Hampered by smashed controls, Solomon gingerly felt his way back to the aerodrome and managed to flop the machine down on it.

Gradually the German front weakened. American troops and munitions were pouring into France; Ludendorff, at

German Imperial Headquarters, was a broken man. October came, and with new heart we flew low over the Lens coalfields and saw British soldiers waving to us from German trenches.

We got up in the dawn and machine-gunned the rearguards of the retiring German army, as they struggled over muddy fields; they were full of fight.

I was due for leave, and on a lovely autumn morning came over a hilltop to see Paris shining below me. Paris! The very word was a silver bugle call. I spent enchanted days, drank champagne, ate raspberries and cream, went to the Folies Bergères. Paris was gay, full of uniforms and pretty girls. I had never seen anything like it, and reluctantly I took the dusty road back to Camblain l'Abbé. When I got there the squadron had gone, hard on the heels of the enemy, who was now far behind Valenciennes. I chased after it and on November 10th was peering curiously down from an aeroplane cockpit on Mons, that legendary town where the war had begun for the British Army. Now Belgian civilians jubilantly waved to us black-gold-red tricolours that they had kept hidden for four years. A German aeroplane took me unawares — I thought he was English — and put some holes in the fabric near me before I got my gun to bear on him.

Next day the war was over. We sat in a tiny Belgian schoolroom and drank whisky immoderately. Afterwards I leaned against a farmhouse wall in the dusk, to cool my head, and watched horse-gunners going by, rain streaming from their helmets. Silence, save for the jingle-jangle, clip-clop of harness and hooves. Set jaws in the fitful light of a street lamp.

I thought of the future. The causes and effects of the war were then unclear to me, but afterwards I read and thought it over and saw that the Russians had saved us in 1914 by pressing the Germans so hard in the east that they had had to halt their drive towards Paris and the Channel ports in the west, and that the Americans in 1918 had saved us again from a German drive that otherwise we could not have withstood.

45

I have to this day a feeling for Americans and Russians that no talk of Yanks or Reds will ever diminish.

One thing seemed clear to me on that dark and drizzling night when the war ended. For four years the Germans had ridden roughshod over Europe, laid waste other countries. Now for the first time, save for the brief East Prussian episode in 1914, the war was approaching their own country. At this very moment we had called it off and granted an armistice. An instinct told me that to leave any doubt in the German mind about a military defeat was a fatal mistake. Years afterwards, in Germany, I became sure of it.

I went to Lille and shared the unforgettable joy of a freed people. I went to Brussels, and saw the Allies march in, the Americans then surpassing all others in bearing and looks. I walked in awful boredom along the single slushy street of a tiny Belgian village and thought dismally of my future. I was consumed with impatience to be out of the army. I could have clung to my commission, and its pay, for some weeks or months, but when an icy plunge has to be taken I like to get it over. I agitated to be demobilized, was sent home and dispatched to a dreary frostbound camp near Grantham, where my fellow-officers passed demoralizing days playing billiards, while I, mutinous, took my bags down to the good George Inn, ate and drank well, took no thought for the morrow, dashed up to London to see girl friends and only looked in at the camp once a week to see if I were still a soldier. One day in March I came down the hill holding a paper which made me a civilian. The brave days were over. The world lay before me, and a grim place it looked.

I came to London, drew my officer's gratuity of several hundred pounds, had my first evening clothes made, and began an expensive round of theatres, restaurants and dance-clubs. I still had one or two friends from the army who did not know my private plight and thought that I, like they, could now look forward to piping years of peace. Invitations came. I found myself in unaccustomed country houses, privily bothered about

46

tips and manners. With a few pounds left I lazed in June in a rose-contained garden overlooking the Needles and played tennis with a boy who was England's premier Duke.

One day in July the silver and copper coins in my pocket amounted to less than ten shillings. The future had to be faced at last.

CHAPTER 3

GREEN AND PLEASANT LAND

IMPROVIDENT as ever, I paid twopence for a chair in Kensington Gardens and counted those few coins. Just there I had sat five years before, waiting for the lady of my then affections, self-conscious in unaccustomed khaki, and somebody whom *Punch* inevitably would have called an Elderly Party or Dear Old Lady asked kindly, 'And can you sing the "Marseillaise"?', whereon I blushed and hung my head. Much had happened since then, I had been far and seen many things, and now it was all sponged out and I was back where I had been, with two suits, one blue and one grey, a few shirts, evening clothes, and no talents.

I cannot understand now why I was so unenterprising. I could have got on a ship and gone to Malta or Capetown or Ceylon, or one of a hundred other places where an Englishman could find some work. I could have exploited my evening clothes and become a dancing partner. I could have done dozens of things. But instead, when I had no money left, I looked desperately for a clerk's job. I had a one-way mind then.

The bank was ready to take me in, but at a price that was not my price, and when I said so it made crushing remarks about young officers who would have to modify their ideas. So I walked out. Afterwards I longed to walk in again, but pride forbade. After lean and despondent weeks I found myself hired to type letters, in the French I had learned in the war, for a wine merchant, an ebullient foreigner known to all pedestrians in Piccadilly, for he would stand at his door and beam on the passing throng, and a part of his technique was to lunch and dine at some expensive restaurant that sold his wares.

London had got me again. From my Piccadilly window, as I tapped on my typewriter, I saw war-time acquaintances

48

strolling to their clubs. Eggs were at first sixpence each, and butter five shillings a pound. London's streets were full of armless and legless ex-soldiers trudging round with barrel-organs. My two suits wore threadbare and I saw no hope of going to a good tailor again. My days were spent communing with dozens of port and sherry, with clarets that boasted of having been bottled at some château, with fussy burgundies that were self-important about their rank — premier crû, or première cuvée.

It was hell. It lasted eighteen months. Then I was ushered out with a cheque for four weeks' salary. I forget why I was dismissed, I think I had asked for a higher salary, and this was the answer. The manager, who had spent a lifetime among vats and was wont to apply irrelevant adjectives like 'robust' and 'vivid' to the wines he tasted, told me as he handed me my cheque that many a career had been spoilt by a thoughtless act, a baffling remark that irritated me like an itch, and then I found myself strolling aimlessly along Piccadilly, thinking 'How now?'

This time the luck failed. The eighteen pounds dwindled rapidly to nothing. Something had to be done. I answered an attractive advertisement offering a large income, easily earned, to ex-officers, and found myself being interviewed, with many others in like plight, by a map-maker in Fleet Street. We had only to go out into the English country-side, hire a bicycle, call on rich men and sell them motoring maps of England, handsomely bound in imitation leather, and the commission was so munificent that we should live, as the Germans say, like God in France. It was a grim prospect but it was baited with an advance of four pounds, and I had no money. The next day I breakfasted in a cheap lodging in Salisbury with Captain Eustace Mountebankes, the map-maker's star salesman, a merry fellow who sang a good song and accompanied himself on the jingling piano in our lodging.

Eustace was marvellous. His manner overbore the most pompous butlers and daunted dukes. A man conferring a favour, he played his order-book into the hands of baronets and squires like a conjurer forcing a card and he took their signatures for several pounds worth of maps practically by sleight of hand. He had to show me how it was done. He certainly showed me that it could be done. He earned some £600 a year at it. One Sunday long afterwards I saw him in the Row. He escorted a fashionably dressed woman, wore a silk hat and a morning coat, and in his right hand he carried, with complete assurance, a lady's umbrella, one of those slender, almost shoulder-high things with a long, straight handle.

After three days he left me alone. I bicycled miserably along the roads about Salisbury. I could have steeled myself to walk to the gallows with not much more difficulty than to pedal along those rhododendron-lined drives, to ring at those grimly forbidding doors, to start talking about my ridiculous maps and watch the look of apprehension come into rich men's eyes.

But I did it, and made some strange acquaintances; a jovial landowner who would have none of my maps but sat for hours smoking cigars and drinking port with me who had hardly enough money for my next meal; a solitary lady who had no interest in maps but extended a flattering invitation to a *tête à tête* lunch, from which I stupidly fled; well-to-do farmers who unexpectedly ordered eight guineas' worth of maps, gave me cider and took me to see the pigs.

Sometimes I could not bring myself to go on and bicycled aimlessly along the lanes or lay on a river bank watching the swallows. I had always longed to see primroses growing and here they were abundant. I picked quantities, and squandered shillings posting them to my mother and girls in town. I dallied in the cathedral close, watched the pigeons circling round the mellow roof and wished I need never leave the peaceful place again. Now, I shun that cloistered tranquillity; I am happier in a Bierstube in Moabit, in a wine-garden in Sievering, in a gipsy restaurant in Belgrade, or almost anywhere away from that remote, repressed life of the English countryside, all cluttered up with golf courses and fox hunting.

When I had exhausted Salisbury's appetite for maps I went to Tunbridge Wells, a town of mean cottages and mansions, and from the common looked resentfully down on the rows of great houses, with their parks and gardens. I alone was to blame if I had squandered the money my wounds and service in the war had earned me, if I had recklessly forfeited my clerk's desk. But I had no money, a sharp appetite, no prospects, and a detestable occupation. I hated wealthy Tunbridge Wells.

Somehow, I earned thirty shillings one week, fifty shillings the next, in one unforgettable week eight guineas. On Saturdays I bicycled furiously round the countryside, racing time to get one more order and justify a trip to town, and at three o'clock in the afternoon I set my face Londonwards, rode hard for four hours, arrived dripping with sweat just in time to take a girl to the Military and Naval Tournament at Olympia. Though the stars on my shoulder had waned I was under the spell of the army and had buoyed myself up through an exhausting week with the thought of that Saturday dash to town and Olympia. It was glorious. I loved the regimental marches and the bravely stepping companies. Since then I have watched military parades all over Europe, and like them less.

Soon after dawn on Monday morning I was on my way to Tunbridge Wells again. I pedalled and peddled through the summer. I rode up an endless drive to a great castle, rang at a ponderous door which was opened by one footman for another footman and a moment later was bowed politely out. I remounted and rode with dignity down the drive, but found afterwards that I had worn a large hole in the seat of my army breeches, through which my shirt was waving like a banner.

I had shot my bolt. I was as thin as a rake, my energy spent, and I knew I could not go on with this revolting struggle.

London had won again. I came back, answered advertisements, dragged about the streets, ate a poached egg and drank a cup of coffee occasionally, and after some time I sat in a cellar in Fleet Street, now typing letters for a travel agent about hotel accommodation in Switzerland, conducted parties, train-fares and time-tables. I seemed to be inescapably back in my London corridor.

I was wrong. I was in the street of adventure. I had never been able to understand why Fleet Street was called that. I had spent years in and about Fleet Street and had vainly explored it for adventure. It seemed dull, dirty, noisy and narrow. But it was the doorway to the world for me.

CHAPTER 4

PARISIAN ATTIC

ALL these years I had vainly tried to write. The articles and stories I wrote found no buyers, but the itch to write was unappeasable. Now, in my Fleet Street cellar, I was in the world of letters, but not of it. I was completely surrounded by publishers' and newspaper offices.

Shorthand is commonly regarded as a petty accomplishment, unworthy of a gentleman. But if you have no old school tie you have to look around for some side entrance to betterment, and this insignificant key opened the doors for me to a wider life, to travel, to the profession of writing. I bless it now as I detested it in the days of my office-boyhood, when the publisher demanded that I should know it and a young clerk came to my home two evenings a week to teach it to me and a couple of fellow-sufferers, while my mother made cocoa for us all.

In my cellar I racked my brains to find a means of escape. I wrote to an anonymous advertiser who wanted a good shorthand writer to take down long messages over the international telephone. Within a week I had a new desk, in Printing House Square.

It was a grand life. For the first time since my early days as an officer I had something to do that interested me. I loved working at night, I loved being a small link in the long chain of news, hearing great tidings from Berlin and Paris and Vienna flowing into my mind through the earpieces and seeing them flow out again at my pencil's tip. I loved the hum of the printing presses towards midnight, I loved the moist copies of the paper that the fetch-and-carry boys casually flipped into my basket about midnight.

News transmission by telephone was then in its infancy. You waited interminably for calls; when they came cracklings

53

and buzzings kept you in a white heat of profanity. Now you can casually ring up New York or Melbourne or Baghdad, and count on quick connection and clear understanding.

The Times was then founding its telephone news service — it now covers all Europe — and after a few weeks I found myself on a cross-Channel steamer, bound for Paris, where I was to be part of the network of telephonic communication between correspondents abroad and Printing House Square.

I found a very different Paris. Paris on a lovely autumn morning, with the war going well and all the girls smiling at a British officer, was one thing. Paris on a dank autumn evening, for a humble clerk without acquaintances, was another. I had a tiny stone-floored room with an iron stove *au sixième*, on the sixth floor, with the moon and chimneypots for my neighbours, and thither I retired at two o'clock in the morning, after the telephone from Madrid or Milan had rung for the last time.

My neighbours were a young man and a girl, a pair of quarrelsome lovers, who were wont to fight like cats, until one day one of them threw a burning lamp, and the girl was so badly burned that she died. Across the courtyard was a table full of laughing *midinettes*, to whom I would heliograph with my shaving mirror, and in one corner a little seamstress, who would entertain me with aniseed liqueur when I had a free evening, discourse with the simple fluency of a river flowing to the sea on this and that, and inevitably tell me I was *gentil*.

And near by lived Mademoiselle Sautier, who personified the brave and thrifty and hard-working France that I loved. She was over seventy, and went out at 5 o'clock every morning to char a bank. It was hard, she said once, to crawl round scrubbing and shifting heavy furniture when you were over seventy. In her little room she had a big French bed, where her brother Jean had slept when he came to Paris on leave during the war, and a stove, and lots of shining copperpots and pans, and she was eternally cleaning.

She had her economies, beyond a doubt, and I was happy to add a little to them then and later, when I was in other lands.

You could tell she had them from the respect shown by her legions of relatives who came to visit her, all dressed in unalleviated black, on Toussaint, the day of the dead, when they all set out together for the resting places of other relatives who had gone before and left their economies in the right direction. She must have been a grand girl once, and I wondered that she was only Mademoiselle Sautier. She tolerated Madame from me, poor foreigner, but would snap 'Je n'ai pas de Monsieur' at cronies who, hearing me say it, tried to ingratiate themselves by calling her that.

In the evenings, I began to see how the news is made. Sweating lavishly in an upholstered cabin, insulated against noise, I strained my ear muscles to catch between the noises what little exasperated voices were saying in Madrid and Rome and Berlin. Strange things happened. A voice from Morocco whispered to me of a gallant and successful attack on a Rifi position 'by two Italians'. I did not notice anything strange. It ought to have been 'by two battalions'. A correspondent in Geneva spoke of 'the famous Ali Baba arbitration case', and that was all right with me, who had never heard of the good ship *Alabama*. And once when the multi-murderer Landru was being tried my colleague in London dropped the word 'beard' from an allusion to his 'long black beard', and the sub-editor in London put 'hair' into the gap. Landru was as bald as a coot.

I went out to Versailles to see him, and sat among the avid Parisiennes scoffing their sweet cakes and sandwiches and scoffing audibly at his protestations of innocence. He had killed and burned a dozen women for their economies and the police had evidence that about two hundred and fifty women in all had been his dupes. I watched the fiery Corsican de Moro-Giafferi, simulating intense moral indignation at the suggestion that his client was a murderer, the public prosecutor sitting in his pen and gazing unblinkingly at Landru, whom he reminded from time to time that his head was at stake, and Landru himself, turning in quiet dignity to reprove the jeers

55

of the spectators with the words, 'There is nothing to laugh about'. He was the most dignified figure in court, this pale, thin-faced, bearded, bald, unsmiling man with the dark eyes, and he could have sat well as model for one of the apostles.

I began to pick up the tricks of the journalist's trade — the advantage of stating the news in the first sentence, the value of a neat phrase, the importance of brevity, the feeling of satisfied craftsmanship that a soundly constructed message leaves. Sometimes things happened in Paris late at night, after the correspondents had passed beyond the ken of the office. I was able to fill one or two small gaps and achieved print.

Then the spring came and I was ordered back to London once more, to take charge of the telephone system.

CHAPTER 5

NORTHCLIFFIAN EPISODE

Out in the channel a spout of water flung high into the air. The captain of the cross-Channel steamer, lying alongside Folkestone quay, said it was probably a whale blowing, and I contemplated his clear eyes, tanned skin, neat beard and long row of medals won on the Dover Patrol with great respect, for I had not known that whales ever blew so near the English coasts. Then the wireless operator came running with a message, he scanned it quickly, and next moment the gangways were hurriedly drawn up and the ship steamed quickly out to sea. An aeroplane had crashed into the Channel dead ahead.

The ship listed hard over as the passengers gathered on the port side and craned their necks. Among the wreckage floating by, unrecognizable, I could see two bundles. I knew they were men; not long before the thought of ending like this had been constantly in my own mind. A boat put out from the ship, a Harley Street doctor among the passengers accompanying the crew, and rowed over to the wreckage. First they pulled out the pilot, a Frenchman, and then the passenger, and as they turned up his face the doctor recognized one of his patients.

I often have to restrain myself from remarking that the world is a small place; this particular coincidence impressed me as deeply as that other strange marine encounter, when a man called Aloysius Pendlebury Plum, or something equally rare, plunged into the Thames at Blackfriars and rescued a man called Aloysius Pendlebury Plum.

The ship continued on her course. Once more, though England had seemed to loom indefinitely ahead of me, I was leaving it behind. Lord Northcliffe had just returned to France from an anonymous tour in Germany and had cabled urgently to London for a secretary. I had been chosen.

A strange adventure lay before me. I had been dispatched at a moment's notice, primed with instructions that I was going to meet a most remarkable man and that I must strain my wits and energy to the utmost to satisfy him. A picture of a journalistic god had been given me — The Chief, ruler of Fleet Street, all-seeing and all-wise, quick to reward devotion, ruthless in punishing infidelity. Immoderate devotion inspired this picture, which misled me so that I was prepared to see in every action, however strange by normal standards, only the incalculability of genius, the eccentricity of the great.

We met in a little hotel in Boulogne, whither Mr. Leonard Brown, as he chose to be known, had come from Cologne. He lay in bed, a very sick man, as I should have known if that priming had not fogged my judgment, a man disappointed, disillusioned, distrusting everyone, with rare moments of gentleness, knowing himself to be mortally ill and hating the knowledge that neither his brain nor his energy nor his wealth could overcome this enemy. The shadows were already closing relentlessly in on him and he had ordered a little back bedroom, to match his mood. The hotel manager, a young man who was anxious to make this distinguished guest as comfortable as possible, had thought to know better and given him the best bedroom, in front. The first summons was to this young man and the brief interview ended with, 'Get out!'

'Get out!' was his cure for many evils.

Then he turned to me. A disproportionately massive head lay on the pillow, a greying forelock hung dankly down, greenish eyes contemplated the world in general and myself in particular with malevolence. A series of strange exchanges began. What public school had I attended? I answered that I had had no schooling after the age of thirteen, and had had the bulk of my schooling at free schools before it. This seemed to flabbergast him. At intervals during the short time we were together he remarked that not everyone would have dared to confess to being a council schoolboy, or complained that I should not have been sent to him.

We began to send daily telegrams to the great newpapers

58

he owned — *Old One, Young One, Nightingale*. Guess for yourselves which was which. We criticized, with the telegraphic terseness of the great, their contents or make-up, we rebuked their staffs with the brevity that is telegraphese. To one eminent journalist we telegraphed, 'You are fired', to another, 'Hear you have been seen walking down Fleet Street in top hat. Don't do it'. We wrote long letters, which mercifully never appeared, in which we discussed in satirical vein all manner of things, from the skinny shanks of a famous society lady to the Jewish influence in English life. We began to write that series of articles, 'Incognito in Germany', in which he described his German journey — Northcliffe, the German-hater, alone in Germany — in the manner of a bold, adventurous undertaking. The first two were published; a third was written but did not appear; and the series came to a sudden end.

He discoursed of many things, of his early struggles and later successes, of his friends and enemies, of his Government mission to America, of Mr. Lloyd George and Mr. and Mrs. Asquith.

He felt himself surrounded by treachery. He put his hand under the pillow and brought out a little black silk bag. 'Look at this', he said, 'it was left here for me, for Mr. Leonard Brown, by a man who wouldn't give the porter his name. How do they know that I am here? You see the colour? It is the colour of death!'

For the first time I saw something of the system of spies with which great men sometimes surround themselves. Sleek young men with sinecure posts in his London undertakings arrived to report on the doings of their chiefs.

So these were the ways of the great! My mind was in a whirl, but so deeply had I been impressed with the necessity to humour his every mood that I never thought anything was amiss and when the valet, a really good and devoted man, stopped me in the ante-room to ask me what I thought about his master's condition I put the suggestion from me like a poisonous snake. Unquestioning devotion, I had been told, and that was going to be my rule.

59

In later years I came to know the signs of mortal illness. I have seen them in men who had the destinies of nations in their hands, and have speculated about the consequences that this might have for a country or a continent. They thought they were still masters of their souls and minds, and they were making plans accordingly. This twilight period is the greatest argument against dictatorship. No man who had been present at Napoleon's autopsy would be likely ever to vote for the absolute rule of a single man.

My salary was rocketed up to £500 a year, a figure that had always seemed to me to mark the Becher's Brook of the Betterment Stakes. And after a few days of this whirlwind atmosphere I was dispatched hot-foot to London, with £150 to buy myself a silver-fitted crocodile leather suitcase. I don't know why. He had asked if I had one, and of course I had not.

I could not bring myself to buy a silver-fitted crocodile leather suitcase. I did not need it. I needed other things. My two suits were on their last threads. I bought a wardrobe trunk and ordered some clothes and paid some bills and still had some money left.

This was a fatal mistake. I had to admit that I had come back without a silver-fitted crocodile leather suitcase. I had failed in unquestioning compliance, and suspicions were aroused. He began to find in me too much or too little zeal. I was approaching the moment of dismissal, which a long line of my predecessors had experienced. The words 'Get out!' or 'You're fired!' trembled on those close-clamped lips.

In between we worked, went for drives to Wimereux or Paris Plage, and at night we took some book of biography or politics and I read to him. 'As the poet Cowper wrote . . .' I read. 'Stop a minute', he said. 'How do you spell that?' 'C-o-w-p-e-r', I answered. 'But you pronounced it Cooper,' he rejoined. 'How did you know that?' 'I thought it must be so,' I said. 'Good, I like that.' Then silence. Then, drowsily, 'It's extraordinary how well you read for a board school boy.' A few seconds later he slept like a child, and I stole out.

The end, but for the background of a most unhappy man, would have made a comic film. Continually complaining of pain and poison, he became more and more irritable. One morning we went for a long drive, and on returning he went to bed, while I went to the hotel dining-room to snatch a quick lunch. He sent a servant for me to my room and was violently angry to find that I was not there. Summoned from the dining-room, I was bitterly reproached and a servant, with the wooden face of those trained to conceal their feelings and opinions, was called into the room, and asked if he had carried out some order or other. The little scene had been rehearsed and he answered, for my benefit, 'Not yet, sir, I haven't had my dinner yet. Food first is my motto'.

'You're fired' was the next step, accompanied by the intimation that I could keep the £150. I had not asked for it and said I would repay it, whereon he answered with the contempt of the moneyed man, 'You'll never earn enough'. He was wrong. Traps were being packed and before he drove off to Boulogne Station and Paris he said to me, 'Good-bye. You will never see me again in this world'.

Few people saw him again in this world. Cryptic daily bulletins told the public that he was ill and finally that he was dead. I watched the funeral service in Westminster Abbey. Many thousands of people had part in it. The funeral procession was miles long, the wreaths were innumerable. He had felt himself a man without friends.

Nothing much else happened to me in 1922, save that I married.

CHAPTER 6

MUSCLING IN

I HAD barely had time to survey the pleasant prospect that lay beneath me from the dizzy heights of £500 a year and now I was back in the depths, nursing my bruises.

Years of struggle followed. I needed money, to buy furniture, to rent some habitation fit for man. Post-war England was the paradise of the profiteering houseowner. The men back from the war were getting married and wanted houses. Outer London was throwing off new slums in eccentric circles, like the rings of a tree trunk, to add to those of the Victorian era, jerrybuilt settlements of mass-produced houses with niggardly little coal grates, up-and-down windows, primitive bathrooms without any adequate means of heating water. Speculative builders could buy land and dump what they liked on it. Co-ordinated control of building in the general interest, co-ordinated effort to beautify London, there were none. Even these suburban outcrops lagged far behind the demand.

In inner London, in the gloomy squares around Bayswater and Paddington, gaunt Victorian mansions were being converted into small dwellings. You took a nursery floor, two or three small bedrooms and the children's playroom, put a gas stove into one room, a bath tub and a geyser into another, threw in a couple of thin partitions for luck, called it a maisonette, and as a favour accepted tenants at £3 a week.

The Londoner had the choice of paying a high price for discomfort in one of these claustrophobic dwellings or trekking out to a distant suburban house three walls of which he might call his own, for semi-detachment was still the jerrybuilder's golden rule. There he had neither the benefits of the town nor the delights of the country, and he used up his income and energy in long journeys to and from his daily occupation. Privacy in his home, beauty in his surroundings, were things beyond the hopes of the bulk of workaday Londoners.

For some time we counted ourselves lucky to find two un-furnished rooms in Praed Street, which is just a slice of the hundred miles of dreary streets that you find between the inner and outer circles of London, and we fetched water from an outside tap. Then we moved into a maisonette in a Paddington square; it was like a prison cell, but you could see trees from the window, great plane trees in the railing-guarded square, where a lugubrious gardener and a few geraniums fought a losing battle against the dingy soil. The tenants of Norfolk Oblong — London squares are seldom square — had keys to the garden, but a square-watcher appointed jointly by all the house-owners kept a stern eye on it, and if a child threw a ball or a tenant took a puppy for a walk there the watcher at the window sallied forth and forbade these goings-on. So the square, imprisoned behind its soot-blackened railings, remained always empty, and remains empty, I dare swear, to this day, save for the disgruntled gardener.

Later I discovered that in Germany, where all things are supposed to be forbidden, such a private tyranny as this would be unthinkable; there pieces of open ground between houses are the joint property of all men, they are made pleasant with flowers and fountains and sandpits for the children, and rail-ings would be an intolerable affront to the common public conscience.

What did Mr. Gladstone say in 1886 — about London squares? From the window of Margot Asquith's boudoir, he 'admired the trees in the square and deplored their useless-ness'. And when Margot asked him 'if he would approve of the square railings being taken away and the grass and trees made into a *place* with seats, such as you see in foreign towns, not merely for the convenience of sitting down, but for the happiness of invalids and idlers who court the shade or the sun', he said, 'Yes', but the only people who could do this — prevent it — were 'the resident aristocracy'.

Forty years later in 1926, when I lived in such a square, the residents, though their blue blood had thinned, were still preventing it, and in 1966, as things go in England, they are likely to be still entrenched there, resolved to sell their railings dearly.

However, in 1937, when I was in London for a few days and walked through St. James's Square, I suddenly realized that these railings have their uses after all. They keep you from approaching nearer than a hundred yards to the equestrian statue of William III, dressed as Nero.

I worked like a mole to find an outlet from this existence. My night work began at seven and ended at two a.m. and I took up private work to augment my means, so that for months I worked from nine in the morning until two at night, drawing heavily on reserves of health.

I met Sir Roland Bourne, who had gone to South Africa as a young officer to fight the Boers — I listened enthralled to his tale of the blue-bearded Boer who came at him with a bayonet shouting 'Burgher Offizier', but Bourne got him with his revolver in the nick of time — and stayed there afterwards to build the Union with them. A disappointed man, he was trying late in life to carve a new career for himself by directing from a little flat in St. John's Wood, where I typed his letters and sub-edited his appeals and card-indexed his correspondence for him, a scheme for settling retired officers and pensioned civil servants in communities in South Africa and the other Dominions. A great gentleman, he loved to go shopping with a string-bag in the Edgware Road and to chat with the shopkeepers. His energy was amazing and, though his scheme was impracticable, he did by irresistible force succeed in getting together a committee and extracting a Government grant. But the burden of his disappointments and of this hopeless venture was too much and he afterwards shot himself, in his bathtub. I seldom had warmer respect for anyone.

I fought hard to find a bridge across the great gulf fixed between the men who wrote and the clerks. It was a great battle. A university, or at least a public school education was normally essential. The gulf seemed unbridgeable. The

64

Northcliffe episode, which at first promised to open all doors, had ended ill. I had a few slender hopes. Far back in the Paris days the correspondents, Wentworth Lewis, Ralph Deakin and W. F. Casey, had found me worth backing. My French was fairly good. But the years were passing.

At last a chance came. Long-distance telephony bridged the Atlantic. Men in New York and in London could converse as easily as men in Putney and Pimlico. The opening of the London-New York telephone was a nine days' wonder in 1927. The first public conversation was between my paper and its American opposite number — the *New York Times*. A quite ordinary tinkling of the telephone bell heralded the great moment for me. At the other end was Adolf Ochs, proprietor of the *New York Times*. I wrote the account, and it was a distinct success. For the first time I experienced the warm touch of that friendly helping hand which journalists are quick to give when they can. The London Correspondent of the *New York Times* came up to say that, for once, he had read a turnover article through 'to the bitter end'. Members of the editorial staff caused congratulations to come to me by devious ways.

I had gained a slight foothold. After some time I modestly suggested that I had the makings of a good journalist. The suggestion fell flat. I went downstairs prepared to struggle on. Suddenly, a note on managerial paper told me briefly that I had been promoted to the writing staff.

All those stubborn doors were open. A great moment. This tiny achievement, measured by the things that men accomplish every day, was to me an inexhaustible source of satisfaction. At last I had found confidence in myself, and I thought thankfully of the men who, with never a word to me, had backed my cause. Presumably they thought first and foremost that they were serving the paper, but they helped me too and I never forgot it.

For three years I learned to write. We found a house, restful and perfect, within sight of Harrow spire. Even during our

E 65

few months' tenancy it was submerged by the tidal wave of jerrybuilt settlements, but it was so secluded that within the hedges of its garden complete peace reigned, save for one or two serpents. I loved it, I loved the almond tree, the apple blossom outside the kitchen window, the view of Harrow-on-the-Hill from the bedroom windows, the intervening group of elms with the rooks cawing around them, the market gardens through which we used on summer evenings to stroll, accompanied not only by our dog, but also by our cat, a strange animal.

At Christmastide 1927 the moving men came and took our few pieces of furniture, which I had so sweated to procure, and carried them away to storage. We packed our modest wardrobe in our cheap trunks and sent them to the station. The rooms we had loved so well were empty. As we went down the lane we took a last look at the house. The snow lay heavy on it and on the trees; at that rare Christmastide snow fell abundantly. I was 32. The house was my first real home in England. I had had it a few months. I left a piece of my heart in it, for now I was leaving England again and, as I instinctively felt, for good.

We were bound for Germany. I was torn between ex-hilaration in a new career, and regret at losing England, which I loved but of which I had never been able to feel myself a part. That pain lasted for three years. Then changes began to occur in me.

CHAPTER 7

GERMAN JOURNEY

A BURLY, green-bloused porter pushed our trunks across from the Friedrichstrasse Station to the Continental Hotel, heavy with red plush and chandeliers. A sleek, morning-coated and inscrutably suave young man wafted us to our rooms. Everything looked prosperous. With some millions of my fellow countrymen I had spent four years of my life trying to reach Berlin; and now, here I was.

I began to look for the crushed and starving and desperate and bled-white Germany. I never found it. I found a country that had never known war on its own land save for the brief Russian drive in East Prussia in 1914; that had called the war off when inevitable defeat impended and had retired in ostensible submission into its own unravaged land; that by this apparent surrender had warded off decisive military defeat; a country that, scarcely daring yet to believe this, was beginning to hope that it had outwitted its foes. Germany had been spared a knockout. An international heavyweight, proclaimed to be defeated on points, but feeling himself to be the better man and dreaming of a come-back, feeling his biceps.

The next seven years were the fullest and most stimulating of my life. I should hate to have lived without knowing Germany. At the end of them the fears I had felt on Armistice Day in France, as I watched the gunners clip-clopping by, were confirmed and branded in my soul. It seemed likely that the Great War had been fought in vain, all that human energy and idealism and life and treasure squandered fruitlessly. Seventeen years after the Armistice all Europe, bordering on Germany, was in a fever of fear again. She was mightier in arms than ever. Seventy years after the first Prussian year of expansion — against Denmark — the threat to Europe was greater than ever.

I went to Germany without knowledge, but with prejudices, born of the sinking of the *Lusitania*, the execution of Nurse Cavell, the shooting of Belgian civilians at Louvain, the bombardment of Paris, the bombing of London. Seven years later, though an enormous admiration for Germany had taken shape in me, these prejudices had become convictions founded on knowledge.

There is in Germany a class of ruthless man, and this class has now again mastered the State, that acknowledges only the law of Germany's right to prevail by force of arms. These very men have harnessed the nation to a mighty fighting machine. You will find the type drawn to the life a hundred times in non-Jewish German literature — in Heinrich Mann's *Der Untertan*, in Remarque's *All Quiet*, in Peter Martin Lampel's *Outlaws*, in Wolfgang Langhoff's *Rubber Truncheon*, and many more.

After six years in Germany I stood Unter den Linden with a famous American journalist. We had been together to see a woman who had been beaten senseless by Nazi Storm Troopers. He had come to Europe, full of anti-German prejudices born of war-time propaganda, with the American Army, and after the war had come to Germany of the pre-Hitler period and had come to love Germany, deciding that the war-time propaganda had been lies. 'After what I've seen lately,' he said, 'I believe all I was ever told about them.'

Germany in 1928 was still seemingly in the throes of this struggle for the soul of the nation, though actually, as I think, it had been decided on November 11th, 1918, when the German militarists had been left the possibility to tell the nation that it had never been defeated in the field, but had only retired within its frontiers because it had been betrayed, 'stabbed in the back', by the Jews and Marxists — the dejected German sailors, the war-weary population.

Germany had lived to fight another day. The outward signs of defeat were there. Allied armies stood in the Rhineland — until reparations were paid; and in Berlin Parker Gilberts and

Bernarr Macfaddens, with large staffs of highly paid men and women still floating on the cushions of war-time soft jobs, collected these reparations. The outer world saw Germany as a prostrate figure, with a mailed Allied foot on her neck and an Allied hand in her pocket.

It was an illusion. This was no despairing, starving country. There were no devastated areas to make good, but streams of British and American gold, flowing into the country, went to build and equip vast new factories and industries, sports grounds, suburban Lidos, stations — in short, to improve and adorn German real estate.

The Germany I found had been deprived after the war of her entire merchant fleet. Now, ten years later, she had one of the biggest in the world, all new. She was forbidden to build military aircraft and severely circumscribed in her production of civilian aircraft; but through factories in Russia, Denmark and Switzerland, and by ingenious design, she overcame all obstacles and one day I saw the lovely flying-ship DO.X. go up from Lake Constance with 173 people on board — a feat never yet equalled, as far as I know.

I travelled on their maiden voyages in two lithe and graceful German ships, the *Bremen* and *Europa*, that effortlessly stole the Blue Riband first trip across the Atlantic and set wealthy victor powers hurriedly trying to recover lost prestige by building *Normandies* and *Rexes* and *Queen Marys*.

In France, England, Italy, America, airships came crashing down and these countries abandoned the search for the secret of their construction. In 1929 I saw a German zeppelin take the air. It crossed the Atlantic, circumnavigated the world, began regularly to ply to and fro across the Pacific to admiring South America.

German exports rose until she was among the first trading powers of the world. Leipzig and Stuttgart displayed splendid new stations, like proud, municipal smiles. Berlin, Hamburg, Hanover and the great Rhineland cities built vast settlements for workers.

The Germany I discovered in 1928 was a well-found land, going ahead fast, overhauling the world by its prowess in peaceful pursuits. But the political itch left it no rest. The outcasts — the men who had lost rank and privilege through the war, the men who had achieved unexpected importance in the war and found themselves nobodies in peace, the big business men who disliked the power of the trade unions, the small shopkeeper who hated to see a Socialist as mayor, all those classes which traditionally oppose and resent any betterment of the working classes — played incessantly on the nation's nerves with the refrain 'You didn't lose the war, you were stabbed in the back by Jews and Marxists, they are bleeding you white to pay the foreigner'.

Germany had one all-consuming desire — to get the Allied armies out of the Rhineland. That was the essential condition for all further policy. Foreign troops in the Rhineland! That was the shackle on the German wrist. No use stopping reparations while they were there, because they would never go. The Rhineland, occupied, was a pledge for payment. Get them out!

Stresemann was Foreign Minister, Stresemann, who looked like one of the Allied wartime cartoons of a German. I often saw him at the Foreign Office. He sat in the centre of a long table, between Baligand, who afterwards became German Minister in Lisbon and was shot by a German caller, and a Socialist official. They sat among a hundred foreign journalists of all nationalities, a motley gathering, with one woman journalist, the then Mrs. Knickerbocker, as pretty as a picture, in the middle of them. They were forbidding-looking men, and I wondered how far you are justified in taking physiognomy as a springboard for jumping to conclusions.

Stresemann, when the war was going well, was hot for the annexation of Belgium, and he was now the figure head of 'the policy of understanding'. I don't know how he himself conceived the policy of understanding, but I know that the German people in bulk understood by it, not reconciliation with former enemies, but concessions to get the foreign troops out of the Rhineland. Then you would have your hands free; then you could stop reparations; then you could re-arm; after that, well, Germany had never been defeated in the field.

Austen Chamberlain was Stresemann's opposite number in London, Briand in Paris. Chamberlain, rare among Foreign Ministers, really knew his subject. He had lunched with Bismarck, and, still more important, he had sat among Treitschke's students at Berlin University and heard him impart hatred of England and the thirst for conquest. Fifty years later, in 1937, the son of a British diplomat whom I know heard just the same lesson being taught at German universities.

'I fear my generation of Germans,' Chamberlain wrote from Berlin in 1887. 'There is a school growing up here as bad as the French military school, and if they come to the front, why, *gare aux autres*. They are likely to find a friend in Prince William, who is said to be thirsting for warlike distinction and is the idol of the military party.'

His father, Joseph Chamberlain, in spite of his son's reports from Berlin, strove for years for an Anglo-German agreement in preference to an Anglo-French-Russian group designed to contain Germany, and only abandoned hope of it when, a private understanding having been reached between himself and von Bülow, the German Chancellor let him down in a public speech.

Another Chamberlain, Neville, is trying precisely the same thing to-day. He has no personal knowledge of Germany. But the memory of his father's experiences in dealing with German leaders and of his brother's experiences in Germany itself should still be deeply imprinted in his mind.

Austen Chamberlain never forgot the lesson he learned in Berlin, and there was then a strong team of other men in the Foreign Office, men who had really plumbed the German mind and never forgot what they had seen there.

I met Austen Chamberlain years later, in Vienna. The traces of his stroke were perceptible and I felt that he had not long to live, but his intellect was as keen as a Toledo blade and his character seemed as fine as his appearance. I talked with him about Germany and found the perfect truth of the words he wrote: 'There is in my mind no thought of hostility or ill will to Germany. There is, I admit, serious anxiety as to the trend of policy of the present German Government and the effect of their daily propaganda on the people.'

His feeling was that of all of us who know Germany, an unbounded admiration for Germany and a conviction that others must defend themselves tooth and nail against a new attempt to subject Europe to German military domination. These two things are not incompatible.

Austen Chamberlain, from that youthful experience, had preserved invaluable impressions. Yet even he, before Hitler came, had thought to see a change of heart in Germany. I doubt if he was right. He thought Stresemann was Germany. Whether Stresemann ever really changed from the Belgian annexationist of 1916 only Stresemann could say. But Chamberlain misread the German mind when he thought that the Stresemann that he trusted and liked really represented deep feelings in Germany when he worked for 'a policy of understanding', or if he thought that 'understanding' meant 'reconciliation'.

'It is a comfort to us . . .', wrote Austen Chamberlain, 'that Stresemann was mourned by his own people as one whose immense services to the Fatherland were recognized.'

Was he? I saw his funeral. Large crowds attended it, but Stresemann was to them a name without any popular appeal, a name to which the stigma of kow-towing to Germany's enemies attached. Real mourning was little in the public mind. They named a street after him, and Hitler later changed the name again, so as to obliterate all memory of the man whose name, whatever his motives, had the tag 'policy of understanding' attached to it.

But as yet Stresemann, shaven-headed, his cigar between his podgy fingers, worked doggedly to get the foreign troops out of the Rhineland. I saw him most Fridays at the Foreign Office, surrounded by men of the international press. This man, whose outer man was so unprepossessing, who had acquired his doctorate with a thesis on 'The Bottled Beer Trade of Berlin', who in the war had thirsted from his arm-chair for the blood of Belgium, whose political and business career seemed to show the heavy, humourless, suspicion-ridden, petty bourgeois, had in his last years developed a fine and flashing wit, a lively repartee, that kept everybody in a good humour and made him a worthy adversary even for the brilliant Briand, who once answered, when Stresemann asked him what history would say about guilt for the Great War, 'Ah, I am no prophet and will not anticipate her judgment. But there are three things which I think she will not say — she will not say that this time France was the aggressor; she will not say that Belgium invaded Germany; she will not say, like Bethmann-Holweg, that a treaty is only a scrap of paper'.

One Frenchman can say more in a few words than a hundred retired ambassadors, university professors and colonels in letters to the newspapers, and history will be a fool if it quarrels with this answer of Briand.

At last Stresemann achieved his end, and died. In 1930, five years before the due date, the French and British troops marched out of the Rhineland. They advanced the date of the new armaments race, probably of the next war, by five years. A new chapter had begun, for Germany, for the world — the chapter of German rearmament. After that, if history runs true to form, comes the chapter of German reconquest, which at this moment is having a rehearsal in miniature in Spain.

The Rhineland was free. Germany was mistress again in her own household. The Rhineland broke out in a fever rash of flags and bunting. Hindenburg in Berlin prepared for a triumphal progress along the liberated Rhine. I packed my bag and followed in his path.

73

CHAPTER 8

HINDENBURG ON THE RHINE

I watched Hindenburg pace along the Maximilianstrasse at Speyer, between the Dom and the Old Gateway. All around him were the fluttering blue-and-white of Bavaria, students like a human tulip bed in their vivid uniforms of orange and violet and scarlet bravely flaunting the twin gages of their manhood, pimples and scars, elderly Excellencies with their paunches straining at the buttons like hounds at a leash and the Pickel-hauben of their distant youth perched precariously on the distended pates of their ripe old age, as if a cathedral had been given a dome several sizes too small for it, grizzled peasant veterans of 1864 and 1866 and 1870 in frock coats and top hats, and everywhere children, sturdy, brown, well tended, buzzing like excited bees.

Hindenburg's great body was heavy on his aged legs, his massive head heavy on his shoulders, even his top hat seemed to weigh heavily in the hand that laboriously came up and lifted it in acknowledgment of the roaring cheers. I studied his features, the heavy sweeping moustache, the vertical stubbly hair. 'The Wooden Titan', John Wheeler-Bennett called him. He was right: wood was the ideal medium to portray this man. You sought vainly for any outward and visible sign of the inner man. His face, as if carved from a block of wood, was set in heavy, chiselled grooves. The eyes were as empty as a down-side dewpond. They rested without any responsive gleam on obsequious bowing aldermen and posy-presenting children alike.

Eighteen months later I listened to him addressing the nation by broadcast. Some passages he spoke quietly, some louder, some very loudly. Ah, you thought, there speaks the real Hindenburg; see how deeply he feels this, the stress he lays on that. But I had seen the typescript of his address, prepared for him by another hand. Some passages were in small letters. Some were in capital letters. Others were in capital letters deeply underlined. That was how he knew when to raise his voice.

He was a model of devotion to duty they said. In 1914, from retirement in Hanover, he had briefly replied 'Am ready' to a telegram offering him a command. A few weeks later he had thrown out the Russians, the only invaders of Germany during the War.

In 1925, from retirement in Hanover, he had agreed to become President, to take the destiny of Germany again in his paternal hand. The Allies, who had once had him on their list of war criminals marked down for trial and potential execution, had taken alarm; but now, years later, they were reassured. He had proved to be a godfearing and constitutional man; the enlightened German republic was safe in his hands.

Legends. The Legend of Napoleon and his glory — 'Ten million dead and diminished frontiers'. The legend of Mussolini and his glorious Empire. The Legend of Hindenburg. The Legend of Hitler.

Retired generals seldom shrink with reluctance from the offer of a high command. Hanover is a pleasant town, and I recommend the Café Kropke for an agreeable place to sit and watch the world go by, but it is a backwater for a man who has commanded millions and told his Kaiser what to do.

Disgruntled Ludendorff, down in Bavaria, did not agree that his former chief had sacrificed himself to duty. He was frankly jealous and clearly thought the President of Germany should have been called Ludendorff. 'For four years Paul Hindenburg' — not even *von*, you notice — 'did everything I told him', he commented bitterly. 'Didn't even know the disposition of the various army corps', he grumbled. And General Ludendorff worked busily away at his theory that Jews, Jesuits and Freemasons — not German generals, save possibly General Hindenburg — shared the guilt for Germany's defeat, and propagated his new German religion, a druidical faith of sun-and-

75

ancestor-worship which Hitler ultimately admitted to equality with the Christian confessions.

Hindenburg climbed ponderously into his car, and I climbed into another behind him, and we sped across the Rhineland countryside. It was a summer of roses and wine on the Rhine. Between the villages golden points of light marked the helmets of the volunteer firemen, strung out between them so that the President should never be out of sight of his reunited family. Peasants in blue and red came hurrying across the fields of ripening corn and through the vineyards to see him. In the villages the lovely German children, due soon to grow into Hitler Youths and soldiers of the new German Army, clustered thick about the garlanded houses and joyfully waved him by.

And in one village young men, brown, well-muscled fellows, stood posed in a symbolic tableau on an archway. The central figure, a broken chain falling from his wrist, held a sword triumphantly aloft. The Rhineland was free; the fetters were burst, the German sword was unsheathed again. The President's car slowed down, stopped. His vacant eyes ranged slowly over the group, slowly took in its meaning. He shook his heavy head slowly, approvingly. Ah, he liked that!

The Haardt Mountains came in view, and the quick passage through jubilant wine-growing villages was like a glance down a wine-list — Deidesheim, Forst, Ruppertsberg and Nierstein. I was under the spell of a deep admiration for the loveliness of the countryside, the prosperity of the farms, the cleanliness and dignity of the cities, the looks and spirits of the people, the unremitting effort to keep everything well tended and to improve property. Germany in these things excels all other countries I have seen. But for the spirit of ruthless militarism which now prevails again I might long to be a German. It is a spirit artistically expressed in the Victory Column in Berlin, where a buxom gilded angel with enormous wings and a voluminous nightshirt glides with elephantine tread over a squat column, the flutes of which contain gilded cannon barrels captured in the three wars of 1864, 1866 and 1870.

At Mainz Hindenburg drove through tumultuous cheering streets to the Grand Ducal Palace, where the French had had their headquarters a few weeks, Napoleon a hundred years before. In between, the Germans had been to Paris and, with young Lieutenant Paul von Hindenburg watching, had rubbed their vanquished enemy's nose in the dust by proclaiming the German Empire in the Mirror Hall at Versailles.

Then we began an unforgettable journey down the Rhine, with Hindenburg in the prow of the steamer *Mainz*, and myself watching him. Before waterside villages of which the earliest historians had written, a thousand years ago, the children were ranked in white-clad rows. The youths, in shorts and singlets, built brown-limbed human pyramids on the banks.

On all sides were the black-white-red of Imperial and the red-black-gold of Republican Germany, the emblems of the struggle for the soul of Germany which the old man in the prow of the *Mainz* was to decide. On the banks ancient abbeys, and before them, waving handkerchiefs to the President, brown-robed monks. Dutch barge skippers coming upstream from Rotterdam, the Dutch eel fishers who had leased the Rhine fishing rights, Swiss bargemen homeward bound for Basel, all dressed their craft with flags and bunting, cheered the German President as he passed. The Rhine castles, ruined Rheinfels, stately Marksburg and the others, awoke to dim memories of former sieges as salutes were fired from their ancient battlements and echoed by others from the barges and the shore, so that the echoes joined with the pealing of church bells and went rolling down the hills towards Coblenz. At the foot of the Lorelei, where the Rhine maiden combs her golden hair and lures luckless sailors to their doom, crowds of children cheered shrilly, and on the headland itself tiny human figures waved white specks.

Then Coblenz, where the Rhine and Mosel join hands at the Deutsches Eck, with its monument to the First German Empire, in the shadow of the towering fortress of Ehrenbreitstein, now lined with tiny dots that were human heads.

Hindenburg stepped heavily ashore. The Burgomaster's daughter, pretty, flushed, a little breathless, advanced and said her little lyrical piece about the liberation of the Rhine and the joy of being a German. The President listened, heavy, motionless, shook her hand when she finished. Later, after the drive through a town so packed with people that it seemed to burst at the seams, she sat near me at the official celebration at the town hall and excitedly discussed her great moment with two attentive young men, who well understood the deference due to a Burgomaster's daughter.

'I was so nervous', she said. 'You didn't show it', they answered politely. 'And what was your impression of the President?' *'Ach, der Mann hat ein steinernes Gesicht'*, she said. ('Oh, he has a face of stone.') 'Hush, here he comes.'

Three years later, when the man with the face of stone opened the German sluice to the floodtide of Hitlerism, her father was thrown neck and crop out of office.

While the Rhine rang with cheers and bell-clangour and gunfire, the outer world, listening to the speeches, received the first shock to its comfortable belief that withdrawal five years ahead of time had fostered the spirit of amity and reconciliation in Germany. It was a false calculation, based on misanalysis of the German character. A few weeks later six million Germans voted for the hitherto obscure Hitler and his gospel of the martial come-back.

Now Hindenburg, reading his carefully prepared manuscript, proclaimed that the Rhineland was not yet free. It was still subject to humiliating penalties — the ban on fortifications and military garrisons on the bank nearer to France. Germany was still denied her rights, her full freedom, her full equality.

A tremor of apprehension went through Germany's neighbours. But in Coblenz the sun shone and the great crowds laughed and cheered, and drank the golden Rhine wines and sang 'Ein Rheinisches Mädel zum Rheinischen Wein', and the day wore on and dusk fell and we all went down to the river.

Ehrenbreitstein lay far above our heads, its solid black walls silhouetted against red festive fires, that set the Rhine aglow. Scores of craft plied to and fro, canoes, rowing boats, launches, Rhine steamers, all beflagged and festooned with coloured lights that cast a myriad green, red and yellow spirals into the dark rippling water. Music and singing came across from the boats. On the banks scores of thousands watched the scene. I pushed my way among the crowds and felt as glad as they.

The night wore on, the red fires on Ehrenbreitstein faded, the craft on the river went home, taking the red, green and yellow spirals with them, the singing and music dwindled, the great throngs poured back into the town. At a narrow wooden foot-bridge over an arm of the Mosel a surging mass of people was checked, then poured across in a narrow jostling stream, then widened out again and hurried on. In the darkness came the crack of splintering wood, a great splash, then many small ones, floundering, shouts for help, the shrieks of children.

When I got to the scene soon after midnight all the signs and sounds of festival had died. Ehrenbreitstein was a black, over-hanging shadow, the Rhine a dark, silent stream, the streets were empty, all was still.

Only around the broken foot-bridge was a little pool of light made by flaring torches, that cast flickering reflections into the oily water and dimly lit a circle of sombrely watching faces. In a flat-bottomed boat a man sat astraddle and probed the water with a long barbed pole. As I watched he carefully drew it out; hanging on the barbs, crucified, was a young man, his mouth stupidly agape, his dank hair streaming into staring eyes, a grotesque, ridiculous figure. What fools our bodies make of us when we are done with them. They caricature our carefully mannered, well tended, well disciplined living selves. We ought to evaporate in the moment of death.

Stretched on the bank near by lay a dozen young school-girls, a little boy from America, come to see his Rhenish grandfather, who lay next to him. All through the night they angled, and brought out twenty, thirty, forty, forty-five dead revellers.

The carnival was over. Hindenburg cancelled his tour and,

79

in a darkened room, commiserated with the city elders, white-headed, grey-bearded, shaven-pated, about this disaster to Coblenz. A Rembrandtesque scene, I thought, as I watched him. Then he went back to Berlin.

The Rhineland was free. For me the stench of death hung over it all. I had shared the joy of the Rhinelanders in their freedom regained but I felt instinctively what it was going to lead to. The liberation of the Rhineland, though the actual struggle for power was to continue awhile, marked the end of the young German Republic, which, with many defects, was a humane and enlightened community of men, moving upwards and onwards. It opened the door to a future which held for Germany martial madness, mass hysteria, of the kind to which England gave way on Mafeking Night. Germany was to develop a kind of permanent Mafeking spirit, an obsession of bellicose self-aggrandizement and self-commiseration.

At the end may lie glory, as Napoleon understood it. Ten million dead, possibly; enlarged or diminished frontiers, who knows? For me the grotesque figure hanging on the barbs, dead in the moment of patriotic festival, was the emblem of the Germany that grew out of the liberation of the Rhineland. Cannon-fodder; parade-fodder; cheer-fodder; plebiscite-fodder. Germany threw away with both hands the right to reason why.

CHAPTER 9

GERMAN FREEDOM

I FOUND Berlin a stimulating capital, Germany a stimulating country in these last years of the brief period of enlightenment.

The fate of Europe was being decided here between the Rhine and the Vistula, the Baltic and the Danube. If sixty-six million Germans could be kept to the paths of peace all was well for long to come. No other candidate for European domination offered.

England, gorged with colonies, wanted only that tranquillity to which people with vast possessions habitually aspire.

France, invaded three times within a century, desired only to put some insurmountable, bombproof, gastight barrier between herself and the Germans, to banish this eternal nightmare of invasion by a neighbouring people of whom there were 'twenty million too many', as Clemenceau said in one of those perfectly succinct summaries of the European situation which only the French mind and the French language seem able to achieve, to keep Germany 'in plaster of Paris', as a British Ambassador wrote.

Russia, already straggling amorphously over a sixth part of the world's land surface, was likely to be busy for a century digesting her Soviet revolution. To attack her was as unsatisfactory as fighting Carnera. She, with her ruined railways, her half-hatched industries, could not attack Europe — that was an old wives' tale for nervous maiden ladies in cathedral towns, a nightmare for a corpulent plutocracy, a useful line in sales talk for the armaments industry.

In Germany the battle was fought out, apparently in the full light of day, in Parliament, on election platforms, in the press. There were five main parties — the Hitler Nazis had as yet hardly appeared above the horizon — and in terms of England they corresponded approximately to Conservatives, Liberals, Catholics, Socialists and Communists. But the Conservatives

F   81

were, in English parlance, Jingo diehards of the fieriest hue, though they were yet to be outdone in patriotic hysteria by the Nazis; the Liberals more resembled moderate English Conservatives; the Catholic Centrists were more akin to British Liberals, though on a Catholic basis; the Socialists, like their British opposite numbers, were mainly trades union bureaucrats; and the Communists were typical, well-disciplined German Communists, with a passion for desk-work, organization and detail, and the typically German abhorrence of domestic disorder.

The battle seemed to be open, but it was an illusion. The paramount power lay in the hands of a Prussian Field-Marshal, and when the time came power would not be won by fighting at the barricades, or by the ballot box and parliamentary debate; it would be handed, on a silver salver, by the President Field-Marshal to Hitler. The failure to inflict a decisive military defeat, the infliction of the penalties of defeat on the German moderates instead of the German militarists, had left the former ruling classes with a precarious grip which they stealthily and skilfully transformed into a stranglehold.

The Reichswehr, with its secret funds and its exemption from parliamentary control, had remained a state within a state, ready to turn against the Republic, from the day when the Socialist leaders, fumbling with their unaccustomed power, had called on it to shoot down the Communists, when it had shot the Jewish Labour leaders Karl Liebknecht and Rosa Luxembourg and contemptuously tossed their bodies into the Landwehr Canal, so that they went floating past the Reichswehr Ministry, just opposite which hangs a life-belt, always freshly pipeclayed and well ordered, for those in peril on the Landwehr Canal.

The judiciary had been left untouched and now, with non-committal faces, applied the law of the Republic, but these men, with their students' scars and memories rooted in the days of Wilhelmian Germany, wanted nothing better than to turn on the Republic and administer a fierce concentration-camp and bump-off law of class hatred, and they gleefully applied themselves to this task when the time came.

The great industrialists of the Ruhr and Rhineland, the great landowners of East Elbia, sat undisturbed in their factories and estates and concerted plans for the overthrow of this detestable regime, in which a working man might become Chancellor, Speaker or Burgomaster, in which wages were fixed by collective agreement for entire industries and not at the sole will of the master, in which Republicans, Socialists and Communists were allowed, equally with Monarchists, Nationalists and Fascists, to march about the streets in uniform, to speak their mind in the press and parliament, to stage plays giving their point of view of social problems.

I travelled about Germany from Düsseldorf to Danzig, from Hamburg to Hanover, absorbed in the struggle. Freedom prevailed. For centuries the nation had been battened down by conscription, regimentation, the tradition of servility, rigid class barriers, the glorification of the State in the persons of those who derived profit from its glorification — the officer caste, the bureaucracy, the police, all State servants down to the municipal dustman.

Now the hatches had been taken off and freedom had burst its bounds. A man might do what he wished with his own life. He did not have to serve in the army. The approaches to the high schools and universities had been broadened, so that the arts and professions were no longer beyond the reach of the young man without money or influence.

The Jews, through their native talents and more particularly through close mutual collaboration, had profited enormously. They largely ran Berlin and the great provincial cities. Max Reinhardt counted as the leading representative of German, not Jewish, theatrical art, and I watched his classic interpretations of that good anti-Semite, Shakespeare, at the little Deutsches Theater.

I watched Elisabeth Bergner play a sweet Jewish Juliet to Franz Lederer's romantic Bohemian Romeo, Grete Mosheim dying pathetically as Margarete — I often wonder why the Nazis haven't rewritten *Faust*, with Faust as a Jew — Bruno

Walter, Otto Klemperer and Leo Blech conducting at the Opera, Otto Wallburg, Max Hansen and Siegfried Arno playing the chief parts in *The White Horse Inn*, that Jewish operetta of Austrian life, at the enormous Schauspielhaus, Gerda Maurus in the *kolossal* films of Fritz Lang. In the stalls sat a phalanx of Jewish dramatic critics, headed by Alfred Kerr, and wrote laudatory notices for the most widely read newspapers, the Jewish *Berliner Tageblatt* and *Vossische Zeitung*. In the lobbies of the theatres and picture houses *schwärmerische* German mothers and daughters fought for the signatures of their Jewish favourites. Have all those autographs been ceremoniously burned, in solemn family conclave, since the eyes of Germany were opened?

When I had a toothache I went to a Jewish dentist, and when I was ill a Jewish doctor cured me quickest, and that, I suppose, was why they were so numerous and prosperous. The most fashionable and wealthiest lawyers, well advertised by the press of their co-religionists, were Jews. Jewish architects, Erich Mendelssohn prominent among them, were busy building new villas for the wealthy along the pleasant avenues leading out to the woods and lakes. To the disgust of the fine old crusted type of German Tory, they had abandoned the stucco pineapple, turret-and-gable type of architecture which had been generally held best to express the greatness of pre-war Germany and were putting up severe white structures with flat roofs, sun parlours, roof gardens and wide window spaces, among the green trees of the Grunewald. This was regarded by the diehards as a sign of the decadence of the period.

Freedom! It took many forms. Before the war, on the Baltic and North Sea coast and on the lakes round Berlin, those who went down to the sea in slips were wont to be hauled out by a helmeted and besworded Prussian policeman, who fined them on the spot. Germans might be well developed, but they might not be over exposed.

Now they went down to the sea in nothing at all. In the lakes around Berlin they had their own reservations, these sunbathers. But there were also amateurs of sun-bathing, and you sometimes encountered them unexpectedly. I came upon seven of them one day, five men and two girls. They took no notice of me and I took no notice of them.

And one Sunday morning at the Volksbühne in the Bülow-platz — where the two police captains were shot dead one stormy night — I saw several score naked people, men and women, boys and girls, doing rhythmic exercises, dances and gymnastics on one of the biggest stages in Berlin. A stout and motherly woman member of Parliament, clothed, apostroph-ized the audience on behalf of the assembled nudists, among whom was her daughter, a splendidly built girl. She appealed to her hearers to abandon convention. 'We welcome life', she proclaimed, with outflung arm, 'Wir begrüssen das Leben,' and the great audience cheered vociferously.

The strangest item in this programme, by small town standards, was a faun-and-nymph interlude between the woman deputy's daughter and a young man, clad only in a pair of incongruous horn-rims. They were both such magni-ficent specimens that I felt it a pity they should ever have to wear clothes; but just this, possibly, is the weak point of the nudist movement, and if we all looked like these two the eccentrics would probably be the clothes-wearers. The young man made a series of faunlike rushes; and the girl recoiled nymphlike. They had been schooled to give free play to the instinctive reactions of their bodies, within the limits of rhythmic and graceful movement. The beating of a gong kept their movements in time and gave a suitably tom-tom-like accom-paniment.

I came away puzzled, but with an open mind. I would have liked to look like the people on the stage and, unless I was an Armenian, they were healthy in mind and body. These were no sexual lunatics, of the type of which Germany had many, but Germans of the best type. Nevertheless, I could not see what they gained by gathering on a Berlin stage on a Sunday morning.

True, it was winter, and they had to be nude indoors or not at all. If the display had been under a blue sky, against green trees, I should have had only an aesthetic admiration for it. As it was, I was in the evening immediately prejudiced in favour of the nudists when a paunchy man in a tight dinner jacket with a cocktail-beaten face, to whom I described the scene, said briefly, 'We put people like that in lunatic asylums', and resumed operations on behalf of his paunch, unshakably certain that he had uttered wisdom's last word.

This freedom! For Germany, that depressingly thorough country, half-measures seemingly do not exist. Either you give a man entire liberty to do what he likes with his life and body, or you deliver him body and soul to the State and make him the bondslave of the particular clique which happens to be lining its purse at the moment through the possession of power. In matters of morality a certain rigour is probably best, though you are tempted to doubt this when it produces such oddities as policemen who hide behind trees in public parks and town councillors who go about running a yard measure over the bathing costumes of the adolescent.

Berlin, after decades of secret and suppressed indulgence, was sowing its wild oats with a vengeance. I went to a base-ment tavern near the Schlesischer Bahnhof, Berlin's Limehouse, where you paid a mark and saw an extraordinary cabaret programme of sexual freaks, harumphrodites that were far from giddy, and the like. Young male prostitutes walked the streets. A dozen, a score, resorts where homosexuals of both sexes could meet plied a thriving trade, the young men dressed as girls, the girls trying to look like men and looking actually like caricatures of Harold Lloyd.

I offer no opinions about homosexuality. I only mention it because in Germany, where it is more prevalent than any other country I know, although I notice that it is spreading in Eng-land, it seems to have some indefinable influence on politics. Before the war there was a great homosexual scandal at the German Court.

86

Who knows from what source it springs? Its consequences seem more important. In Germany the thing seems to be wedded to that other incalculable sexual phenomenon, sadism.

Several foremost leaders of the National Socialist Party, fighting its way to power, were known homosexuals and sadists. Röhm was *schwul*, a lost libel action had publicly proved it; Ernst was a *Berliner Junge* who owed his post as Brown Army Commander for Berlin to his relationship with Röhm; Heines was a homosexual sadist who, as the Party exultantly advertised, had killed a man.

But the Party, which subsequently gave 'moral depravity' as one of several reasons for shooting scores of its leaders without trial, then indignantly denied that they were morally depraved. It was all infamous calumny, said that Dr. Göbbels who in June 1937 was to broadcast a speech to the German nation accusing the Catholic priesthood wholesale of homosexuality and recalling that in June 1934 'We shot sixty leading National Socialists for this same vice'.

Sadism, a far more important thing, flourished openly. If you want to know about sadism, read Wolfgang Langhoff's *Rubber Truncheon*, the story of a German concentration camp. Or read the triumphant account by Julius Streicher, the chief Jewbaiter of Nuremburg and Hitler's personal crony, of his visit to a prison cell, with a bodyguard of trusty friends, to beat up a prisoner.

That is one side of sadism. The other side is sexual. They spring from the same root, delight in inflicting or receiving pain. In Berlin, about 1930, hundreds of establishments sprang into being called massage salons. The market for human beings was at its lowest ebb then and at these places every form of indulgence could be bought for a few marks.

It stands to the ineradicable discredit of the Socialist-Liberal regime that, in their fight for the priceless thing that freedom is, they allowed this abuse of freedom — the freedom of the free fox in the free henroost.

The National Socialist regime did a national service in

suppressing them; but under it sadism in other forms — the concentration camps — was practised in a measure never known in the massage salons, not from motives of material necessity or of sexual self-indulgence, but from motives of animal cruelty alone, and on helpless victims.

In 1930 sadism prospered in the massage salons and private establishments — that grotesque, ridiculous, revolting sexual sadism of flagellation, bought and paid for. This delight in inflicting and receiving pain is a thing I have encountered in no other country. You can find it in scores of non-Jewish German books written during the period of free literature. It is an inexplicable, monstrous, sinister thing, out of all rhyme with the noble cities of South Germany and the Rhineland, with Hamburg, Bremen and Lubeck, with the magnificent German culture; it is barbaric and bestial. That the very people who practise it are capable of a tearful sentimentality about birds, flowers, and small children, and especially about patriotism in all its aspects, makes it more terrifying and more revolting. Read Langhoff's account of the man who had charge of Lichtenberg prison, who was wont to torture his captives to death, and whose cold blue eye softened to a warm, mankind-loving azure as he contemplated the prison Christmas Tree and murmured *'Deutscher Christbaum, Deutsche Weihnachten!'*

The Socialist-Liberal Republic did its best to commit suicide through its judicial system. The Socialists, whose ranks at the outbreak of war had been split on the vital issue whether they should stand up and shout 'Hoch' for the Kaiser or only stand up, at the collapse of the monarchy fumbled the catch which fell into their hands, and did not build themselves an armed Republican Guard but retained an army steeped from Field-Marshal to Drummer Boy in anti-Socialist and anti-Republican tradition. They retained a pre-war judiciary of just the same mind. Not only that, but they politely handed the judges a dagger wherewith to stab the Republic in the back. This was their new system of 'humane justice', born of the conviction that the criminal was largely the product of his surroundings and his ancestry, by no means wholly responsible for his crimes. They improved prison conditions, promoted schemes for the moral redemption of the criminal, suspended the death penalty, all things desirable or at least debatable in matters of crime, but suicidal in politics.

Thus Hitler, having grown plump, as his jailer recorded, during the few months of cushioned and well-fed captivity with which he expiated his Munich rising of 1923, was let loose on the Republic again.

Thus Heines, having bumped off somebody whom he chose to consider a traitor in one of the secret anti-Republican battalions at the maintenance of which successive German Republican Governments, from fear of the Reichswehr, connived after the war, while protesting that they were disarming according to peace treaty, was soon liberated, and later became police chief of Breslau, with life-and-death power over the population.

Thus Ministers, like Erzberger and Rathenau, who were accused of favouring reconciliation with Germany's enemies, were killed with impunity by patriotic gunmen, who had only brief imprisonment to fear.

Such a Republic could not live.

The Republic did, I believe, thrice bring itself to inflict the death penalty in its fourteen years of life.

The first victim was the sexual sadist Haarmann of Hanover, who in 1925 was convicted of killing twenty-two youths and young men.

The second was the sexual sadist Karl Angerstein, convicted of eight murders in 1925.

The third was the sexual sadist Peter Kurten of Düsseldorf, who was captured in 1930 by an extraordinary chance after killing ten or eleven little girls and young women and threw in a confession about a child killed while sleeping in its cot before the war. In the dock he spoke calmly of his irresistible impulse to commit murder and described drinking his victims' blood.

But while Berlin lavishly sowed its belated oats, Germany was busy at work, making and mending. I went to Kiel to watch Hindenburg name Armoured Cruiser A, the first big warship to be built by Germany since the war. The German navy was rising from Scapa Flow, and I thought back to the war as I contemplated her. She was lovely, with perfect lines. Sixty thousand Germans, with top hats and brass bands, stood about me.

At this time the main aim of German policy was to get reparations payments stopped and the outer world everyday was getting a picture of a Germany prostrate, broken and starving. It was rubbish. I compared that picture with the one before me — a fine and costly ship, well-nourished German crowds, German sailors of fine physique and bearing, the bright harbour busy with beflagged craft, the prosperous town behind.

Up on the dais Brüning made a speech, and Hindenburg, beside him, waited to name the ship. Suddenly she ran away. Hindenburg tried to grab the dangling champagne bottle that trickled through his fingers. Sixty thousand heads turned in flabbergasted silence as she went. Hindenburg called after her from afar 'I name thee *Deutschland*!'

'A bad omen', said the seamen, shaking wise heads, 'that she should take the water unnamed.' 'A good omen', said the optimists, 'that she should be so eager to be off.' 'Did you notice', remarked a wit, 'that she moved away just as Brüning spoke of the League of Nations?'

The seamen were right. An ill-omened ship.

Seven years later, just after the new German air force had won its first wings by destroying the ancient Basque country-town of Guernica, two Spanish Government airmen mistook the *Deutschland* for a Franco ship and dropped bombs on her as she lay in the roadstead of Iviza, in the Balearics. Two days later a German squadron shelled Almeria, a Spanish coastal town which in its wildest nightmares would have been more likely to foresee an invasion of Martians than its destruction by Germany. The town was razed, many women and children were killed, scores of small existences were destroyed, and the surviving Almerians stayed out camping on the hills for days, eventually creeping back to try and rescue a kitchen table or chair from their ruined homes. This was the first action of the new German Navy. It justified the feelings I had when I watched the launch of the *Deutschland* and meditated about the spirit that was abroad in Germany. The world has yet to see the first exploit of the new German Army, which will be impatient to blazon on its maiden standards some honour worthy to rank with those of Guernica and Almeria, won by its sister services.

But in Kiel on this fine and sunny day no thought of collapsing tenements and terror-stricken Spanish women and children clouded anybody's pride in the rebirth of German naval power.

Hindenburg, the rest of us in his trail, went out to the fleet review and Germany paraded her naval poverty before us. Through the lane of old battleships, cruisers and destroyers we steamed, floating monuments to the lost war and the peace treaty, still waiting for Hitler to tear it up. A few years later those old ghosts of Imperial Germany's naval power — 'The Admiral of the Atlantic greets the Admiral of the Pacific', the Kaiser had wired to the Czar — were quickly disappearing, and German shipyards were rapidly building a new fleet.

Then I went all over Germany, marvelling at the richness of the countryside, the well-to-do-ness of the peasantry in Mecklenburg and Pomerania and Oldenburg, the dignity of the cities, the cleanliness and order everywhere. These things are inherent in the German character, permanent in Germany, they survive all regimes. The casual visitor to Hitlerist Germany puts them down to Hitler, not realizing that they were always there.

I found no slums, as I knew them in England. Read this: 'Many of the smaller villages consist of a straight row of slum houses built only to serve the pit. They have no church, no inn, no village hall or any facilities for community life. With the pit closed, they are not only derelict but have no chance of revival of their original industry or the introduction of new occupations. W—, with a population of two hundred and fifty, has only six men in employment. A typical cottage contained a living-room, a scullery, two bedrooms, a backyard, an outside earth closet. For twelve years it had been the home of a man, woman and six children.'

In Germany, defeated in a world war, you could not have found that. That is in Durham, in England, victorious and wealthy, twenty years after victory in a world war, according to the Durham Community Service Council.

In Germany such conditions would not be tolerated, neither under the Kaiser, nor under the Republic, nor under Hitler. Private charity, subscription-begging hospitals with highly-paid 'Appeal Secretaries', do not exist, and I liked that too: I always detested Lady Bountifuls, munificently distributing cast-off clothes and petty largesse. The German hates straggling, untidy, unorganized things. For him the relief of distress is the duty of the State, not a hobby of the individual, calling for a kiss-hand from the recipient. Thus the care of the poor, the sick, the children, the aged, the unemployed is all organized by the State, and admirably organized. In the big cities the Lord Mayor, or Oberbürgermeister, is not a chain-wearing tradesman but a highly paid municipal specialist with wide powers. And when the trade slump became so bad, about 1931, that cast-off clothing and petty largesse were urgently needed, their collection and distribution were organized by the State. This was the *Winterhilfe* scheme, introduced by Brüning, developed by Hitler.

Pursuing my travels, I came to Essen, where Krupps were making ploughshares until the Rhineland evacuation, Hitler and rearmament should enable them to resume making swords, day and night, year in year out. I was consumed with admiration for the idyllic garden settlements that Frau Bertha Krupp had built for Krupp workers. I found coalmines screened by rich fields of grain, miners well housed, a bright and busy town without squalor, full of flowers. I thought rancorously of Durham and South Wales, black scabs left on England's face. My own eyes saw what I had always felt, that the Black Country

did not need to be, but was the product of carelessness, callous-
ness and rapacity. You tore up and blackened large chunks of
England's green and pleasant land in order to get at the coal
underneath, leaving the people to decay in their hovels when
the coal was exhausted or became too expensive to work. All
you had for that mass of human energy and misery was a few
stately homes how beautiful they stand in Surrey and Hampshire and large areas of squalid wilderness peopled by permanent unemployed in the North and Midlands, and you called them
the Distressed Areas at first but Special Areas later, so that the
poor should not be always with you, just as you decided to take
sanctions against Italy in Abyssinia when you thought they
would work and decided to take sanctions off when you saw
that they wouldn't.

But in these great industrial settlements of the Ruhr and
Rhineland — practically one big city, as large as London —
pitheads did not mean grime and squalor. Slums in the English
connotation were none. Factories were great bright mechanical towns. The workers were well cared for. Tables showing
that their wages were lower than those paid in other countries
meant little, because they had more from their lives; they could
buy better quarters for the rent paid, electric light, central
heating and running warm water were available to most; the
countryside around the towns was not allowed to be ruined by
the private speculative builder, since all building had to con-
form strictly to long-laid town planning schemes; great leagues
of cyclists by subscribing a few pence a head laid and maintained special paths for cyclists through the endless State forests
and woodlands; the young people hiking over hill and dale at the
week-ends had a choice of forty thousand hostels in which they
could sleep and eat for a few pence.

Wandering about Germany between 1928 and 1933 the
Englishman of my origin was constantly forced to ask himself
three questions:

What does England gain from centuries of prosperity, security
from invasion, and victory in a world war?

What has Germany lost from losing a world war?

Would it not be in the long run a good thing if Germany were to dominate Europe, since she runs her country better than the rest of us?

I am still looking for the answers to the first two questions. After Hitler came I put 'No' against the third question. Then the thought of European domination by this Germany became abhorrent.

Travelling about Germany, I came to have a great respect for the part that had been played in building up this almost perfect State by the little kingdoms, the petty principalities, the grand but diminutive duchies, all of them for centuries vassals of the Habsburg Emperor in Vienna, after 1866 and 1871 lieges of that bold military upstart the King of Prussia, and now all swept away.

All about me Germans complained incessantly that disunity was the besetting evil of the Germans; but as I contemplated Germany it seemed to me that Germans might well have reached their greatest happiness during this patchwork quilt period, when they were Bavarians, Saxons, Württemburgers and the like, each with a ruler whose State was not too big for him to oversee and who had sovereign power in his domestic affairs.

I loved Munich and Dresden with their pleasant kingly courts and priceless treasures, the two Mecklenburgs, with the grand ducal palaces overlooking idyllic lakes at Schwerin and Neu Strelitz, the little main streets where court hatters and court wiggers, their occupations gone, still hung out their signs that told of past glories, the sleepy gentility of the little cobbled streets about the palace with the pretentious villas from which fussy Court Chamberlains had been wont to puff forth to bow before the Grand Duke, ladies-in-waiting to attend upon the Grand Duchess.

Take Oldenburg, the capital of such a tiny grand duchy, once splashed over Germany in enclaves hundreds of miles apart — such were the tricks that princely bequeathment and inheritance played with the German map. The Grand Ducal

94

Palace, dreaming of the brave Oldenburger grenadiers and dragoons who used to people its pleasant forecourt, slumbers in the sun, and near at hand a little river softly slips past. All around are the pleasant villas built by the generations of retired officials and prosperous farmers who were wont in former days to come and live as close to the court as they could get and end their days in a gentle round of visits to each other and to the little State Theatre, which still proudly displays the Grand Ducal crown. In the palace is a marvellous museum of peasant costumes and arts and crafts and old shop signs and shop fronts that shows you the lovely, hard-working, craftsman's Germany of the petty dynasties. How much more these places, Munich and Dresden and Hanover and Stuttgart and Schwerin and Neu Strelitz and Oldenburg, seem to belong to Vienna, lazy, courtly, elegant, good-humoured, cynical, baroque, Imperial Vienna, than to goose-stepping, drum-beating, trumpet-blowing, sabre-rattling, stiff, confident, parvenu Berlin.

In Oldenburg, against this incongruous background, I saw the Communists — for this little town has a little industry and therefore a small proletariat — come marching from the station, shabby, with Thälmann in their midst, Thälmann who now lies in perpetuity in a German prison, never tried, never likely to be tried, because his only crime is that he was leader of a party that was legal until Hitler declared it illegal. He came, fist clenched in the Communist greeting, at the head of the underdogs of Oldenburg, where a few factory workers live entirely surrounded by prosperous *bourgeois* in a countryside inhabited by prosperous peasants. Stout, with shaven head and coarse features, he might, by physiognomy, have been the brother of Stresemann, of Ley, of Streicher, or of Röver, the taciturn, glowering leader of the Oldenburg Nazis, who had the local Communist leader put to death as soon as he was in a position to do so. Thälmann looked a typical German.

As they went by a young upstanding man in Nazi uniform watched them from the shadow of the station, making mental notes of faces for future reference. The Nazis were feverishly active. Their propagandists were busy in every township and village and hamlet and farm and cottage. I met and talked to their leaders everywhere.

In Essen and Hamburg and Cologne and Dresden I watched them at work. They were all glooming, glowering men, boastful of their war service, all thirsting for revenge on the traitors at home who had stabbed the German army in the back and on the foreign foes who thought they had beaten Germany. Many of them were men without occupation, who had not made good in civilian life and who could only hope again to have the money and power they had enjoyed in the army through the victory of their party. When it came to power most of them performed wonders in rapid self-enrichment and self-aggrandizement.

Some had a record of violent crime. Some were almost penniless save for the doles they received from the party. Others were living on women. A few years later they were all Little Hitlers in their local domains, partaking avidly of the fleshpots, wielding power of life and death over their submissive compatriots, who applauded them just as heartily as they had cheered Kaiser Wilhelm, the Republic, Grand Old Man Hindenburg.

They lived on hatred. They hated their enemies at home and abroad, with a consuming hatred, and titillated their imaginations with visions of the things they would one day do to them. They were, as I saw them, lustful, savage, sadistic, virile, resolute.

One glowering fellow in Essen particularly hated a local police official and was longing for the day when he could 'shave him with a blunt razor'. That policeman must have had a bad time when Hitler came, unless he went while the going was good.

For these men, politics, soldiering and war were obsessions. They lived so entirely in the last war and the next that I put them down as cases of incurable trench fever.

One told me that the Great War was nothing to the spectacle

that Germany would offer the world in the next. Thirteen years after the Armistice his mind was still rambling, in its beloved officer's uniform, about the trenches around Ypres and Verdun. Beelzebub knows how much he had in years of brooding added to his wartime exploits, but I grew so tired of them that when he told me how he met unarmed a Scottish soldier face to face in a shellhole and induced him to surrender by threatening him with a bottle, the only thing ready to his hand, I suggested that the Scot had thought the bottle to contain whisky and had willingly given himself up. He went pale with perplexity at this modest jest, and stared stupidly at me and at the girl sitting with us, on whom he was living; the cuckoo seal of the Prussian bailiff, pasted on her car, in which he drove about Essen, was the price she paid for the society of this Capitano Horribilicribifax.

This habit of exchanging terrific reminiscences of their prowess in war, like the captains of the harlequinade, was prevalent among the Nazi leaders. The Nazi Angriff one day said that Hitler had won his Iron Cross in the war for the singlehanded capture of fourteen Englishmen ('No doubt he surrounded them', remarked the Socialist *Vorwärts* sarcastically), and Sefton Delmer of the *Daily Express* went to Hitler to ask for further details of this exploit, whereon Hitler answered modestly, no, they weren't Englishmen, that would have been too much even for a Hitler, they were only fourteen Frenchmen. The deed that won this Iron Cross was long shrouded in mystery, but on Hitler's 48th birthday, four years after his advent to power, the German War Ministry suddenly produced a document stating that it was the reward of general good conduct under fire. It made no mention of the fourteen Frenchmen.

I met Röhm, Hitler's best friend and first lieutenant, at the flat of a friend. A swollen head, with a little island of hair atop, porcine features, small eyes, the nose smashed by a shell fragment. He came attended by several young men of the type he habitually had about him. When he was in Bolivia after the war, building the Bolivian Army, he had written letters to a friend openly discussing his homosexual love affairs. Political enemies acquired and published these letters in the Socialist *Vorwärts*. Röhm brought an action, which he lost, the court finding that the letters were genuine. This was years before Hitler came to power. I shall never forget the accents, literally trembling with shocked horror, in which little Göbbels, the morning after Hitler had had Röhm bumped off, disclosed to the nation the awful discovery that Röhm, Heines and the others were addicted to homosexuality.

Now Röhm sat next to me, with Helldorf opposite him, Helldorf who had organized the first anti-Jewish riots on the Kurfürstendamm. Röhm spoke of the funeral of a Nazi Storm Trooper. Nazis, Socialists and Communists were then killing each other daily in street brawls, two Socialists or Communists to one Nazi. The leniency of Republican justice was the real cause of this readiness to draw a gun. Röhm said how moved he had been by the funeral. The day before half a dozen Socialists had been killed in Brunswick and I pointed that out to him. 'Pity it wasn't twenty', he remarked briefly.

Then I met Hitler, the hero of a hundred platforms. With his gigantic aide Bruckner he sprinted up the stairs of the Brown House, flipping his arm seal-like in answer to the salutes. I was ushered in. He sat behind a table, with a portrait of Frederick the Great hovering in the offing. He wore the gloomy and glowering mien of all dictators and candidates for dictatorship. Hess, of the unbelievably deep set eyes and the extraordinary jaw, wider even than his forehead, but one of the least unsympathetic of the leading Nazis, sat by him.

He talked to me just as he talked to his audiences, beginning quietly, then growing louder in tone and more emphatic in gesture, then generating an awful righteous wrath and a bright flush as he discoursed of Germany's wrongs. I knew the platform technique by heart. All the other Nazi leaders, big and little, that I had met on my travels had used the same manly effort to control a strong man's feelings until the floodtides of indignation burst the dam, but now I saw that they had even copied his gestures. I was at the fountainhead of Nazi eloquence.

All the way round Germany I had found Nazi leaders using the same gestures. Two in particular impressed me. When you wanted to lay clear your mind in all lucidity you bunched the points of all your fingers together and plucked thoughts from your forehead, as if you laid bare your innermost soul. You drove a good point home by stabbing the right forefinger against the left palm. Thoughts had been plucked and points hammered home for me all over Germany. Now Hitler did it again.

He addressed me as if I were the Sport Palast packed to bursting. The quiet self-control; the rising tide of righteous indignation; the impassioned outburst, the voluble gestures, the baneful glare. He would have made a marvellous sergeant-major and I wondered that he had only become a corporal in the war. He spoke bitterly of France, the peace treaty, the League of Nations, as the sources of all original sin, of Germany's unrequited love for England. France would squeeze England like an orange; and woe betide England when France turned upon her. Frederick the Great, the patron of Voltaire, smirked down on us.

I heard this argument often enough from Nazis in my seven years in Germany. But I formed the opinion that the real hatred of that warlike Germany which eventually prevailed is for England, first and foremost. England took the German fleet, England took the richest German colonies, England confiscated German property, England's intervention prevented a lightning German victory in 1914, for without her France would have been rolled up like a piece of linoleum. Then England could have been tackled singly, later. England was the real obstacle to world domination. Any Englishman who can convincingly pass as a Dutchman, an Austrian or what not can test this statement; he will hear other things about England than the unrequited love story which so titillates the palate of the casual English visitor, come to see for himself.

99

I had seen the Nazis at work all over Germany. I believed that if these men ever acquired power in Germany Europe would see a Greater War. They had told me so, and I believed them. Force was their creed and bible. Only by force could Germany get what she wanted in the world.

I thought then that there was hope of saving the moderate regime. I believed in the legend of Grand Old Man Hindenburg, staunch guardian of the constitution. After I saw what happened to Germany I made few mistakes in appraising politicians and their actions.

In Berlin the struggle approached its climax. Hindenburg, well into the seventh age of man, was the centre of a hornets' nest of intrigues that made his palace in the Wilhelmstrasse like one of the Italian courts of the Middle Ages.

The foreign troops were gone from the Rhineland. The moment to suspend reparations was coming. Rearmament would be the next step; after that, the come-back? Who was going to rule Germany at this vital moment in her history? The President could not live much longer. Care must be taken to see that the power passed into the right hands before his death. The façade erected for the delusion of the outer world could be pulled down, the period of Liberal and Socialist and Centrist Chancellors ended.

Von Papen, his name and extraordinary exploits as military attaché at Washington during the war long forgotten by the world, stood in the shadows of the palace; von Schleicher, reading the reports of his spies and listening by dictaphone to Centre Chancellor Brüning's conversations, sat at the Reichswehr Ministry and pictured himself as the real ruler of Germany. The great landowners gathered round the failing President and inflamed his mind against Brüning through their emissary Oldenburg-Januschau, a corpulent squire who many years before had cried that the Kaiser ought to send an officer and ten men to close Parliament and for this rare and beautiful phrase had for twenty-five years been a revered and legendary figure to all the Diehards. In Potsdam, a monarchist fieldsman hoping to make a catch in the slips, sat the Crown Prince Wilhelm, tall, drooping, always smiling, whom I often saw lounging about on the terrace of the Wannsee Golf Club or driving to Berlin in his blue sports car, a well-massaged, old-young man, with grey-blond hair, automatically smiled on by the girls Unter den Linden.

In Munich, entirely surrounded by swastikas, sat Hitler, whose first whole-time job in life was to be German Chancellor and absolute dictator, with power exceeding that of Bismarck or the Kaiser.

CHAPTER 10

BRENDA MARY

My German landlady came quickly down the corridor as she heard my key turn in the lock and said: 'Mr. Reed, you are wanted in London at once.' A good soul, a Jewess, the wife of a former rector of Berlin University and the grandmother of a boy who could have stood model for one of Frl. Leni Riefenstahl's film shots of Hitler's young, blond, blue-eyed, Nordic Germans. On his looks he qualifies for any post in Germany, but in Germany nowadays they ask you who your grandmother was. You can see the fill-out forms in the stationers' shops, with a sales ticket: 'Who was your grandmother?'

Twenty-four hours later I was at Victoria, and my father met me with the words, 'It's a girl'. A London April, windy, cold, dampish. I found my wife in a dingy bedroom in a dingy nursing home, in a dingy Marylebone square, tended by two nursing midwives of such awesome appearance that you had to take their hearts of gold on trust. They were the sergeants-major of childbirth, the little nursing home was their parade ground, where they hauled the new recruits into the world, smacked them, stood no nonsense.

My wife had felt her time come one morning and gone hot-foot to them, and they had cast experienced eyes over her, told her to come back next day. At night the pains were unbearable; she went to them again; they took one glance and said, 'Come back to-morrow'. On the morrow they took her in and the oldest drama in the world began, while a two-man band mournfully played in the drab square.

It took hours and hours, and the doctor and the nurses had to work hard. That baby gave them no help at all. The perspiring doctor put a handle suspended from a rope into my wife's hands, for her to bear on, and said, 'Now push, push hard'. The band outside, in the railinged square with its meagre buds, began to play 'Pull for the shore, sailor, pull for the shore.' My wife tried vainly to comply with conflicting instructions.

Then at last the baby came, while the band was playing 'Sonny Boy'.

They were wrong again. It wasn't a boy. It was Brenda Mary, with a mat of black hair that turned to pure gold and then dwindled to a nondescript dark-blonde.

Marvelling, we took her to a humble lodging in Highgate, and while we slept in the big bed she slept the first night in a chest of drawers and the second night in a suitcase, and then we drove down through Kent to Whitstable and a cottage, with bluebells and primroses in the garden, on a hilltop among the woods, and she had a cot of her own.

For the last time I felt that longing to stay in some quiet corner of England like this, to watch the spring come and the autumn go, to bring up fine healthy children and have a few good friends, and to feel that my roots were in England. I would have given anything then to stay for ever. From one window of our little sitting-room we looked over Canvey Island, Laurence Irving's picturesque windmill, and the mouth of the Thames; from the other we looked down over endless Kentish hills that spring was lacing daily more lavishly with green. In the garden jays and magpies and woodpeckers were busy, and I discovered with a telescope unsuspected details of their plumage and their occupations. The road past the cottage ran to Canterbury, and I ran with it and loved the old cathedral, dreamed of Chaucer's pilgrims, looked with awe on the tomb of the Black Prince. But the queen of this May was Brenda Mary.

These were happy weeks, overclouded by the thought of leaving England, of the spirit that was abroad in Germany, of the new war that was looming ahead. The weeks went like a flash and one morning, just after Brenda Mary had smiled for the first time, I went bumping down the road in a taxi, the waving handkerchief and the bundle that was Brenda Mary quickly receding in the distance. Twenty-four hours later I was back in Berlin, with politics buzzing about me like bees, the peace of that Kentish countryside an almost unimaginable thing.

We grew apart later, my wife and I, which was a nuisance, because you both feel like unwashed dinner plates. She remained as she always had been. I changed, intellectually and almost physically, with my changing surroundings, far and frequent journeys, nerve-absorbing occupation. I became a nomad. I lost England, which I understood less and less, and developed an interest, that became almost a passion, for the study of foreign peoples and foreign places.

The worst of that was that it ultimately meant losing the companionship of Brenda Mary, a lovely, cheerful child, with whom I delighted to go tobogganing in the Grünewald outside Berlin or skating at the Eisverein in Vienna or shopping in Lugano. She was bilingual from the time she learned to speak at all, and talked good Berlinisch to our Dienstmädel in Berlin and sang 'Mei' Mütterl war a Weanerin' in good Wienerisch to the charwoman in Vienna, and she had no inhibitions but developed a quick intelligence through seeing so many places and people and chatted with lively self-confidence to everyone she met, from my old friend the old Minister on the Ice Rink to the woman who used to go walking with a hen in the Cottagegasse.

GRAND OLD MAN

I SAT at my loudspeaker and heard Hindenburg's national broadcast appeal for re-election as President. Sometimes his voice vibrated with emotion. I knew when it was going to vibrate. I had his speech before me and this is how it looked:

'. . . I have resolved to offer myself for re-election. As the request does not come from any party but from the broad masses of the nation, *I feel it my duty to accept.* Not one of my critics can deny that I am inspired with the most ardent love of my country AND WITH THE STRONGEST POSSIBLE WILL THAT GERMANY SHALL BE FREE.'

Meissner had done a good job. Hindenburg spoke with his Meissner's voice.

The Gods in High Olympus must have held their sides when they looked down on Germany in 1932.

Hindenburg now had all the Catholics, Socialists, Republicans and Jews solid for him, who had foreseen the end of the liberal Republic when he was first elected in 1925. They saw in him the saviour of the Republic, of the Constitution, of justice, humanity and peace, their guardian and prop against Hitler, who immediately after the Rhineland evacuation had flabbergasted the confiding outer world by increasing his vote from 800,000 to 6,000,000.

The Nationalists and National Socialists, who had put Hindenburg in the Presidential chair in 1925 to wreck the Republic and restore the monarchy, were solidly and rabidly against the man who had countersigned the Young Plan. The Young Plan, as you will not remember, was the final reparation I O U which Germany signed to get the foreign troops put out of the Rhineland five years before the due date; as an equivalent for her signature to this 'final settlement' several noughts were struck from the amount she was to pay in instalments spread over 59 years and the troops were withdrawn.

Ludendorff, brooding down in Bavaria, even demoted Field-Marshal von Hindenburg, tore his shoulder straps off and drummed him out: 'Field-Marshal von Hindenburg', he wrote, 'had forfeited the right to wear the field grey uniform of the army and be buried in it. Herr Paul von Hindenburg has destroyed the very thing he fought for as Field-Marshal.'

The nobles, the landowners, the ex-officers, the Nationalists and Nazis differed only in describing him as senile or a traitor. Göbbels, the diminutive clubfoot whose heart bounded so readily to the brave music of that distant drum to which he would never march, Göbbels whom the Socialists caricatured as a ranting dwarf 'chest measurement 36, mouth measurement 63', asked malevolently, 'Is Hindenburg still alive?'

Hindenburg was elected and the Republicans breathed again. The constitution and the rights of man were safe.

A year later the Young Plan, with all its noughts, had dissolved in thin air, like so many smoke rings.

And here I should like to say what I think about the peace treaty, as a man who saw the war that made it and the way it worked, both on the spot.

Firstly, if you refrain from inflicting a decisive military defeat your peace treaty is an illusion, a house built on shifting sands.

Secondly, you cannot keep a conquered people permanently in armed inferiority unless you occupy their country. To tell them they mustn't have arms is vain. If you still fear them the only thing to do is to outarm them and, if you are numerically weaker than they, to ally yourself with fast friends who will make good the deficit — to face your enemy with the certainty of defeat by an overwhelming coalition if he attempts to reverse the verdict.

Thirdly, it is wrong to expel from the conquered country the people you consider guilty of the war and to inflict the penalties on their liberated subjects. This means that the peaceable and moderate incur the unpopularity for the sins of their predecessors.

Fourthly, it is vain to think that a country like Germany

will make good the havoc she has wrought by buying absolution on the instalment system over a period of 59 years. If you want compensation you must march in and take it, in treasure.

So everything is bad about the peace treaty, except the most important thing of all — the frontiers it made. I mean the European frontiers; I always regretted that England should have enriched herself from the war more than any other country by taking the German colonies, and the moral indignation that so many English people display about the treatment of Germany by other countries is the joy of the satirist. But, travelling about Europe, I became convinced that, in its territorial results, the war had been a good war. It had freed 80,000,000 people who had been for centuries under alien domination, and the over-lapping areas it had left, where minorities still lived under alien rule or had come under it, were inconsiderable compared with the total enslavement of entire nations before the war.

Lastly, it brought a whiff of freedom to the domestic life of the peoples. These domestic ideals of freedom, parliamentary rule, and social progress, were soon overthrown again; but in Austria and Germany they lasted many years, the masses for the first time had a real part in the government of the country and caught a glimpse of a new world of self-respect and wider opportunity.

Internal freedom — that is, government by an elected parliament, a free press, public control by these means over the acts of the country's rulers, free access to universities and professions, the security of the individual against arrest, maltreatment and imprisonment without trial, free literature, art and theatre — has now vanished in all the defeated countries. Of the new countries that sprang from the war Czechoslovakia alone, surrounded by enemies who hate her for that very reason, remote from lukewarm friends, retains some measure of democracy and is fighting a lonely battle in Central Europe to maintain it in some degree.

The issue was decided in Germany. What 70,000,000 Germans do to-day, in the heart of Europe, millions of people around them do to-morrow. When Hindenburg was elected President a second time, Europe breathed again.

Millions of freemen, in Germany and beyond, thought the day had been saved. They were wrong. Ten months later Hindenburg sold the pass. Germany became again a nation of conscripts, bondmen, yes-men. She had gained the world of freedom from alien dictation, but she had lost her newly-found soul. The Great War had opened a vista of an enlightened age of social progress, of humanity and justice in Europe, racked throughout the centuries by the wars of dynasties and dictators. Hindenburg slammed the door on that vision, and left Europe facing another era of war.

Twenty years after the Great War, all that remained of it was the frontiers, and the next attack would strike at them. The Great War, with its umpteen million dead, was due to be written off as a bad debt. Politicians and newspaper lords who in 1914 had told the youth of England to go and make the world safe for democracy were already smiling upon the new great martial dictatorships and the wars they were planning.

CHAPTER 12

BRÜNING'S FALL

On a May morning in 1932 I stood in the Wilhelmstrasse and watched a detachment of German bluejackets come marching down to Hindenburg's palace, men of fine physique and bearing, accompanied by that sheeplike crowd of marching civilians which in Germany always follows the drum.

It was the anniversary of Skagerak, of the Battle of Jutland. I thought back to the day, sixteen years before, when we stick-in-the-muds in France had heard, with a shock, of the British losses in the greatest naval engagement of the war. 'Thank God we've got a navy' we had been wont to say, contemplating the deadlocked armies on the Western Front. Now, as we read the story of Jutland, we were not so sure about that navy.

Afterwards both sides claimed the victory. The Germans invoked the heavier British losses, in ships and men. The British replied that the German fleet had run for home and never come out again until it surrendered at Scapa Flow. On balance I think the British admirals can justly claim the victory. The man who remains in possession of the field is the victor. But he who fights and runs away lives to fight another day — at sea as on land.

Anyway, the Germans celebrated Skagerak as a great victory each year, and on the anniversary the bluejackets came marching down the Wilhelmstrasse to stand guard for a week outside the President's Palace, instead of the field-grey Reichswehrmen.

As I waited, I saw Chancellor Heinrich Brüning come out of the President's Palace, looking grave and preoccupied, and go down the Wilhelmstrasse towards his Chancery. A Catholic politician and wartime machine-gun officer, bespectacled, going bald, hard-working and full of nervous energy, he was the man who was trying to free Germany from the burdens of the war by negotiation and treaty with Germany's former enemies — the method that Hitler ridiculed.

A moment later, while sharp commands rang through the air, Hindenburg came out, heavy on his stick, to inspect the naval guard.

Brüning had been dismissed. I did not know it then, but learned it soon afterwards. The die had been cast for another era of German militarism. The doom of the German Republic had just been sealed in Hindenburg's study, the war of the German Succession begun. The fate of Germany and Europe was to be settled in the next ten months — ten months that shook the world.

Brüning, as I saw him disappear down the Wilhelmstrasse towards political obscurity and a long life of exile in Switzerland, England and America, had lost his race with time. He had spent himself, six weeks before, in rallying nineteen million German Republicans to vote for their old enemy the Field-Marshal President, who alone could save them from Hitler. Brüning knew that when Hindenburg died, and that could not be long, Hitler must succeed unless he, Brüning, could wear down the Nazis before then by successes abroad, trade improvement at home.

Both things were within his reach, he had thought as he waited on Hindenburg that morning. The cancellation of reparations impended, the fruit of the Hoover Moratorium. Ramsay MacDonald and the others had at last agreed to German rearmament by mutal consent and had recommended France to agree also. Trade showed some signs of improvement.

If he could hold on a little longer he would be able to show Germany results for the policy of negotiation and understanding, he could offer something to that large body of wavering opinion which was beginning from hope deferred to turn to Hitler and his ceaseless cry that Germany would never obtain anything from her enemies save by her own strength and the sword.

At that moment he was overthrown. For there were other men in the shadows of the Palace who did not want gradual rearmament or agreement with the other Powers, but high-speed rearmament without a by-your-leave, and they, too, saw the importance of getting power into their hands before Hindenburg died. Thus the schemers gathered round Hindenburg. If Hindenburg had died three years earlier the German Republic might have been saved. His stern sense of duty kept him alive.

The men who had his ear were Kurt von Schleicher, the politician-general at the War Ministry, who made and unmade Chancellors, had his spies and dictaphones in every Ministerial department, had decided on Brüning's overthrow and had his successor ready, Franz von Papen, who had been forgotten by the world since his expulsion from America during the war; Oskar von Hindenburg, the President's ambitious son and Papen's friend; Otto Meissner, permanent head of the President's household, who had been political valet to the Socialist working-man President Ebert before Hindenburg and was to perform the same office for Hitler, a political Vicar of Bray, as John Wheeler-Bennett called him. Meissner's memoirs, if they are ever published, should be beyond price. I used to sit next to him at the barber's in the Behrenstrasse.

But even more important than these were the Prussian squires, leagued by the common interest that binds rich men with their urban brethren, the big businessmen of the Rhineland and Ruhr, and headed by the corpulent Oldenburg-Januschau.

Years before, the squires had subscribed together to present Hindenburg, who was being too loyal to the Republican Constitution for their liking, with Neudeck, the former estate of the Hindenburgs in East Prussia. By that astute move they made him one of themselves, calculating that at the vital moment he would be on their side. By making out the title deeds in Oskar von Hindenburg's name they not only insured that he, who had much influence with his father, should also be on their side, but that he should be spared death duties. The Socialists discovered this transaction, which no Jew could have bettered, and published it in *Vorwärts*. 'Bolshevism' muttered the squires in Hindenburg's ear.

In 1925, when Hindenburg was first elected President, his electoral promises had included one of land in East Prussia to ex-servicemen smallholders, and money to help them settle there. The Field-Marshal had not forgotten the men he had led back from the war! The great landowners grumbled together about 'agrarian bolshevism', for the land could only be found by splitting up bankrupt big estates — and they bought Neudeck for Hindenburg. And Hindenburg five years later, as a condition of signing the Young Plan, extorted a written promise from the Socialist Chancellor Hermann Müller that £12,000,000 from the savings falling to Germany under this lesser reparations burden should go to the great landowners, his fellow squires, to order their affairs.

Hindenburg, installed at Neudeck, felt the call of the land. You will begin to discern the real reasons why things happen in politics, why moderate regimes are overthrown and dictatorships set up.

Now, in 1932, Brüning, in his efforts to hold the fort, had proposed the confiscation, against compensation, of bankrupt estates in East Prussia and their division among smallholders. The Field-Marshal's own promise to his men was to be redeemed. A Reichstag Committee had inquired into the use of the millions granted in 1927 and 1928 to those great landowners for whom Hindenburg in 1930 had demanded another £12,000,000, and had uncovered appalling scandals. One landowner, said the investigators, had whored, drunk and gambled away the public money advanced to him.

The landowners knew of these things and clustered round the President, murmuring 'agrarian bolshevism' in his ear. Brüning, they said, was the instrument of the internationalists, a man of Geneva, the enemy of property, the chosen spokesman of all those Marxists and Republicans and Jews and Papists at home who had stabbed Germany in the back in 1918, the trusted friend of those foreign foes who kept Germany in chains, the enemy of everything Protestant and Prussian and true blue German.

That was why Brüning that morning, just before the sailors came marching down the street, was curtly dismissed by Hindenburg. He had expected it, for the day before Hindenburg had received him with a sheaf of notes in his hand, on which were written in block capitals legible to his failing eyes the things the schemers had told him to say to Brüning — 'Bolshevik Ministers in your Government', 'Bolshevik Policy', and the like more.

On this day Hindenburg had scarcely bothered to look at the man who six weeks earlier had rallied nineteen million German voters to his cause, but had turned his back on him and gone out to inspect the guard, muttering, 'Now I can have a Cabinet of my friends'.

The fate of Germany had once more been decided, in favour of an absolute military despotism, by the great landowners of Germany east of the Elbe, the class which had always ruled Germany and led her from war to war, which had gathered in pious loyalty about the Hohenzollern kings and emperors:

> Unseren König absolut
> Wenn er unseren Willen tut.

> Our unchallenged King and Lord
> So long as he obey our word.

As I watched the naval guard present arms my mind was busy with thoughts of that day in the trenches at Ypres sixteen years before when we learned of the Battle of Jutland. How long would it be before Germany again had a formidable fleet, I wondered, and would England again allow herself to be outgunned and outarmoured? I did not know, as I saw Brüning come out and Hindenburg pace off the guard, what had happened inside the palace, or I should have known that the rebirth of Germany's naval might was not far off.

CHAPTER 13

PAPEN APPEARS

I LOOKED with interest at Franz von Papen, as he shook hands with us. The ever-ready smile, the curiously shaped head. The Iron Cross, won in the drawing-rooms of the Washington Embassy, modestly adorned the frock coat of this man who lyrically sang the beauties of a death on that battlefield which he would never see. I saw him afterwards many times, and never ceased to wonder at this trick that providence played on Germany. 'A curious choice', said the British Press on the morning Papen and his Cabinet of Barons — Hindenburg's 'Cabinet of my friends' — burst on an astonished world.

Papen's sole appearance in world affairs before this eventful day in 1932 had been that awful gaffe in 1916, when, as German Military Attaché in Washington, he was expelled from America for sabotage activities — and allowed the cheque counterfoils for payments to shipwreckers to fall into the hands of British naval officers who stopped his ship and searched his trunks. Germany, whose fate was now in his hands, knew nothing of that episode. The wartime censorship had suppressed all news of it and now, when the opposition press began to turn over the yellow pages of the past in search of data about Franz von Papen, he issued a decree threatening with dire penalties any editor who referred to his past.

Now, thanks to intriguers behind the scenes and to the liking of a bemused old man, he, whom nobody in Germany knew, took over the helm of affairs at a moment vital for Germany, for Europe, for the world. Thus is the destiny of nations shaped.

You will know about Franz von Papen. You will have read how he left compromising documents in a New York tram-car or elevated railway train. And you will be wrong. He didn't. A certain Geheimrat Albert did that, not Papen. There are writers who like to pass on pieces of gossip as authentic history.

But Papen did have a strange weakness for mislaying compromising or valuable documents. In Washington, before his expulsion, he had a private office for that business which the German Military Attaché could not conduct at the German Embassy, and the American police raided it and seized certain papers; when the German Ambassador protested, American Secretary of State Robert Lansing amiably offered to return any document which Papen cared to identify as his property. In 1918 he was serving on the German Staff in Palestine and, hurriedly departing at the approach of Allenby's cavalry, left in his tent papers of great value to the British General Staff. In 1932, when he had suddenly reappeared from oblivion as German Chancellor, to wage that brief and inglorious struggle with Hitler, Hindenburg gave him a warrant to dissolve a Reichstag which was implacably hostile to him and he mislaid it, so that it was found only just in time to avert a ludicrous crisis.

One day in Vienna I talked with him about a German correspondent who had been expelled. He was indignant, said the man had done nothing wrong, but had simply written frank accounts of the Austrian situation to his editor in Germany and that carbon copies of these letters had been found.

'Ah,' I said, 'that is the old German fault — thoroughness. Why keep carbon copies?'

Followed a moment's silence, filled by the crash of falling bricks, and I hastily changed the subject.

Well, there he was, Franz von Papen and his Cabinet of Barons — seven ministers from the nobility, none from the Republican and working-class masses, all got together and blessed by Hindenburg within six weeks of his re-election by nineteen million Republicans, Democrats and Socialists. The world then still had tender sensibilities — later they became blunted — and it was dumbfounded. The old Field-Marshal had reverted to type.

Providence finds strange tools, but could hardly have entrusted the welfare of Germany's millions to a stranger pair than the aged von Hindenburg and the debonair von Papen, cavalry officer, gentleman jockey, scion of the Westphalian gentry, by marriage a brother of the big business fraternity in the Saar, obscure member of Brüning's Centre Party.

He was as buoyant and indestructible as the cork that out-lives Atlantic tempests. He juggled blithely with problems laden with high explosive and when they burst they hit every-body but himself. The peasantfolk of Guernica, the towns-people of Almeria, with their roofs and walls crashing about them, their womenfolk and children wounded and dying, may never have heard of Franz von Papen. Yet but for him their walls might still be standing, their children still playing in the sunshine.

For he, who smiled and smiled and was a good man at a tea-party, and for sixteen years after that crashing debacle in Washington had been a rich clubman, squire and amateur politician of no account, now took the fate of Germany and Europe in his hands. He was to save Germany from Hitler and the Marxists; for the monarchists, militarists, squires, big busi-nessmen and reactionaries. Through him the real power in Ger-many did pass into the hands of precisely these groups, though von Papen himself had to climb down and let Hitler into the Chancellorship, where he remains, as yet, the prisoner of these groups.

All these things were yet in the lap of the gods that day as Papen came towards us across the thick pile carpet, smiling affably, chatting genially. What pleasant manners he has, we thought. How hail-fellow-well-met. No Prussian stiffness about him!

CHAPTER 14

HITLER'S VICTORY

I HAVE seen many strange sights, all over Europe, but none stranger than Franz von Papen's first Reichstag, which Hindenburg had given him authority to dissolve even before it met, so hostile had the country shown itself at the July elections.

By Reichstag custom the oldest deputy presided at the opening session. The Communists, seeing a good propagandist opening — normally the Nazis and Nationalists walked out when a Communist speaker rose, but this time they would have to stay put — included among their candidates Klara Zetkin, a sturdy woman Socialist who had all her life fought in the working-class struggle in Germany against Kaiser Wilhelm, and was now eighty-four years old and lived in Moscow.

Klara Zetkin, marked 'Fragile, with care', was brought from Moscow on this September 12th, 1932, helped up the stairs to the Speaker's chair by Torgler, the Communist Parliamentary Secretary and parlour-Bolshevist who a few months later, to his astonishment, was to be charged with burning down his beloved Reichstag, and made a blistering revolutionary speech. The Nazis, all in uniform, sat grimly through it. The atmosphere produced by 230 strong men all being silent against their will was strangling and I almost sympathized with them.

Klara Zetkin's performance was astounding. She was dying and her powers were failing fast, but somehow she had memorized a fierce revolutionary oration and she delivered most of it by heart, Torgler prompting her when she faltered. Propped on a stick, swaying, gasping for breath, she hurled her taunts at the Reichstag. She listed the sins of the President and said he ought to be indicted before the Reichstag, but that would only be 'to indict the devil before his grandmother'.

With that speech the voice of the German masses was

heard, as I think, for the last time for many, many long years to come. Then Klara Zetkin, tenderly helped by stalwart women Communists from the working-class constituencies, tottered down the steps, and Göring, the new Speaker, marched up them. A remarkable scene, I thought. But you could only play this trick once. Once it was known, the Communists were no match for a party with so many elderly generals among their followers as the Nazis. At the next election Hitler included among his candidates General Litzmann, a very old and bloodthirsty gentleman who had once expressed regret that Hindenburg could not be bumped off for signing the Young Plan. General Litzmann was unconquerably old and, weak on his pins but erect in the inevitable frock-coat, he opened the next Reichstag.

When Klara Zetkin had gone, that comedy of errors followed which began with Papen's forgetfulness to bring with him Hindenburg's dissolution warrant and ended with a vote of censure on Papen carried by 513 votes against 32 and the dissolution of the Reichstag amid uproar and pandemonium.

The tumult was but the echo of Germany outside. I shall never forget those critical weeks. Germany was in a turmoil, a brass band of a million instruments all playing furiously against each other, with Papen blithely conducting the disharmony. The entire country was against him, but divided against itself. Hindenburg, who alone could restore order from the chaos he had made, sat in his palace, surrounded by intriguers. Nazis and anti-Nazis shot each other in the streets, one or two every day, but more anti-Nazis than Nazis.

The killings became so frequent that Papen tried to play the strong man. After the Nazis had killed a few anti-Nazis in their beds at Königsberg he introduced emergency courts and threatened the death penalty.

The Nazis immediately challenged him. At Potempa in Silesia six Nazis had killed a man. Village jealousies may have been the motive, but they called him a Communist; nowadays it is always safest to say your victim was a Red.

The six Nazis broke into the hovel where he slept with his aged mother and brother. While the old woman stood terrified against the wall she saw her son murdered in the flashes of a pocket torch. He had an eye poked out with the blunt end of a billiard cue, his throat trodden in with a boot heel, he was shot, stabbed and bludgeoned, and in all received twenty-nine wounds.

At the trial the judge said, 'The gravity of the crime is aggravated by its monstrous barbarity', and sentenced the six men to death. Hitler began a national campaign to save them. He telegraphed assuring them of his 'undying loyalty', proclaimed that their liberation was 'a point of honour for the Nazis'. The blonde Magda Göbbels, Göbbels's wife, who was expecting about then, told the wives and mothers of Germany that it was 'an elementary duty of humanity to secure the release of these men'. I wonder what the old mother of the victim thought about it, with those flashlit glimpses, those shots and shouts and blows still in her eyes and ears.

Papen yielded and reprieved the six men. When Hitler became Chancellor he released them. Applauded by the population, the pride of their fellow townsmen, they were marched in triumph through Potempa and presumably received that preferment to which their sufferings had entitled them.

I wrote about that time that a period of jungle justice or revolver rule impended for Germany. I don't think I was far wrong.

Papen's method of saving Germany from Hitler was to attack the Constitution, to make gaps in the defences for Hitler subsequently to walk through. He began with Prussia. Prussia was in area and population nearly two-thirds of Germany, and the Socialists were still paramount there. They had the Prussian Premiership and Ministry of the Interior, which meant the efficient Prussian police force. Police chiefs and Prefects everywhere were Socialists. Resolute men, given this power, could have resisted. But the German Socialists, who called in the officer caste to suppress the Spartacists in 1919, had always been unsure of themselves; conscription and serfdom were in their blood.

Hindenburg authorized Papen to dismiss the Socialist Ministers — the representatives of his own electors — and take over the Prussian Government. Otto Braun, Prussian Premier and 'strong man of German Socialism', departed quietly into the shadows; when Hitler came he slipped into Switzerland for his health. Karl Severing, Prussian Minister of the Interior, proclaimed that he would yield only to force; a corporal and two men applied the requisite amount, to the delight of old Oldenburg-Januschau, the leader of the squires. Long before the war he had called for the Kaiser to send an officer and ten men and dissolve the Reichstag, and for the rest of his long life he enjoyed an imperishable fame in the reactionary strongholds for this rare and beautiful phrase. But even he had never dreamed that you could do it with a corporal and two men.

Papen, the country solid against him, then set about out-witting Hitler. He called him to Berlin to see Hindenburg. Hitler, led by the intriguing von Schleicher at a clandestine meeting at Fürstenberg to believe that he would be offered the Chancellorship, came to Berlin in high spirits. I saw him arrive. He menacingly set up his headquarters in the Hotel Kaiserhof, overlooking the President's and the Chancellor's Palaces, the strongholds of his adamant adversaries, Hindenburg and Papen.

On August 13th, 1932, came the famous interview, first with Papen and then with Hindenburg. Hitler demanded the powers of a Mussolini, only to find that Papen did not think of resigning and merely offered him the Vice-Chancellorship. Hitler became almost hysterical with disappointment.

Then he went to see Hindenburg, who had not much use for the National Socialist leaders, though he liked the militarist methods and organization, the patriotic ranting, the flags and drums and uniforms. He disliked the bawdy Röhm, whom Hitler brought with him. Göbbels had called him senile.

Hitler he regarded as the kind of man you hadn't much use for in the army, and he spoke of him as the 'Bohemian Corporal', a contemptuous phrase in the mouth of a Prussian officer. It means a second-rate individual, with a touch of the Czech or God knows what about him, from the border districts where all the streams of European blood and language meet and mingle — German and Slav and Latin and Jew and the like more.

Hitler said he wanted the Chancellorship or nothing, and Hindenburg read him a lecture which left Hitler emptier of words than he had ever been. He would not make Hitler Chancellor, said the Old Gentleman categorically. His duty and conscience would not allow him to hand over the Government of the country to the exclusive control of the National Socialist Party, which would wield this power onesidedly. He rebuked Hitler for breaking promises and recommended him to exercise greater chivalry in his future campaigns.

On August 13th, 1932, the millions of Germans who had voted for Hindenburg were vindicated in their trust, Germany was saved from National Socialism by one staunch unyielding man. Hitler fell into one of his characteristic periods of lachrymose self-commiseration and, as Göbbels testifies, talked of shooting himself. The vale of European tears is paved with the suicidal threats of dictators; these, like their other promises, remain unfulfilled.

Watching day by day, I found the Party declining. It had passed its zenith. Hindenburg's rebuff had had its effect on the electorate. Hitler and his lieutenants knew it. Read their books. At the next elections they lost two million votes. Germany was over the worst. Papen and his cabinet could have been liquidated and a way found to restore popular government.

A few weeks later the Prussian Field-Marshal ate his words and made the Bohemian Corporal Chancellor.

I never worked harder than in 1932. The world was avid for news of the struggle for power in Germany. The world instinctively knew what it meant — for the world. But with the best of wills we of the world's newspapers could not see more than an occasional writhing of the serpentine intrigues that finally settled the fate of Germany. The thing was all done backstairs and underground, the weapons were whispers and dictaphones and keyholes.

The Nazi leaders wrangled among themselves. Better half a loaf than no bread, said some; after all these years of waiting and campaigning, better accept a share in power than stand out for the whole and go from defeat to disaster. Hitler saw Hindenburg again, in November, and again was refused the Chancellorship, with the words 'I cannot give a leader of a party my Presidential power, because such a cabinet is bound to develop into a party dictatorship and increase the state of tension prevailing among the German people. I cannot take the responsibility for this before my oath and my conscience'.

Noble words, eaten and swallowed six weeks later, with oath, duty and conscience.

Hitler, sunken in pessimism, went back to the Brown House, leaving the field to his adversaries across the street, Hindenburg and Papen. But his time was coming.

Papen had the entire country against him. He had no hope of a Parliamentary majority and now, with less than one German in ten behind him, he was preparing to do the only other possible thing — to erect a Papen dictatorship, to sit on bayonets in Berlin. He proposed to dissolve Parliament, parties, trades unions; and if necessary to use the army to that end.

But here his calculation broke down. The army would not interfere in politics except in the last resort, and certainly not for a man with so little backing in the country as Papen. Hindenburg's chickens were coming home to roost. Schleicher, the Chancellor-maker, saw that Papen would have to go, that there was only one hope left of saving Germany from Hitler and restoring order from the chaos that Hindenburg and Papen had made. The wire-puller must take office and responsibility. He went to Hindenburg and told him that the army had no confidence in Papen.

Hindenburg, in his eighty-sixth year, found himself forced to drop the only Chancellor he had ever liked — a gentlemanly fellow, after all these Socialists and Papists. Papen went, with a signed photograph of his benefactor to comfort him. Schleicher, the puller of strings, took office. Most of the barons joined his cabinet. Hindenburg's experiment had broken down. He had dismissed Brüning, who had never been beaten in Parliament, destroyed parliamentary government in Germany, in favour of a man without political experience, credit or backing, who now, detested by the country and distrusted by his colleagues, had had to throw in his hand.

The curtain rose on the last act of the German Republic. I watched Kurt von Schleicher rise in Bismarck's seat in the Reichstag, with his hairless cranium, shrewd grey eyes, not unpleasant features. He was a doomed man, with a few weeks of inglorious Chancellorship, a few months of life before him, then a dog's death, shot down by hired assassins in his lodging. The master keyholer, the prompter in this stupendous drama, suddenly found himself the principal player, with the spotlight full on him, a condemned man who thought to make German history, the last Chancellor of the German Republic, whose Chancellorship was to last forty days.

Had he a clear-cut plan, this man who had shown so sure a touch in his wirepulling from behind the scenes? No sign of one emerged. Generals, terrific as opposition politicians, are generally disastrous failures in office.

Schleicher's main idea was to split those Nazis who were crying that half a loaf was better than no bread from those who were for holding out and fighting on. He offered Gregor Strasser the Vice-Chancellorship. Strasser, Hitler's first lieutenant and right hand man, headed the compromise group. But Hitler's hold over the party was still firm. He stripped Strasser — who seems to have behaved quite loyally, but was pessimistic — of all his offices, sent him into outer darkness.

None followed Strasser. By this vain move Schleicher dug his own and Strasser's graves, which received them eighteen months later. Hitler already distrusted Schleicher for sending him to the disastrous interview with Hindenburg in the belief that he was to be made Chancellor. Distrust turned to hatred after the Strasser episode.

Schleicher's second venture was even more undexterous, it was suicidal. He apparently hoped to win over a large body of moderate and middle-class opinion by adopting the project that had chiefly been used by the intriguers to bring about Brüning's downfall — the project for the confiscation, against compensation, of the subsidized but still bankrupt East Prussian estates and their division among ex-service smallholders.

The great landowners had not overthrown Brüning to be pestered by Schleicher. They rose as one man and swarmed about Hindenburg, their co-opted fellow landowner, like angry bees, buzzing 'Bolshevism' into his ear.

Schleicher then played his trump card, as he thought. He threatened to publish the report of the parliamentary committee that had investigated the use and abuse of the millions advanced to great East Prussian landowners to order their affairs, that report which until now had rested securely in a Reichstag pigeonhole and which disclosed how bankrupt East Prussian noblemen had spent the grants given to put their estates in order on new motor cars and trips to the Riviera, on 'whores, drinking and gambling'.

The scandal revealed by it sprawled over the whole large estate area of East Prussia. The Hindenburgs, too, had their estate there, and had not forgotten their own little transaction, by which the payment of death duties had been thoughtfully forethwarted, the deeds for the estate presented to the President by grateful and far-sighted East Prussian landlords having been made out in the name of the aged President's son.

The Prussian Army, the stone on which the German Reich had ultimately been built, has its deepest roots in the landed estates of East Prussia. Here the tradition of blood and iron was born that made out of a tiny Margraviate one of the most powerful Empires the modern world has known. And now a Prussian General, using stupid words like 'insolvency' and 'bankruptcy' and 'squandering public money' and 'settlements for ex-soldiers' proposed to dispossess landowners indebted to to the public purse. The landlords in their thousands beleaguered Hindenburg's palace and his manor at Neudeck, through their emissary Oldenburg-Januschau and others.

Schleicher allowed the newspapers to publish a little of the report. After his downfall it vanished into a Hitlerist pigeon-hole, never to be heard of again. The great landowners remained comfortably sitting on their estates and loudly applauded the vociferous campaign against Socialist, Marxist and Jewish corruption with which the Nazis ushered in their rule over Germany.

Schleicher was doomed. The only question was, who should succeed him. Papen was still Hindenburg's favourite, and Papen, smarting at his overthrow by Schleicher, longing to revenge himself on the man who had made and unmade him Chancellor, was in touch with Hitler. He still hoped for some arrangement which would give himself the possibility of putting the brake on Hitler, even if he became Chancellor. But his dominant ambition was revenge on the traitor Schleicher.

Thus the famous meeting came about, on January 8th, 1933, between Papen and Hitler at the house of the banker von Schröder in Cologne. It was arranged by Joachim von Ribbentrop, the political champagne merchant who thus staked such a claim on Hitler's gratitude that he later became Ambassador and Foreign Minister. Here at last, Papen agreed to recommend Hitler to Hindenburg for the Chancellorship. In return Hitler pledged his word not to break the Constitution. If he took any liberties, that is, he was to be overthrown by the President and Papen. With the simple faith that is more than Norman blood Papen came away, well satisfied. He did not know, or had forgotten, how Mussolini in Italy was also in appearance the prisoner of a majority of elder non-Fascist politicians in his first Cabinet after the March on Rome. He did not reckon with a Reichstag fire.

At Cologne, under the rooftree of big business, the Papen-Hitler alliance was forged. Schleicher's fate was sealed. On January 28th, realizing at last that he could neither split the Nazis nor cow the landlords nor persuade the Socialists and Centrists to back him, he went to Hindenburg and asked for power to dissolve the Reichstag. His request was bluntly refused. A discredited man, with relentless enemies waiting for him in the shadows, he went down the steps of the President's Palace, out into the bleak January Wilhelmstrasse.

How came it that Hindenburg at last, on the morning of January 30th, 1933, examined his oath, duty and conscience, and found nothing in them to prevent him from making Hitler Chancellor and giving him that authority to dissolve the Reichstag which he had denied to Schleicher? In spite of all the intrigues, all uproar about the report on the East Prussian landowners, his fellow squires, he apparently still hesitated.

Two years later Göring drew back a corner of the veil from the events of that day, from the last crowning piece of intrigue by which the old President was induced to betray the faith of his nineteen million electors.

The atmosphere between the two camps — that in the President's Palace, where Papen, Oskar von Hindenburg, and the emissaries of landed property and big business gathered about the old Field-Marshal, and that in the Kaiserhof Hotel, where Hitler sat in unbroken conference with his lieutenants while telephone bells rang incessantly and messengers dashed in and out — was of the utmost tension.

Somehow this last obstacle had to be overcome. The cup of power could not again be dashed from Hitler's lips, that would be intolerable. 'It seemed', said Göring two years later, 'that our laborious efforts were to be thwarted at the last moment through a violent intervention of Schleicher . . . In the evening we heard that the Reichswehr was to be mobilized, that Schleicher was preparing a regular revolt to prevent the constitutional formation of the Government. But the Führer saw to it that the execution of this plot was made impossible.'

This was the last story whispered into the ear of the aged President. Schleicher was going to march in from Potsdam with the Reichswehr and arrest him, Oskar, Papen, Hitler, put them all in a fortress, in order that power might not fall into the hands of National Socialism. The story was presumably the product of the same minds that conceived the Reichstag fire and other like exploits.

So that fellow Schleicher was thinking of sending troops to arrest him, Hindenburg? The excitement in and about the Palace and the Kaiserhof Hotel was terrific. Without further ado Hindenburg signed the decree making Hitler Chancellor.

That is how it all came about on January 30th, 1933. So is history made. Berlin was buzzing like a beehive from morning till night, the nerves of four million people were quivering like harp strings. Only the very ill, very poor, or the deeply enamoured were not moved on this day by lively hopes or fears for the future.

I walked Unter den Linden to the Wilhelmstrasse, thinking back to Armistice Day 1918 and forward to what might be coming. I felt that this was the final breakdown of the peace.

The Brown Shirts were hilariously jubilant. The last trench had been taken, the brown armies had the freedom of the streets, even of the coveted *Bannmeile* — that square mile of streets in Central Berlin where the Ministries and other Government buildings are situated, within which political demonstrations had never been allowed.

I stood at a window of the Foreign Office that night and watched them tramping endlessly past, the Brown Shirts, while their bands played Fridericus Rex and the Horst Wessel March. Hour after hour they poured with their torchlights through the once forbidden Brandenburger Arch into the promised land of Unter den Linden and the Wilhelmstrasse, marching with the triumphant ecstatic air of soldiers taking possession of a long-beleaguered city.

Opposite me were two palaces — the old and the new Chancellors' Palaces, one a grey, ponderous building in the Wilhelmian style of architecture, the other a clean-cut, four-square building, a typical product of the Germany of 1918-1933.

Behind a lighted window of the old building stood a massive old man. The night air was chill and they wouldn't let him have the window open. His dim old eyes saw the river of torch-lights flowing past, his ears heard the crash of the bands and the tramp of the Storm Troopers. What visions of Königgrätz and Sedan and Paris and the proclamation of the German Empire at Versailles and long years on the barrack square and Tannenberg and Verdun and the Somme did he see at this moment, some seventy years after his first parade?

I saw him nod his head continually as the bands blared and the Brown Shirts goose-stepped past, throwing their heads back and their eyes to the right to salute him. But they were not there to honour him. His day was done. The salute to the old man, dimly seen behind the lighted window, was perfunctory.

Fifty yards farther down the street in the new Palace was another window, on a higher level, open, with the spotlights playing on it, a younger man leaning out. An American Jewish newspaper man, an acquaintance of mine, soon after-wards to be expelled from Germany, found beauty in the scene — the tumultuous brazen music, the tramp, tramp, tramp, the ceaseless cheering of the crowds, the blazing torches, the bellowing of the loudspeakers, the old man behind the lighted window and the younger man who leaned far out of the spotlit window, saluting.

'Hitler looks marvellous,' he said.

The old and the new. Field-Marshal and Bohemian Corporal. Hitler and Hindenburg. Tramp, tramp, tramp, blare, blare, blare. Hour after hour they came tramping through the Brandenburger Tor down the Wilhelmstrasse. *'Die Strasse frei, die Reihen fest geschlossen — Hoch, Hoch, Hoooooch!'*

The lighted window went dark. Hindenburg had gone to bed. I went off to write. Hitler, the spotlight still fastened on him, old General Litzmann dimly seen behind him, leaned far out into the Wilhelmstrasse, surveying his Reich. The Vienna destitute, the man of all trades and none, the battalion message-runner, the political hired man sent out by the Reichswehr after the war to spy on his kind, the man who by his own account had never done a real day's work in his life, had got his first job — Chancellor of the German Reich.

CHAPTER 15

REICHSTAG FIRE

To be in the contemporary fashion I ought, in the course of this tale, to take you through the boudoirs of my love life and introduce you to the Sonias and Veras, the Javan princesses and Hungarian dancing girls whom you would expect to meet there. It is remiss of them if they are not there, for they should know that all diplomats and newspaper men sooner or later feel the urge to write a passionate novel or a coyly candid book about themselves, and turn their thoughts to their past loves, whom they expect to find dutifully lined up and waiting to be made into literary capital.

I should not take you with me on this round of calls even if these lovely and invigorating ladies existed, as I hope they do, for two is company and three is none and you would be in the way. But Nadya, a turbulent person, intrudes forcibly at this point, whether we like it or not.

She was born on the Black Sea, which I have not yet seen, but if it is as black as her hair and eyes it is very black, and one of her earliest memories is of a German airman who took her joy-riding with him until she was very sick, so that he brought her down quickly, and gave her some tinned meat to take home as a consolation prize. Her father was killed in a long-forgotten Balkan War and almost her only memory of him is of being held up to look at him as he lay in his grave. Then she was married off when she was about fifteen, as girls are, or were, wont to be in the Balkans, and soon she saw the stranger, her husband, drowned; and then, somehow, she began dancing and travelled all over Europe until one evening in Berlin she was going along the Kurfürstendamm to work, gawdy and sparkling as a humming-bird in a flame-red dress, when I drove rather carelessly round a corner and knocked her down with my mudguard, so that she couldn't dance for a few days, and this naturally led to a lasting friendship.

Thus it happened that I drove through the Brandenburger Tor on my way to inquire after her on the evening of February 27th, 1933, and saw the flames burst through the cupola of the Reichstag. I had a ringside seat at a most important event in European history. So you see how valuable these connexions are.

I lived with the Reichstag fire for about a year, from the moment the flames burst through to the passing of sentence; followed the investigation, attended the trial, and studied every detail of it. I even wrote a book about it, rather spoiled by pressure of other work, but the facts are all in it for anybody who still is interested in old far-off forgotten things.

Hitler told Sefton Delmer, *Daily Express* Correspondent, that the fire was a sign from heaven, and as it happened just four weeks after Hitler was made Chancellor and a week before the elections and solved the problem of usurping absolute power this shows how swiftly heaven intervenes when it sees a man on earth who is really worth supporting. Memories of that evening are the great bulk of Göring, swathed in trench-coat, dashing into the burning Reichstag, where I already was, and the bemused expression of von Papen, who arrived later and found that, though he was titular Premier of Prussia, his energetic Minister of the Interior had on his own responsibility taken measures which meant the end of all constitutional Government in Germany — the end of dreams of a Hindenburg-Papen partnership that would always hold Hitler in check.

The Reichstag fire was important because it was the ostensible justification for erecting a National Socialist dictatorship on a seeming basis of constitutional action, Parliamentary support and popular approval. These are the things you should know about it:

It was proclaimed to have been the work of Communists. Under this pretext thousands of people — Communists, Socialists, Pacifists, among them even Carl von Ossietzky, who years later was in captivity awarded the Nobel Peace

Prize and was at first intended to be among those charged with the arson! — were rounded up by Storm Troopers and thrown into concentration camps.

Alarming accounts of impending Communist revolution were issued. In this confusion Hindenburg, either swallowing everything he was told or deliberately condoning the rape of the law, signed a decree 'for the protection of the nation from the Communist danger' which handed over Germany to Hitler. It legalized arrest and imprisonment without trial of anybody you did not like, the seizure of his property, the suppression of his newspapers, raids on his house, eavesdropping on his telephone, opening his letters, his execution 'while attempting to escape'.

With elections only a week distant, it enabled the country to be panicked by tales of Bolshevist terror which were ridiculed even by that staunch Diehard newspaper, the *Deutsche Allgemeine Zeitung* in its last independent utterance. It enabled the elections to be held under terrorism, ensured an enormous increase in the Nazi vote, and by authorizing the cancellation of the Communist votes gave Hitler what he could never otherwise have won — a majority in the Reichstag. Not much more than one German in every three ever voted, or ever would have voted for Hitler at any free election.

At the trial before the Supreme Court of the Reich, of the five men accused, no proof whatever was brought that Communists had caused it. Four of the accused — Torgler, the Communist Parliamentary leader, Dimitroff, Popoff and Taneff, the three Bulgarian Communist refugees, proved their innocence and were acquitted. The case against them rested on depositions by Nazi agents, police spies, stool-pigeons, convicts, lunatics, garrulous charwomen, hysterical women typists and *agents provocateurs* which crumbled to ashes in the white heat of world publicity.

The fifth accused, the half-witted young Dutch vagrant with the injured eyes, Marius van der Lubbe, who was found guilty and executed, was not a Communist.

The court found that van der Lubbe alone could not have caused the fire, that he might have made the two insignificant fires in the restaurant, but that the great conflagration in the session chamber was the work of many hands, carefully prepared, probably with little heaps of inflammatory waste placed on each of the deputies' desks, and connected by strips of celluloid, and set ablaze by 'a self-igniting fluid'.

An underground tunnel ran from beneath the session chamber to General Göring's palace. This was probably used both for bringing in the incendiary material and for escape. Göring, candid soul, himself suggested in court that the incendiaries so escaped. The night porter at his palace, where Göring's personal SS Bodyguard was wont to lodge, said he had frequently heard steps in the tunnel at night, in the week preceding the fire. He had been curious enough to paste strips of paper and threads over the two iron doors and had sometimes found them broken. Yet he had not troubled to find out what was going on.

Walter Weber, the commander of that 'Hermann Göring SS Bodyguard', himself admitted in evidence that he went through the tunnel during the fire, taking with him three police officers — who were never called in evidence. Although I and other newspaper men, in daylight and under leadership, only with great difficulty found our way through the labyrinthine underground of the Reichstag to and through the tunnel, he had immediately found it and dashed through it, looking for Reds. How come? Well, when he was on duty at Göring's palace he had noticed the trail of melted snow (caused by the heating pipes which the tunnel carried) leading across the street to the Reichstag. He had, indeed, often discussed the tunnel with the porter — that curiously incurious man who had heard steps in the tunnel at night and pasted threads over the iron doors and often found them broken but had never reported the matter.

The Berlin Fire Chief, Gempp, dismissed after the fire for some reason I should like to know, said he saw a torch lying in the corridor leading to the session chamber and a petrol-trail on a carpet near by.

The Reichstag night porter, Albert Wendt, a former Socialist, in giving evidence quietly disclosed that a deputy of whose presence in the empty building he had not been informed and who must have entered it before he came on duty at 8 p.m., left the building as if in flight while the fire was at its height. Wendt's disclosure was the first mention in the trail of this deputy as the only person seen to leave the Reichstag after the fire had started.

Following Wendt's statement this deputy, alleged to have left the Reichstag 'hatless, collarless, breathless, excited, as if in flight' while the fire was at its height, was called as a witness.

He was Dr. Albrecht, a Nazi, who had fought in the Free Corps against the Communists in 1919, been with Hitler from Hitler's earliest days.

An electric thrill went through the courtroom when Wendt made his statement, another when, a month later, the court finally brought itself to call the unnamed deputy and he proved to be a Nazi.

I looked at Dr. Albrecht, a young and spectacled man of a nondescript type, with burning interest. In the dock sat a lunatic vagrant who had been captured in the burning Reichstag and four men who had been conclusively proved to have been far away from it. Here, an honoured witness treated with every consideration by the choleric red-robed justices on the bench, stood a man alleged to have been seen to leave the building while it was burning — without hat or collar, out of breath, violently agitated, 'as if in flight' — and he was a Nazi deputy and might never have been heard of but for the quiet statement of a taciturn Reichstag porter and the spotlight of the world press. On his flight out of the Reichstag he had indeed been captured by the police — and immediately released when he was found to be 'a National Socialist deputy'.

Dr. Albrecht was allowed to tell his own story, without interruption by an affable bench. An extraordinary story it was.

He had been lying ill in a lodging near the Reichstag, was told that it was burning by the maidservant, rushed across, half-clad and hatless, to rescue important papers from his deputy's locker.

It did not tally with Wendt's emphatic statement that the fugitive deputy did not enter the building during his time on duty, which began at 8 p.m. (the building burned after 9). Albrecht was not confronted with Wendt, nor was the discrepancy mentioned by the court.

At the end of the trial, the Public Prosecutor — in his dual capacity as Public Defender of National Socialism against the charges which were being made all over the world — announced that Night Porter Wendt had been dismissed for neglecting his duty. He had been found drinking beer when he should have been watching the door. You see the inference of this statement? No? Allow me. It was that Wendt had been drinking beer and neglecting his duty on that night of the fire, so that he had not seen the excited Dr. Albrecht fly into the burning building in quest of his important papers. The neglectful Wendt, however, had seen him fly out, and, all unbidden, had said so before the Supreme Court, at the risk of having very unpleasant things happen to him, of which dismissal would be the least, and, equally unbidden but with calm certainty, he had said that Albrecht 'did not enter the building when I was on duty'.

I watched scores of witnesses in the Reichstag Fire Trial. Many of them were liars. Wendt did not look like a liar. He was of a species now apparently extinct in Germany, a Socialist, a hard-working, taciturn fellow who believed in the rights of man and in truth. Possibly he did not know the dangers he ran. Possibly he did. In that case he was an even greater hero than Dimitroff. I wonder what he is doing?

Believe it or not, but these facts came out in open court, in a trial staged and manipulated to prove that Communism was the culprit. This seems almost incredible. I myself could sometimes hardly believe my ears. But the reasons are simple, and two in number.

The first reason is Dimitroff, a man who could not be intimidated by five months in chains, threats of death from zealous examining magistrates, a lurid promise of a private hanging from Göring in court, repeated exclusion from his own trial, of which he only had fleeting glimpses at some periods.

A lone Communist entirely surrounded by seventy million Nazi Yes-men, all itching to kick him, Dimitroff fought the German Reich and at the end stood morally as high above his adversaries as the Eiffel Tower stands above the encircling Champs de Mars. You could only quieten him by killing him, and that was difficult, because you had undertaken to hold this trial in the full light of day and show the world that the Reds had fired the Reichstag. As long as Dimitroff was in court nothing could stop him from pouring his fierce contempt upon the wretched procession of lying witnesses and upon the charge against himself and his fellow accused, from openly suggesting what no other man in Germany dared more than whisper — that the Nazis had fired the Reichstag — and from putting questions in this sense even to the terrible Göring himself, so that for the first time in my life I saw a man literally bouncing with rage.

An unforgettable scene, this encounter between Göring, obese, ravingly angry, lobster-red, pounding the air with his fists, and Dimitroff, being pushed and pulled out of court, but straining back towards his adversary, with burning eyes, undaunted, crying through the din, 'Are you afraid of these questions, Mr. Prime Minister Göring?' Above them, on the bench, Lord Chief Justice Bünger, completely unnerved and jittery at the awful idea that anyone should say such things to the great Göring, shouting 'Out with him!' In the well of the court, the spontaneous ovation squad, scores of yes-men, bravo-ing Göring's most extravagant feats. They would have bravoed if he had stood on his head and waved his legs in the air.

The second reason for the unexpected course taken by the

Reichstag Fire Trial is that if you hold a really public trial you cannot convict innocent men. You may be able to cloak the truth and shield the guilty, but you cannot prove a crime against a man who has not committed it. Your case is built up on the false statements of witnesses who are either suborned or lie for private reasons and when the accused, fighting for their lives, point out the obvious fictions in the evidence against them and the spotlight of the world press is turned on them, your case collapses.

With van der Lubbe and Dimitroff extremes met in the dock. Torgler, Taneff and Popoff were shadowy figures, unlucky men drawn into the trial only by an ill-prepared attempt to stage a spectacular indictment of Communism. Van der Lubbe displayed the well-known symptoms of manic depressive insanity. He sat with his head sometimes bent, sometimes bowed almost between his knees; he slavered at the mouth and ran at the nose. He was in the Reichstag but did not fire it — he may have played about with firelighters in the restaurant. He was captured in the same condition that he displayed in court.

Who put this young mentally deficient vagrant, with his damaged eyes, into the Reichstag to be captured? He had tramped over many parts of Europe and the day before the fire had left Berlin to return to Holland. But after spending the night at a destitutes' home at Hennigsdorf, not far away, he turned back to Berlin — and that night was found in the burning Reichstag. It seems clear that the Mephistopheles of 'this shabby Faust', as Dimitroff called him, found him in the destitutes' home. Van der Lubbe's answers to questions were often unintelligible; but once, asked where he was on the day before the fire, he answered 'With the Nazis'.

Why, then, did this pitiable, slavering dummy, usually maintain that he had fired the Reichstag unaided? True, he did once in examination speak of 'the others' — and the examining magistrate left that remark out of his record, on which the indictment was based. But in court, when an answer could be wrested from him, he usually said that he alone was guilty. It was proved that this was a physical impossibility. The answer can only lie in van der Lubbe's mental condition. Once, when he asked to be sentenced to life imprisonment or death, he rambled off into curious statements that stimulated the curiosity of onlookers to know what treatment he had behind the scenes. He said he 'could not carry on this struggle in prison any longer', spoke of 'visions in my cell', 'voices in my body', 'meals five and six times a day', and the like.

The known facts are that he was taken in the Reichstag, that he did not fire it alone, and that he did not know or would not say who were his accomplices. Drugs, said some. Hypnotism, said others. His mental condition, as I saw him in court, was enough to account for anything. And the expert witnesses certified him sane and responsible!

On a day they took him out into the prison courtyard at Leipzig, a gloomy town, and he shambled obediently and apathetically, slavering and with sunken head, to the block. The headsman, restored to Germany by Göring because the guillotine in its name and conception was too Gallic and un-Prussian—German heads needed to be removed by the good old German axe—was there in top-hat and tailcoat and gloves. Methuselah knows why German headsmen have to wear this uniform unless the explanation is to be found in Wodehouse's story of the golfer who, desiring for private reasons to lose a match, dressed himself in the clothes of ceremony only to find that the tight coat and top-hat had cured him of his besetting fault — raising his head on the top of his swing.

Thus van der Lubbe died, and Dimitroff is now Secretary-General of the Communist International and a big man in Moscow, and Torgler was released several years after his acquittal and is happily back in his dear Moabit, and Popoff and Taneff are cut by all the best people in Moscow because they did not put up so good a show for Communism as Dimitroff.

A divinity shapes our ends, and this divinity, having a sense of humour, probably ordained that about the time of the

Reichstag fire two burglarious brothers named Sass were much in the Berlin news. They were repeatedly arrested but always released for lack of proof, and the newspapers jollied the police unmercifully about their immunity. Their particular speciality was their method of defeating interrogation, which they frustrated by a mixture of silence, bland innocence and inconsequent answers until Police Commissioners had strokes. A German film made them famous. They were suspected of a great bank robbery in the Wittenbergplatz, when the strongrooms were entered through an underground tunnel, but had to be released for lack of evidence. Then came one or two other big robberies and each time the brothers Sass were arrested and released by the exasperated police. Then somebody discovered that an underground tunnel was being driven, whither and for what purpose was never made clear, from a bush-hidden spot in a Berlin cemetery, and immediately the brothers Sass were arrested, interrogated, cursed and released.

If they had not existed they would have had to be created for without them the world would have lost the best of the thousands of whispered mouth-to-ear political jokes which were coined when newspapers were muzzled and free speech killed: 'Have you heard who fired the Reichstag? The brothers Sass — SA and SS.'

The SA and SS are the two parts of the Nazi Brown Army; the SA are the mass of brown-shirted Storm Troopers and the SS are the smaller *élite* formation of black-uniformed Nazi guards. SS means *Schutzstaffel*, a designation difficult to translate; Black Guards is a free but fair rendering which one occasionally used until it attracted the attention of those who always look for a *double entendre*. The SS acted the part of firing-squad against the SA in the greatest double-cross operation yet known to history — the clean-up of June 30th, 1934. Though closely following the methods of Chicago gang-warfare it was on a much larger scale, indeed, on a scale only possible when you are not outside the law but are a law unto yourself.

The Supreme Court of the German Reich made a sorry showing and I came away from it with a loathing for the spectacle of inhumanity and cruelty masquerading in the red caps and robes of justice. The justices on the bench knew, as every habitué of the trial knew, that four of the accused were innocent and the fifth a half-witted dupe.

They knew that men on whom overwhelming suspicion of guilt rested had not been even arrested, were not even mentioned in the indictment, were only called as witnesses when this could no longer be avoided and were then allowed to tell a glib tale without questions or cross-examination and go their way. They knew that in outer Germany men could be thrown into prison without any trial at all, for no crime at all. Why all this paraphernalia of justice? The outer world had to be convinced, and they had to convince it. They knew what was expected of them. Lord Chief Justice Bünger did not long outlive this trial. I often feared he might have a stroke on the bench.

After this trial the National Socialist State took care that its prey should never again escape it by the Communist trick of proving innocence, that the searchlight of world publicity should never again pry into a German trial.

A People's Court was founded to try cases of treason, sedition, treachery, espionage and the like. In this court the professional judges, hampered by their legal training and respect for paragraphs and penal codes, were in a minority. Lay judges formed the majority — military and naval officers, senior SA and SS commanders, stout Nazi citizens generally — and what they said went.

These trials were held behind closed doors, where death sentences were passed without any outer public prying, domestic or foreign, into innocence or guilt. I attended the first of them, quite a minor affair. The company on the bench was impressive. There were two black-robed justices and three lay judges. One was Christiansen, that wartime German seaplane pilot who afterwards took the lovely flying ship DO.X half-way round the world and is now an Airman-General; another was von Jagow, Nazi Storm Troop commander for Berlin; the third was a Reichswehr colonel.

In the dock stood a miserable man, undernourished, under-developed, stunted, from Berlin's East End. Two years earlier, before Hitler had come to power and when the Communist Party was legal, he had distributed Communist pamphlets, they said. The black-robed presiding judge busied himself with papers and paragraphs and procedure. The three lay judges sat stiffly at attention, as military men should, only their eyes travelling indifferently from Public Prosecutor to accused, their hands on sword- or dirk-hilt. The Public Prosecutor briefly sketched the enormity of the crime. The accused's defender, a typical German jurist with a fair paunch, scarred cheek, bald head and squeaky voice, said he was not in a position to contest his client's guilt, indeed it was too obvious, but might he plead for a little clemency in view of the fact that the prisoner had grown to manhood in the Dark Age preceding National Socialism and thus had imbibed pernicious doctrines.

The court retired. The prisoner had an epileptic fit. His wife, a hardworking *Berlinerin*, looked with anguish in her eyes at the writhing collection of rags and bones that was her most cherished possession. Defending counsel watched indifferently, suddenly remembered, with an exclamation, that he had a telephone call to make, and rushed out. The prisoner recovered and exclaimed, while his beefy custodians looked contemptuously at him, 'When I come out I'll do it again'. His wife pleaded with him to be quiet. The court came back and passed sentence of two years hard labour. The court dispersed. I went out. Down the street before me went Christiansen and the colonel, very swagger in their uniforms, chatting and laughing, lunchward bound.

This is a long digression. I started out to tell you how I was driving through the Tiergarten to inquire how Nadya was recovering from my car's encounter with her, and have gone rambling all over the Reichstag, the Supreme and the People's Court.

Well, three or four hours later than I expected, I did find time to telephone, found that she was still up, and went along. I told her that the Reichstag had burned, that grave things impended for Germany, perhaps for Europe. She was sitting by a stove, reading, and listened more or less attentively between poking the fire. 'Well, well,' she said. 'There's always something happening, isn't there? Do you know, the doctor was here this afternoon and says I can dance again next week.'

CHAPTER 16

SPIRIT OF POTSDAM

'OH, did you see? He has quite blue eyes.' A girl, who had been straining her tiptoes to peer between the helmets of the Reichswehrmen, turned excitedly to her mother. Hitler had just gone by, to join hands with Old Hindenburg over the tomb of Frederick the Great in the Garrison Church and pledge Germany to 'the spirit of Potsdam'.

His eyes were about as blue as the Blue Danube, and anybody who ever sees the Danube blue should take a colour photograph and frame it. The Danube has every virtue that a river should have and I love it; it is for me a friend and a brother, and a peerless highway; it is magnificent, but it is not blue. If Johann Strauss only wanted a rhyme to Au he might just as well have taken Grau.

> Donau so Grau, tum-tum, tum-tum,
> Durch Tal und Au, tum-tum, tum-tum.

No, you can't do it. You can't waltz to a grey river. It hadderbe blue.

So with Hitler's blue eyes and the young lady of Potsdam. They had to be blue. It was the beginning of the cult of Hitler among German women. Nothing succeeds like excess, and the female population already had a terrific *Schwärmerei* for him. Afterwards I saw women crowding around him in hundreds, trying to kiss his hand, touch his garment, weeping from a surfeit of bliss at being in his presence.

Weeping women will accompany Hitler on his way through this vale of tears. Women must have wept at Guernica and Almeria, though possibly they did not even know his name; the peasant folk of Guernica and the fisherfolk of Almeria did not bother themselves about politics. A century ago the tears of women were accompanying Napoleon on his campaigns. Not that it matters. Tears soon dry, and your dictator can be sure of his legend. Whether Hitler conquers Europe and is buried in the biggest marble mausoleum of all time or whether he fails and ends his days peacefully on an island, films, theatre, radio, literature, painting, and sculpture will unite to ensure his immortal popularity. And with the passing of a generation the millions who periodically die for Europe's Strong Men are as forgotten and uncounted as the sands of the desert.

I looked about me curiously on this fitfully sunny day, March 21st, 1933. The bells of Potsdam, with Leipzig and Halle one of the few depressing towns in Germany, were clanging, the flags waving, and an enormous concourse of people had come out.

As I watched Hindenburg came, stepped out of his car, looked slowly round and stiffened as he saw the soldiers. That always galvanized him into life. Here were no perplexing politicians but ranks of field-greys, entirely immobile save for their heads, which turned like the leaves of a book as he went past, the eyes of each man bent on him as he came and went. A blazing orange order slashed his great chest, the cupola-like Pickelhaube glittered on his massive head, one hand rested on his sword and with the other he raised the field-marshal's baton in salute.

Sinking his head in humility, Hitler met him, Hitler, whose Göbbels had derided Hindenburg's senility, asked 'Is Hindenburg still alive?' Now little Göbbels sat in hushed reverence inside the church with the other members of the Cabinet, waiting to see the marriage of the old and the new Germany.

Göring, too, stood at the door of the Church, monumental in morning clothes. Nearby, the object of my particular interest, was a wooden pen, reserved for the *Generalität* — the members of the Generalhood. Here were the figures from that past which the Allied Powers thought they had killed and buried in 1918 and which now fifteen years later was returning to haunt them. Here were the representatives of the Spirit of Potsdam, of the doctrine that Germany has the divine right to expand by force of arms, venerable Excellencies in bestarred and bemedalled uniforms. For years these men had been figures of fun in a disillusioned Germany; now they had come into their own again.

What was all this about, this pilgrimage to Potsdam? It was a clever piece of mind-reading, probably inspired by that same ingenious Göbbels who hit on the idea of leaving the League, proclaiming rearmament and reoccupying the Rhineland always on a Saturday morning, rightly calculating that the shock effect of such bombshells on a Western world accustomed to regard the week-end as exclusively reserved for golf would be doubly great.

For Hindenburg was neither quite clear what he had done nor whether he had done right. This Potsdam ceremony was designed to reassure him. In the misty recesses of his darkling mind the question still prompted itself whether by making Hitler Chancellor in January and by approving the rape of the Constitution in February he had really honoured his oath 'to do justice to all men'. In March Hitler had found a way to allay his doubts, one of those ceremonies of symbolic patriotism so dear to the German mind.

Potsdam was identified with the rapid rise of German military might. From Potsdam, by means of blood and iron, the little Margraviate of Brandenburg was expanded by conquest to make the stout Kingdom of Prussia, and the Kingdom of Prussia strengthened by conquest to make the mighty German Reich, which became the greatest single power in Europe, spread overseas, built a great navy and in 1914 made a bid, which only just failed, for world domination.

From Potsdam Frederick the Great, pouncing on Silesia in times of profound peace and partitioning Poland for the first time, had doubled his inherited dominions. From Potsdam the Prussian Kings had gone out to acquire fresh territories: Schleswig-Holstein over the body of Denmark in 1864, Hanover, Hesse and other lands over the body of Austria in 1866, Alsace-Lorraine over the body of France in 1871. The very name Potsdam stood for the process of expansion by conquest checked in 1918. Frederick the Great was buried there. Lieutenant Hindenburg made his first pilgrimage to the tomb after the victorious campaign of 1866, his second when he came back, after seeing Wilhelm I proclaimed German Emperor at Versailles, from the victorious war against France in 1871.

This was the meaning of the Potsdam ceremony. Before the new Reichstag — returned at the elections held immediately after the Reichstag fire — met in an Opera House in Berlin a dedicatory service was to be held in the Garrison Church, the new regime was to be pledged to 'the spirit of Potsdam', and Hindenburg and Hitler were to shake hands over the tomb of Frederick the Great. The torch of German ambitions for world power, not extinguished in 1918 but still smouldering, was being passed on, from Field-Marshal to Bohemian Corporal.

Such thoughts stirred the heart of Hindenburg as he entered the church, sixty-seven years after his first visit. Tears filled his eyes as he saw around him all the symbols of the old martial Germany. He nodded ponderous approval when Hitler said that, thanks to him, 'the marriage has been consummated between the symbols of the old greatness and the new strength'.

Then came the famous handclasp, which meant, to Germans, that the years between 1918 and 1933 had been blotted out of the German history books, that Hindenburg, who led the German armies back from the war, had handed over his command to Hitler. The Armistice was over. The illusion that it was a Peace dissolved.

With the bells clanging again, out they came, Hindenburg, Hitler, Göring, Papen and the rest. Directly opposite me stood two sons of the former Kaiser, Hindenburg's liege lord, and as Hindenburg saw them he gave them a special salute. They were the portly Eitel Friedrich and the slimmer Oskar. Each wore the simple field grey of a private German soldier and stood with others similarly dressed, members of the Stahlhelm ex-soldiers' organization.

This display of the comradely spirit among soldiers of all ranks — we-are-all-brothers-in-the-trenches — prince-and-peasant — was an after-the-war-thought, for in the war Eitel Friedrich and Oskar both nominally held high commands, had their headquarters far from the front, and they survived it unscathed, like all the Kaiser's many sons. The Stahlhelm, however, was a good monarchist organization and in the Papen period had been a potentially powerful political force, so that it was worth while even for Hohenzollern Princes to endure the hardships of an occasional propaganda march or *Bierabend*. Subsequently the Hohenzollern Princes put on the Brown Shirt and became good Nazi Storm Troopers.

After all, Hindenburg in his testament enjoined Hitler to restore the monarchy and Hitler has never committed himself against it. He is likely to do this one day. He will probably be made to.

An hour later I sat in the gallery of the Kroll Opera House and watched Hitler take his place in the Chancellor's chair. He first entered Parliament after every possibility of opposition or counter-argument had been ruthlessly suppressed. I marvelled as I looked down on him, who had changed into the brown uniform and sat with Papen beside him.

According to his own story he drifted aimlessly about Vienna before the war, as do innumerable pieces of human flotsam and jetsam to this day, and never found a job he could keep for very long, never toiled hard with his head or his hands for meagre pay as other men do, to keep themselves alive and decent. His Socialist fellow workmen threatened to throw him off a scaffolding unless he went quietly; in private conversation Hitler must be infuriating.

In the war he was an obscure battalion orderly. After the war he was used by the Reichswehr as a spy to keep the military authorities aware of what political movements were hatching in Munich. Then, still afire with the Great-German, Anti-Jewish politics he had absorbed in Vienna, he joined the little group of men that was later to become the National

Socialist Party, came to be their leader, and for the next dozen years spent his time addressing meetings of his own supporters, accompanied to and from them by an Al Capone bodyguard and surrounded at them by Storm Troopers. The only difference in them was the degree of applause, which became greater as his supporters multiplied.

Open debate with an adversary he never knew, except on a small scale at the beginning. He avoided it, for he cannot debate. It upsets him to be challenged and he gets angry and loses control. In a real Parliament he could not have lasted, so that the timing of his first appearance in Parliament to coincide with the suppression of all opposition commands admiration.

The Reichstag on that day felt just like a bomb must feel immediately before it explodes. Only one thing — short of the death of Hindenburg, which could not be long delayed — now stood between Hitler and absolute power: — a Bill giving him authority to do what he liked, without Parliament and without regard for President or Constitution. Such a bill needed a two-thirds majority in the Reichstag.

The elections, in spite of terrorism, concentration camps, beatings-up, and the bamboozlement of the population by the Reichstag Fire, had only given the Nazis 44 per cent of the votes, or together with their Nationalist allies 51 per cent. The Communists could not come to the Reichstag at all; having been declared the authors of the fire, they would have been taken off to concentration camps forthwith, such of them as were not already in one. The Socialists could only vote against. The decision lay with the Centre Party — a Catholic Party, liberal and democratic when liberalism and democracy were in fashion, anti-democratic when the tide turned.

Hitler introduced his Bill, in his famous 'Give us four years' speech. His Parliament was in a theatre, and all the theatrical trappings of National Socialism surrounded him. Göring, massive and glowering, towered over him in the Speaker's chair. High up, the heads of two stalwart SS men poked through

148

a hole in the wooden curtain over the stage; no doubt good shots, they kept a close watch on the people in the public galleries. The brown-shirted phalanx of Hitler's deputies, among them several men whom he was to have shot a year later, tumultuously cheered every sentence. The Centre, under Kaas and Brüning, sat prim and decorous, trying to look as if they really dared vote against the Bill. The Socialists, who had to vote against it or become the laughing stock of history, were a picture of dejection. Against the wall by them lounged a thick fringe of armed Nazi SS and SA men. Outside the House masses of Storm Troopers, posted there by a thoughtful stage manager who forgot no detail, shouted in chorus threats of the things they would do if the Bill were not passed.

It was the last appearance of the great German Socialist Party, that had fought the Kaisers and Bismarck, had in the war kept alive the idea of humanity and peace in Germany, and for its pains had been saddled by the Allied Powers with the task of carrying out the Peace Treaty and kicked hard in the pants for fourteen years while engaged in doing so.

When Hitler came to power he inaugurated in Germany a military despotism far more menacing for the outer world than that of the Kaisers, and yet he was treated with infinitely more consideration and respect than the German moderates by Germany's former enemies. How can Germany fail to learn the lesson of this? How can the cause of peace and justice and humanity ever flourish in Germany?

Wearily Otto Wels, the Socialist leader, in response to Göring's barked invitation, mounted the dais. Afterwards I saw him, and Scheidemann who had proclaimed the Republic, and Stampfer the editor of *Vorwärts*, and other Socialists eking out a dreary exile in Prague. The Socialists had a little office there, where they printed anti-Nazi information about Germany and sent it back over the frontier, and Nazi agents bribed their house-porter to take photographs of their files and card indexes, with unpleasant effects for many people in Germany. But even in the hundred-per-cent Hitlerist State a few people are apparently always ready to take the risk of smuggling these newspapers, which are as dangerous to carry as a live bomb, across 'the green frontier' and distributing them among the faithful.

They would vote against the Bill, boomed Wels through his beard. They were defenceless, but they had their honour. *Wir sind wehrlos, aber nicht ehrlos*. Even at this moment of disaster the Socialist leader found comfort in one of those meaningless rhymed clichés which the German language provides for almost every contingency in life.

Wehrlos, aber nicht ehrlos. Wels had missed the spirit of the times. In the new Germany the man who was *wehrlos* was indeed *ehrlos*. Hardly had he stepped down, with heavy feet, before Hitler, with elastic tread, was at the tribune. For the first time he had the chance to answer an adversary in Parliament — in a Parliament packed with and surrounded by armed Storm Troopers, with the constitution torn up and with concentration camps filling on the verges of the town. He poured vituperation on the Socialists, who sat dumbly while the Nazi deputies frantically cheered his every word.

Then the Prelate Kaas got up, a son of that Mother Church which can always yield and always wait, which in history has so often been on the side of inhumanity and cruelty if only these were arrayed in the robes of a Most Catholic Majesty or something of that sort. The Catholic Centre, modestly announced the Prelate Kaas, would vote for the Bill.

The battle was won. The Centre votes just gave the Bill its two-thirds majority and the Nazi regime the semblance of a constitutional foundation. Absolute power was Hitler's, cloaked for the nonce only by the thin shroud of a non-committal deference due to a failing President.

I walked through the Tiergarten and Unter den Linden. Hitler, standing bare-headed in his car, drove between thick hedges of Storm Troopers to the Wilhelmstrasse. The crowds surged to greet him. The cheering crashed about him like salvoes of gunfire. Germany had 'given him four years'.

CHAPTER 17

NO JEWS IS GOOD JEWS

A BURLY Brown Shirt, stupid and bespectacled, blocked the doorway of the shop as I entered. I tried to push past. He leaned his weight against me. I pushed harder. He leaned more heavily — he was a heavy man. I forced my way past, saying 'Ausländer'. He slightly relaxed his weight, and I found myself inside the shop.

I was testing the Jewish boycott, on All Fools' Day 1933. The boycott was to be entirely one of gentle moral suasion, and peaceful picketing they said. No force would be used. Shoppers would just be politely reminded that the threshold was a Jewish one.

I don't know why I showed such zeal. It wasn't my quarrel. But I am glad I did, for while I was buying an unwanted stick of shaving-soap from an entirely non-committal Jewish proprietor, who must have wondered why I should wrestle with a Storm Trooper on his behalf, one of the few things happened that I remember with respect from this period in Germany.

A young servant girl came, one of those buxom, strapping Berlin servant girls who work like bees for their *Gnädige*, keep the flat spotlessly clean, cook, look after the children, and still have neat hair and a smiling face. I suppose she was a regular customer of this Jewish druggist. When the Brown Shirt blocked her way she told him roundly to move and when he sought to prevent her entering she said 'Quatsch' ('Rubbish') and pushed him aside, came in, made her purchase and went, to continue scrubbing her floors. This was courageous and hazardous on All Fools' Day 1933.

So I remember her with affection, together with Dimitroff, Albert Wendt the Reichstag porter, and Geheimrat Planck and those other learned men of the Kaiser Wilhelm Institute at Dahlem who in 1934, watched in respectful admiration by myself from the gallery, publicly commemorated Fritz Haber, the Jewish scientist who by his process of extracting nitrogen from the air enabled Germany to maintain her supply of explosives in the war and withstand the world for four years. Haber left Germany when Hitler came, and died in Switzerland.

But the little incident in the shop seems to me typical of this anti-Jewish racket. Inside the shop the Jew, temporarily inconvenienced but secure in the inward certainty that when this particular political swindle has had its day he will still be selling scent and soap in the Kaiserdamm. In his doorways Gentiles brawling with each other about him. If anybody had been hurt it would have been a Gentile; 99 per cent of the people who have been bumped off in Germany or by German bombs and machine-guns in other countries since the anti-Semitic swastika became the State flag of the German Reich have been Gentiles.

Moreover, I strongly fear that millions more Gentiles are going to bite the dust before the universal victory of anti-Semitism is achieved. By the accident of birth a Gentile myself, I am opposed to this, for by this process the proportion of Gentiles to Jews in the world will ultimately be reduced to that of the Jews to Gentiles in Germany at the time Hitler came to power — say five in every hundred — and at that point the Jews will probably realize that we are a menace and exterminate us. But they will do it thoroughly.

Thus I wonder who were the fools on All Fools' Day 1933. You can fool all the people some of the time, and perhaps on that day everybody in Germany believed that the Jews were really going to be eradicated from Germany. Perhaps even the Jews believed it. In that case we were all fools together and the day was well chosen.

I seldom found Berlin so unattractive as on that April day. In the early morning I watched the Brown Shirts going from shop to shop with paint pots and daubing on the windowpanes the word 'Jew', in dripping red letters. In some places I saw them pasting up black placards with the yellow spot of the Ghetto. The Kurfürstendamm was to me a revelation. I knew the Jews were predominant in business life, but I did not know that they almost monopolized important branches of it. Germany had one Jew to one hundred Gentiles, said the statistics; but the fashionable Kurfürstendamm, according to the dripping red legends, had about one Gentile shop to ninety-nine Jewish ones.

But statistics, even official German statistics, are untrustworthy about Jews. I do not know how it is done, whether large numbers of baptized Jews or non-practising Jews or Jews with foreign passports do not show in them, but nobody who trusted the evidence of his eyes could believe that Germany had only one per cent of Jews, and the same thing holds good today about the statistics for the Jewish populations of Austria, Czechoslovakia, Rumania, Yugoslavia and other countries — including England.

I watched a fat Storm Troop Commander directing operations on the shop front. He strode up and down the Kurfürstendamm smacking his leathered calves with a dog whip — a trick begun by Hitler himself, taken up by Julius Streicher, the Nüremberg Nazi leader and chief Jew-baiter, and imitated by many other little Hitlers, just as they copied his gestures and his moustache. Here he placed a picket before a shop, there he ordered the locking of a shop door and stood by while the Jewish proprietress silently complied, there again he had the paint-pot squad come and daub some new legend on the panes. Then he strode with Napoleonic mien to his waiting motor car and was driven off to hearten his men at some other sector of the front.

At night the boycott ended. It was not meant to last longer. It was a sop to the Storm Troops. They thought that by painting red letters on shop windows between dawn and dusk they could rid Germany of the Jews, a race which had endured and survived infinitely more rigorous repression in every part of Europe through the centuries and had always emerged stronger and more powerful. The Storm Troops were the fools of this All Fools' Day.

In Kiel, however, they lynched a Jew. Single-handed, he had provoked and threatened to attack a large crowd.

A month before Hitler a Jewish doctor had brought my son into the world. His nursing home was a model of cleanliness and kindliness and efficiency and I can wish no son of mine a more comfortable entry into this life. After Hitler came he was deprived of his practice among State-insured patients but his private practice continued, and even improved, and he continued to live well, a little less prosperous than before, but suffering far less material loss under the anti-Semitic regime than investors, for instance, had suffered from the inflation. Another Jewish doctor cured me of an ear trouble acquired from swimming. He moved into a smaller flat and adapted himself to a more modest income, but his private Gentile patients continued to come to him, for he was a good doctor, and he earned an ample livelihood.

I rented a house from a Jew, a house built after the war, by a Jewish architect I imagine, in that new district of Berlin near the Stadium where the Olympic Games were held, a lovely house with ivy and a porch and a sun balcony and a marvellous bathroom and a garage and a garden that merged itself in the trees of the Grunewald, where the deer sometimes came up to our fence, and yet it was but fifteen minutes eastward by car from my office in Unter den Linden and five minutes westward to the lakes — a perfect house. In a sane world, I would have liked to live there for ever. My Jewish landlord had been in politics and had gone off to Palestine; he sold his lovely house for much less than it was worth to a Berlin manufacturer who was growing rich on armaments.

My neighbour was another Jew, a prosperous lawyer, who had to reduce his scale of life because of the restrictions placed on the Jews in the legal profession. He let half his house, withdrew into the other half, divided his garden in two. In his half was a grove of trees, a little world screened off. Here his children and other Jewish children, their friends, used on sunny afternoons to gather and sit in a circle, talking quietly. I used

154

to wonder what they talked about. Here they clearly felt themselves *geborgen*, safe. But I noticed that his daughter, a beautiful girl, continued to go on school excursions with the non-Jewish children and apparently enjoyed herself.

Sometimes on a warm morning I would take out the car and drive with Brenda Mary to the ice cream shop off the Olivaerplatz, by the Kurfürstendamm, where a Jew sold the best ice cream in all Berlin, a whacking great wafer for a penny. His ice cream was famous. Scores of people and a dozen cars habitually waited outside his shop. Inside you had to wait your turn, and this Jew waxed so rich under National Socialism that eventually the hours of opening for ice cream shops were restricted.

The Jews were cleared from the theatre and opera stage, from the newspapers, from the teaching staffs of schools, colleges and universities. The worst hardships were suffered by Jews in these professions. So far as I know, no Jew can play, sing, write or teach in Germany — though, a strange anomaly, old Leo Blech was for some reason taken under Göring's protection and, for years after Hitler and the Jewish boycott, remained in the conductor's chair at the Opera, the focal point of Berlin social life. Doctors and dentists were deprived of their State patients but carried on their private practices. Lawyers were placed under crippling restrictions but, as lawyers do, found various ways of circumventing them.

But the Jews have been left almost unmolested in their most powerful stronghold — that of trade and commerce. One or two big Jewish concerns have, by various devices resembling sleight of hand, been filched from their owners and brought under non-Jewish control. The great mass of Jewish traders, big and small, remains, and goes on trading, and you can see them to this day eating and drinking in the Kurfürstendamm without let or hindrance.

The anti-Jewish racket in Germany is a pricked balloon, a hollow bluff, a shop-window exhibit like one of those tempting bottles of Chartreuse or Benedictine that you can see in expensive grocers' shops — they only contain coloured water.

The Jews know it in their heart. They may hate National Socialism as much as ever, but they no longer fear it. They know they have but to bide their time. They know that the bombs and aircraft and tanks of the new Germany were used for the first time against Gentiles, and will be used against Gentiles again. They were used in the name of anti-Bolshevism, which for the Nazis is synonymous with anti-Semitism, but what had the peasants of Guernica and the townspeople of Almeria to do with Jews or Bolshevists?

The anti-Jewish laws of Nüremberg 1936 were thought by the outer world to mark the climax of anti-Semitism in Germany; actually they meant the end of the bluff. Of what practical importance is a law forbidding German maidservants under the age of forty-five to serve in Jewish households? It is a rare insult. It will not drive one Jew from Germany or lessen by one pfennig the turnover of a Jewish trader.

The exodus of the Jews from Germany was confined to Jews in the professions. But their lot is infinitely better than that of non-Jewish emigrants. The German Socialist, Communist or pacifist emigrant has no hope but to eke out a miserable existence in Prague, Antwerp, Paris or London. I have watched him doing it — a depressing sight. He has no friends, no chance of a job, no *Protektion* — a word that plays a big part all over Europe south of the Danube and means the help of relatives or friends who have some reason to intervene for you with those in high places.

The Jew nearly always has relatives and friends in other countries, he often speaks several languages, he sometimes has more than one passport — and he has that priceless asset, the instinctive sympathy of fellow Jews, all held together by the bond of a common struggle against anti-Semitism.

Those Jewish actors, singers, writers, and academicians who went abroad belonged to precisely those professions in which Jews predominate. That is why so many of them were able with little difficulty to step across into the higher places in their professions in other countries. Many of the Jews who had become

156

famous in Germany were not even born in Germany—Einstein was born in Switzerland, Elisabeth Bergner and Richard Tauber in Austria, Franz Lederer in Bohemia.

The Jewish stars had little trouble. Einstein was welcomed in America; Bruno Walter and Otto Klemperer simply took themselves and their batons off to London, New York, Vienna and Salzburg; Max Reinhardt and Fritz Lang went to Hollywood; Elisabeth Bergner and Richard Tauber found fresh fields for their triumphs in the opera, theatre and film studios of London; Franz Lederer added English to German, Czech and French and quickly made a name for himself in Hollywood; Georg Bernhard lost no time in mourning his defunct *Vossische Zeitung* but founded an anti-Nazi Jewish paper published in Paris, the *Pariser Tageblatt*; Leopold Schwarzschild began publishing in Paris an anti-Nazi weekly called *Das Neue Tagebuch* and quickly acquired a circulation all over Europe for it; Gitta Alpar, Fritz Körtner, Pabst, Erich Pommer and many others found England eager to give them lucrative work.

All these men quickly found Jewish patrons and backers in other countries, and the lesser lights were equally successful. Many theatres and most of the cabarets and bars are Jewish-owned in Vienna and Prague, Karlsbad and Marienbad, Brunn and Zagreb, Bratislava and Bucharest. Travelling round these places I found the Jewish second-rank stars of the post-war years in Berlin, playing smaller parts than they had in Berlin but nevertheless working and earning a good livelihood.

Fritz Schultz, a popular Jewish stage and film actor, with whom I had played tennis in Berlin, I found working in a small cabaret show in Vienna. Paul Morgan, another second-rank stage and film star of those days, I saw making a crack in a bar at Marienbad that vastly amused his Jewish audience but enraged the local Nazis for its gibe at the Hitlerist Reich. He told of the snail and the goat that ran a race, which the snail won, so that the snail asked the goat what he had been doing; the goat answered that he was so confident of winning that he had stopped on the way and bleated, whereon the snail answered,

'Oh, you can't win by bleating nowadays, you have to crawl'.

'Bleating' was the name coined by Göbbels for any criticism of Hitler or his disciples and it was a practice liable to lead to the concentration camp; 'crawling', in the opinion of Paul Morgan, was the only way to advancement in Nazi Germany.

In Belgrade I found my Jewish colleague X, formerly of the Socialist *Vorwärts*. He was living moderately well, and already had a finger in Yugoslav-Bulgar politics. Viktor Schiff, of *Vorwärts*, began to write for the London *Daily Herald*. I went into a Prague cinema and saw Paul Grätz in an American film; he was apparently in demand for character parts in Hollywood.

In Vienna, owner of a prosperous women's hat shop, you could see in 1938 the Jew who in 1932 had been a leading attraction at the homosexual Eldorado in Berlin, and was famous for the elegant evening frocks he wore.

In Vienna, Prague, Brünn, Marienbad, Karlsbad, Bucharest, Budapest, Zagreb, and to a lesser extent in Belgrade and Sofia I found Jews growing more and more numerous and prosperous. They predominate in the expensive cafés and hotels and restaurants in these towns and in their theatres and cinemas and bars and newspaper offices and trade. The wave of rearmament had eddied outwards and reached all these surrounding countries by 1936, bringing with it a new wave of prosperity, real or artificial. The Jews in all these countries were riding on the crest of the boom, as they always do because of their commercial genius.

The new prosperity was born in rearmament, and that was begun in the name of anti-Communism and anti-Semitism. Abyssinia, Spain and China have already shown that the new armaments race spells death, not for Jews, but for indiscriminate millions of helpless Gentiles, Africans, Chinese and whatnot. The profits from the armaments race will go largely into the pockets of Jews, because of their preponderant share in retail trade, which in the last resort catches the pounds and pennies paid out by the manufacturers to their workers. Such is Hitler's achievement in the cause of anti-Semitism.

I was talking one day to Z, a Jewish journalist expelled from Germany who has settled in Vienna, where he has a pleasant home and a motor car. He talked with bitter resentment of Germany. 'Ah', he complained, 'the Poles murdered us, but the Germans have robbed us', and it was quite clear from his tone which was the worse thing for him. Then he told me how his son was still working for a big German film company in Berlin and had thrice had his salary raised to induce him not to leave and emigrate, as he desired, wishing to join his father.

The Jews. As I write, in Vienna, they are all about me, watching with non-committal, veiled, appraising eyes the comedy that is going on in Insanity Fair. They know that when Hitlerism has passed away they will still be trading in the Kärntnerstrasse.

CHAPTER 18

MIDSUMMER NIGHTMARE

I SAT on a balcony in the Bayreutherstrasse, just as thousands of Berliners were sitting on their balconies on this Saturday afternoon in June, and drank coffee. Nadya was there and we both felt restless and apprehensive. She was going away in the evening, to Antwerp, and we did not know when we should meet again. We envied the people in the street below, as they strolled about with no thought of impending leavetakings or long journeys.

As we talked and watched them, from between the flower boxes, we saw them crowding about a newspaper seller, snatching his papers, gathering in groups to discuss their contents. I went downstairs to buy a paper, saw a headline, 'Chief-of-Staff Röhm dismissed!'

Röhm dismissed! Hitler's bosom companion and thoufriend, Minister of the Reich, creator and Commander of the Brown Army, brave but bawdy soldier, homosexual in chief, Captain in the German, General in the Bolivian Army.

Back on my balcony, while Nadya packed, I pondered the bare announcement when I saw another newspaper man, with fresh supplies, come round the corner from the Tauentzienstrasse, where the trams clanged unconcernedly by. In an instant a group of people were about him, clamouring for his papers. He could not serve them fast enough, the group quickly grew to a crowd, he turned and ran, the crowd ran after him and hemmed him in against a wall, he turned this way and that, hugging his precious newspapers against him and trying to escape, but they tore them from him. Another moment and he stood there without newspapers, lucky to retain his clothes.

Again I dashed down and after a struggle procured a newspaper. Röhm shot. Ernst shot. Spreti shot. Spreti, Spreti? Ah yes, Count Spreti. Other Nazi leaders had their blonde lady secretaries; Röhm had his blond young aides-de-camp.

Count Pretty, we had called him. I thought with regret of the curly-haired, ladylike Count Pretty. I had seen him a week or two before, in a most becoming uniform, all looped and tasselled and braided, walking with Röhm through the Tiergarten. About the same time I had seen him at Röhm's elbow on the night that Röhm sang us a stentorian song of praise about his three million Storm Troopers. Now Count Pretty had ended in a pool of blood, beside his chief.

Heines shot, Heydebreck shot, Hayn shot. All men who had gone on fighting after the war, against the Poles in Silesia and the French in the Ruhr, men who had been with Hitler from the start, men who understood nothing but soldiering and fight-ing, products of the fifty years of blood and iron that began in 1864 and reached their explosive climax in 1914. The National Socialist revolution was eating its children.

Hullo! General von Schleicher shot. Frau von Schleicher shot. The revolution was devouring some that were not its children.

Nine names were contained in this first list of the dead on June 30th, 1934.

An official statement on July 7th said, 'Although it is known that the number of traitors shot is under fifty grotesque figures are being bruited about.'

Seventy-seven was the number given by Hitler in his speech of self-exculpation on July 13th.

Some years later I lent a German diplomat in another country Konrad Heiden's book about Hitler. In the chapter about the great clean-up of June 30th are the words, 'The number of dead cannot be stated. Three hundred is the probable minimum, one thousand not improbable'.

In the margin against this passage when I got the book back I found the pencilled note '1,176!'

I believe this is the exact number of the persons shot in Germany on June 30th, 1934.

Nadya had a few hours to spare and we took the car and drove through the town to see what was afoot. Groups of Berliners stood discussing the news. Röhm shot, Röhm to whom Hitler on January 30th had written, 'On the first anniversary of the National Socialist revolution I am moved, my dear Ernst Röhm, to thank thee for the imperishable services which thou hast rendered the National Socialist movement and the German nation and to assure thee how thankful I am to Providence that I may describe such a man as thee as my friend and comrade.'

Ernst shot, Ernst who a few weeks before had been sent on the streets with other Nazi stars with a collecting box for some Nazi charity and had been mobbed by thousands of adoring Berlin flappers.

I drove past the Press Club in the Tiergartenstrasse, which had a tennis court in its garden on which the windows of the Reichswehr Ministry looked down. I had played tennis there that morning, with Quentin Reynolds, I think. The Reichswehr Ministry, the father of this mass execution, had towered above us, placid, inscrutable and invulnerable. Sometimes an officer or a woman clerk came to a window and watched the play for a moment, then disappeared, and the Reichswehr Ministry resumed its wonted featureless calm, with no sign of hurry or worry or even life, while at Munich and out at Lichterfelde and even in the Wilhelmstrasse half a mile away men were being shot in bedrooms, in prison cells, against walls, in offices, in their flats.

Then I drove on past the Bendlerstrasse, until there was a block in the traffic, and a taxi coming from the opposite direction halted alongside me. In it sat a woman, weeping. She neither looked right nor left nor dried her eyes, but just stared straight in front of her and the tears ran down her face and I watched her until the jam of cars broke up and she was carried past me. She was young and rather pretty and, I suppose, somebody's wife. That morning, as I imagine, her husband had been a Nazi star, with a smart uniform, an expensive car, cohorts of saluting subordinates, and they were both living in a brave new world and now quite suddenly he was dead and she didn't know why.

I saw on the kerbstone a friend, a Spanish Catholic journalist, and stopped to have a word with him. He was talking earnestly to another man I recognized, a young diplomat who was a collaborator of Herr von Papen, who as a Catholic and a Papal Chamberlain was regarded with some hopes by those who complained of the alleged persecution of the Catholic Church in Germany, a thing of which I saw little sign. My Spanish friend came and told me that Bose and Jung, other collaborators of Herr von Papen, had been shot, and asked if I could take in and hide the young man he was talking to. But I had no quarters to offer.

That night all Germany sat at the loudspeaker, waiting and waiting for some explanation of these events and at long last we heard Göbbels's voice, describing that fantastic midnight flight of Hitler to Munich, his motor-dash to the conference of all high Nazi Storm Troop commanders which he himself had summoned at Bad Wiessee, the shooting of the men who but yesterday had been the white flower of German chivalry — Röhm the soldier of fortune, Ernst the bell-boy, Heines the murderer and homosexual who as Police Chief of Breslau and Silesian Storm Troop Commander had had power of life and death over millions of his fellow countrymen.

I had seen Heines, often enough, but the most interesting occasion was eight months earlier, at the Reichstag Fire Trial, where his murder and his homosexuality, both general knowledge but always denied, had both been openly proclaimed before the Supreme Court of the German Reich.

You will find some of these things hard to believe, but you can check them up.

He was a big, blond fellow, good looking but for the indefinable something that betrays the homosexual. In that astounding trial he told the Court, 'I now admit that I dispatched a traitor to that place where traitors ultimately belong'. He had now been sent, as a traitor, to that very place, together with Röhm, who in unveiling a memorial to the assassins of Rathenau a little earlier had praised their act as 'a manly deed'; and had now seen what a manly deed looked like from the muzzle end of a revolver. ('The National Socialist Party repudiates political murder as a weapon', said Hitler in his funeral oration about Gustloff, the Nazi leader shot by a Jew in Switzerland in 1936.)

The way Heines's well-known homosexuality was flourished before the Supreme Court was amusing. He had been accused, wrongly, by the anti-Nazi Brown Book published in London of having been one of the Nazis who entered the Reichstag through the underground tunnel and fired it. He came before court with a newspaper cutting and photograph showing that he had on that night spoken in Gleiwitz and with a hotel keeper to prove that he had slept there.

This hotel keeper produced the receipted bill paid by Heines. That unfortunate Dr. Bünger who presided over the great trial and was during the course of it faced with so many unexpected problems, bless his innocent heart, in examining it said to the witness, 'There are two names on it — Herr Heines and Herr Soundso. Who is Herr Soundso?' The hotel keeper shuffled his feet, coughed and said, 'Er, Herr Soundso shared Herr Heines's room', the red-robed justices modestly dropped their eyes, and Dr. Bünger, suddenly seeing a yawning chasm before him, hastily passed on to the next point.

Now little Göbbels stood at the microphone and told us all about that midsummer night's nightmare. His voice trembled with some emotion, possibly pent-up indignation, I don't know; bloodthirsty little Göbbels, who talked so bravely of cannon and wars, had that day for the first time rubbed shoulders with murder and sudden death. He was the loudest spokesman of the discontent for which Röhm and the others had now paid the death penalty, the loudest prophet of the 'second revolution', and he had only in the nick of time changed over to the side that held the butt end of the revolver.

He told us, in accents of hushed horror, of Hitler's raid on Munich and Wiessee, of the awful discovery of Heines in bed with a youth — 'this throws a vivid flash of light on conditions in Röhm's circle' — and the arrest of the 'mutinous Storm Troop Commanders'.

164

Not so Göring, when he strode into the room the next day to address the assembled legions of the international press, invited by himself. His week-end had done him as much good as a holiday in the country.

Here was no longer the raving, red-faced incoherent Göring of the passage at arms with Dimitroff; he was clear-eyed, brisk, in perfect control of his nerves. He told how he had suppressed, at Hitler's order, the Berlin end of the alleged mutiny, how he had 'extended his mission' and had his fellow Reichswehr General von Schleicher shot — and Frau von Schleicher. He had in the preceding forty-eight hours ordered the death of dozens of men, many of them his comrades for years in the struggle of National Socialism for power. He was as cool as a cucumber.

Twelve days later, on July 13th, I again looked down from the gallery of the Kroll Opera House and watched Hitler getting up to make his speech of self-exculpation. There were eloquent gaps in the ranks of deputies. The atmosphere of the House was as taut as a bowstring.

I looked curiously at the people in the packed public galleries, breathlessly waiting for Hitler to begin. There were priests, Reichswehr officers, old women, young women. I was staggered afterwards by the unanimity with which they all rose at him in jubilant ecstatic approval. I knew that the Nazis had been growing more and more unpopular in the country, and that there would be a fierce exultation among masses of Germans at the thought that some of the more detested figures had been hoist with their own petard. But, after all, these very men had been cheered to the echo by enormous crowds wherever they went but a fortnight before. Now these same millions just as rapturously cheered the smashing of yesterday's idols. None asked 'Were they guilty?'

Hitler's speech that day really needs a book to itself, a book which would marshal against each statement the evidence for and against. It is a mass of demonstrable mis-statements. The great plot, from which Germany was supposed to have been saved by this midsummer massacre, had as little real existence as the great Communist rising for which the Reichstag fire was supposed to have been the signal, and from which Germany was saved by similar measures.

Three years later Stalin in Moscow had a very similar clean-up, shooting or imprisoning numbers of his bosomest friends and closest collaborators and also some Red Army Generals. The German press described that operation, in terms of unmeasured contempt, as political gang warfare springing from the basest motives of fear, treachery and lust of office. But when the same things were said abroad about the great Hitler clean-up of June 30th the rulers of Germany were stung to the quick.

Dictators, these men of blood and iron, are highly sensitive to criticism. Protected from it at home, they wince like a salted snail, to quote a Wodehousean simile, when the outer world puts their domestic methods under the microscope. Thus Hitler was really upset by Low's 'Double Cross' cartoon, which showed the Storm Troopers standing with hands up before a Hitler with a smoking revolver and said 'They salute with both hands now'.

Hitler unfolded to an enthralled Reichstag the story of the great plot. It was a long rigmarole, but the gist of it was that Röhm, wishing to acquire control of the army, had plotted with other senior Brown Army Commanders to rise at five o'clock on Saturday afternoon, June 30th, seize all Government buildings, arrest Hitler, and murder non-Nazi members of the Government. Ernst, Brown Army Commander in Berlin, was to lead the rising. 'Under these circumstances', cried Hitler to our rapt selves, 'I had only one course open — ruthless and bloody intervention'.

Well, well. I have hardly any illusions left, but when I look back on those days and that speech I am still staggered by the gullibility of mankind. The mutinous Brown Army Commanders who were to storm Berlin on the afternoon of June 30th, were in the morning of that day all gathered at Bad Wiessee, a remote Bavarian spa about as far from Berlin as any place in Germany, whither they had come hotfoot at the personal order of Hitler himself, who there had the ones who were to be shot arrested and the others sent home. They were hundreds of miles from Berlin and from their own Brown Shirts.

Ernst, who was to lead the attack on the Wilhelmstrasse on June 30th, was on June 30th at Bremen with his newly acquired wife, about to embark on a honeymoon trip to Madeira. The *Bremer Nachrichten*, which could not foresee on July 3rd what Hitler was going to say on July 13th, announced his arrest on June 30th at Bremen and transport by air to Berlin — where he was shot.

So much for the great plot. Many other picturesque details were woven into the bloodcurdling story. Schleicher and Strasser were both in it, having conspired with Röhm. Both were shot.

Schleicher and Strasser on June 30th paid the price of an intrigue which, whether by accident or judgment, they had never begun. Von Schleicher, incidentally, was sitting writing letters in his flat at Zehlendorf on that pleasant June afternoon when the SS forced their way in and shot him and his wife. Their maidservant, a good, simple soul who was not used to such goings-on, afterwards rushed downstairs in a hysterical state and talked loudly about what had happened in the shops of the local tradespeople, but after an hour or two she disappeared and was not seen again. I hope nothing unpleasant happened to her.

All sorts of other dark figures appeared in the great plot, as related to us by Hitler that day — Communists and reactionaries and an unnamed foreign power generally assumed to be France. Everybody seemed to have been in it.

For instance, there was Dr. Klausner, a high government official, who would not have been seen dead with Röhm if he had had any choice in the matter, and would probably have been among the first victims if Ernst and his Brown Shirts had really seized government buildings, for he was an ardent Catholic churchman and head of the Catholic Action and the spokesman of that body of militant Catholic opinion which actively resented the attitude of the Brown Army towards the Church.

He was shot in the Ministry of Communications and the Minister, Baron von Eltz-Rübenach, a retiring nobleman who had been left at this non-political Ministry in virtue of the promise to Hindenburg to keep the Government one of 'National Concentration', rang his Nazi colleague Frick at the Ministry of the Interior and said plaintively, 'They've just shot Klausner in the next room', and Frick answered, 'Yes, and they'll be shooting a good many others', and rang off.

In Papen's office Bose was shot and Papen himself was led away in arrest and only owed his life to the patronage of Hindenburg, a coat of mail against which the Nazi leaders still feared to strike. For Papen on June 17th had made that famous speech at Marburg where he warned Hitler against 'the second revolution' for which the bolder Brown Army leaders, irritated by the sight of big business and inherited privilege and military exclusivity still deeply entrenched, were clamouring — the speech in which he said, 'A free press ought to exist to inform the Government with open and manly statements where corruption has made its nest, where bad mistakes have been made, where the wrong men are in the wrong place, and where the spirit of the German revolution has been sinned against. A third revolution can easily follow a second and he who threatens the guillotine comes the sooner under its knife'.

It was a speech mainly aimed at Göbbels, the most hated of the Nazi leaders, who furiously hit back at Papen through his newspapers with references to 'armchair critics', 'effete aristocrats', and the like, but by June 30th Göbbels had in the nick of time seen the danger and he was at Hitler's side in the midnight aeroplane dash to Munich. And Papen's collaborator Jung, who wrote the speech, was shot, just having the time to scribble the letters 'SS!' on the inside of his bathroom cupboard before he was led away, to be returned later to his relatives inside a small urn of ashes, but Papen, the buoyant, the cheery, the indestructible, went free.

All sorts of other ancient scores were paid off on this day. For instance, old General von Kahr, who had suppressed Hitler's 1923 Putsch, was now seventy-eight years old and living in retirement in Bavaria, was taken out and shot.

So was Scheringer, a fine-looking lad, idealist to his finger-tips, the best type of German. At the famous Reichswehr trial in 1930, when three young officers were charged with spreading Nazi sedition in the army, Hitler was called as witness and made his famous promise that 'Heads will roll when we come to power'. One of the three officers, then held up as national idols and martyrs by the Nazis, was Scheringer. He little thought, as he listened to his Leader, that his own head would roll. In prison he had ruminated about things and discarded his National Socialism, deciding that Communism alone could save Germany. He had openly said so, and now he had paid.

At Hirschberg in Silesia a local SS commander, hearing that shooting was going on, took out four Jews and shot them, this being one of the relatively few instances in which Jews actually lost their lives.

The most unfortunate man in the great plot was that Dr. Willi Schmidt, who was music critic of the *Münchener Neueste Nachrichten*, and had never had any connection with politics but whose godfathers and godmothers at his baptism had unwisely conferred on him the same not uncommon name as a black-listed Brown Shirt commander. He was executed, to make sure. But generous amends were later made to his widow and four little children; a personal aide-de-camp of Hitler called and expressed regret for a painful mistake.

Hitler on that day offered a choice of reasons for the executions. Not only the great plot, but homosexuality — he laid emphasis on that. The private habits of the Röhm clique were intolerable, he said.

When men become rich or powerful their shabby friends are a nuisance. Röhm's homosexuality, openly proclaimed and angrily denied, had not bothered his chief during the struggle for power, nor prevented him from recalling Röhm from Bolivia to become his Chief-of-Staff.

I hope you haven't heard this one, stop me if you have, but I should like to tell you what the great clean-up of June 30th was really about.

On one side you had millions of Brown Shirts angry at the failure of National Socialism, after eighteen months of power, to fulfil its promises. The working-class parties had been suppressed, their leaders imprisoned, the trades unions had been dissolved and their property confiscated, the workers had lost the right to strike or collectively to bargain about wages — yes. But big business had been left alone, the big landlords sat undisturbed, the army remained the close preserve of the generals and the military caste, into which no stranger might venture, and wages were falling. The Brown Shirts felt they had been fooled and sang on the march this parody of their Horst Wessel song:

Die Preise hoch, Kartellen werd'n geschlossen,
Kapital marschiert mit ruhig, festem Schritt,
Bankdirektoren werden Parteigenossen
Und für den Sozialismus sorgt Parteigenosse Schmidt.

(Up with prices, form your trusts,
Capital is on the march, steady, firm and fit,
Directors of Banks now march in our ranks
And Socialism's in the charge of Mr. Comrade Schmidt.)

The good Herr Schmidt, Minister of Economics, was the able representative of big business who looked after Germany's economics under National Socialism until Dr. Schacht came.

On the other hand you had big business deeply suspicious of the increasing clamour of the Brown Shirts for Socialism, the big landlords still mindful of National Socialism's promise in pre-power days to expropriate big estates, and the army determined not to yield control to interlopers like Röhm. You also had millions of private citizens detesting the behaviour of the Storm Troop commanders, their self-aggrandizement and self-enrichment, their expensive motor cars, their squandering of public money, their interference everywhere.

Then bear in mind three things:

(1) Hindenburg could not live long. He was commander-in-chief. When he died Hitler would become commander-in-chief. The army did not know whether Hitler was for Röhm-Göbbels-Ernst-Heines and the discontented Brown Army or whether he was with the army, big business, big banking, big landlordship. If he were on the side of the 'second revolutionists' he himself would have to be displaced. That was only possible so long as Hindenburg, the commander-in-chief, lived. Otherwise the army would have to revolt against its own commander-in-chief and it had never done that. Therefore the blister must be pricked, Hitler's submission sealed in blood, before Hindenburg died.

(2) German rearmament impended. Instead of a few score thousand Reichswehrmen Germany was to have an army of millions, with a vast and entirely new air force, legions of tanks, hundreds of batteries — a soldier's dream of the most roseate hue. The generals were determined not to let control of the army pass out of their hands into that of the Party and the Brown Army, least of all when this marvellous prospect of promotion and new battalions was just opening to them.

(3) Röhm and his group feared that National Socialism would repeat the mistake of the Socialists and leave the army as the exclusive property of the military caste, a weapon that might one day backfire. They wanted the formation of a revolutionary people's army, in which the Brown Army and its leaders should have the last word. They wanted measures against capital. They had no plot to rise in Berlin, seize Government buildings, arrest Hitler, murder Papen and the like. The facts of June 30th prove that. It is a fairy-tale that could only find credence in a country where the bulk of the population is of a child-like gullibility and has no access to information. But they did want control of the army, and said so. They thought Hitler could be brought to see things in this light.

If you put these three things together you will understand

the clean-up. The generals knew that Hindenburg, their commander-in-chief, was dying, that Hitler would be their next commander-in-chief, that in a few days or weeks they would have to obey him or openly mutiny—a thing the Reichswehr had never done. It was a race with time. Röhm and his upstart commanders must at all costs be disciplined, Hitler be brought to heel, before the Old Gentleman died.

They timed their move perfectly. Hindenburg died four weeks later.

Not treachery, not homosexuality, not a plot, was the reason why Hitler killed Röhm. Hitler had the choice of disappearing himself, dead or alive, who knows, but at all events of going, of stepping down from his hardly-won Chancellorship, or of ruthlessly disciplining the Brown Army and smashing its dreams of interference with the army, once and for all.

That is why Hitler's speech to which I listened that day, though tremendously long, contains only one all-revealing passage, which tells everything. Speaking of the alleged Röhm-Schleicher plan to make Röhm Reichswehr Minister in place of General von Blomberg, he said:

'It would never have been possible for me to approve of a change in the Reichswehr Ministry and to appoint Röhm . . . My promise to President von Hindenburg to preserve the army as an unpolitical instrument of the Reich is binding from my deepest conviction and from my given word. But such an act in respect of the Reichswehr Minister would have been impossible for me as a man. I and all of us are happy to see in him a man of honour from tip to toe . . . Any such idea would have been an act of disloyalty to Field-Marshal Hindenburg and to the Reichswehr Minister and also to the army itself. There is in the State only one bearer of arms — the army.'

You could not desire a more complete submission than that. Röhm paid the price of hoping to do what the Socialists never dared to attempt. By the clean-up Hitler insured himself against the only force that could overthrow him, the army, at the very moment when, with Hindenburg's death impending, it would have overthrown him rather than suffer any interference with its prerogatives and with plans which it considered vital for Germany.

Thus General von Blomberg, twenty-four hours after the clean-up, praised in his order to the army 'the soldierly resolution and exemplary courage' with which Hitler had laid low 'traitors and mutineers'.

'The army', he said meaningly, 'as the bearer of the entire nation's weapons will prove its thanks by devotion and loyalty.'

Thus Hindenburg's last telegram thanking Hitler 'for saving the German nation from a grave danger'. That may be true, but the danger was not the Great Plot.

And when Hindenburg died von Blomberg's first act was to have the army sworn in undying loyalty to its new commander-in-chief. William the Second, watching from Doorn, must have thought back to wartime days when he, the Supreme Warlord, was the prisoner of those imperative Generals Hindenburg and Ludendorff at Headquarters, who had also sworn undying loyalty. In February 1938, when Hitler dismissed a dozen generals, the Party got some of its own back on the Army, but the last word has not been said.

But on this day in the Reichstag Hitler curdled Germany's blood and swept Germany off its feet. How they rose at him when he said, 'In this hour I was responsible for the destiny of the German Nation and for twenty-four hours I was the supreme court of the Reich myself'. They loved that. Near me was a stout woman with a shining, good-humoured face. She drank in his words in deep draughts and looked at her neighbours to see if they were enjoying it too and beat her hands together, which were encased in black kid gloves, and the Protestant Priest sprang to his feet and gave the Hitler salute, and the grim-faced Reichswehr officers jumped up and stood at attention and there was a thunderous Hoch! that nearly took the roof off at that passage about Hitler having acted as avenging angel himself for twenty-four hours. As he sat down he wiped something from his eye. It may have been a tear.

That was the end of it. I had overestimated the effect of June 30th on the German people. I thought some of them had had a lasting shock. Not a bit of it. Nobody had really cared about Röhm and the rest, although scores of thousands of Germans had cheered them wherever they appeared. Nobody, except a few widows, cared about Schleicher and Strasser and Scheringer and old von Kahr and the unhappy Willi Schmidt.

It was all quickly forgotten. As I drove back to my rooms the streets were quiet again. The trams were clanging to and fro, people were thronging to the theatres and cinemas, the guests in the cafés were already turning from the startling front pages to the sporting news, the boys and girls were coming in on their bicycles from the countryside and stopping off at the ice-cream shops to refresh themselves. How small a thing is the killing even of several hundred people in the life of so great a country. And except in war itself the great majority of the people suffer no direct consequences from the vendettas of the politicians. They just marvel, and go their way.

I went with Nadya to the station. We were both unhappy at the severance, possibly for good, of a valued friendship. The late train, the one that I had so often caught for England, bore her away from the Bahnhof am Zoo, and we both waved until we could see each other no longer. Then I strolled back to my rooms. It was a perfect June evening.

CHAPTER 19

MECKLENBURG IDYLL

Uncle William sat on his chair by the lakeside, his enormous straw hat over his eyes, drowsing in the sunshine. A good-humoured old gentleman, very popular with the children of the farmer who hired him in England, when he was a prisoner of war. He led an idyllic life now, by this Mecklenburg lakeside. He just pushed his boats off, and as they drew away he folded his hands over each other and flapped them like a bird's wings, in farewell; it was his one little joke. When they came back he tied them up and went on drowsing, until his busy wife called down the garden that his dinner was ready.

The whole village was like that. True, the grocer, who had sailed about the world as a sailor on North German Lloyd ships, had a wider horizon and some interest in Insanity Fair. He was just intelligent enough to be stupid, suspected my camera, with which I took snapshots of the bathing beach and the lake, gave me, for some private motive that I distrusted, a hint that a big aerodrome was being built 'just over there'. German rearmament wasn't my business, except such news of it as the Germans themselves published, and I kept clear of him. Perhaps he was a peace-loving man, who disliked these new preparations. Perhaps he was a spy maniac; the nation was being reared to that mania.

The only other man who had seen the outer world was old Hans Sturm, the bathing-beach attendant, with his Kaiser moustache, who had served in German East Africa. Now he dozed, in his shady corner, like Uncle William in his.

All the rest were just village people, who thought only of fishing and farming and milling, and not even the *Völkischer Beobachter* or the *Lokal Anzeiger* could really ripple the even tenor of their ways.

I loved it. The lake was wide and long, the sun warm, you

could bathe where you wanted, you felt yourself growing fitter every minute. In the evening there was a restful inn, and a glass of beer and a glass of korn mix well together before you go to bed with a book. The storks were everywhere. Out in the lake was a little island, with an English princess buried on it.

You couldn't have found a more sleepy and peaceful place for a fortnight snatched from a turbulent summer.

CHAPTER 20

HINDENBURG GOES TO VALHALLA

In the early morning I listened to little Göbbels's voice announcing 'The office of the Reich President is united with that of the Reich Chancellor, and the former powers of the Reich President are now invested in the Führer and Reich Chancellor Adolf Hitler', and then I turned a knob and heard an emasculated voice from London proclaiming the death of Germany's Grehnd Old Mehn.

Somebody should found a society either for the abolition of Grand Old Men or of meaningless clichés indiscriminately applied to anybody who is sufficiently old, just as the Nobel Peace Prize is automatically awarded to the Foreign Minister of any Great Power which has not actually declared war in the preceding year, but if it is given to a pacifist like Ossietzky after years of martyrdom in concentration camps, a storm of protest immediately arises.

Hindenburg had died in the night of August 1st. Hitler, having cleaned up the Brown Army and made his submission to the Grey Army, now seemed to reign supreme. But his power was not boundless. If he ever breaks that pledge to the army Hitler, as I think, will have to go, unless the spirit of the German changes vastly. Göring realized that from the beginning and that is why he, son of a general and himself an officer, quite early in the National Socialist regime made himself a Reichswehr General and habitually wears that uniform. Thus he early booked himself a place on the right side for June 30th.

Hitler became the master of Germany, pledged to respect the wishes of the army, big business and big landlordship. Papen's calculation proved right in the end, though by delayed action, and though he himself had come near to losing his life, had lost all immediate hope of office in Berlin, and was

M

marooned in Vienna. Papen, who flew to Germany for all the big festivals and was always prominent on the platform, never lost hope of a come-back, but was eventually recalled.

But on this morning, when events were too near to be seen in perspective, Hitler seemed to be absolute lord over sixty-six million Germans. Twenty years to a day had passed since the German armies had set out to fight the world and now the old Field-Marshal, their commander, was dead, and the Bohemian Corporal was Führer of the Reich.

A week later I watched him rise to deliver the funeral oration. An unforgettable sight. There we all were, gathered together within the octagonal walls of the bleak fortress-like memorial to Hindenburg's victory over the Russians at Tannenberg in East Prussia. Here the enemy had for the only time in the war trodden German soil. Here Hindenburg had driven them back — but not before the Russian incursion had compelled the Germans to withdraw troops from France, and stop the drive on Paris and begin the retreat from the Marne. I thought back to the retreat from Mons in 1914 and to the German drive that nearly reached Paris even in 1918. I too paid my silent homage — not to the Prussian victors of Tannenberg but to the Russian losers. But for them I might not have been sitting there, citizen of a prosperous victor State.

The eight square towers of the memorial, built on cold, hard, Prussian acres, cut hard, cold lines against a clear blue Prussian sky. I had never understood the spirit of Prussia so well. On the ramparts between the towers stood immobile German blue-jackets. On the greensward enclosure stood immobile Reichswehr regiments, the best-looking troops I have ever seen, square jaws set against the fine lines of the German steel helmet. All around me, on tiers of encircling seats, sat officers of the old Imperial Army.

It was as if the German Army of 1914 had sprung from the earth. Swagger lancer helmets sat jauntily on heads from which every scrap of hair had vanished. Pickelhauben glittered over clamped lips, monocled frowns, scarred cheeks. Gold-encircled paunches dwindled down to thin legs encased in dainty shining kneeboots. Pomp and circumference. But here and there sat a young lieutenant in the grey of the new Reichswehr or the blue of the new Air Force, bronzed, fit, hard as nails, fine-looking lads.

Down the steps, a blazing mass of colour, came the Ambassadors and Ministers-Plenipotentiary with their military attachés, and the foreign military delegations — the scarlet and gold of the Brigade of Guards, the sky-blue and emerald green plumes of the Imperial Austro-Hungarian army, and many more.

Ranked before Hindenburg's coffin sat the men who had made the new Germany. They were all there, Göring in his general's uniform in the front rank, Oskar von Hindenburg, soon to be relegated to country squiredom, old Oldenburg-Januschau in a tiny helmet and a uniform swathed round his corpulence until it cascaded down into leather gaiters, Papen with a flaring green sash, Blomberg erect and soldierly, little Göbbels chatting away somewhere at the back, Mackensen with the gleaming silver death's head on his hussar's busby and his own face looking like a painted death's head with the sunken eyes and the lurid patch of colour on his withered cheeks.

And Hitler. With the eyes of the world upon him he strode across the greensward to the dais before the coffin, the manuscript of his speech in his hand. He glanced at it, paused and said something to the aide-de-camp behind him, who hurriedly fumbled in the leather wallet from which he had taken the speech, found nothing and whispered a reply. Hitler paused uncertainly a moment, then mounted the dais. They had given him the wrong funeral oration. He began to repeat the speech I had heard him deliver the day before in the Reichstag. An excruciating moment. He only spoke a couple of paragraphs of it and then, apparently feeling that to read the whole thing again would be too stupid, he laid aside his manuscript and spoke freely.

But he could not remember much of what he had prepared, so that after a few improvised sentences he let off his great set-

179

piece, 'Dead Field-Marshal, now go to Valhalla!' That was Hitler's own, or I am a Martian.

And Hindenburg's body, with Reich Bishop Müller of the Evangelical Church and a Roman Catholic Bishop reverently watching — was removed to Valhalla — one of the eight towers of Tannenberg Memorial, after the shortest funeral oration on record.

The great concourse split up and surged down the tiny village street to the station, and the great special trains drew out, until Tannenberg was left again to its few hundred inhabitants and to Hindenburg.

I had travelled all the previous night to Tannenberg, and had had an exhausting day and now had another night journey ahead. In the late evening, I got out at Schneidemühl to write and telephone. As I left the station the Hitler Youth went marching past, and suddenly several lusty youths were all around me, threatening violence if I did not salute the Nazi flag. The weary explanation 'Foreigner' made them withdraw, sullenly.

A small town, a dark street, a search for a hotel, tip-tap, tip-tap in a small room, a long wait for a telephone call, a hurried meal, back to the station in the small hours, a train, Berlin at breakfast time. A wire was waiting for me to say that my mother was dying. I caught the midday train and travelled all night to London.

When I arrived she was dead. She had had little happiness. But when I came on leave, from the war, from Europe, she had always been there, sitting at the window, watching the buses go by, eagerly peering at the passers-by to see if a crony were among them. I walked behind the modest coffin, with its few flowers, saw it lowered into the ground. I felt bitter. I walked out of the little flat for the last time, down West End Lane, past Fortune Green, went back to Germany.

CHAPTER 21

GERMAN LEAVETAKING

I STOOD in the street at Cologne, in the shiny polished street where the reflection of the street lamps soaks in like golden paint. I had a couple of hours to wait between trains, about midnight, and was using the time for a last look at Cologne,

The great cathedral towered above the station square, faintly luminous in a starry night. At the corner coloured lights gleamed in the window of the Gegenüber shop, where Eau de Cologne was born. I took leave of them both. I strolled down to the Rhine, which remembered me at once, and we exchanged reminiscences of that voyage with Hindenburg from Ludwigshafen to Coblenz, of the disaster in which our mutual friend the Mosel was concerned, when the bridge collapsed at the Deutsches Eck. I said good-bye to the Rhine. 'Heil Hitler!' it seemed to call after me. 'Grüss Gott!' I replied.

I walked at random through the streets, and paid my last tribute to them. The dignity of these German cities, on the North Sea and Baltic coasts, along the line of the Rhine, in South Germany. The order, the cleanliness. No muddle, no litter, no slums. Good houses, good flats, everywhere baths and sports grounds, cheap rail and tramcar fares and easy access to woods, lakes and rivers. Above all, a noble cleanliness, an immaculacy in every detail that to me was the finest thing in Germany.

I thought with depression of the vast areas of slum and semi-detached squalor in my native London. Years afterwards, in Vienna, a friend of mine who had come from Haifa in Palestine told me how he had heard Jewish emigrants there singing German patriotic songs. In spite of everything they could not conquer their longing for Germany. I know how they felt.

Heinrich Heine, the Jew, after twelve years of exile in Paris wrote:

If in the night I think of Germany
Sleep flies from me,
I cannot close my eyes again,
Hot tears run down my cheeks.

Wolfgang Langhoff, not a Jew but a German whose bestial sufferings in a concentration camp you may read, left Germany only because he could not work there again and then sick at heart, so that he wrote:

'What is happening in Germany now is not truly German, or at least only part of it, the ugliest part. Those who speak to-day of their love for the Fatherland, of German virtues, and German character, and who in their fight use murder, treachery and all the dark methods of barbarism as weapons, are not justified in calling themselves the best sons of my country.'

And you probably know the story about the two Jewish fugitives from Germany who came out of the station just as Starhemberg's anti-Nazi Heimwehr were marching by. They watched a moment and then one said to the other: 'They're not a patch on our Storm Troopers, are they?'

I was leaving Germany, after many years. I took my last walk through the streets of Cologne, went into a bar and had a drink with a smiling Kölnerin, went into a café where the solid and stolid citizens were watching a late mannequin parade of the provincial type, continued my way to the station, contemplating the few people still abroad.

As my train pulled out, and I watched the lights of Cologne receding, I realized with a sudden shock that my feelings on leaving Germany were of envy for this country and the people that lived in it. I sat up and took myself seriously to task. Had I been dishonest with myself in my abhorrence of Hitlerism? I put my feelings under the microscope and with relief detected the flaw.

The envy I felt was for the Germany I had learned to know and love long before Hitler came to power, the Germany that is in many important things a model for the world and preserves these qualities and virtues intact, whether under the paternal eye of the little Grand Dukes or the rule of an Emperor, an Ebert, a Hindenburg, a Hitler.

This Germany, whether she conquer Europe in a new war or be defeated — really defeated, this time — will always be there. Life within her boundaries will be more or less pleasant, according to the way things go.

In present circumstances I was on balance glad to go. All the good things did not compensate for the feeling of being battened-down and gagged. And so, much as I loved her, I did not murmur *Auf Wiedersehen* as after seven years I left Germany behind.

CHAPTER 22

YEARS THAT THE LOCUST

A FEW months after Hitler came to power I had gone to England on leave. Before leaving London for the country I sought out a certain important man and told him what I knew — that Germany was rearming day and night, that a fierce desire to stage a come-back was being instilled into the Germans, that the danger of a new war was looming larger and nearer, and that England should not delay a moment in rearming herself.

It was all true. In Germany the entire energy of the nation is concentrated on militarization. I should doubt whether a nation has ever been so completely and thoroughly reared to think exclusively of arms and warfare. You start when you wake up and stop when you go to sleep, provided you do not dream about these things. Your education in these matters begins in the nursery and finishes with the grave.

The child that learns to read gets as a birthday present a book, which might be called Little Adolf and The Big Bad World, describing how Little Snow White (Germany) was set upon by wicked neighbours (England and France) jealous of her beauty, prowess and possessions, how she nevertheless would have overcome them but that she was stabbed in the back by an Evil Spirit (Marxism), and how one day Prince Charming (Adolf) freed her from her abasement. Adolf ('Ah, the lad was doughty!') had been accustomed in his youth to play war games with his comrades, and the other boys played the Frenchmen and Adolf and his friends the Germans, and Adolf always won!

Then it goes on, through schooldays, when you begin your military training as a member of the Hitler Children and then of the Hitler Youth and learn from teachers who have all had to pass the test of political orthodoxy and racial purity, until the time comes when you serve your year in the Labour Corps, which makes you a complete soldier except that you carry a

184

spade on parade instead of a rifle, and then come your two years conscription, and after that, if you want to get on in life, you probably become an SS or an SA man. If you are anybody at all you do not stop wearing uniform all your life. Even the good Baron von Neurath, after five top-hatted and tail-coated years as Hitler's Foreign Minister, was put into SS uniform when Mussolini went to Germany in September 1937, so that he should not spoil the picture by being out of dressing.

Your morning, midday and evening newspapers depict the world for you as a battlefield, with Germany engaged in an endless struggle with relentless, vindictive foes, whose only aim in life is to keep Germany down. From time to time the foremost foes of yesterday — Poland and Italy — become overnight the bosom friends of to-day, but you do not find anything strange in that, you know that Hitler often moves in a mysterious way his wonders to perform but is always right, and you stop hating Poland and Italy and worrying about your German brothers oppressed in the Polish Corridor and the South Tyrol and hate somebody else. Unspecified but implacable enemies are always about you plotting your downfall.

Your illustrated newspapers feed you, year in year out, with pictures of soldiers and warfare and tanks and aeroplanes and artillery. When you go to the cinema the news reel is full of similar scenes. Turn the knob of your radio and the same story fills your ears. Parade follows eternally upon parade. Heil Hitler Deutschland Über Alles Die Strasse Frei Die Reihen Fest Geschlossen Fridericus Rex Fest Steht Und Treu Die Wacht Am Rhein. 'Germany needs space to live and breathe'; 'Germany needs bigger families — bonuses for young newly-weds, bonuses for babies.'

Like the massed brass bands of a thousand regiments, the patriotic cacophony beats about your ears, numbing all thought. You read periodically that the People's Court has sentenced spies to death. Sometimes they are women. They are beheaded. Spy mania becomes a part of your life. One fine night at a Hitler Youth holiday camp little Hans Schmidt goes out to relieve himself. Little Fritz Meyer hears him and calls 'Halt! Who goes there? The password'. Little Hans Schmidt giggles. Little Fritz Meyer shoots him dead. 'I thought it was a spy.'

Your organization against air attack is a marvel of perfection. The lofts and garrets of every house in the city have been cleared of inflammable material. Every house in the city has its Air Raid Warden, its Fire Fighting and Nursing Squads. Your gas- and bomb-proof shelters are ready. Every man has his allotted post, every woman her allotted basin.

You do not throw away a cigarette packet or an empty milk tin, because these things are needed for pulping or melting down for re-employment by a Germany surrounded by foes who would like to starve her out.

And your army grows bigger and better, your tanks and guns and aircraft more numerous. You are ready.

These were the things I told my influential acquaintance in London on a summer's day in 1933. He listened to me indulgently, warming his behind at an empty grate in the English fashion.

'I think you are wrong,' he said. 'I believe Hitler will prove to be a force for peace in Europe, like Mussolini.'

For the first time I fully realized clearly the spirit of ostrichism that was abroad in England. From that refusal to face the facts all the present trouble has sprung — yesterday, Abyssinia; to-day, Spain and China; to-morrow, who knows what? My warning was only the warning that all Englishmen living in Germany gave early in 1933. In November 1936, when British rearmament had at length got under way, Stanley Baldwin, answering in the House of Commons charges that the Government had 'failed to make any preparations in 1934', said he had not told the country 'Germany is rearming and we must rearm' because 'I cannot think of anything that would have made the loss of the election from my point of view more certain'. By waiting until 1935, he added, 'We won the election with a large majority'.

So now you know why you are not told things. It may have been good strategy, I don't know, the future will show. 'A democracy is always two years behind a dictator', added Mr. Baldwin. I don't see why that should be true; in this case the democracy was not allowed to make up its own mind.

A nation that in wartime was told the full truth about the battle of Jutland, and took it without a tremor, in peacetime is treated by its leaders as an elderly aunt might treat a flapper; 'hush dear, it isn't necessary for you to know these things'.

The question of the near future is whether we shall be able to make good these two — in my opinion three — years in time.

CHAPTER 23

HITLER AND EDEN

Sir John Simon was in a facetious mood and falsetto voice. 'You must not expect', he said, 'to get anything out of me, I am an old hand at dealing with the press.' We of the world's newspapers smiled dutifully. Ha, ha, ha, ha. Now we knew why we had been summoned.

We were in a reception room of the British Embassy in Berlin. Unexpectedly I found myself there again. Sir John had just come from the famous interview with Hitler. Behind him sat Anthony Eden, deep in thought. Sometimes he got up, paced restlessly about, sat down again. We wondered what the German dictator had said. 'Anthony looks to me as if he had had a bad time', said Victor Gordon-Lennox, standing next to me.

A shrewd piece of intuition, and right. Little by little, sometimes months or years later, you get at the truth. Long afterwards I met a diplomat in Paris who had met Sir John when, returning to London, his aeroplane landed at Amsterdam, and in the few minutes before the flight was resumed had heard from him how the floodtide of Hitler's oratory had swept over and dismayed himself and Eden. His demands for Germany and his information about Germany's rearmament had been alarming beyond their fears. England's future Foreign Minister, if he had had any doubts, learned that day what he was up against. He had heard hair-raising things. No wonder that Eden was restless and worried. Even then he did not know the worst. For Hitler had assured them that, although he had torn up the Peace Treaty, he would respect the Locarno Treaty, and a year later he tore that up too.

The great European line-up had begun. For two years the British Government had stilled the country with the milk of reassuring statements about German rearmament. Now the fat was in the fire—and is still in. A few weeks before this day somebody, Heaven reward his confiding heart, had in an English newspaper pleaded compassion for a Germany 'unarmed and defenceless amid a world of foes'. Statements about Germany of the same stratospheric ignorance are frequent.

Now, the spring of 1935, the facts had to be faced. The rearmaments race had begun. Europe began to look like a two-headed, bewildered figure remarking breathlessly, 'That's rearmament, that was!'

On March 4th the British Government issued its White Paper expressing the anxiety aroused everywhere by the dimensions of German rearmament and the spirit in which Germany was being bred, and announcing that it would really have to think about rearming soon if this went on.

On March 5th the French Government announced its decision to increase the term of conscript's service from one to two years to make good during the five lean years the decline in the strength of the French Army arising from the fall in the French birthrate during the war years from 18.8 to 11.3.

On March 10th Göring announced that Germany 'already had an air force', *und was für eine*, and began to build the biggest Air Ministry of all time in the Wilhelmstrasse, 3000 rooms in all.

On March 16th the German Government reintroduced conscription, which meant on paper a standing army of 600,000 men, but actually many more.

And on March 25th Simon and Eden went to Berlin to see if anything could be saved.

Before they went I looked down from the press gallery of the House and listened to Simon's statement about his coming visit.

It was not inspiring or reassuring. A bird's-eye view of Baldwin, looking bored and scratching his nose, was not impressive. Sir John Simon said something uninformative — 'Whatever comes out of this Berlin visit it is not going to be some sudden and surprising result', and so on. Lansbury, Dear Old George, said something about peace and the bestiality of war. Sir Herbert Samuel, suave and Jewish, expressed cultured misgivings about this and that. Maxton alone said something that really showed knowledge and the courage both to face facts and speak the truth, but then he was a one-man party and you knew that the House only listened to him because he was impotent.

So it went on, with murmurings of dissent or approbation, and somebody in a wig said something, and on a back bench sat a lady member with whom I had lunched in Berlin and on another back bench sat a young man with whom I had played golf, and I thought of Germany and contrasted what I had seen there with what I saw here.

Was salvation to come out of this assembly? Twice an enormous majority — which meant that for years to come the Parliament would in effect be simply a lecture platform — was secured by a device not altogether dissimilar from the Reichstag fire. The first device was the Zinovieff letter, an old wives' tale, and probably a fairy-tale at that, which stampeded the electorate. The second device was the undertaking to lead the world against Italy in the Abyssinian episode, an undertaking dropped as soon as the election was over. And the result was that you got a House with an impregnable majority and an impotent and ineffective minority, in which fatuous questions were asked (Mr. Thurtle: 'Is it not against Standing Orders to impute motives?') and important questions were calmly ignored (An Hon. Member: 'Is it true that German howitzers have been mounted on the Moroccan mainland to cover the British forts at Gibraltar?' — No answer was returned) and in which Ministers expounded one policy one day and exactly the opposite policy a few months later but on both occasions professed the highest moral indignation against the critics of their policy.

When I was in England I had always voted Conservative, but as I looked down on the House of Commons, with the picture of Germany in my mind, I could not think for whom I should vote if I ever voted again. I would have voted Winston

Churchill or Maxton or A. P. Herbert, or even Lloyd George, except for his temporary aberration when he went to Germany and swallowed the Hitler-is-sincere bait, hook, line and sinker. They seemed to me the only men with intellects and feelings comparable with those of the great Parliamentary figures of the past. I could not imagine myself voting Conservative or Liberal or Labour. In this Parliament voices were often raised in defence of cruelty and injustice and against humanity and freedom, statements were made about vital matters in foreign affairs that I knew to be untrue, Government speakers often hoodwinked the public, the masses outside were like children groping in the dark for lack of accurate information — for instance, about German rearmament — and yet the Government always claimed to have acted in this way or that from deference to public opinion.

Then the House rose, and I rose too, and we all went off to Berlin.

And Hitler told Simon and Eden that Germany was already as strong in the air, within her frontiers, as the British Royal Air Force throughout the world!

Just four months earlier Baldwin had told England, 'It is not the case that Germany is rapidly approaching equality with us. If Germany continues to execute her air programme without acceleration and if we continue to carry out ours at the present approved rate, we estimate that we shall have in a year's time in Europe a margin — in Europe alone — of nearly 50 per cent.'

My flesh crept when I read that statement. Consider it carefully and you will realize some of the perils England has been spared as yet, you will realize why Anthony Eden looked worried when he left Hitler. And even then neither he nor Simon had realized the awful truth. They thought Hitler meant that the German air force was as strong as the home air force of Britain. But he meant the British air force throughout the world — and as strong as or stronger than, was what he said. This was only realized a fortnight later.

Later Baldwin stated that he had been 'completely misled'. The Air Minister, Lord Londonderry, resigned, but after the lapse of another year he announced that he had not misled Baldwin. So if you want to know who was responsible, close your eyes and take a pin. At all events, you now know what you get for your income tax.

Such was the plight into which ostrichism had led England three years after Hitler. Nobody who lived in Germany in those years can ever understand how that extraordinary under-estimate of German rearmament and the spirit behind it came to be made and authoritatively presented to the British people.

That was not all Hitler told his visitors. He confirmed Germany's intention, revealed by the proclamation of con-scription, to have the biggest land army in Europe. And he said that Germany, with her modest coastline, required one-third of the strength of the British Navy, which has a world-wide Empire to defend.

So the great Berlin interview was over. A fruitless meeting, except that it had opened the eyes of British Ministers. Simon flew to London. Eden and the rest of us took train for Moscow, and the next stage in the European line-up.

CHAPTER 24

MOSCOW EXCURSION

At first I felt more as if I were going to a fun fair than entering
Soviet Russia. Across the railroad was a flimsy metal arch
that carried the words 'Under World Communism Frontiers Will
Disappear' written in electric bulbs. It was like Hampstead
Heath or Coney Island. For the present, this particular
frontier was very much in evidence.

Once across, that battened-down feeling fell upon you that
the discerning traveller experiences in a State based on terror
and the secret police. You have the same feeling in Germany,
Italy or any other dictatorship State, if you live there. It comes
from the knowledge that you must keep your mouth shut,
that you have no real liberty and are liable to arrest and
imprisonment without trial if you do not keep your thoughts
to yourself.

All around stood soldiers and police wearing long-skirted
greatcoats that reached nearly to the ground and gave them
a curious air of immobility exactly matching the inscrutability
of their faces. On either side of the track, stretching as far as
you could see, and beyond that I suppose to the Baltic and the
Black Sea, ran barbed wire entanglements, and whether their
primary use is to prevent people from entering or leaving
Russia I don't know. I went into the station to send off a
telegram and immediately made the acquaintance of Mother
Russia, for there, instead of a slick clerk with some more-than-
human machine for counting out money and delivering change,
sat a flurried woman in a shawl who did all her calculations
with the aid of beads on a wire frame, the sort of thing that
children play with in England.

So this is Russia, thought I, as we sped on our way through a
featureless, cold and darkling landscape. Our coach was a
special one that the Tsar had used, very gilt and plush, and

one of the loudest speakers I have ever heard lavished the Moscow radio programme upon us, and we ate chicken and drank wine and talked with Ralph Barnes and Bill Stoneman and some other American correspondents who had come down to meet us from Moscow, and it was all very warm and cheery, and I only hope lots of other people in Russia that night were as warm and well-fed, but I doubt it.

Moscow Station was all beflagged with Soviet Banners and Union Jacks, affectionately linked together. Neither the blue nor the stripes of the Union Jacks was quite right; they had evidently been made in Moscow for the occasion, and a pretty thought too. On all sides stood Red dignitaries and Red soldiers and Ogpu soldiers, and far across the Station Square, under ample police supervision, stood a fringe of Muscovites, poorly-dressed, agape, nondescript. I wondered what they thought, these Russians in the distance, about England, England who had fought them in the Crimea, who had so often been on bad terms with them in the next fifty years, whose ally they had been and whom they had helped to save in 1914, who had sent troops against them in 1918.

Perhaps they did not think at all, they seemed irrelevant to the scene, these expressionless, drab crowds in the distance, silently watching. They were the first Russians I saw, and they immediately got me into trouble.

The two great British institutions represented by Eden and myself had never sent a representative to Soviet Russia until now. The British Government had never, until Germany proclaimed conscription and brandished her fist publicly, had to consider the awful possibility that England might one day in self-defence have to take Soviet Russia as an ally, so that British statesmen had never gone to Moscow. My paper had never sent a correspondent to Moscow because of the Soviet censorship.

Thus our two visits were both great events, each in its sphere. The Soviet Government had repeatedly complained about Russian news being published from Riga and asked why a correspondent was not sent to Moscow To See For Himself, and the answer was always Censorship. So my arrival was in the nature of a prospecting tour. Before I had been there five minutes the Soviet Government started quarrelling with me about the most trivial thing. For I wrote that Eden had passed through streets lined with 'drab and silent crowds', I think that was the expression, and a little Jewish censor came along, and said these words must come out.

I asked him if he wanted me to write that the streets were filled with top-hatted *bourgeoisie*, but he was adamant. Such is the intellectual level of censors. The censorship department, and that means the whole machine for controlling the home and muzzling the foreign press, was entirely staffed by Jews, and this was a thing that puzzled me more than anything else in Moscow. There seemed not to be a single non-Jewish official in the whole outfit, and they were just the same Jews as you met in New York, Berlin, Vienna and Prague — well-manicured, well-fed, dressed with a touch of the dandy. I was told that the proportion of Jews in the Government was small, but in this one department that I got to know intimately they seemed to have a monopoly, and I asked myself, where were the Russians? The answer seemed to be that they were in the drab, silent crowds which I had seen but which must not be heard of.

I went to Moscow with feelings of strong sympathy for Russia — not for Bolshevism, which I guessed to be a political racket like Fascism and National Socialism, but for Russia and the Russians, a sympathy born of that great service they had rendered my country in the war, for without them, I thought, we should have been lost.

Moreover, I felt that their revolution was good in its origins and motives. The Bolshevist Revolution was born in the agony of Russia, an agony endured in a common cause. It was a revolt against intolerable tyranny, and at first was inspired by brilliant economic theories.

It was the convulsive upheaval of a nation tortured and exploited beyond endurance, a desperate effort to throw off an

195

age-old tyranny and achieve better things. In the event power passed from one gang to another gang, and none can yet say what will ultimately come out of the Bolshevist Revolution for Russia. But the books of Bruce Lockhart and Negley Farson show how Russia was driven into this revolution by her own leaders, how in Moscow and St. Petersburg profiteers and swindlers and trollops and all the other poisonous scum that comes to the top in wartime wallowed in champagne and furs, while Russian soldiers were being driven on to the barbed wire without decent boots.

The desperate longing for peace of a people bled white, plundered and starved by the ghouls that fatten on war produced, in a world at war, the Bolshevist Revolution.

Ambitions for conquest, revenge, and the resubjugation of the masses produced, in a world at peace, the Fascist and National Socialist regimes.

I thought about these things as I wandered about Moscow, and although Mussolini had not then begun to make Abyssinia a land fit for Neros to live in, and the Germans and Italians and Moors had not started to save Spain from the Spaniards, and the Japanese had not yet begun to defend themselves against the Chinese in China, I felt what was coming in the world. The European line-up had begun, and the signs were that the British Empire would have to let itself be saved by Russia again, with loud protests from Hove and Harrogate, or hand over the British Empire in instalments to Germany.

Thus I was particularly interested to meet our potential ally. The Bolshevist Revolution is not yet old enough for the upper classes in England to appreciate the musical merits of the 'Red Flag' and the 'Internationale', as they do those of the 'Marseillaise,' nor has the Crimean coast yet had time to attain the popularity of the French Riviera, which plays an extremely important part in international politics, as I think, for the equanimity with which many people of large possessions regard war seems due to the fact that war has never yet spread to the Riviera.

I strolled about the Red Square and looked at Lenin, who they say is a wax model, if not he keeps remarkably well, and marvelled at the Kremlin from without and afterwards from within, when I was shown its amazingly fine collections. I felt I would have loved Russia, but I could see that you would never be allowed to love Russia. I knew the signs of a police State, from Germany, and saw that here too a foreigner, though entirely surrounded by Russians, might stay for years and never enter the life of the people. They would be too scared to know him. He would remain perpetually alone, his circle confined to other foreigners, his life limited to Legation teas, an unfelt flea on the hide of the colossus Russia.

But nevertheless I loved it as I drove past the Kremlin on a fine March evening, with the towers black against a darkling sky of cold and brilliant blue, and I said how the place impressed me to Victor Gordon-Lennox and Ewer, who were with me, and Norman Ewer, mistaking my meaning, said 'Yes, they have done something', and Gordon-Lennox, with an urbane glance at the golden cupolas of the Kremlin, said imperturbably, 'Well, they didn't do that'.

He is a most urbane man, and his comments on men and affairs, always to the point, always amusing, never laboured, never malicious, brightened these and other hours. He was treated by the Soviet dignitaries with the especial esteem due to a member of a ducal house.

We were a goodly company on this journey. A. J. Cummings, a good friend of democracy, freedom and the rights of man, had on a previous visit to Moscow felt that there was much to be said for the Soviet case in the trial of the British engineers, and had plied a powerful pen in that belief, so that he was received with ostentatious respect. After that incident he became something of an expect about trials, and during a visit of a few days to the Reichstag Fire Trial confided to me his conviction that van der Lubbe had fired that massive stone structure alone.

In my hotel I had a bed of heroic dimensions and the biggest though most ancient bath tub I had ever seen, with the hottest water, and meals of such ostentatious plenty that I began to suspect them.

Also I had a series of telephone calls from unknown but friendly ladies, a thing that mystified me, because my colleagues were not similarly honoured, and my face, although it had healed well from the burns of 1918, is not of the kind that makes the female population abandon all reserve for the sake of knowing me, but afterwards I found that my predecessor in this room had been an enterprising American, the news of whose departure had not yet reached the outer world.

It was an efficient hotel, one of the two or three still maintained for the shelter of foreigners, I believe, and in the hall was a list of the excursions you might make. Bars and beauty spots were lacking, but it contained such items as a visit to the home for reformed prostitutes, a thing I had no time to see.

The one urgent hint I had had from Soviet circles before leaving London for Moscow was not to forget a tail-coat, white tie and medals, and in the proletarian capital I spent a great deal of time in these clothes. My war medals, indeed, I wore for the first time in Moscow. In the evenings there were receptions, and vodka and caviare, and all around just the same crowd of tall and short, fat and thin people, all looking rather absurd in evening clothes and orders, that high society produces anywhere.

And then Litvinoff proposed the health of His Britannic Majesty King George V, and somewhere in darkest England Colonel Blimp wrote to the papers to say that the news had nearly made him sick at breakfast. I wonder why. Because Litvinoff was Russian? Russia was our ally. Because Litvinoff was not Russian, but a Jew? His Britannic Majesty had had Jewish Ministers. Because people were shot out of hand in the Soviet Union ('Hand in hand with Murder')? Innumerable British peers and baronets found their way to Hitler's dinner-table not long after the great clean-up; Hitler's most constant admirers in England are found in these classes. No, I think

Colonel Blimp must have felt sick because to him Litvinoff stood for that gang of cloaked and bearded foreign crooks far away who were conspiring to take away his two-seater.

I broke away for an hour or two from Central Moscow and the beaten tourist tracks and went looking for the real Moscow. I found it. Streets long out of repair, tumbledown houses, ill-clad people with expressionless faces. The price of this stupendous revolution; in material things they were even poorer than before. A market where things were bought and sold that in prosperous bourgeois countries you would have hardly bothered to throw away; dirty chunks of some fatty, grey-white substance that I could not identify, but was apparently held to be edible, half a pair of old boots, a few cheap ties and braces. Shades of the Caledonian market!

And then, looking farther afield, I saw the universal sign of the terrorist State, whether its name be Germany, Russia, or what not. Barbed wire palisades, corner towers with machine guns and sentries. Within, nameless men, lost to the world, imprisoned without trial by the secret police. The concentration camp, the political prisoners. In Germany the concentration camps held tens of thousands, in this country hundreds of thousands.

This was the thing that I detested in every country where I found it, this cruelty, this inhumanity, this injustice, and this was the reason that, whatever else I found to admire in them, and whatever else I found to criticize in other countries, I always came back with relief to those European countries where so much of reason and right at least as yet remained that men cannot be imprisoned or killed without trial — to England, France, Belgium, Holland, Switzerland, Norway, Denmark, Sweden, Czechoslovakia.

Then the Soviet Union gently but firmly took hold of us all again, Eden, Litvinoff, the attendant journalists and the rest, and took us for a drive through Moscow's one and only underground. Moscow Overhead was tumbledown and out-at-elbows; in Moscow Underground we travelled through gleaming marble halls with blazing lights in the charge of spick and span officials. The splendour of it took our breath away, and at last we came to the surface again to breathe. It was the best Underground I had ever seen, and when it was opened, a little after, the Muscovites spent their time and pennies travelling round on it for the fun of the thing. Next to being thrown off a tower in a parachute at the Culture Park, Moscow's Fun Fair, more or less, it was their most popular amusement.

Then we were all wafted away again, and the next thing you knew I was sitting in the Moscow State Opera. Eden, very Balliol and well groomed, was in the ex-Imperial box, the band played 'God save the King', and the house was packed full with men and women, boys and girls, who, judged by Western standards, I put down as members of the proletariat, but no, I was told, the proletariat isn't so lucky, these were the members of the privileged class which the Proletarian State is throwing up, higher officials, engineers and experts.

On the stage far below they danced 'Swan Lake'. It was one of the loveliest things I ever saw, a superb performance that held me spellbound. The ballet has survived the revolution in glory not much diminished.

By day Eden talked about the outlook in Europe, with Germany becoming mightier in arms than ever before, to Litvinoff and then to Stalin. Few people in the western world would recognize Stalin if they saw him in the street, whereas Hitler or Mussolini would immediately be mobbed, and yet he seems to be in many ways the greatest of the world's dictators, he rules over a sixth of the world's surface and 160,000,000 people, and as far as you can judge from outside he seems to be more of a tyrant in his own right than they and less the instrument and prisoner of powerful groups.

Stalin lives immured in the Kremlin and is seldom seen. Very few people were present at his meeting with Eden and a camel might more easily pass through the eye of a needle than a journalist enter the Kremlin or learn what transpires there. But the advantage of my profession is that you make many friends. You meet to-day at Athens a man you knew yesterday in Paris, to-morrow in Peking a friend you once had in Madrid. I had such a friend in Moscow and he told me some of the more interesting things that had transpired.

So that night at the British Embassy, while Lord and Lady Chilston sat talking before the fire in the big drawing-room, Eden with Lord Cranborne and Strang and young Hankey received us in a little room with chintz-covered sofas and chairs, and I said, 'Mr. Eden, I can't ask you to tell me what Stalin said to you, but I have heard from another source something of the conversation. I'll tell you what I have heard. Will you tell me if it is wrong?'

'That's fair enough,' he said. 'Go ahead.'

'I'm told,' I said, 'that Stalin asked you if you thought the danger of war greater or less to-day than in 1914, that you answered less, and that he gave reasons for holding the contrary view, saying that in 1914 there was but one nation whose expansionist ambitions held the danger of war, while to-day there are two, Germany and Japan. Is that wrong?'

'No,' he said, 'it's not wrong.'

'And I am told,' I added, 'that he expressed respect for the German people and their qualities and the conviction that an attempt to hold down or isolate such a nation in the middle of Europe would be vain, but that nevertheless Germany was in a dangerous state of mind to-day and precautionary measures were necessary for the peace of Europe.'

He nodded.

'And,' said I, 'I hear that at one moment in your conversation he glanced at a map which showed the little island in the Atlantic which is England and the sprawling mass over Europe and Asia which is Russia, and in reference to England remarked that it was strange to think that the issue of peace or war lay in the hands of so small a country.'

'Isn't it uncanny,' said Eden, turning to Cranborne, and then to me, 'How do you do it? Were you hiding under the table?'

Thus is the news born. So much of what Stalin said was known next morning to people reading their breakfast newspapers in England. Eden found in Stalin, the most closely cloistered dictator of them all, remote in his Kremlin, a man with an astonishingly intimate knowledge of what is afoot in Europe.

The Moscow talks went on, with indignant cries of 'What about Communist propaganda?' coming from the Diehard strongholds in distant England. I took the opportunity of passing propinquity to ask Litvinoff, at one of those white-tie receptions, 'What about Communist propaganda?' 'Ah,' he said, in his guttural English, 'Communist brobaganda is a vord that beoble use when they vant bad relations with Soviet Russia.'

How right he was. Communist propaganda in twenty years has not made a revolution in any single country. Indeed, the world revolution cannot come through propaganda, but only through a world war. The Soviet Government does not break off relations with States which maltreat their Communists. It enjoyed excellent relations for many years with Italy. Personally, in all my experience in many parts of Europe, I never found any evidence that streams of Russian gold flowed in to foment unrest, but if I had been Prime Minister of any of these countries I should have been only too glad to see the Russian gold coming in, knowing that my police were fully able to look after my Communists.

Thus Eden did not ask Litvinoff 'What about Communist propaganda?' because he knew that Communism is among the least of the anxieties of the police throughout the British Empire, and that, although the Soviet Government could not be expected to make penance at the shrine of Mammon in a white shroud, Communist propaganda financed and controlled from Russia is in these days about as dangerous to England — in peace — as an attack by Martians.

At the end that historic declaration was issued containing, among more formal and less important things, the statement that:

'There is at present no conflict of interest between the British and Soviet Governments on any of the main issues of international policy.'

That is the key to the matter. Russia does not want anything that England has. Germany does. She wants British colonies, to begin with. Russia has too many troubles, too many problems, too many people, too much territory. She can only lose by war. Germany claims that she has too little territory for too many people; her avowed aim is territorial expansion.

When Eden went to Moscow he found the age-old suspicion, now more deeply rooted even than under the Czars, that England is behind every threat to Russia's frontiers. The Soviet rulers had not failed to notice that many prominent people in England and some newspapers were in sympathy with the idea that Germany should have 'a free hand in the East' if she would only keep the peace of the West.

Now this Russo-German war, as the map shows, is an extremely difficult thing to bring about. I don't see how the two can get at each other. They are like Kipling's East and West — never the twain shall meet. But still, leading Nazis have expounded this idea of carving slices off Russia, and the Soviet was naturally suspicious about it, and convinced that the British Cabinet itself was not of one mind in this matter.

Eden's visit, and the statement about 'no conflict of interests' somewhat reassured them. England, under the shock of German conscription and Hitler's bombshell about the German air force, was at that time leaning to the belief — imprinted on the butter pats at a lunch given by Litvinoff to his guests — that 'peace is indivisible', that collective European resistance to aggression anywhere must be organized.

But now, after Abyssinia and Spain, who knows? By 1937 he would have been a clever man who knew just what was British policy. It often looked like the policy of the jelly-fish, which is to be trodden on and sting faintly in expiring, or like that of the Gadarene swine, which is to hope that you will stop running.

Like an old gentleman drowsing with a handkerchief over his face on an English lawn in June and made irritable by the noise of distant thunder across the channel, British Toryism has begun to think about foreign policy since Germany, rearmed, re-entered the lists, and, making a simple calculation, has decided that England ought to make friends with Germany ('The Great Bulwark against Bolshevism') and let her have her 'free hand in the East'. Let Nazi dog eat Bolshie dog. Then we can arrange the handkerchief over our face again and resume our nap. Hitlerism will thus save us from Bolshevism and Bolshevism from Hitlerism.

I don't think it will work out like that.

But the next time Hitler received a British Minister, two and a half years after Simon and Eden's visit, Lord Halifax had no longer been charged to invite Germany into an all-European collective peace scheme, but only to 'explain to Herr Hitler the desire of the British Government for the swift completion of a new Western Pact, as a guarantee of the security and *status quo* in that part of Europe'.

That sounds like 'Leave us alone and we shan't watch you too closely elsewhere'.

True, the periodical clean-ups in Soviet Russia do make it a little difficult for a British Government to make up its mind about Russia.

But the basic fact remains — that Germany wants something that England has and Russia does not.

At Moscow station the drab and silent crowds had gathered again. The Union Jacks and Soviet banners remained affectionately linked. We all shook hands and boarded the train. Litvinoff took leave of Eden with the words, 'I vish you all success, for your success vill be our success now'.

CHAPTER 2 5

FEATS OF MEMORY

F. W. MEMORY versus the Soviet Union; an impressive sight. Memory is as big a man as the Soviet is an empire, but no fat, all muscle, a journalist of rare robustness. He is the man who for weeks on end trailed the monster of Loch Ness, a beast so elusive that his colleagues invented the slanderous theory that the Monster of Loch Ness was Memory himself.

He will not share a sleeping-carriage with anyone else. I don't like it myself but did not feel equal to undertaking something that Napoleon had failed to do, but Memory searched the hotel until he found someone who was supposed to allot sleeping berths and insisted on a compartment to himself between Moscow and Warsaw, and this man, wise in his generation, said smoothly, 'Yes, yes, that will be all right', and cashed in, and when we got to the station there we all were packed into the one sleeping-car two-by-two, like the animals in the ark, with nobody on the train who spoke English or cared a hoot about Memory's lien on a compartment to himself.

Then an angry Memory appeared at the door of the sleeping-car, oblivious of the Red Army and the Ogpu and the Soviet Government and all the paraphernalia of leavetaking that was going on around, and called on God and man to witness that he had paid for a sleeping compartment to himself and meant to have it. Russian train officials looked vaguely in his direction and said Nitchevo or whatever Russians say and then looked away, but gradually the awful majesty of his mien attracted them and they began to look at him with interest, as if he were some strange animal, and the upshot was that, with Memory speaking only English and nobody else understanding anything but Russian, Memory was left in triumphant occupation of his compartment and somebody else's luggage was cleared out and somebody had to sleep on the roof as far as Warsaw, I suppose. A famous victory.

Memory could lift a fifteen-stone man with either arm, and later, on Warsaw station, we made him do it, and then we experimented to see how many men were needed to lift Memory, and I think it was fifteen.

CHAPTER 26

NEWSPAPER MEN

TRAVELLING swiftly through a Russian night, behind steamy panes, we drank vodka and talked of newspapers and newspaper men, of journeys in the Near and Far East, of politics and wars. We compared our passports, chock-full of visas in Latin, Cyrillic, Arabic, Japanese, and Chinese characters. Between us, we had been all over the world.

The House of Commons is called the best club in London. The confraternity of journalism is the best club in the world. It is the most comradely of crafts. You have friends wherever you go. There are no barriers of race or creed. You fly on some mission, and when you land you find men you know. You speak several languages, the hopes and fears of Croats and Ruthenians and Walloons and Basques become as familiar to you as those of your own countrymen.

You speak with kings and dictators and statesmen in the full pride of power, and you see them sitting miserably in exile in a dingy coffee-house in Prague. You see a man, the almost forgotten ex-ruler of a Balkan country, dining quietly in a London hotel, and then you see him as King George of Greece in his palace in Athens. You see vast crowds thronging to acclaim King Edward VIII of England as he drives to the Abbey, you eat your schnitzel in a half-empty Vienna restaurant while the Duke of Windsor eats his at a neighbouring table.

At the Stresa Conference I met an American journalist who a dozen years before had reported another Italian conference, at Genoa, with an Italian colleague, called Mussolini. I don't think he would have changed places. I know I wouldn't.

You travel about Europe by car and train and ship and aeroplane and gradually the chaotic pieces of the jigsaw puzzle form themselves into a complete picture before your eyes. And gradually you realize how little you know.

If ever I have to leave journalism I shall say with real regret *Adieu la très gente compagnie*. Good friends, good colleagues, great journalists. The best journalists of them all served their best years in Germany after the war. No other country so stimulates a man to write as did Germany between the Armistice and Hitler. There was Edgar Mowrer, who had to leave under open threats against his life, after he had written *Germany Puts the Clock Back*. The Americans, for some reason, write better books than the Britishers, and this book of Mowrer's, published just at the moment of Hitler's advent, was perfectly timed.

The Americans have a great gift for timing. John Gunther's *Inside Europe*, published just when the great British public was thinking that it would really have to get out the atlas and see where Czechoslovakia is — or is it Yugoslavia? — was a miracle of timing. After its appearance the international expresses and the main streets of Europe's capitals became filled with English families firmly grasping their *Inside Europe*, to show that they had primed themselves with Inside Information, and that Europe had better not try any nonsense with them. Peace hath her horrors no less renowned than war. After it was published, an angry German journalist of my acquaintance, who held that Gunther's book was just another Marxist view, went about saying that he intended to write a book called *Inside Gunther*.

Knickerbocker's *Germany, Fascist or Communist?* was another well-timed book. It was always a joy to see that Texan's red head, now in the restaurant of the Gare du Nord at Paris, now in the lobby of the League of Nations, and the next day you heard of him in Abyssinia, and after that in Spain, and then again in China. Their books, like Vernon Bartlett's writings and talks, are monuments to their knowledge and judgment and to the service that good journalists render their countrymen.

Norman Ebbutt's dispatches were paid the greatest of all compliments — they were read by his own colleagues all over the world. A man with a profound admiration for Germany, who in pre-Hitler days was often held up by the German Press as a model foreign correspondent, he was expelled from Germany amid torrents of abuse and anonymous threats on his life after the British Government had requested three Germans to leave England on account of their political activities.

Sefton Delmer, Karl Robson, and Gilbert Panter — the last two also expelled, Panter after a spell in prison without the preferment of any charge — were others of that company, and Pembroke Stephens, also expelled and later killed at Shanghai.

Those great days of journalism have faded. The American Press continues to give a freely-drawn and accurate picture of European events. British correspondents, less staunchly supported by their Government than their American and French colleagues, have become fair game for anybody who wants to vent a little bad temper.

'The German Ambassador was informed that a deplorable impression would be created by Mr. Ebbutt's expulsion' — this means in modern diplomatic parlance, 'Go ahead if you must, it will all be forgotten next week'. Not even the domiciliary rights guaranteed to British citizens under the treaties with foreign powers are upheld for British journalists. They can be kicked out at will, without any specific charge, just as a propagandist stunt.

Doing the job for which they are sent out, they are coming to be treated rather like spies in wartime — people you must have but for whom you take no responsibility and to whom you give no succour. Thus the news about dictator countries is coming to be supplied to British newspaper readers less and less by specialists and more and more by titled or other dilettanti who go out for a few days, without knowledge of language or conditions, to see for themselves, and are feasted and Cook's-toured.

Viscountess Snowden, the widow of that Socialist leader who was a good Socialist as Socialists go, and as Socialists go went to the House of Lords, made the following discoveries about Germany in 'five days' intensive search for the truth at the centre of affairs in Germany':

'There is no antagonism to England in this country.'

'On the contrary, there is an earnest desire on the part of Herr Hitler and his people for friendship with England and if it should rest with him and them there would be no war.'

'But there is a sad and growing conviction that nothing the German spokesmen can say or do will advance by one iota those fraternal relationships which . . . are so ardently desired if they can be honourably achieved.'

'The secret of Herr Hitler's power lies in his selflessness and his sincerity.'

'He is a simple man of great personal integrity.'

'I would not hesitate to accept his word when promised.'

'Labour has achieved a new dignity.'

These things are all there, waiting to be seen, as plain as a pikestaff, by anyone who takes the trouble to go to Germany for five days and find out 'the facts about this new regime'.

But on this night in the Moscow-Warsaw train these things were far away. The vodka was invigorating, the dining-car warm, we were good company; somewhere in another part of the train Eden and his staff sat busily working out dispatches for H.M.G.; Warsaw, Prague and London lay ahead of us, and after that, who knew, but at all events something interesting.

CHAPTER 27

EDEN

'Do you know who your pilot is?' said Memory to me. 'He's the man from whose machine the two sisters jumped the other day and the man who lost the gold flying over France.'

'Help!' said I. *'Alle gute Dinge sind drei.* All things go in threes. Something is going to happen to us.'[1]

We were on Prague Aerodrome and for the first time since the Armistice I was going to fly. For seventeen years I had taken pains to avoid the air, but I badly wanted to be in on the last stage of that famous trip round Europe. Of all the Foreign Officials and journalists that had left London ten days before all that were left, in the aeroplane bound for London, were Eden and young Hankey, his secretary, and Gordon-Lennox and myself.

With an eye for prospective misadventure that seventeen years on the ground had not dimmed I studied the lay-out of the aerodrome, the direction of the wind, and the weather, and then I looked at the pilot to whom such curious things happened and hoped that there was no danger of falling out of his machine.

Prague lay behind us, with President, then Foreign Minister, Benes waving good-bye on the aerodrome. Eden had seen him and heard what the people who lay within twenty minutes' reach of Germany's mighty new air force were feeling nowadays.

Behind Prague lay Warsaw, where Eden had seen a very different kind of man, the head of another country liberated by the war, Poland. The old dictator Marshal Pilsudski, the man who

---

[1] A little before this time two American sisters, who were said to have been in love with a British flying officer, committed suicide by jumping, clasped in each other's arms, from a British air-liner somewhere in Italy; and the same pilot who suffered this bizarre adventure was flying over France one day when his cargo of gold fell through the floor of the machine and was subsequently found in a peasant's field.

had been imprisoned both by the Germans and Russians in the days of Poland's struggle for freedom, was a dying man when Eden visited him. All that could be learned in Warsaw was that Poland, since she had made a favourable standstill agreement about her own frontiers with Germany, was pretty well satisfied and did not intend to join any line-up against Germany, whereas Czechoslovakia, with German aerodromes springing up like mushrooms on her frontiers, was looking for a powerful friend as quickly as possible and, with France, soon found one — Russia.

I studied the man who, as I then felt sure, would before long be England's Foreign Minister. I had lunched with him at the Carlton before we left London, watched him as we toured Europe. Everybody knew that Sir John Simon would not remain Foreign Minister. He may not have been responsible, but he had been Foreign Minister during the period when England, having escaped by the skin of her teeth from the greatest war in history fifteen years before, leaving a million dead, had allowed the defeated enemy to rearm and outarm her overnight. The first fruits of that period of quivering inertia have been Abyssinia and the seizure of the Rhineland and the tearing-up of treaties and the German and Italian invasions of Spain, and the last fruits — well, we shall see.

I knew that Eden must be Foreign Minister before long, his record was good and his school tie right, and that he might even be Foreign Minister when the next war came.

Now, as we left Prague behind and made towards the German frontier, behind which the countryside was buzzing with military preparations, we flew over land that bade fair to become the next cockpit of Europe. He pored intently over the English newspapers, fresh out from London, to see what England was saying about that cordial encounter in Moscow. This was the chink in the armour of any British Foreign Minister. What would the England of Blimp say to the prospect of having one day to combine in arms with the country that had tampered with the laws of private property — for that was what 'no conflict of interests on any major international issue' meant. What was the Press saying, what would the Cabinet say, what would the House say, the Party, the Constituencies?

On this magic-carpet tour of Europe I saw a man who worked like a bee, who carefully spared his strength to be fit for his job. He had been a Brigade Major, he knew something of Europe and European languages, which was a gain. He had seen Hitler and Stalin, knew what to expect from Germany and Russia. I felt that he had a grasp of realities, but I wondered whether he would be able to surmount a task calculated to daunt any but a statesman of granite.

He succeeded to a fiasco in Abyssinia which has left all Europe on the rack of apprehension, and that was not his fault, and the Spanish tragedy grew out of the Abyssinian one, and both were the offspring of that period of ostrichism in British policy between the advent of Hitler and the belated beginnings of British rearmament.

That day in the aeroplane, with Berlin and Moscow behind him, and the pitfalls of Abyssinia and Spain still hidden in the future, it must have seemed to him that England and France would have to get Russia on their side quickly if they were to survive against Germany rearmed. Because the obvious alternative at that time — a German-Russian alliance — was too awful to contemplate. Since then Germany has so committed herself to her triangular anti-Russian front with Japan and Italy that that danger has receded — but not vanished quite.

We headed north, bound for London and the House of Commons and explanations and debates that would change nothing. At Leipzig the British Consul and his pretty wife paid their respects to England's Lord Privy Seal, and then we were off again, bound for Cologne, and in a few minutes I was kicking myself hard for ever having been foolish enough to break that Armistice pledge and take the air again.

It was a foul trip, the worst I ever made, for in the war you

213

flew by sight, and when the weather became so bad that you couldn't see the ground you came down, quickly. But now we flew into thick cloud, and then suddenly snow was beating about us, and the machine was thrown here and there and let down with a bump into a deep void and then again rocketed upwards and given a smack on one wing and a smack on the other and a bang on the solar plexus and a kidney punch that sent the tail spinning round.

No channel crossing had ever turned my stomach, nor did this flight, though it was worse than the worst channel crossing I had ever made, but that was not what worried me. I knew that we were flying over wooded and mountainous country, with no hope of a forced landing, and although I knew that pilots nowadays had wireless and instruments that told them exactly where they were and exactly how to get to Cologne without seeing the ground once, still I did not believe this and when Gordon-Lennox passed me a slip of paper, which he still has, with the words 'Do you think we can get down?' I wrote 'Yes' without any conviction, and I was not far wrong, for the very next day, in precisely the same weather and over this selfsame stretch of country, a Dutch air liner, for all its instruments and directional wireless, banged into a hill and was destroyed with seven occupants.

But just as I was thinking '*Alle gute Dinge sind drei*' again, the pilot throttled back his engines and dropped through the clouds and there was Cologne beneath us, clairvoyance rather than piloting it seemed to me, and inwardly I blessed him.

The flight was abandoned. Eden was badly knocked up and the doctors ordered him to retire from world politics for some weeks. This flight, coming after harassing weeks of rushing dispatches to H.M.G. in trains and bedrooms, and generally trying to catch up with a European avalanche which was already in movement for lack of forethoughtful propping-up, had temporarily finished him.

So I found myself once more for a night in Cologne and said good-bye all over again. Since I first took leave I had been farther and seen more than I expected, but the Rhine, greeting me with a surprised look, by its lack of interest in my experiences reduced my ideas to proper proportions. 'Gad about and gad about, little man', it said, 'but I go on for ever. Your gaddings about and your opinions and your politicians are all less important than you imagine.'

Next morning I looked down at the cross-Channel steamer ploughing through grey, white-flecked waves. The white cliffs and green fields of England came in sight. From the air I loved them. The amorphous, meaningless mass of London, Croydon, a maze-like drive through interminable suburbs, a taxi, White's. A great shining mahogany table laden with joints and tongues and pies and salads and cheeses. A cold collation on the heroic scale. Champagne and ale in a silver tankard.

Remote seemed Moscow with its drab and silent crowds, Berlin with its eternal parades, Warsaw with its caftaned Jews, Prague with the sun shining on the Moldau. There people lived next door to the realities. Here people lived for whom Hitler and Stalin and Germany and Russia were just irritating names that carried a threat that one day you might be disturbed in the enjoyment of your quiet daily stroll along Piccadilly and down St. James's Street to your club.

Champagne and ale in a silver tankard. I shall never forget that meal.

CHAPTER 28

ENGLISH APRIL

I HAD a few days in England and it was April and cold and oh to be anywhere but in England now that April was here, for what can you do with a few days in England in April? Telephone all the people who have lunched with you in Berlin and Vienna and said 'Do let me know when you come to England'? That meant prolonged cross-examinations about The Situation and I was tired of The Situation, as a doctor who does nothing but remove appendixes must become tired of appendixes; I once met one, from Australia, who said he had removed 65,000 Australian appendixes and I said, 'Well, you have certainly left your mark on Australia', and for some reason he took umbrage. You lay The Situation on your lunch or dinner table and take out its innards and agree that it is a foul situation and ought to be operated on at once, and then you put back the innards and go on eating and The Situation is removed and gets worse. The Situation is interminably dissected by Well Informed Circles and always gets worse. I hate The Situation and I wish Low would draw a Well Informed Circle.

So, as it was Easter Monday and this seemed the natural thing to do, I went to Brighton. From the train I watched lots of other people going to Brighton, by car, all travelling at the regulation thirty miles an hour, each car nosing the car before it, and Teas proclaimed everywhere and petrol stations innumerable, and I wondered what the joy of motoring was.

On the seat opposite me a gaunt woman with rabbity teeth and her legs tied round each other like a schoolgirl's plait discussed the Royal Family in enraptured tones with a friend. All the young women in the train seemed plain and all the young men had unkempt hair and wore the national uniform, corkscrew grey flannel trousers and a raincoat with creased collar upturned. At Brighton we all oozed down streets bright only

216

with the brilliant pink of Brighton Rock, in all sizes from that of a cigarette to a telescope, to the grey thing called the sea and the other grey thing called The Front. I had known another thing called The Front. I wondered, as I surveyed this one, which was worse.

The Front around the West Pier was a solid mass of Jews down from London. Their cars, put end on end, would have reached probably to the moon. On the verandas of the big and flashy hotels they sat, the older ones, and the younger ones, in snappy clothes, strolled to and fro along the pavement and exchanged cracks with a film flavour. 'Hullo, big boy', they called, and 'Sez you' they answered. England. Not even in Vienna have I seen so many Jews together. In few foreign towns have I felt so completely alien.

In search of England, I went to the Palace Pier, and found it. Palace is Palace and West is West and never the twain shall meet. It is a strange thing, this invisible but real dividing line between the Palace and West Piers, which lie only a few hundred yards apart. It is the legacy of the old rivalry between genteel Hove and plebeian Brighton, between the residential town of prosperous retired people and the trippers' town of winkles and 'Who's for a sail?'. The Jews that day had banished the Hovians from the West Pier; England remained in possession of the Palace Pier.

Here came scores of sleek, fat-bellied charabancs, bringing the Londoners for a hard-earned day at the sea, for a few hours of riotous amusement among the slot-machines. We plunged into the gloom of the Aquarium; how many shillings have I spent in pursuit of that mythical octopus, so largely advertised but never seen. We surged along the pier and watched the fishermen at the end; how many hours have I spent in watching them, and never seen anything larger than a sprat caught. We spent pounds with the slot-machines. We bought sweets.

And the litter! This litter! When I have finished writing *Insanity Fair*, about Europe, I shall write *The Picnic Papers*, about England. Bus tickets and paper bags and newspapers

217

blew about, and winkle shells and orange peel filled the gutters. In desperation I fled to the little railway and took train for the cliffs. I would get away from this unbelievable ugliness. I would get up on the Downs.

So I hastened eastward, but Brighton had grown even bigger since I had seen it last, and I could not get away from it. The space between Brighton and Rottingdean had always been pretty well filled by the derelict factory and the enormous school for the daughters of the great, but I seemed to remember glimpses of green turf, but now Brighton and Rottingdean were reaching out to link arms with each other and when I came to Rottingdean, which I had once found picturesque, it was entirely surrounded by charabancs and tea-rooms and no spot where a man could find anything to cheer him, and I plunged desperately through it and up the hill beyond, thinking here I shall find England, England of the clean white cliffs and green turf and the wind blowing in from the sea and the seagulls floating on it.

But what I found was called, so help me God, Peacehaven. Here, in one of the loveliest spots in England, on green-carpeted chalk cliffs, they had dumped down a nightmare town consisting largely of wretched bungalows, miserable villas, tin cinemas, with broken and gaping fences, coarse and weedy gardens, a thing that took all beauty out of the grey sky and gusty wind and combined with them to make a symphony of ugliness and misery.

I thought of the well-tended German coasts, by nature far less beautiful than this, of Swinemünde and Travemünde, of the French coasts around St. Malo and Dinard, of the Adriatic and Italian coasts. This would have been allowed nowhere that I had been. If this was freedom and democracy, I thought, then give me an efficient tyranny. It was incredible. If this was the result of honorary mayors and freedom for the speculative jerrybuilder, then give me highly paid municipal specialists and state-control of town-planning. If this was the fruit of centuries of prosperity and freedom from foreign invasion, of victory in a world war, this and a few stately homes in ring-fenced parks, then give me defeat and a new start.

As I looked at Peacehaven I would have liked to abolish everything in England, save A. P. Herbert and Low and Beachcomber, and begin again.

J. B. Priestley, in his *English Journey*, tried to open English eyes to these things. It is a good book, received by the majority with that irritation which England reserves for anybody who writes about anything other than love affairs among titled people, but in reading it I felt that even he had quailed before the task he set himself, had felt that the things he saw in the slums and the manufacturing towns and in the Black Country and the Midlands could not really be so bad as they seemed to him. But they were and are. In England you have conditions like these, and yet you don't use your Empire. It stretches all over the world and you don't want anybody else to have it, yet you leave it fallow and unexploited, so that Australia, a continent, has fewer people than London.

I fled from Peacehaven as if the devil had been behind me. Somewhere, I thought, there must be an end to this; on, Stanley, on. I came to Newhaven, a dreary little port, and found my only consolation that day in the man who ferried me across the harbour. He earned but a few shillings a day and had lived all his life in Newhaven, save for a few sea voyages, but he had a clear mind and a sense of right and from his cockleshell boat he saw the world as it was, and he was bitter about England and Hitler. He was an Englishman.

I trailed on and came to some terrible seaside place, for all I know it may have been called Seaford, I don't believe it had any real existence, by this time I was probably seeing things, and there, rather than go on and experience Eastbourne, which I did not know but now feared, I turned tail and fled to London.

CHAPTER 29

THREE JUST MEN

An emerald islet, with a marble palace and cypresses, set in an aquamarine lake among snow-capped mountains. Warm spring sunshine laden with the scent of azaleas, hyacinths, oranges and magnolias.

The town is Stresa, the lake Maggiore, the islet Isola Bella, the palace that of a noble Italian family, the Borromeos. Napoleon slept in it in 1797, and it is filled with paintings by Tempesta, who was given asylum there by Count Vitaliano Borromeo when he fled from Genoa, falsely charged with murdering his wife.

The town gay with the flags of Great Britain and Italy, the foes of six months later, lovingly entwined, and of France. 'God Save the King' played by an Italian Grenadiers band as Ramsay MacDonald arrives at the station. Mussolini greets him, in English. They shake hands warmly. Two Socialists.

'The Marseillaise'. The monumental Flandin, the saturnine Laval. It is a great occasion, the first conference of the three Western Powers, the European victors in the Great War, presided over by Mussolini. Germany, the bad boy of Europe, is absent. Germany has been tearing up the peace treaty, and we are gathered to discuss what we shall do.

As our train pulls in at the station Ramsay MacDonald steps down into a large central space cordoned off by the guard of honour, and at either end by a hedge of sinister looking men in soft hats and raincoats with a hand in either pocket and, as I strongly suspect, a revolver in either hand.

They face us, the camp-followers of the conference, with their pocketed hands suggestively pointing towards us until the great men have been driven away. Outside Carabinieri lurk among the bushes and flowerbeds of every garden. Hundreds of plain men in plain clothes hang around the streets and hotels.

Detachments of Fascisti march to and fro. At night searchlights scour the sky and lake front. As you go about the town your face is so often scrutinized that your ears burn; when you get near the conference hotels you have to show your documents continually.

Europe's rulers are taking no chances. Revolvers have been going off all over Europe of late, and not always in the right direction. Eleven months before came the great bump-off in Germany. Ten months before Dollfuss was murdered. Seven months before King Alexander of Yugoslavia and Barthou of France were assassinated at Marseilles. Nowadays we take rigorous precautions.

The islet in the lake is as safe as anything could be. Stresa has more guardians than inhabitants, the islet itself is full of police, and nobody is allowed on the lake but the representatives of Italy, England and France, on their brief dash across by fast motor-boat.

Isola Bella! 'Splendid Isolation!' says a wit.

Ramsay MacDonald and Simon, black-hatted and tail-coated, walk down the little causeway to the motor-boat in the forenoon and return in the evening. Flandin and Laval too. Nobody sees Mussolini. He remains in seclusion on the tiny islet a few hundred yards from the water's edge, until he is rushed ashore one night for a banquet. The adoring Stresans are herded off at a distance. Hall and banqueting chamber of the hotel are ablaze with Fascist uniforms. The roof, the corridors, the lavatories and the basement are packed with the plain men, still in their plain clothes. The searchlights from the lake still rake the hotel, disturbing flies and sparrows in their slumbers.

Reports filter across from the emerald islet to the waiting newspaper men. Simon receives us and tells us of progress made. One of my useful friends, a French newspaper man, receives me and tells me much more. Mussolini and Suvich, Ramsay MacDonald and Simon, Flandin and Laval, are all agreed that this must be stopped, that treaties must not be torn up, that Germany must be arraigned before the League and there condemned as a treaty-breaker, that measures against future infractions must be preconcerted. Peace must be preserved. Pledges must be kept. What is left to us, Italy, England and France, the leaders of the League, to whom nations great and small are looking for a lead at this moment, if we do not stand shoulder to shoulder for peace, for the sanctity of treaties?

Among the British delegation is an expert on Abyssinia — Thompson. Abyssinia, Abyssinia? Myself regards him curiously. What is he doing at Stresa? Abyssinia, that is the country that Italy sponsored for membership of the League, against British opposition. Italy has some dispute with Abyssinia, about a place called Wal-Wal. A sandy desert region, with scattered wells used by nomadic tribesmen. The name always reminds me of that silly story. 'Do you know the story of the two holes?' 'No.' 'Well, well.' Wal-Wal. What can Thompson be doing here? Mussolini is taking his stand with the others for the sanctity of treaties, for united action against an aggressor. The dispute with Abyssinia cannot be serious. Why Thompson?

This six months before the Italian invasion, twelve months before the Italian annexation of Abyssinia.

Then comes the final moment, on April 14th, 1935. Mussolini in riding breeches and riding boots, without a hair on his head, stocky and brisk and unaffected; Ramsay MacDonald, bonhomous and radiating geniality; Flandin smiling, Laval a mask, Simon attorney-like. All good fellowship and gratification. Most gratifying. All difficulties overcome. We shall support the French request to the League to condemn the action of Germany in violating a treaty. We shall concert measures against new infractions. We are completely agreed to oppose any one-sided repudiation of treaties which may endanger the peace of Europe.

'Of Europe'! And Abyssinia? Perish the thought, here in sunny Stresa.

And we, England and Italy in particular, who have

guaranteed the Treaty of Locarno, and thereby the mutual frontiers of France, Germany and Belgium, we 'formally re-affirm all our obligations under the Treaty and declare our intention, should need arise, faithfully to fulfil them'.

Hullo, think we of the world's press, decorous and expectant, that is important. The Locarno Treaty contains the obligation 'to take immediate action' if Germany sends troops into the demilitarized Rhineland zone, and France fears that Germany intends next to do that very thing, even though Hitler has told Eden that he will not tear up the Locarno Treaty. The French have carried their point, then. England and Italy have categorically reaffirmed their undertaking to come to her aid if Germany does that and if she tries to throw the Germans out.

The sun goes down in a golden curtsy and the Stresa Conference ends with a sigh of thankful reassurance from Europe. The Stresa front has been formed, the common front of the peace-loving powers, with Russia in the offing, against the potential peacebreakers. The knights of the pledged word, Italy, England and France.

I tap out my dispatch in a tearing hurry, and wait frantically for a telephone call — I have to catch the evening train for Geneva. At last it comes, the news is telephoned, I rush up-stairs and pack, tear off to the station, exhausted after a hard and foodless day.

Just as I get there the beflagged official cars push in front of me. Ramsay MacDonald is being seen off by Mussolini. 'Giovanezza, Giovanezza, primavera di Bellezza God Save our Gracious King Long Live our Noble King'. They're at it again.

Impossible to get into the station, the plain men with their ominously pocketed hands are everywhere. At last I find a back way in, but the ticket clerk is too rapt in contemplation of the scene, he won't be bothered selling tickets. The whistle sounds, the Lord of Rome salutes the Laird of Lossiemouth. I'm not going to miss that train for all the tomfool dictator-ships in the world, ticket or no ticket. Hung with bags like a Christmas Tree I hurtle across the rails, holding off, like a

Rugby player, officials whose conception of Fascist efficiency is to make as much unnecessary trouble as they can, and fall into the rear carriage just as the train moves off.

A foodless day, and a longish train journey ahead. We make for the dining-car. No meals until the Swiss frontier has been passed. The Swiss frontier arrives and falls behind us. We make hotfoot for the dining-car again. It is empty but for Ramsay MacDonald and three of his entourage. The waiter hastens towards us with protesting hands. No meals until Monsieur Ramsay MacDonald has finished eating. I am in the company of three of America's leading newspaper correspondents and blush inwardly as I see their expressive faces — H. R. Knickerbocker, that ubiquitous Texan; Frederick Birchall, that extraordinary veteran who has the hands of a girl of fifteen, the gait of a lad of twenty, the intelligence of youth and the experience of age, who still has his British passport, who after a lifetime spent managing the business affairs of the *New York Times* has decided at the age of something over sixty to return to writing and hops about Europe with the agility of a chamois; Walter Duranty, hobbling on his stick, another Englishman, who has spent a decade in Moscow, whose conversation is as clear and sparkling as an Alpine stream.

I beckon to Neville Butler, Ramsay MacDonald's secretary, and ask whether four good men and true, who have not eaten all day, may not be allowed to get a meal in a public dining-car. He yields. We take our seats. A hungry Swiss colleague who has seen us enter follows and lights his pipe while waiting for his meal.

An embarrassed Neville Butler appears at my elbow. The Swiss gentleman is smoking, and if he smokes everybody else will smoke. Would we be good enough to leave? I go, for the sake of peace. My three American companions, saying the things you would expect Americans, born or adopted, to say in such circumstances, go too, for the sake of collegiality. The Swiss journalist, ordered out of a smoking car in his own country, goes too, fuming and smoking. England's Labour Prime Minister, the man of the people, is left to eat alone.

We gather in the corridor outside. Other passengers come and join the queue. Time passes. The corridor fills and the corridor of the next compartment too, with men and women of many nationalities. They get restless. They stamp their feet. They shout in chorus 'à manger, à manger'. The door of the dining-car remains closed. Time passes. The crowd gets angry. The train is chock-a-block with would-be diners. There is an irresistible surge towards the dining-car, impelled by the weight of hungry people behind. The door bursts open. Ramsay MacDonald is just finishing. He rises and disappears through the opposite door, narrowly escaping the floodtide that sweeps in behind him. There is a fight for seats.

We eat. Geneva. The Stresa Front of the Three Just Men, England, France and Italy, has been formed. The curtain rises on the Special Session of the League of Nations, summoned at the request of France, supported by England and Italy, to condemn the treaty-breaking methods of Germany and concert measures to ensure the peace of Europe against future threats.

CHAPTER 30

GENEVAN SHADOW SHOW

In my necessitous days just after the war in London I had once, at the cost of a few hard-earned shillings, bought a curious box and a pair of earphones, and was wont, irritably telling other people in the room to keep quiet, to probe a small and unresponsive piece of crystal with an exasperatingly wobbly filament, and sometimes, between the scratches and shrieks, while I marvelled at this new product of the mechanical age, I heard diminutive voices singing or speaking, and occasionally among them one that I came to recognize as that of Uncle Arthur, telling bedtime stories or the like.

I never then expected to meet him in the flesh, but now I was with him, in Geneva, and he was Arthur Burrows, an official of the League and *nebenbei* a newspaper correspondent, and I spent pleasant hours of relaxation with a delightful English family in a restful English home in a lovely country. In the daytime I went out with his son Reginald and we tramped down the road and past the French customs house, where the gendarmes neither overwhelmed us with undue obsequiousness nor irritated us with bureaucratic officiousness, but just sat on their benches and indifferently watched us pass without even asking to see our passports, and the next moment I was in France, for the first time for many years, and had that feeling of inward warmth for that country which not the most surly of French taxi-drivers or the most rapacious of French hotel-keepers can kill.

France. The one country where, in spite of incomprehensible occasional cruelties like Devil's Island, the ideal of humanity survives. Once, in Montreux, I played tennis with a Frenchman and his wife, a rich man who owned a large factory, and he spoke pessimistically to me of the disordered conditions in France, of the extent of Communism, and said that France needed some sort of Fascism and ought to stand with Germany, the sort of statement you hear everywhere from men of large possessions, and his wife agreed with him.

'Would you then go into a war at the side of Germany?' I asked him. His wife answered, 'Ah, war,' she said, 'rather Communism than war'. Thinking of other women whose political views I had heard, of the hysterical dowagers who fear a Bolshevist under every bed, the infatuated Hitlerist flappers, and the repressed spinsters budding into a belated passion for the politics of strong and lusty he-men based on the principle of rape, I inwardly salaamed deep before her.

So I breathed deep of the air of France, as we climbed Mount Salève, and ate a French omelet and French *pommes frites*, and then, when I had got my breath, I took a look at Geneva.

The great blue lake bedded between the border mountains of France and Switzerland, with their snowcaps. The pleasant town clustering at the western end. Behind, among the trees, the great new palace of the League of Nations, dazzlingly white and gigantic even from the top of Mount Salève. It was not yet quite finished, and what was its future to be? Was it but a whited sepulchre, another monument to the futility of men's efforts to prevent war, a temple of lost causes, something that in twenty years would seem as dead and useless as the Hague Peace Conference of 1907, a lifeless and empty shell like the great Imperial palace in Vienna, that would one day be turned into a museum.

Or was it, in spite of the duplicity of dictators and the mendacity of politicians, the beginning of a process that would eventually unite the peoples of the world in the cause of peace, the expression of a human longing that would ultimately prevail over the leeches that fatten on wars.

Next day I saw the League from inside. Here was another world than that of the dictators, with their heel-clicking robots, their legions of yes-men, their hordes of police and detectives, their eternal uniforms and orders. Here were politicians and journalists of all nations and creeds and shapes and sizes,

227

rubbing shoulders in the lobbies, smoking, chatting, drinking, fat men, thin men, tall men, short men, men in tail coats and men in light summer suits, bald men and men with shock heads of hair, all expressing their own opinions, a sight to arouse the contempt and anger of the mass-produced German journalists, the Nazi button in their lapels, who had come to send disdainful reports about the Marxist-Jewish-Bolshevist International comedy of Geneva to their newspapers. Litvinoff, paunchy, bespectacled and rubicund, talked in a corner with Laval, saturnine and inscrutable. Titulescu, monstrous and misshaped, exchanged flawless French with the laboured public school French of Simon, heavily genial through a protective veneer of British repression.

And among the throng I noticed once more the Abyssinian expert. 'Why Thompson?' I asked myself again.

Then the great sitting began. Of the fifteen Council seats one was empty — that of Germany, the bad boy, who had given her two years' notice to leave the League eighteen months before but was still a member. The French resolution was put to the vote, that Germany 'has failed in her international duty', that the League 'condemns all unilateral repudiation of obligations', and would establish a committee 'to devise measures against future unilateral acts likely to endanger European peace'.

'European peace'! That lets out Baron Aloisi, for Italy, and his 'Oui' follows the others, as the vote runs round the horseshoe table. England — 'Oui'. France — 'Oui'. Russia — 'Yes' — Litvinoff is proud of his English. Spain, Portugal, Mexico, Australia, Argentina, Chile, Turkey, all 'Oui'. Germany stands condemned as a treaty-breaker.

Only Denmark stands aside. Denmark is the only small and defenceless power at the Council table which has a common frontier with Germany. Denmark remembers 1864, when Bismarck began his series of territorial grab-wars against Germany's neighbours. Nobody helped Denmark then. Denmark, says M. Munch, must reluctantly abstain.

'European peace!' Litvinoff seizes on these two words. Why only Europe, he inquires blandly, why not other continents? Possibly Litvinoff has seen the Abyssinian expert, possibly the Soviet Government wonders why Italy is to be allowed to break treaties in Africa if Germany is to be condemned for breaking them in Europe. Possibly Denmark had thought of that too, and distrusted the sincerity of this solemn arraignment of Germany at Geneva. Will the great states really help the small ones when their turn comes? Isn't it better to be on the safe side?

Litvinoff's interjection brings Simon to his feet, the flush of indignation on his cheek. Sir John is the worst possible man for dealing with foreigners. He does not understand them and thinks they are always up to some scurvy trick. They do not trust him and think him a salaried attorney without convictions. He is a Skittle Minister. Knock him down in one post and he bobs up in another; does he not command a few Liberal votes? He has been almost everything in the British Government except Prime Minister. The Gods in High Olympus have made him Foreign Minister of England at a critical moment in the history of the British Empire.

Sir John sees clearly that Litvinoff is trying by some un-principled trick to wreck that model of sincerity, the Anglo-Franco-Italian resolution condemning Germany as a treaty-breaker. Extend the resolution to breaches of the peace outside Europe? Where is any threat to the peace outside Europe? 'Let us address ourselves to practical problems in a practical spirit. Let us not spread our aspirations and endeavours so wide that the whole of our efforts be lost in miseries and shallows.'

Sir John, long oval face with shining cranium and white hair fringe perched on a lean neck, sits down, aflush with the heat of a good man stung. The French translator, without turning a hair, quietly puts this Shakespearean quotation into perfect French. I should love to know who else at the Council Table understood it. They all remain perfectly impassive. They know Sir John, they know the British habit of righteous moral indignation, of lecturing foreigners. Litvinoff, unmoved, gives

229

a characteristic shrug and says, 'In these circumstances we are all agreed'.

Germany is condemned. Of her own will, she has torn up a treaty and proclaimed her intention to rearm, although she had pledged herself not to.

In the lobbies I meet another of my useful friends, who murmurs to me that he hears that the British Government has seized on that demand of Hitler's, made to Simon in Berlin, for a third of the British naval strength. The British Government, he tells me, rather likes the idea. It is already negotiating with Hitler for an agreement.

I do not believe it. England five minutes before has voted for the condemnation of the treaty-breaker, who has proclaimed her rearmament without the consent of the other signatories to the peace treaty; now England herself is negotiating with the treaty-breaker, without reference to the other signatories, to have a limit put at least on that branch of rearmament, naval rearmament, which particularly threatens herself?

No, that can't be true. But it is, murmurs my acquaintance.

Sir Robert Vansittart passes, permanent head of the British Foreign Office. Simons may come and go, but the Crowes and Tyrrells and Vansittarts last quite a long time, though not for ever. I ask him if the news is true. Oh yes, he says immediately, quite true. A few days later it is known all over the world. Sir John himself had invited Hitler to send delegates to London without a word to France.

Those foreigners imputed duplicity to England on this account. In France they have an obsession, as you know, about England being perfidious, and a few weeks later M. Laval, Sir John's neighbour of the Council Table, told a French audience that he had given England a piece of his mind about this transaction 'and even those who consider me too moderate would perhaps think I had gone rather far if they knew the exact terms which I used'.

Whereas all the world knows that France and M. Laval always let England down, and never more so than in the

Abyssinian conflict a few weeks after this time, when the collapse of League action against Italy under British leadership was entirely due to French perfidy.

At Stresa and Geneva I still had a confiding trust in conferences and resolutions. Later, when I knew what had been going on behind the scenes there, I felt as if I had been a dinner guest at the Borgias'.

I wonder what happened to that committee 'to devise measures against future unilateral acts likely to endanger European peace'. Is it still sitting somewhere in Geneva, unwept, unhonoured and unsung, thanking its stars that Abyssinia was in Africa and that China is in Asia and resolving that the Italian and German invasions of Spain are not unilateral acts likely to endanger European peace?

CHAPTER 31

BOUND FOR DANUBIA

You need never go to sleep at all in Antwerp, if you prefer to be awake. The innumerable dance bars begin reluctantly to close down about 7 a.m. and then you see the captains rolling back to their ships and the waiters sleuthing after them to collect the bill, and the dance girls, rather faded and tawdry in the morning light, going back to their lodgings to sleep off during the day the vast quantities of tobacco and alcohol they consume at night. But long before that time the cafés on the main boulevard are open so that life in Antwerp goes on like an ever rolling stream.

I had gone once or twice to Belgium from Germany and felt that sense of relief, as of a weight being lifted from your back, that you have when you pass from one of the dictatorship countries into France, Belgium, Holland, Switzerland, Czecho-slovakia, or even Austria, where *Gemütlichkeit* softens dictator-ship to vanquishing point.

The soft French accents rested me. The Belgians in the train were quiet and unobtrusive and smiled pleasantly if you trod on their toes. I went into the dining-car and ordered an omelet, and instead of a soulless thing of yellow flannel I had a real omelet, a thing that only French and Belgian cooks know how to make. If only the Germans would learn to make omelets and the French and Belgians to tidy up their streets the world would be perfect and there would be no more wars. When I had finished my omelet I lit a cigarette, and then I noticed that I was in the non-smoking part of the dining-car, but as I was alone I kept on smoking and the Belgian waiter politely brought me an ash tray. Life is pleasant when people understand that rules and regulations are made for man and not man for rules and regulations. In Germany you must not smoke in a non-smoking car, and that's that, and only

Hitler could give you permission and he would rather die than do it.

This time, with Germany still fresh in my mind, I enjoyed Antwerp and Bruges and Ghent and Brussels. I liked sitting on a café terrace and reading the *Indépendance Belge* and waiting for the Paris papers to come in and drinking excellent burgundy and eating real *pommes frites* and being able to buy English cigarettes and Sandeman's Port, which seems to be a staple food of the Belgians, I can't think why, and chatting with courteous elderly gentlemen with neatly trimmed beards who neither tried to *imponieren* nor to ram their opinions down my throat, but seemed to have a broad and intelligent and humane view of the world and its problems.

It was over all too quickly, and duty called, so I dropped down to Berlin to pick up my car, which I had left there, and set down the road to Dresden and Prague and Vienna. It was my last flying trip to Germany and the Lord knows if and when I shall ever go there again, more's the pity, for in many ways it is the finest country I ever saw or ever shall see.

Once again I bowed to the loveliness of Dresden, to the immaculate villages and tidy fields, the brown, well-tended children. Ahead, only a few minutes away, was my new world, the Czechoslovak frontier, and behind that all Danubia and the Balkans.

Everywhere were military preparations. Prague, the Czechoslovak capital, is but half an hour by air from this southeasternmost part of Germany. Astride the Dresden-Prague road great aerodromes were springing up. On all sides were marching men, barracks, batteries, labour camps and labour conscripts. The countryside was buzzing with military activity.

I ran up a hillside into the clouds and found the frontier station in a damp white mist. Once more the impeccable uniforms and clicking heels of the German Reich, and then I was in Czechoslovakia, running the belt of country that is inhabited by Germans, 70 per cent of them fanatically Hitlerist. Bodenbach, the frontier town on the Czechoslovak side, was full of German customs officers and railwaymen in uniform and wearing swords, a sight that made me rub my eyes. Would Germany ever allow French or Polish or Czechoslovak officials in uniform on her territory?

I spent a day or two in Bohemia, among these Sudeten-Deutschen, long enough to see how busy National Socialism was at work among them. The waiter at the hotel, reassured by the Berlin number on my car, told me that trade was pining because the Czechs were discriminating against the German areas; the best thing would be for Bohemia to unite with Germany. The same old story. On the road one or two young countrymen gave the Hitler salute when they saw my Berlin number.

Then Prague, and a quick run through to the Austrian frontier, where a genial Austrian customs official found a copy of Hitler's *Mein Kampf* in my luggage, a book that was then forbidden because the Austrian Government was fighting to keep the Nazis under, and he looked at it and then at me and my Berlin number, and then again at it and without a further word he put it back in my case and closed the lid and signalled me through.

Austria. I couldn't foresee it, but some of the happiest times of my life lay before me, for I came to love this country more than any other I know. It was April, the fields and hills were green and full of flowers, the orchards white with blossom. I drove lazily along and wondered what adventures the future held for me. In the hazy distance a slender finger probed the sky, a landmark for the traveller seeking Vienna from north and south, east and west — *der alte Steffel*, St. Stephen's Cathedral. I came in over the Danube, up the Rotenturmstrasse, said good-day to Steffel, whom I had met before, and sat down on the café terrace opposite to contemplate him and this agreeable world.

CHAPTER 32

THE OTHER GERMANY

Der alte Steffel looked down on me benignly as I drank my coffee and said, 'Habe die Ehre!' 'Servus!' I answered blithely, wishing to put him at his ease. We had met before and liked each other immediately. He is a very good judge of affairs, with a good-humoured Viennese contempt for the fretting anxieties of the midgets he sees coming to him in their nurses' arms to be christened and then in beflowered carriages to be confirmed and soon afterwards in a box to be buried. 'Ruhe, Kinder, nur Ruh',' he says. 'You should take it all calmly, like I do.'

The Holy Roman Empire has gone but *der alte Steffel* goes on for ever. When he was little his parents told him of the Romans, and their legions encamped just down the street, where the Hoher Markt now is, and he himself has seen the Turks and Napoleon, and now, when he sees the Nazis surging down the Kärntnerstrasse and chanting in chorus 'Ein Volk, ein Reich' ('One people, one State'), he looks across at his friend the Capuciner Church, where one hundred and forty-three Habsburg Emperors and Empresses and princes lie in stone coffins in the vault, among them the very son of that long-mouldered upstart Napoleon himself, and then he looks across at his other friend the Charles Church, which combines the dome of St. Peter's in Rome and the portico of the Temple of Theseus in Athens and Trajan's column and a few other things, and oddly enough they all fit in, and he says, 'The little men are noisy again to-day, meine Herren Kollegen, I begin to fear that they never will learn', and they answer, 'Ganz recht, Meister, ganz recht'.

When I was in Paris the *chanteuse* used to sing lyrically of the joys of the stroll between la Madeleine et l'Opéra. She should have strolled with me from the Stefansplatz to the Opera. Here you are in the heart of Europe. Sooner or later everybody passes this way, and you sit on your café terrace, or behind the steamy panes, and watch them — Mrs. Roosevelt, Wales-

Edward-Windsor, Queen Marie, Titulescu, Litvinoff, Hodza, Indian Maharajas, Hollywood film stars, Napoleon, Mussolini, Hitler — in the flesh or the spirit they all walk these streets.

If you turn your back on *der alte Steffel* and follow your nose in one direction you come soon to Budapest, in another to Prague, in a third to Trieste, in a fourth to Munich. Here you are at the confluence of the streams of German and Latin and Slav blood and of the Jewish migration, pouring ceaselessly across Europe to the promised lands—Germany (before Hitler), Austria, France, England, and, the great goal, America across the sea.

Vienna is the only really international city I know. The shop-names round the cathedral and in the Rotenturmstrasse give you a cross-section of the cross-bred population. Jewish names, taken from places in Poland and Bohemia and Hungary, predominate, and then there are German and Czech and Slovak and Croat and Italian names and many more. Whether you like it or not is your affair. This Vienna made Hitler what he is and the streets still swarm with that mixture of races, 'among them all the eternal fission-fungus of humanity, the Jew', which the youthful Hitler, contemplating them, found 'repulsive, the incarnation of incest'.

Above all towers St. Stephen's Cathedral, the outward and visible sign of the paramount power in Austria — the Roman Catholic Church. For a thousand years the devoutly Catholic Habsburg Emperors and Empresses in Vienna kept the Holy Roman Empire together. Voltaire, that cynic, asked in what respect it was Holy or Roman or an Empire, just as you might ask in what respect is the *Christian Science Monitor* Christian or scientific or monitorial, but Vienna during all these centuries ruled over peoples of a dozen different races and languages and religions and somehow or other kept them all together, and even up to a few days before the Armistice Croats and Czechs and Poles and Hungarians and Italians and Slovenes were all fighting for the Emperor in Vienna, and the real cement was the Catholic Church.

To-day Vienna is an Imperial City without an Empire, its

236

gaze fixed on a curtained future. It is an international city, the ideal capital for the polyglot Habsburg Empire, and you ought after the war to have put the League of Nations here and filled up the empty palaces, but that opportunity has been lost, and now Hitler, looking down on the lovely valleys of his native land from his Bavarian chalet at Berchtesgaden, just across the frontier, is filled with nostalgia for Austria and for Vienna, which he pretends to detest, and actually longs for, like every man who has lived in Vienna, and the coming years are going to be filled with this fight for the possession of Austria between Hitler's Nazis, in Germany and Austria, and Vienna, where the spirit of toleration in race and religion that kept the Habsburg Empire alive for so many centuries still pervades the air.

'Happy Austria, while others make war you marry', they say, and like all such sayings, which may be true and witty when they are made and in application to specific circumstances, this became untrue long before anybody realized it.

True, the great domains of the Holy Roman Empire were largely acquired by marriage, and Napoleon was bought off by giving him our Marie Louise, who wasted little time in mourning him when he died on distant Elba, but actually Austria came to disaster through marriage. For the last Emperor but one, old Francis Joseph, who had an incredibly long innings and was already reigning in Vienna long before England fought Russia in the Crimean War and yet died only in the third year of the World War, married a Bavarian Princess, Elisabeth, whom he loved with an extraordinary constancy and who was one of the most beautiful women the world has seen but who did not love him and continually fled his society, so that for years she was seldom seen in Austria.

Desperately seeking substitutes for the happiness she did not find with him, she developed passions for many things, travel, languages, Corfu, Greek culture — and Hungary. When Austria, until then the leader of the German States, had this leadership wrested from her by Prussia in the war of 1866 Hungary, seeing her weakness, pressed for self-government in

Budapest, as distinct from rule from Vienna, for the coronation of the Emperor in Budapest as King of Hungary, and the like.

The Hungarian nobles, a particularly astute clan, had remarked Elisabeth's unhappiness and her liking for Hungary, and a most handsome and winning Magyar nobleman, Count Andrassy, was sent forward to plead the cause of Hungary with her.

The method is one in which the Hungarians are experts and sixty years later, when Hungary was eagerly courting foreign support of her complaints against the territorial cuts that she suffered in the World War, influential British visitors were wont to find their gratification that they had inspired ardent passions in the hearts of beautiful Hungarian ladies whose other main topic of conversation was the wrong that had been inflicted on Hungary. The British public would often have a shock if it knew the origin and motive of the news and views that are set before it.

Andrassy succeeded beyond the dreams of the Magyar magnates. The harassed Francis Joseph in Vienna received a stream of letters from his absentee Empress in Hungary imploring him to grant the Hungarian demands, or the Empire would go to pieces. There is a great resemblance between these letters and the arguments that have been put before the British public in the last twenty years — 'Justice for Hungary or something awful will happen.'

Anyway, the result was that Francis Joseph, a lovelorn, lonely and unlucky man, allowed himself to be talked over and Hungary was given a full half-share in the Empire, which became the Austro-Hungarian Empire, Hungary becoming the Overlord of Slovakia and Croatia, and this was a thing which the other subject races, Czechs and Slovaks, Croats and Slovenes, Ruthenians and Poles, could never swallow. 'Either we must all be subjects of the Emperor, ruled from Vienna', they said, 'or we must all have self-government. Why should the Hungarians be picked out from among the rest of us for preferential treatment?'

That was the main reason for home-rule and secession movements which bore their fruit in 1918, when all these people broke away and formed their own states. Many of them had a deep inbred affection for the Emperor in Vienna and would have been glad to stay within a Habsburg, but not with an Austro-Hungarian Empire.

You will not find any great cult of Elisabeth in Vienna, for all her beauty. The Austrians resented the way she treated Francis Joseph, whom for all his bad luck they loved, but in Budapest, not far from your snob hotel on the Danube, you will find a large bronze Elisabeth enthroned beneath a marble canopy.

But Francis Joseph they remember in Austria with affection, for all that he brought that great Empire to the dust. What a life! When you consider Francis Joseph you could almost believe in the evil eye.

A reign begun with two disastrous wars and the loss of Austria's pride of place in the councils of the German nation; continued with the suicide of his son, the murder of his brother as Emperor of Mexico, the death of his sister-in-law in a Paris fire, the mania of his wife for travel abroad and her assassination by an Italian anarchist at Geneva, the murder of his nephew at Serajevo, which led to the final fatal mistake, a world war at the side of Germany and the collapse in ruins of the Austro-Hungarian Empire. Francis Joseph died just too soon to see that culminating disaster and say once again 'Nothing is spared me', but he knew it was coming.

Unhappy Francis Joseph. His love letters to his globe-trotting Empress, continued for decades, show a man of almost unique constancy to a woman who did not love him. She was an extraordinary woman, afire, as it seems to me, with the longing for a great love and sent rushing round the world by the frustration of this desire.

Read how she went to the masked ball in Vienna and sought out a good-looking young man there, to whom she held out every promise of an amorous adventure of a kind that only comes the way of one man in millions, but he recognized her behind her mask and was stupid enough, as young men are, not to hold his tongue, so that she took fright. She had evidently been reading the life of Marie Antoinette and knew how that Habsburg Princess found her handsome lover — Fersen.

Francis Joseph had to have somebody to talk to and he and Elisabeth together found the right person — Katherina Schratt of the Burgtheater, buxom, blond, gay, sensible, a Viennese in the best sense of all that word implies.

Every morning early you could see Francis Joseph, who was wont to rise at four a.m., driving out to Schönbrunn to breakfast with Frau Schratt and confide his cares to her, and the Viennese knew where he was going and sympathized with him and raised their hats, and Frau Schratt was called with the members of the Imperial Family to see him as he lay on his deathbed, and to-day she still lives out there in her villa in Hietzing, doing good.

When I came to Vienna all that was gone. The great chestnut avenue through the Prater, which on summer afternoons used to be filled with brilliant uniforms and pretty frocks, was bare and empty. The Prater Fun Fair, with its antediluvian entertainments and half-empty garden restaurants, was a dejected ghost of the gay past. The Tabarin, where Francis Joseph's Polish officers used to throw a hundred guilders to the band to play a Mazurka and his Hungarian officers quickly capped that with another hundred guilders to stop playing the Mazurka and play a Czardas, and his Austrian officers capped that again with another hundred guilders to stop playing the Czardas and play a Waltz, the Tabarin was a gloomy modern bar that went bankrupt every spring. At Sacher's, where so many state secrets were made in the *séparées* and where the Habsburg archdukes came with their lady friends, Madame Sacher, who was wont to smoke cigars and box her waiters' ears, was dead.

The Blue Danube, with its unhurried and unworried melody, was the musical expression of life in Vienna before the World War. The Danubian Blues, with saxophonic wailings and syncopated explosions, would be the musical expression of life in Vienna after it.

But I loved it. It was, is and will be, for me, the best city in the world and when I come late at night into the dirty old West Bahnhof, and hear the soft Viennese accents of the porters and taxi-men, I feel as if I were coming home.

It is the one city in the world, as far as I have seen the world, where a foreigner need not feel himself a stranger, if he behaves himself decently and has a little mother-wit—and how badly they sometimes behave, the foreign visitors. Wit and understanding will procure you more happiness there than money; if you only have money you will quickly be parted from it and immediately forgotten.

But don't take that to mean that you can walk into a bar and invite a girl to sit with you for several hours and drink a lot of stuff that she doesn't want and be glad to have had the opportunity to sit with you; she is there to earn her living, and her time and company cost money, and you are not so handsome or amusing that she can afford to waste her time on you for nothing, though if you are she probably will.

I could sometimes wish to be a Viennese, even in these days of Vienna's decline. I think of my youth in London, of those endless areas of dreary Dionne quintuplet streets, of the wide belt of near-countryside through which you endlessly tramped trying to reach the mirage of the real country beyond. Vienna, even in its days of poverty, seems to have much that I then lacked, and still lack when I go to London.

True, you will see neither white shirts in the Opera nor bare shoulders in the Burgtheater, the champagne-and-caviare circle is very small, and if these things distress you Vienna is not for you. But within five minutes of the Opera you can breakfast on excellent coffee and fresh rolls and whipped cream and have the morning papers in all languages brought to you on a sunny terrace, you can dine in a delightful garden with a band playing, you can dance under the trees, you can listen to Viennese operetta played in the open air (this a little under standard as yet, it is true), you can swim in an open or a closed pool, you can play tennis, in winter you can skate, you can see art collections equal to the finest in the world, you can take a tram for

Czechoslovakia that will carry you past a Roman amphitheatre where Marcus Aurelius wrote his meditations, you can take another tram with a snack-car attached to it and go to Baden and lose your money at roulette if you prefer to get rid of it that way.

In the Old City, lying within the semi-circle formed by the Danube Canal and the Ring, where the walls of Vienna formerly ran, I wandered for hours. The old streets, with their palaces mouldering into business premises and shops, are inter-locked by innumerable alleys and passages and courtyards, all of which I haven't discovered even yet, and everywhere there are antique shops full of fascinating things, and in the shadow of the Stefansdom are the old monasteries of the Dominicans and the Franciscans and the Ursulan nuns, and it always amuses me to see a monk in his begirdled and hairy brown cassock go by sucking an ice-cream wafer.

Everywhere the black robes of priests or the brown ones of the monks or the blue ones of the theological students, the signs that the Catholic Church still retains its hold on the capital of the Holy Roman Empire.

Everywhere churches and abbeys and monasteries — the Charles Church, glowing like a green lamp in the Viennese dusk, the Pöstlingberg Church on the hillside by Linz, like an emerald suspended in the sky.

These are the things you see in Austria, instead of marching men and eternal parades and saluting Storm Troopers. But up in his hillside chalet, a stone's-throw across the frontier, sits Hitler, the Austrian, able almost to reach out and touch his Austrian birthplace, so near and yet so far, and yet frustrated as yet, a dictator thwarted in his dearest wish, that triumphal entry into Vienna.

Everywhere in Vienna you see the Jews — in the waterside district around the Danube Canal the bearded and ringletted orthodox Jews with their spectacles and black hats, in the Rotenturmstrasse and the Ringstrasse the smart emancipated Jews of trade and commerce, and the theatre and the press, with narrow waists and oiled hair, filling all the best seats in the theatres, thronging the more expensive hotels and restaurants, packing the showier cafés.

In the political cabarets young men and woman, many of them Jewish emigrants from Germany, make wise-cracks about the Third Reich to appreciative Jewish audiences. I never saw a more brilliant piece of political satire than a sketch played by such young *émigré* artists, earning only a few schillings a night, in which they adapted the fairy-tale of the tardy tailor to contemporary political conditions in Europe. You remember the tale of the tailor who was late with the King's new coat and, not wishing to be beheaded, hit on the idea of pretending that the coat was ready but made of a marvellous new cloth which only the completely loyal could see, so that the King presently appeared naked and all the courtiers were loud in their admiration of the new coat.

In Vienna in 1937, in this little political cabaret in the shabby back room of a cheap café, the King's coat was only visible to those whose patriotic enthusiasm and racial purity were above suspicion and the result was not a caricature, but a photograph, staggering in its accuracy, of conditions in a Yes-man dictatorship. And when the simple peasant girl exclaimed, 'Why, the King's naked!' there was universal horror and her trial, with self-righteous judges and sanctimonious State attorneys and police spies, stool-pigeons, lickspittles and other hired men all giving evidence against her in the jargon of self-abasement, was so much like the Reichstag Fire Trial that it left me gasping.

Surveying Europe to-day, with its Black and Brown and other shirts, I have often thought of that other fable of the King in search of happiness who was told by a soothsayer that he must wear the shirt of a completely happy man and sent out his courtiers to scour the kingdom to find such a man. But the only completely happy man in all that realm, when they found him, hadn't a shirt.

While the Jews sit talking and gesticulating in the cafés and the priests and monks go sedately about their business, the young Nazis of Vienna ironically watch them and make bitter jibes about the hold that the Church and the Jews have on the country. They call the Government the 'K.K.' Government. 'K und K', before the war, meant *Kaiserliche und Königliche*, or Imperial and Royal; 'K.K.' to-day, in Nazi accents, means '*Kutte-Kaftan*', or 'Cowl and Caftan', to indicate their belief that the Jews and the Jesuits work hand in hand. And the little red-white-red riband which all supporters of the Government have to wear, to show that they belong to the orthodox Patriotic Front founded by Dollfuss, the Nazis call the 'Pour le sémite', for the same reason.

Amid this throng of Jews and Clericals and young ardent Nazis longing to have Hitler come to Vienna, strolls the average Viennese, kindly, courteous, cynical, witty, often bored about politics, unless he be a monarchist longing for the repeopling of the Court, or a Socialist still bitter from the events of 1934.

The foothills of the Alps run down to meet the Danube at Vienna and within an hour of the Opera by tram or car or bicycle you have sub-alpine scenery, with the Hungarian and Czechoslovak border mountains and the first snow-caps in the distance, and the Danube running beneath you on its journey between the Black Forest and the Black Sea and all around you the endless Vienna Forest, where Beethoven and Mozart and Strauss found the inspiration for their music.

You come back lazily in the dusk, with the fireflies dancing round you and the young men in their leather shorts and white stockings strolling along with their arms round the trim waists of the girls in their *Dirndls*, and pause at one of the wine-growing villages before you resume your homeward way. For the good God, who thought of everything when he made Vienna, has put vineyards on the surrounding hills, where the suburbs end, so that Vienna has only to reach out its hand when it wants a drink, and in these wine-growing villages, one lovelier than another, Grinzing and Nussdorf and Sievering and Gumpolds-kirchen, every second house has a green light on a pole and a garden or a courtyard where you sit and drink this year's wine, from last year's grapes, while musicians play Viennese songs.

244

But be careful of that wine. Like the Viennese themselves it is friendly and smiling but has unsuspected fires in its depths. It does not deprive you of the power of movement, indeed it promotes it, the homeward way being downhill, but it induces extraordinary lapses of memory and you awake the next morning feeling perfectly fit but remembering nothing from the moment you got from the table.

And a little farther afield the Viennese, luckiest of townsmen, has the Wachau, where the Danube runs between terraced orchards and vineyards and wooded hills crowned with magnificent abbeys and ruined castles perched on crags to the gates of Vienna. Here is one of the loveliest places in Europe, completely unspoilt either by dog-in-the-manger landlords or unthinking trippers. There are neither bombastic commercial exploitation nor ribbon-building nor petrol stations nor indiscriminate advertising nor boards to threaten you with prosecution for trespass nor charabancs, only a drowsy countryside with well-built village lads and girls with trim hair and the broad Danube going swiftly to the Black Sea and a great log-raft with a little house on it being steered deftly down-stream, a rare canoeist toiling up-stream.

Beyond that lies Austria — Upper Austria, Salzburg, Salzkammergut, Tirol, Styria, Carinthia, one lovely place after another. If you will come with me for a drive along the lakeside road from Ebensee to Gmünden you will learn one of the reasons why I love Austria. On that road my car developed a petrol stoppage far from a repair shop, and I found that I had not the right tools to clear it, so I stopped a lad on a bicycle and asked if he had the right spanner. No, he hadn't, but he would ride back to Ebensee and borrow one. He went, and a minute later a motor-cyclist drove up and stopped and asked if I were he who wanted a spanner. I was, and he dismounted and cleared the block in my petrol feed, and while he was doing it the lad on the bicycle went by, waving cheerily, and then the motor-cyclist repacked his tools, shook hands and went off, and I followed.

Don't ask me, if we ever meet, if the friendliness of the

Austrians is sincere. I shouldn't know what you mean, any more than I know what people mean when they say Hitler is sincere. I don't expect to be loved for myself alone at first sight. I like their friendliness, and in a world where manners seem to me every day to be more and more important, I like their manners, and *Habe die Ehre* and *Küss' die Hand* and all the other baroque flourishes with which they adorn the structure of their conversation, and I like listening to their continual grumbling and contradicting them and telling them that all Austrians ought to be thankful to live in Austria and playing up to their national delusion that all Austrians have no money.

The extraordinary thing about the Austrians is their dissimilarity from the Germans. They are, as far as I can make out, Germans, and feel themselves so, within limits, but the French and Bulgar are not more dissimilar than the Austrians and Germans. Go and study them in Salzburg. You will recognize the Austrians because they are simply dressed; the people in fancy clothes are the foreign visitors, who have been to the shop opposite the Café Bazar to be made up like Tirolean mountaineers and Styrian huntsmen.

Salzburg station is half Austrian and half German — Hitler, you will remember, lives only half an hour from here — and the Germans have their own customs and platforms at Salzburg. In the Austrian half of the station, where a bust of the murdered Chancellor Dollfuss gazes pointedly across at the German half, Austrian railwaymen in easy-fitting Austrian uniforms take life easily, the trains, though they may come and go punctually, do so casually and without being self-conscious about it.

In the German half, though you are still in Austria, you immediately feel yourself battened down; here the arrival or departure of a train is a defiant gesture of Germanic efficiency to a world of implacable enemies, the immaculate and well-filled uniforms of the Reich induce a feeling of civilian inferiority in you, the railwaymen are less locomotive drivers and guards than cogs in the gigantic machine of National Socialism.

Salzburg itself, where in the Café Bazar, under the paternal eye of the old head waiter, Toscanini and Bruno Walter rub shoulders with Wilhelm Furtwängler, Marlene Dietrich with Michiko Meinl, Max Reinhardt and Helene Thimig with Wales-Edward-Windsor, is a monument to that real German culture which finds its highest form in Salzburg and Austria, of which Salzburg and Austria are the last outposts. If you are interested in Salzburg I commend to you an amusing little book called *This Salzburg*, which is well adapted to the mentality of the snob tourist and is devoid of illusions other than that, of which I have already told you, that all Austrians, and particularly all Austrian counts, have no money.

This brings you back to Vienna, and its hopes and fears. What is going to happen to us? Are we going to be overrun by war, is Hitler going to swallow us, is young Otto, now vegetating at Steenockerzeel in Belgium, going to return one day and take up the Habsburg throne? The unspoken question pervades all life in Vienna. It is the city of suspense. Nearly everybody hopes for the one thing or the other.

Come with me up to Coblenz and drink a cup of coffee on the terrace. Vienna, with the broad ribbon of the Danube curving by and gradually losing itself in the distance, lies outstretched below you, the story of centuries of siege and famine and pest and prosperity told in stone. Sobieski, starting from almost where you sit, threw the Turks back here and thus began their expulsion from Europe, completed over 200 years later. Over there at Aspern, where you see the great air liners arriving and departing, Napoleon suffered his first setback. The erstwhile capital of a great empire, which has played a foremost part in European history, is now the capital of a tiny state battling for its independence. Will it also be absorbed into the great Germanic family, so that a new and mightier and greater German power will arise in Europe on the ashes of the Hohenzollern and Habsburg empires?

Over there, and there, and there again you will see great gleaming blocks of buildings — the Socialist tenements for the workers of Vienna, the latest chapter in its history. After the

247

war the Socialists had power in Vienna. They put taxes on the more expensive restaurants and bars, on rents above a certain figure, on servants over a certain number, and from the proceeds of these taxes they built new homes for the workers, writing off the cost of building and charging insignificant rents to cover only upkeep and maintenance.

They rehoused almost a sixth of the city population, about 200,000 working-class people, giving them for the first time in their history light and air and sunshine; housing conditions in Vienna had been particularly bad. They aroused the bitter enmity of the classes that are traditionally opposed to all efforts to improve the lot of those less fortunate than themselves. I once knew a wealthy young Englishman who could find a hundred arguments against this Socialist housing scheme. 'Putting the people in barracks, taxing labour, undercutting private enterprise', he said, and then in the next breath, 'You know, the prices at the Femina are scandalous. They charged me eighty schillings for a bottle of champagne last night'.

He was a dapper young man with an upgrowing moustache which I suspected he imprisoned at night in a net fastened to his ears.

These Socialist houses in Vienna form almost the only constructive achievement born of the war that I have found in Europe — apart from the liberation of subject peoples and the creation of independent states for them. But the Socialists were also pacifists and incurred the enmity not only of the reactionaries in Austria but of Mussolini's Italy.

For Italy, who in 1935 was at Geneva to condemn Germany's action in proclaiming rearmament, in 1933 was sending arms through Austria for the rearmament of her protégé Hungary, and Austrian Socialist workmen intercepted a consignment and made the affair public. Thus in 1934, when Austria was fighting for her independence against Germany, and a crisis clearly impended, Mussolini made his support conditional on the suppression of the Austrian Socialists. That was the message he sent to Dollfuss by his emissary Suvich in January 1934.

It may prove that Mussolini, though he withheld Austria from Hitler for a year or two, destroyed the last hope of real Austrian independence by this action. Up to that time two anti-Nazi parties in Austria, Catholics and Socialists, held an overwhelming majority of the votes, about eighty per cent. A man really convinced of the need for Austria's independence should have forced them to coalesce on the anti-Nazi issue and then the world would clearly have seen what was at stake. But Dollfuss could not or would not do it, possibly no man could have done it, for their mutual hatred was great. The Socialists detested the clerical hold on the country, the enormous wealth of the Church with its myriad abbeys and churches and monasteries, as compared with the poverty of the workers. The Church detested the workers' tenements, with their birth-control clinics and anti-Popery teachings, and could not see that Imperial and Catholic Austria, with its palaces and abbeys, had never produced anything finer than these Socialist homes for workers.

So the army and Prince Starhemberg's and Major Fey's Fascist Heimwehr, financed with Italian money, were sent against the Socialists, and the famous workers' houses, which students from all parts of the world had come to Vienna to see, were bombarded by an Austrian army awfully arrayed. I was in Berlin when I heard the news and my heart sank at it; I knew that this was a major disaster for Europe. Little Dollfuss, the Austrian David fighting the German Goliath, had been uproariously cheered by the world's statesmen at a conference in London a few weeks before, now he had turned on his own workpeople, the one class that from inmost conviction would have gone with him to the barricades to keep Hitler out — for the Church was not against Hitler from conviction, only on grounds of interest.

The pretext, as in the case of Germany and the mythical rising which was to have been let loose by the Reichstag fire, was that 'a Bolshevist rising' had impended in Austria. How true that was you can judge by the fact that Major Fey, speaking the day before the bombardment of the Socialists in their homes, said 'To-morrow we are going to clean up Austria'.

But even in this disastrous affair the Austrian character brought redeeming features. The Austrian gunners placed their shells with as much humanity as they could, the great tenements were only holed and not destroyed and were quickly repaired, and the loss of life, though high, was at least as low as you could hope for in such circumstances.

Since that day nobody knows just what the state of feeling in Austria is and Austrian independence can never again be a thing for Austria to claim and defend in her own right, but only a bargaining pawn between Mussolini and Hitler. And the more Mussolini finds himself in antagonism with England the more likely he is to sell out to Germany in Austria, in order to keep Hitler's support.

Austria can only look helplessly on. As the reward of her suppression of the Socialists she got, in the Roman Protocols of 1934, the promise of Italian support, and when Hitler went to see Mussolini at Venice in June 1934 he agreed, as Mussolini's son-in-law Ciano announced, 'that Austria should be enabled to live in full recognition of her independence'.

Just five weeks after Hitler, the sincere, had given his brother dictator this assurance, the Nazis rose in armed insurrection in Austria and Nazi raiders murdered Dollfuss in his own Chancery. If you have any doubts about the German responsibility for this action read the official Austrian Brown Book, giving the evidence, photographs of explosives supplied by the German War Ministry to Austrian Nazi terrorists, and the like.

Mussolini redeemed his promise of political and economic support on that occasion. As a warning to Hitler not to seize the opportunity and grab Austria he mobilized an army on the Italian frontier. As an antidote to the tourist- and trade-boycott with which Germany was trying to starve Austria into submission he gave trade and financial concessions to Austria. The things he said about Hitler, as I am told, were unprintable. For the nonce he had, indeed, saved Austria.

But a year later he was invading Abyssinia and had the world against him, and a year after that he had conquered Abyssinia but was sending armies to Spain and again incurring England's hostility and Germany's friendship began to look desirable to him. So that two years after Dollfuss's murder he made Austria sign a truce with Germany, by which Hitler 'acknowledged Austrian sovereignty' but Austria promised 'to pursue a policy consonant with her position as a Germanic State', and thus Mussolini, giving another dose of anaesthetic to the patient Austria, which had already survived alternate doses of strychnine and morphia, strangely enough, shook hands with Hitler across the operating table and the Mussolini-Hitler partnership began, of which the world has yet to see the end.

It was the thin end of the German wedge in Austria, and when or whether it will be driven deep enough to split Austria asunder depends on Mussolini's plight. If his adventures lead him deep enough into the mire, if he is hard pressed enough, he will have to sell out in Austria in order to keep his German partner. He will only do that in a desperate emergency, and watch Austria if you want to know how Mussolini's stock is standing, for he will need to be in a very bad way indeed to put up with Germany as a next door neighbour, within grabbing distance of the blue Adriatic and Trieste, which Italy only acquired from Austria through the war.

Hitler has often pressed for 'a free plebiscite' in Austria. They say that this was one of the suggestions put to Lord Halifax, when he saw Hitler, as a fair offer. It is skilfully attuned to the British mentality; it has a democratic ring. Statesmen far away do not realize, even if they cared, that there is no such thing as a 'free plebiscite' in a country of seven million people coveted by a neighbouring military dictatorship of seventy millions. The means of pressure and intimidation are too great.

If Hitler gets his plebiscite the moving finger will inexorably write 'Finis Austriae' across the European map, and Austrian man-power and munition-power will be harnessed to the mighty German military machine.

Austria lies precariously under the lee of the Rome-Berlin partnership, and wonders what the future holds. The cheerfully cynical Viennese, as they look out on this strange world of double-crossing dictators, alternatively threatening and embracing each other and springing week-end bombshells on the world, remark, 'Well, war certainly seems to be coming, but we can't foretell where or why, all we know is that it will begin on a Saturday.'

In Vienna Schuschnigg sits in Dollfuss's chair, reserved, entirely untheatrical, austere, unemotional. I have often seen him there. Outside in the corridor is the old messenger who saw Dollfuss killed, and tells you how he tried to run out of the room by another door, but met the raiders coming in and they shot him down. In the corner, over the sofa on which he died, is a weeping Madonna, the work of an Austrian peasant woodcarver who, by a strange chance, had made it and given it to Dollfuss just before his death. A light burns beneath it. In this chancery Metternich sat and span his tangled webs, the Chancellor of an Empire that in its day had spread all over Europe from Spain to the Netherlands. Outside is the Heldenplatz, the most noble place I have seen in Europe, framed by the Imperial Palace and the great buildings of the Ringstrasse, and behind them the Vienna hills and above the blue Vienna sky.

It is an enchanting city, with the melancholy of departed glory lingering in the air. I wish I could take a magic wand and give its people the only thing they lack — common emotion, something to be enthusiastic about. I believe they would cheer anybody they saw entering Vienna on a white horse, whether he were Habsburg, Hitler or what not. From a purely selfish point of view I hope that Vienna will always remain Vienna as I have known it in one sense at least — a city of music and toleration, with a distrust for extremes.

I spoke about these things with my friend *der alte Steffel*, but he was wary and non-committal, as the Viennese always are if you try to bore them with serious problems. 'Schaun S', Verehrtester,' he said, 'es wird sich schon alles finden, warum soll'n ma uns den Kopf zerbrechen über diese Dinge. Wien bleibt doch Wien.'

'Vienna won't alter.' I wonder if Steffel was right. He is getting old now and rather senile, in fact they had to raise a fund for an operation on his steeple.

One day in February 1938 Hitler invited the earnest Schuschnigg to visit him at his Bavarian chalet and there, with German generals standing ominously in the background and tanks and infantry and aeroplanes everywhere, he told Schuschnigg that, of course, he respected Austrian independence, but it would be as well if Schuschnigg would hand over the police to a new Minister, Arthur Seyss-Inquart, in whom Hitler had confidence, and he might as well release all his imprisoned Nazis and change the tone of his press, and he need not delude himself that England or France or Italy would give him any help and Germany could occupy Austria with far less misgiving than she had occupied the Rhineland two years before. That happened, inevitably, on a Saturday, and Mussolini, inexplicably was somewhere deep in the Italian countryside, and London shook in its golf shoes, and Schuschnigg, who had stood face to face with stark, relentless, overwhelming force, came back to Vienna and did all these things.

So by the time you read this book Hitler's nominee will have the Austrian police, and you remember that Göring's control of the Prussian police, although he was only Prussian Home Minister and Papen was Prussian Premier and the Nazis were in a voting minority in the Reich Cabinet, was enough for him to exploit the Reichstag fire in a way that vanquished all adversaries and made Germany into the Third Reich.

By all the portents Steffel will see some changes soon. You could feel the tension in Vienna that Saturday.

CHAPTER 33

SERB SOLILOQUY

I STOOD in the orthodox Cathedral at Belgrade and two bearded young deacons with lusty thighs and sinews sang a sonorous chant in a rising cadence of half- and quarter-tones in magnificent bass voices. It was a spectacle of virile masculinity that clearly fluttered the emotions of the English ladies who were standing about. I should think the priests of the Serbian Ortho-dox Church must be one of the finest-looking bodies of men in the world.

It was the thanksgiving service of the Orthodox Church for the jubilee of King George V of England, who had just com-pleted the twenty-fifth year of his reign; a simple and retiring man who in other circumstances would have left little impression on the world's memory, he had by the accident of time come to symbolize, for England and the world, the ordeal of the war and the survival of the British Empire, and now the whole world was honouring in his person that successful business proposition.

I was by chance in Belgrade and in the morning I thanked God for King George at the Cathedral and in the afternoon I gathered with other miscellaneous Britons in the garden of the British Legation. Sir Nevile Henderson said the customary few words in the tone of reverent emotion that is reserved for kings, until they kick over the traces. In the evening I sat in the bar of the Srbski Kralj and listened to a gentleman whose family in the course of their westward migration had picked up a Bohemian place-name and who himself had acquired a British passport; he was saying what a great day this had been for England.

But now, as I listened half-heeding to the magnificent singing of the deacons, my thoughts were far from King George. Before me stood Prince Paul, the Regent, and his Princess Olga, and behind them were the members of the Yugoslav Government, and among them, the War Minister, and my thoughts were fixed on him. As I watched him the cathedral and Prince Paul and the foreign diplomats and the singing deacons faded and I saw officers, with revolvers and swords in their hands, rushing through the rooms and corridors of a darkened palace, saw panic-stricken fugitives hiding in cupboards, shots, shrieks, shouts of triumph. . . .

He was a little plump now, the War Minister, plumper than he had been on that evening just thirty-two years before, but still a fine-looking man with a thick head of hair and a massive, muscular frame. I think the Serbs must, in proportion to their numbers, be the handsomest men in the world, and their womenfolk are lovely; the average expectation of a beautiful wife must be higher in Serbia than almost anywhere. The men are often still young at fifty, and mostly avoid pouches, paunches, bald heads and the other diseases of age far longer than the males in other lands.

The Royal Palace is not far from the Cathedral, two or three long stonethrows. The War Minister, I thought as I looked at him, standing rigidly at attention in his well-fitting grey uniform, must pass it almost every day of his life when he is in Belgrade. His hands shook, they say, on that evening, thirty-two years before, when he, Lieutenant Zhivkovitch of the Guard at the Palace, fumbled for the keys to open the gates and let his brother-officers and fellow-conspirators in, and they all rushed through the palace vainly seeking for King Alexander and his Queen Draga, and at last detected a crack in the wallpaper that meant a secret chamber, and when they got them out, Alexander and Draga in their long white nightshirts, they killed him with 'nineteen revolver bullets and five sabre cuts' and her with 'thirty-six revolver shots and over forty sabre cuts', and the bodies were thrown out of the window into the forecourt of the palace, where they lay sprawling until the Russian Minister, peeping through the blinds of his Legation opposite, ventured to send out some servants with sheets to cover them, and His Britannic Majesty's Government was so shocked that it withdrew its Minister from Belgrade for three years and all the world shuddered.

Now, thirty-two years later, the bloodstains have long since faded, and after the thanksgiving service at St. Sava's we all go back along the main street past the spot where Alexander and Draga lay, and nobody thinks of them, possibly not even the War Minister. (You remember Anatole France's marvellous story, the best short story ever written, I think, of the two retired Roman Governors who meet and discuss old times and one of them says, 'By the way, Pontius, what happened to that fellow you had such trouble with in Jerusalem, Jesus of Nazareth, I think they called him?', and Pontius, in his palanquin, says, 'Jesus, Jesus, I cannot recall the name'.) Opposite the palace still stands the Russian Legation, yellow and unkempt and out of elbows and now empty these twenty years, for the Czar is also dead, murdered, and we of the Yugoslav Court detest this Bolshevist regime of regicides and Yugoslavia has not yet recognized Soviet Russia.

Possibly the War Minister does after all ponder these things as he passes the palace, for his chief on that night thirty-two years before, the chief plotter, is also mouldering in a distant grave with bullet-holes in his skull, that industrious Colonel Dimietrievitch, nicknamed The Bee, who planned the whole thing, in order to rid Serbia of the intolerable shame of Alexander and his mistress-queen, and bring back the Karageorgevitch.

Apis, the Bee, that was a man, big and strong as a bull, a Serbian patriot in the great tradition, the father of the dynasty. They say that he prepared the assassination of the Archduke Franz Ferdinand at Serajevo in 1914, too, in the hope and intention to bring about a European war in which the declining Austro-Hungarian Empire, the sick man on the Danube, would receive the *coup de grâce* and Serbia, after centuries of oppression and struggle, blossom at last into the great South Slav Reich, in which Serbs and Croats and Slovenes and Montenegrins and perhaps Bulgars would all be united.

But Apis, who murdered Alexander Obrenovitch to put Peter Karageorgevitch on the Serbian throne, was himself shot by Alexander Karageorgevitch, who in his turn was murdered at Marseilles.

It all happened in the war. They say that Apis, head of the Black Hand Secret Society, had come to the opinion that the great South Slav Reich of his dreams could only be realized on Republican lines, but who knows if that is really true. At all events, Alexander Karageorgevitch, then Prince-Regent for his ageing father, feared him and surrounded himself with another group of officers, headed by Zhivkovitch, who formed an opposition White Hand Society. And one fine morning Apis, who died bravely, was taken out and shot on a charge of plotting his third great murder — that of the Prince-Regent. The murder of Belgrade 1903 was certainly and that of Serajevo 1914 almost certainly his; no credible evidence was produced in support of the charge of the alleged third murder, on which he was shot. He seems to have been entirely innocent of it, but those who live by the revolver often die by it.

The truth of the matter, as one of my useful friends told me, and I incline to believe him, is that in 1917, when the hail-fellow-well-met Apis Dimietrievitch was shot at Salonica, the Serbian Government had been pushed out of Serbia and did not know when or whether it would ever get back again. Its army was fighting with the Allies at Salonica, in Greece; the Serbian Government was at Corfu; the Central Powers had vast areas of enemy territory in their hands and were in a strong position to conclude a favourable peace; and the Emperor Charles of Austria-Hungary had just made a peace approach to the Allies through the Pope.

Prince-Regent Alexander and the Serbian Government may well have thought that peace negotiations impended in which the Serbian Government, with the enemy in possession of its territory, would be in a very weak position and would do well to propitiate the Central Powers, moving to a favourable peace, by removing the man who had prepared the Serajevo murder.

I thought of all these things as I came away from the thanks-giving service at St. Sava's and walked along King Milan Street. Alexander Obrenovitch had been a bad king, the doctors who examined his body found that his skull was three times as thick as it should have been and perhaps that had something to do with it, and Draga had done her utmost to make Serbia appear ridiculous by twice announcing that she was pregnant when she was incurably sterile. But was not the method of their removal rather drastic? Could they not have been dethroned and imprisoned? It was a point that interested me, for wandering about Europe the great question which continually confronted me was, is political murder justifiable? Did blood always revenge itself in blood or was it possible that good could come out of what seemed indubitably to be evil, that great civilizations, fructifying the world, could be born in crimes glossed over with the name of patriotism. It was a question that repeatedly prompted itself particularly in Germany.

In Serbia not a soul regrets Alexander and Draga or the manner of their killing. In Serajevo they put up a tablet to Gabriel Princip, who shot the Archduke. An Orthodox Priest spoke to me derisively once of 'the old ladies in England who still talk about poor Alexander and poor Draga'. With my Serb friend X, I climbed to the top of windswept Mount Avala, where Serb conscripts are assembling Ivan Mestrovic's great black marble memorial to the Serb Unknown Soldier, and we looked back over Belgrade and he said, 'Wasn't Yugoslavia worth a world war?'

I knew what he felt and could feel with him. In the new States, Yugoslavia and Czechoslovakia and Poland, this feeling of exaltation at having expelled foreign rulers, this feeling that mastery in your own household is worth any price, is in the very air. You feel that, at last, the air you breathe is your own, and you drink it avidly in.

The killing of Alexander Obrenovitch was an efficient political assassination as these things go, in that, as he was the last of his line, it ended the feud for the throne between the Obrenovitch and Karageorgevitch which began with the rivalry of two Serb leaders of those names for the leadership of their people when the ousting of the Turks began, about 1800. Black George, the first Karageorge, a doughty fellow even for a Serb, who killed with his own hand one hundred and twenty-five people who angered him, including his father and brother, was killed in his sleep by Milos Obrenovitch and his head was sent to the Sultan at Constantinople. After that Karageorgevitch and Obrenovitch alternated on the throne, with occasional assassinations, until 1903, when the vendetta finished, because Alexander was the last Obrenovitch.

So little King Peter, who is now fourteen, has nothing to fear from that direction. The first time I saw him he was only ten and, looking wonderingly from side to side at the wailing and lamenting crowds, he walked behind the coffin of his father, just brought home from Marseilles, as it was slowly hauled past that very palace where the last Obrenovitch met his end. His mother, a tall figure shrouded in widow's weeds, towered over him; behind him came a vast concourse of foreign mourners, with many of the leading figures in the European line-up among them, such as General Göring, King Carol and President Lebrun and Sir Nevile Henderson, and I wondered what lay in store for this child.

His father, although the Obrenovitch were no more, had fallen to an assassin's bullet at Marseilles. Alexander was a most superstitious man. He left the great new Parliament building in Belgrade half-finished for many years because a gipsy woman had told him that his dynasty would fall when it was finished. Immediately after his death work was resumed on the forlorn shell and it was completed, without any ill effects to the dynasty. This superstition makes it strange that Alexander should have disembarked at Marseilles for his great State visit to Yugoslavia's friend France on a Tuesday, for the Orthodox are wont to avoid that day like the plague for any important undertaking since that Tuesday in 1453 when the Turks took

Constantinople, and centuries of Turkish oppression began for the Balkan peoples. But Alexander, although he had for years lived with the thought of assassination always in his mind, this time apparently left his superstition behind him, as well as the bullet-proof mail-shirt which he was wont to wear on such occasions and which might have saved him.

The rise of Serbia, in innumerable wars, from a tiny principality barely free from the Turks to a great modern State is, on a smaller scale, rather like that of Germany, from the Margraviate of Brandenburg through the Kingdom of Prussia to the great Third Reich, but this rapid ascent brought enmities with it to which Alexander fell a victim and at his death Yugoslavia seemed to be riven by domestic feuds and surrounded by foreign enemies, so that little King Peter, as he walked behind the coffin that day, in his grey-and-red Sokol suit with the feather in his cap, seemed to have an uncomfortable time ahead of him.

For within Yugoslavia there was the feud with the Croats, who with their home-rule demands form the most obstinate political opposition in the world, worse even than the Irish. They did not reckon merely to have exchanged rule by the Hungarians in Budapest for rule by the Serbs in Belgrade, they wanted to rule themselves in Zagreb, owning allegiance only to a common kingship. And the Serbs detested Zagreb, with its baroque buildings and indolent coffee-houses, to them it was Habsburg and Catholic and they had been brought up in their schools on the teaching that all the Slavs who were Catholics — Croats and Slovenes and Czechs and Slovaks and Poles — had lain for centuries under foreign oppression, and all the Slavs who were Orthodox — Serbs and Montenegrins and Bulgars and Russians — had fought off the tyrants and were free Slavs.

They hated the spiritual allegiance to Rome, they suspected the Croats, who had fought willy-nilly with the Austro-Hungarian armies against the Serbs in the war, of a sneaking liking for Habsburg. They wanted Yugoslavia to be nationalist to the marrow and firmly ruled from a pure Slav city, Belgrade, by a real Serb dynasty — for the Karageorgevitch are the only kings in Europe to have sprung straight from their own people, all the other dynasties are German and imported, but the only admixture of non-Serb blood in the Serb royal house is that brought in by one or two foreign princesses who had to be enlisted to secure the succession.

This rivalry between Belgrade and Zagreb is very much like that between Berlin and Vienna. In both cases you have a new capital, non-Catholic, strident, modern, rapidly growing, born in wars and victory, and an old one, Catholic, mellow, obstinately but effortlessly self-assertive.

And the upshot of the quarrel was once more — political murder. As in Germany, so in Serbia, the enemies of unity, real or imaginary, are removed. Raditch, the Croat leader, was shot in the Belgrade Parliament in 1929. Alexander suppressed all parties and set up his own dictatorship. His enemies at home and abroad united against him, and after five years he was killed.

That murder at Marseilles is a fascinating thing to study. Read all the evidence, and you will see the Danubian line-up, as it was in 1934, gradually taking shape before your eyes. Apart from her internal enemies, Yugoslavia was surrounded by foes. She had acquired territory as the result of the war from Hungary, who hated her. Italy hated her because she held the Dalmatian coast, which Italy had secretly been promised as the reward of her entry into the war on the side of the Allies. Bulgaria had fought her three times for Macedonia, and lost, and now a Macedonian Revolutionary Organization, sworn to liberate Macedonia or perish, made her eastern frontier so unsafe with raids and bombing excursions that at length it was hermetically closed by a thick wall of barbed wire and concrete machine-gun posts every few hundred yards and trenches. The Serbo-Bulgar frontier looked just like something in the world war.

Now see how these forces joined hands and struck at

Alexander. The actual murderer, the man you saw in the film jump on the running-board of Alexander's car and shoot him, was Vlada Gheorghieff, 'Vlada the Chauffeur', the right-hand gunman of Ivantcho Michailoff, head of the Macedonian revolutionaries. His accomplices, several of whom were caught in France, tried and sentenced, were Croat terrorists, disowned by the great Croat Peasant Party of the murdered Raditch and his present successor Matchek. They had received training in gunmanship and bombing on a farm in Hungary, just across the Hungarian-Yugoslav frontier, about which the Yugo-slav Government had repeatedly complained to the League and Budapest. They were given good Hungarian passports to enable them to get to France for the murder. Their leaders, Perchetz and Pavelitch, were given shelter in Italy, where another group of these Croat extremists, Ustashi, had been trained for terrorist exploits in Yugoslavia, and Italy refused to extradite them.

So the clouds seemed to be gathering thick about little King Peter that day, as I watched him mount the steps to the Kara-georgevitch Church at Oplenatz, fifty miles from Belgrade, to see his father laid to his last rest. The church, with its clustering cupolas, stands on a steep hilltop, and in the valley below lies the village from which the Karageorgevitch began their fight against the Turks. All around us were the brawny fighting men of Serbia. Round and round the hilltop, lower than our-selves, circled Yugoslav and Czechoslovak and French aircraft, the thunder of their engines drowning the clangour of the bells, and they threw out flowers for the dead King.

But actually the clouds were loosening, and a few months later fortune was smiling from ear to ear on Yugoslavia, which was in a fair way to become the spoilt darling of Europe, so did the stars in their courses conspire to favour her. Just before the King's murder Bulgarian officer conspirators, having come round to the view that the feud with Yugoslavia could only lead to disaster, not to a glorious resurrection for Bulgaria, had enforced the suppression of the Macedonian Revolutionary

Organization, which until that time had had open Bulgarian official support, and this was lucky because otherwise Vlada the Chauffeur would by his revolver shot have produced an immediate Yugoslav-Bulgar war, if not a European war, and Europe has had enough wars about that particularly dreary stretch of mountainous land, which has been so ravaged down the centuries that the Bulgars truly say 'Better a Rumanian wife or a ship at sea, than a house in Macedonia', and that is saying something.

Vlada the Chauffeur is for me an absorbing study. I saw a picture of him, naked, propped up in his coffin, that was taken by the French police for the use of their Yugoslav colleagues. He had died a terrible death, his skull smashed by a sabre cut, his body riddled by bullet holes and sword thrusts, and yet in death he seemed as full of fight as ever, his face defiant and truculent. He was not a Macedonian, but South Bulgarian, so that he could not have had the burning resentment against his victim that an actual son of Macedonia might feel. He seemed to have been just a paid gunman, who efficiently bumped off Ivantcho Michailoff's enemies, and got off scot-free through political protection. What on earth could have made the risks he took at Marseilles seem worth while to him? He could not have expected to escape. Or did he cherish that hope, and did his accomplices fail to cover his getaway?

But to revert. The ill wind that blew Italy to Abyssinia brought good to Yugoslavia, and a few months after Alexander's death, Yugoslavia, who had lived in mortal fear of an Italian attack ever since the war and had always wondered whether her allies would really come to her aid, found herself overwhelmed by offers of friendship from all quarters.

Italy, after surviving triumphant one experience of a world united against her, and of Yugoslavia with the other Mediterranean States pledged to support England against her if war came in that blue sea, completely changed her policy and ardently sought her friendship. For the Yugoslavs Italy remains the enemy, with designs on the lovely Dalmatian coast, they have no illusions about that, but for the nonce Italy is most friendly and no more Croat terrorists will be trained in Italian camps, the more so as this suits the book of Italy's associate Germany, which aims at splitting the Little Entente, the trio of anti-revisionist states in Danubian Europe pledged to France, and thinks Yugoslavia the one most likely to respond to a process of weaning away. And Hungary, under the pressure of her German and Italian protectors, has similarly called off her revisionist hounds as far as Yugoslavia is concerned.

So Prince Paul, who was hardly known to the Serbs until their King died, and his Prime Minister, Milan Stoyadinovitch, Batli Milan or Lucky Milan they call him, have been dealt a series of all-trump hands by destiny since they took over the country until King Peter comes of age. The ace of trumps has been a series of bumper harvests.

Prince Paul is the antithesis of his cousin, who had accompanied the Serb army on their retreat through Albania, who knew his generals and politicians like the back of his hand. In Prince Paul the Karageorgevitch blood has been fined down through an aristocratic Russian mother and education at an English University, and the resulting product is worlds apart from that kinsman of a hundred years ago, Karageorge, the herculean cattle-dealer who killed men because they annoyed him and led his countrymen against the Turks and managed even to establish a precarious Serbian independence in a small area, and because of his strength and ferocity and success was acknowledged by them to be the leader of the Serbs.

Prince Paul is the highly refined product of the West, a man of books, music and art. The confiscation of the Demidoff Russian estates has left him with a bitter feeling about Communists, of whom they say he sees one in every corner, and there are few countries where you need worry less about them than in Yugoslavia, but then there are such things as officials who want to prove their zeal and think you will be the more impressed by their vigilance the more reports they bring you about The Reds.

On one famous occasion there was a riot in Belgrade when the police truncheoned a church procession of protest against the agreement with the Vatican. The police statement announced that the demonstrators had been 'Communists'. One or two photographers had taken pictures and these were published soon after all over the world. They showed the 'Communists' as a few hundred Orthodox Churchmen carrying banners and headed by bearded bishops in their robes.

To the Serbs Prince Paul is little more than a name. They seldom see him. They think a great deal about their King, young Peter and about his mother, whom they knew as Alexander's queen, but she also remains mostly in retirement. Peter is usually in the country, being brought up with boys of his own age, and he is growing into a fine young man, who is going to be one of the tallest and best-built Kings in Europe, and not a bad-looking one at that, save for a rather large nose. And Belgrade, the city of awful rumour, seeing so little of them, invents fantastic stories about feuds within the Royal Family and about plots to keep Peter from the throne and plots to put Peter on the throne. It is an unfortunate thing, but it springs from the rigid censorship, which forbids any free discussion of public affairs, and from the rigorous surveillance of the population exercised by the gendarmerie, who walk about hung with lethal weapons like a Christmas tree and are not popular with their fellow-men.

I have never seen primitive passions so starkly exposed as in Serbia. An angry Serb is a man to avoid and if I were Mussolini I should make a pact of eternal friendship with the Serbs. I once saw gendarmes with loaded and bayoneted rifles rushing across the Slavia Square in Belgrade and an infuriated member of the public rushed towards them, planted himself before them, and with shirt torn open yelled to them to stick it in. On the other side of the square a little café was undergoing a siege in miniature. Men with chairs were fighting off gendarmes with bayoneted rifles and truncheons, and the amount of bangs on the head they took was astonishing.

The cause of this unpleasantness, which abruptly ceased soon afterwards because it was the hour at which you go to eat and thereafter to take your afternoon rest, was the unpopular agreement with the Vatican. Once in the Skupshtina the opposition got so angry that I thought the walls and roof would burst asunder. The point at issue was something trivial, I have forgotten what, but I know that I walked round and told the British Minister, Sir Ronald Campbell, that I had heard that some of those angry deputies were carrying revolvers with them and that I felt sure they would start shooting soon.

And sure enough two or three days later one of them, Novakovitch, who now lies in prison, tried to shoot lucky Milan Stoyadinovitch, and another deputy, who had been watching him, knocked his arm up and the bullet hit the wall just by Sir Ronald who had gone to see for himself and was imperturbably watching the scene.

Lusty fellows, one and all, the best companions you could find, friendly and amusing and loyal. If I had to be a king, which God forbid, I would choose to be King of the Serbs. They will be there at the crack of doom, these hardy peasants and mountaineers, in their braided homespun garments and sheepskin caps. My friend X, when he wakes in the morning and is not feeling too good, puts out a sleepy hand and pours himself a good swig of raki, which is just fire-water, red-hot, and after that he is equal to anything.

Belgrade is in the growing-pains stage, between a sleepy Turkish town, with pleasant shady courtyards running off at right angles from dusty streets, and near-skyscrapers, all white and crossword-puzzle-like. Great Ministries rub shoulders and before them stand the sleek American limousines of the bureaucrats. Skysigns advertise radio and aspirin in blue and mauve and pink. Cheap Jewish stores and new hotels are going up on all sides. There is a boom and the astute are making fortunes. But on all sides, poor, patient, plodding, uncomprehending, goes the peasant, the man who is really Serbia, driving his oxen, bringing his wares to market. In the afternoon everybody goes to the main boulevard for the daily promenade, to see and be seen, and that throng, pushing slowly along between the warder-like gendarmes, contains some of the best-looking and best-dressed young men and women you can find anywhere in Europe.

Belgrade will be one of the finest capitals in Europe if they plan it in time and do not spoil it by random and unco-ordinated building. As yet it has not made up its mind what it wants to be. In the hurry of the post-war years it has missed the opportunity to evolve a distinctively Serb architecture, to become a Balkan capital with a character all its own, and has gone racing after American and German ideas in architecture, with questionable success.

It has opportunities unequalled by any other city. It lies at the confluence of two great rivers, the Danube and the Save. In the middle of the main street, Piccadilly in terms of London, the ground abruptly falls away to show a rolling Balkan vista and the broad Save, with busy shipping. But as yet the Belgraders have not made up their minds what to do with this rare opportunity for town-planning. They were rather puzzled, for that matter, to know what to do with Ivan Mestrovic's war memorial, a magnificent nude figure of an armed warrior, many times more than lifesize. The city fathers decided that the closely cloistered wives and daughters of Belgrade were not yet ready for nudes, and the warrior was put away on a promontory overlooking the Danube, right down by the old Turkish citadel, where you can see him only by craning your neck.

Changes beyond their dreams, these twenty years have brought the Serbs. Twenty years ago you looked down from Kaligmegdan Gardens across the Danube and over there, that yellow building, was Semlin Station, the Austrian frontier post. And now Austria is far, far away, and you have taken Slovenia and Bosnia and Herzegovina from her and Croatia from Hungary and you have absorbed the little kingdom of Montenegro and you are well on your way to become a Great

Power, and leader of the Balkans. Now that the river and the land on both sides of it is all yours the French have built you a great bridge across your Danube. Down in the angle, where the river that flows from the Black Forest to the Black Sea, the railway that runs from Paris to Constantinople, and the trans-European motor-road that you have completed by your Danube bridge, down there where these three international highways all meet and intersect, you are putting up the permanent buildings of your great Belgrade Fair. For the Germans and Italians and Americans and Czechoslovaks, and more tardily those slowcoaches the French and British, are at last recognizing the importance of the Balkans as a buyer and seller of goods.

I am always happy when the aeroplane glides in over the Danube and I see Mestrovic's nude and the Turkish citadel and know that I am again in Belgrade. I like to eat at Kolow-ratz, where Apis used to sit, and to go and bathe in the Save and have Apis's brother pointed out to me, and to watch Princip's brother in a café, and to wander by the Royal Palace and the mouldering Russian Legation and ask them what they think of things, and to drive out to the garden restaurant at Dedigne. I like to sit in the cafés and listen to the Bulgarian gipsy girls singing. I like to take a car and go out to Smederevo, on the Danube, where the old stronghold with its twenty-four rectangular towers rising sheer on the river tells of the long struggle with the Turk.

At Smederevo I once met a man who had been at Oxford — during the war some hundreds of young Serbs were sent there, good English friends having hit on the idea that it would be a good thing to have a reservoir of English-educated Serbs to take over high office in the new and greater Serbia that was to arise from the World War. The calculation misfired in one sense. Few of them have risen to high office, but all of them retain a deep affection for England and form a valuable capital of goodwill, well invested in Serbia.

This Serb, although he lived with and for peasants, still had his New College photographs on the walls of his little home and sometimes tuned in to London on his radio. We had an enormous celebration. The Mayor and the deputy and the doctor and one or two prosperous farmers came in and we drank freely of the excellent Smederevo wine. Having occasion to go to the lavatory I found it occupied by a young sucking pig which greeted me with loud squeals, and an hour or two later this same animal, grinning in death, was served and we ate him with appetite, for roast sucking pig, as they know in Serbia, is a thing that the gods themselves would not despise.

And we ate and we drank, and we drank and we ate, and at last, comatose but happy, we set out for Belgrade, and a longish drive of many miles passed like a flash. It was a clear Balkan night, starry and cool. London, the war, Germany all seemed far away. This was Serbia, and I liked it. Perhaps, I should find myself living here some day.

CHAPTER 34

BORIS AND HIS BULGARS

I WATCHED Boris intently and curiously. He had always interested me. He stood, bareheaded, in the midst of his people, with the golden cupolas of Alexander Nevsky behind, and in the far background the peak of Mount Vitosch, with a little dab of belated snow on its shoulder, and above a vivid blue sky. Old Archbishop Stefan, his cumbersome golden crown encrusted with great red and green stones, the bearded bishops and priests all around him, intoned a benediction.

Boris's eyes travelled along the ring of faces. He stood alone, in a little cleared space, his Bulgarians about him, and his eyes never paused in their ranging scrutiny. They are curious eyes, blue, appealing, with a kind of doelike softness, but at the back a hard glint of suspicion.

Boris of Bulgaria is forty-three as I write, bald, with the long, hooked Bourbon nose that the caricaturists of his father made known throughout the world, and he has spent twenty years fighting the twin enemies of every Balkan monarch — abdication and assassination. The dominating memories of his life are of moments when these two implacable foes looked over the walls of the palace.

His father was Ferdinand, that Prince of Coburg who in the teeth of the Czar's and Bismarck's hostility agreed to become Prince of Bulgaria — the little backward Balkan country from which Russia had just driven the Turks. Under his rule Bulgaria cast off the last vestige of her Turkish vassaldom, and in twenty years Ferdinand gained the admiration of all Europe by the reforms he made and the prosperity he brought to Bulgaria. On Boris's fourteenth birthday his father summoned him and told him of the assassination in Lisbon of King Carlos of Portugal and of the Portuguese Crown Prince, who, like Ferdinand and Boris, were of the Houses of Orleans and Coburg.

Ferdinand, who lived night and day with the thought of assassination, wanted to engrave in the brain of young Boris the fact that the King and the heir to the throne were jointly and separately liable to assassination.

That is the kind of present, on your fourteenth birthday, that you do not easily forget. Boris's next dominant memory is of the moment, ten years later, when, amid the crash of falling empires and kingdoms, Crown Prince Boris, twenty-four years old, accompanied the abdicated Czar Ferdinand of the Bulgars to the frontier, and returned, a lonely man, to rule over Bulgaria.

Now another twenty years have passed, with Boris fighting coolly, like an accomplished swordsman, against abdication and assassination. For the present he seems to have fought both his enemies to a standstill. With his background, he knows these two desperadoes find their greatest opportunities in war. Boris's prevailing pre-occupation, as he looks out on the European line-up from distant Sofia, is to keep Bulgaria out of a new war, or if she must come in, this time to make sure that she comes in on the right side.

'The right side.' That is what all the monarchs and politicians in the small states, since the Abyssinian fiasco, are trying to foresee. What will the final line-up be, when the next war starts? Will it be Germany and Italy, with their satellites Hungary and Austria, against France and England and Russia? What will America do? What will our small-state neighbours do? Can we keep on good terms with all parties until we see how things are going, and then come in, at a price, on the winning side? Can we keep out and grow fat on neutrality?

The World War would probably have been over quickly if Bulgaria could have been brought in quickly on the side of the Allies. But British and French diplomacy persistently neglect the Balkans. They do not realize that countries which are small and poor and far away, and which do not buy their goods in large quantities, may be strategically vital. The same mistake is being made to-day. Germany and Italy send their best men, in politics and finance and trade, to the Balkans, spend money lavishly on making Balkan friends. And the Balkan countries are rapidly overhauling the West, building their own industries, exploiting their own mineral wealth, creating powerful armies.

Boris is the astutest monarch in Europe. He has a lonely job, he, the scion of so many princely houses, clinging on to his diminutive and primitive kingdom down there in the bottom right-hand corner of Europe, with its poor, patient and long-suffering population. His achievement in holding and consolidating his throne in these twenty years is epic. He is, in kingship, what Cinquevalli was in juggling and Blondin on a tight-rope.

His technique is quite different from that of his brother monarchs in the Balkans. The thought of assassination — not the fear of it, he is courageous — is always with him, but he does not seek to avoid it by bullet-proof cars, shirts of mail, doubles, seclusion behind a throng of plain clothes men and police. He looks it in the face. He strolls about the streets of Sofia, mixes with his people.

But his eyes and ears are everywhere. None is so well informed as he of what is afoot and what is planned. This afternoon he may appear among the throng that takes its daily promenade, about teatime, between King Boris's Palace and the Boris Park, but to-morrow morning he will not appear at a function where he had been confidently awaited.

By skill and guile he has outwitted all enemies, revolutionary plotters and military conspirators alike. In 1925 somebody blew up the Sofia Cathedral. The King was not present, though he had been expected. I remember reading, how three men who were accused of it were publicly hanged and many years afterwards Nadya told me how she, then a child, had watched their execution, three little dangling figures against a grey sky.

In 1934 officer conspirators threw troops and artillery round the palace at dead of night, entered and made the King a prisoner. Who knows just what was in their minds? Abdication or Assassination, he thought. They denied it afterwards; they only wanted to make the King abolish Parliament and the parties, they said, which he did. But who knows, if he had been found there, panic-stricken, 'a ridiculous figure' in a nightshirt, like Alexander in Belgrade in 1903? But he was not, he was in uniform and sword, sitting at a table, and as they entered he rose quietly and said, 'Well, gentlemen?'

And having forced his signature to their decree, they went away and a few months later they were all tangled up in the knotty business of trying to govern Bulgaria and had to hand the job back to somebody who understood it — Boris — and now their leader lies in durance vile and Boris reigns.

Sometimes he makes long but unostentatious journeys abroad, to see for himself how the European line-up is shaping. You see him Unter den Linden going to talk to Hitler or in London for King George's funeral, or in Paris meeting President Lebrun; you may encounter him all unexpectedly in the foyer of a theatre in Munich, unrecognized by the people around but feeling self-conscious because his appearance is Jewish and he thinks his fellow playgoers are giving him a wide berth on that account. Then he returns one day to Sofia, and you hear no more of him for a while.

His crowning piece of astuteness came in 1937, when Prince Simeon, the heir to the throne, was born. Boris married his Italian queen Joanna, who is a daughter of the King of Italy, in 1930, and in 1933, their daughter Marie Louise was born, and Bulgaria waited vainly for an heir to the throne, for Boris's only brother Cyril is unmarried, and the question of the future of the Bulgarian throne began to loom large.

This is important, because there is still that body of ardent patriots, particularly in neighbouring Serbia, who dream of the great South Slav Empire comprising all Slavs south of the Danube, including the Bulgars. To them belonged, as you will remember, Apis the Bee, of whom relatively few people in the Western World had ever heard, but who had played so great a

part in forming the events of our time. Boris was an insuper-
able obstacle to such plans, but Boris had no heir! Here was a
possibility. The South Slav patriots began to concert plans for
the marriage of young King Peter of Yugoslavia, when he
should come of age about 1941, with little Marie Louise, the
future Queen, in her own right, of Bulgaria.

So that for several years patriotic Bulgars were much worried
about the succession, but in 1937 Prince Simeon of Bulgaria
was born, amid great national rejoicing. Day and night the
peasants, pouring in from all parts of the country, filed through
the palace garden, bringing gifts of goats and sheep and oxen
and flowers and fruit. The succession was assured.

Boris is loved by the Bulgars. They like the way he drives his
own railway engine and shakes the locomotive driver's hand.
He has shaken horny hands all over Bulgaria. That is a trick
he learned from his father, that extraordinary Ferdinand who
always said he expected to be assassinated and once said to
Paléologue, 'How awful it would be if I were to end my days in
Coburg', and now lives, enormously old, at Coburg, and who
detested Sofia with his gloomy little palace and the mauve
satin furniture and loved Paris and the restaurants in the
Champs Élysées, and who once, on returning from a review
with the French President, insisted on shaking the hand of the
engine-driver, so that the wily Briand, another master of the
art of gesture, exclaimed 'What a masterpiece' and thousands
of French working men shouted '*Vive le roi*'.

The Bulgars love Boris. I don't mean the politicians in Sofia.
Politicians in any capital, save for the set in power at the
moment, dislike their ruler and fear he will lead the country
to disaster unless he calls them to power. But the common
people give him a really extraordinary affection. They don't
even bear Ferdinand any bad will, although he never liked
them and actually did bring Bulgaria to disaster; on the
contrary, they would welcome him, if he came to visit them.
What they like about Boris is what they call his simplicity and
what seems to me to be his extreme subtlety.

Bulgaria. What a country for you to consider, you who live in the confident expectation of a peaceful existence on the other side of Europe, on the other side of the Atlantic. Five hundred years under the Turks and not yet sixty years since the Russians drove the Turks out. Watching Boris that day in Sofia, my glance strayed continually to a little group of green-coated veterans, Bulgars who had helped expel the Turks at the Shipka Pass. In the city the mosques still stand, with the crescent moon above them, one of them enclasped in the arms of a great new modern bank. The little underground churches where the Christians crept to pray are still there. And in a bare half-century of liberation, already five wars.

The Bulgar has come to expect but little here below, and in the lean figures and faces of backstreet Sofia you can read the story of oppression and war and famine and plague and suffering. The police and the tax-collector treat you as their common enemy and victim, and their hand is heavy. Come to think of it, the Turks were not much worse in these respects. But in the countryside you enjoy a rude plenty and, above all, you are a Bulgar being oppressed by other Bulgars, and you are frugal and hardworking and intensely patriotic, and although you are not allowed to take much part in the affairs of your country you like your Boris and you hope that Bulgaria is yet going to become a great and rich and important country.

After the war, when Ferdinand's policy had led the country to such disaster, Bulgaria was ruled, with Boris as figurehead, by Stambulisky, who had warned Ferdinand not to join the Central Powers. Stambulisky was a peasant and they call his regime the peasant dictatorship. Well, eight Bulgars in ten are peasants, and I am not sure that the normal Bulgar regime, by which the eight peasants are ruled by two professors or bureaucrats or lawyers or journalists, with the army and police at beck and call, does not better deserve the name of dictatorship.

Anyway, Stambulisky governed the country in the interests of the peasants and was hated by the white-collar minority classes, and the army hated him too, because he saw Bulgaria's only hope in friendship with Yugoslavia, whereas the army regarded Yugoslavia, which had acquired a large slice of Macedonia from Bulgaria, as a deadly enemy, and the Macedonian Revolutionaries, who were fanatically anti-Yugoslav, thought like the army, and so did a large number of unemployed ex-officers who had been thrown out of a job through the abolition of conscription at the dictation of the victor powers. So they got together and murdered Stambulisky, I believe in a very painful way, and his body has not yet been found, and a university professor, Tzankoff, used the Macedonian revolutionaries and the army to terrorize the peasant population into submission, at the cost of two or three thousand dead Bulgars.

Together, amid loud acclamations, they restored parliamentary government to Bulgaria. That was in 1923 and 1924. Ten years later the wheel had turned full circle. The same retired officer who planned the murder of Stambulisky, one Colonel Damian Veltcheff, led the raid on Boris's Palace and forced the king to suppress Parliament and parties, his own gift to Bulgaria ten years before. The army had in the meantime come round to the view of Stambulisky, now unfortunately beyond a glorious political resurrection, that Bulgaria must become reconciled with Yugoslavia, and thus make one gap in the ring of enemies about her, or she looked like disappearing altogether.

On account of this change, the Macedonian revolutionaries, working for a Macedonia either independent or under Bulgarian rule, came to hate the army, and in order to discredit it framed a charge of espionage in the Yugoslav interest against an army officer, whom they kidnapped and tortured. Thus the first thing the officers did, when they made Boris prisoner, was to suppress the Macedonians who had for years been shooting politicians distasteful to them in the streets of Sofia. The officers did this just in the nick of time, for Alexander of Yugoslavia was killed by Vlada the Chauffeur five months later, the last kick of the Macedonians for the time being, and if the

Macedonians at that time had still been sunning themselves in official patronage in Sofia an immediate Yugoslav invasion of Bulgaria would have followed.

Then the officers, who had been deeply impressed by Hitler's methods in Germany and the benefits that the German army was deriving from them, turned Parliament into a Propaganda Ministry, placarded the tramcars with self-laudatory notices about 'the new Bulgaria', which the Bulgar regarded with bleak incomprehension, because the policeman and the tax-collector were giving him just as rough a deal as ever, and generally put up a cheap lath-and-plaster imitation of the National Socialist Dictatorship. But after a few months they were in such a muddle that they handed the job back to Boris, on the condition that there should be no resurrection of party politics, and a few months after that the Government, now all King's men once more, announced that a plot against the King had been discovered, and the good Colonel Damian Veltcheff was sentenced to death and barely escaped with a reprieve. He was luckier than his opposite number in Belgrade, Apis the Bee. I saw him sentenced.

But though the officer conspirators are in gaol, and the other officers are so busy with rearmament that they have little time and little opportunity to conspire against the King and Government, the political blank that they made of Bulgaria remains. Nobody knows now what Bulgars are thinking about, whether they are for democracy or dictatorship, whether they want in the next war to fight with or against the martial dictators. Boris is working cautiously to give the country a Parliament again.

The present regime in Bulgaria began as a copy of National Socialist Germany, and you might take that for an indication that in a new European war Bulgaria would again be on the side of Germany. But the last decision will lie with that astute monarch King Boris, who has no mind to give his prostrate enemies, Abdication and Assassination, another chance at him.

I once watched a parade of the Bulgarian army. The troops

were armed with ancient Schneider guns that had done duty in the two Balkan wars and the World War (can you wonder if officers conspire in such circumstances), but the troops were the finest, in appearance, I had ever seen outside Germany. They were staggeringly good, and at this moment they are getting all the nice new toys that soldiers love and are becoming a very formidable army. And the young cadet officers you see in Sofia are living answers to the maiden's prayer.

Sofia I have found expensive and dull. It combines the main characteristics of an English cathedral city and a German *Residenzstadt*, so sombre is its respectability, so grim its decorum. It is the most primly proper capital in Europe. In Sofia to-day you simply cannot imagine Vlada the Chauffeur shooting his victims, Georgi Dimitroff of the Reichstag Fire Trial planning his armed Communist insurrection of 1923 against the Fascist terror of Tzankoff, the officers and the Macedonians. Sedateness stalks the streets. Night life is none, save for two or three gloomy bars full of Hungarian girls imported, under the clearing system, against Bulgarian gardeners sent to Hungary. The Hungarian dancing girls' wages are paid to the relatives of the Bulgarian gardeners, the Bulgarian gardeners' earnings are credited in Budapest to the account of the Hungarian dancing girls, and I think this must be one aspect of what you call sound finance and I call Insanity Fair. It is a strange thing, the explanation of which I should like to know, that the Catholic countries stock the bars and dance halls and brothels of Europe with girls, while you seldom find in these places a girl from an Orthodox country — a Serb, a Bulgar, a Greek.

As I watched Boris that day, standing in the sun and running his eyes over the phalanx of serving officers and the phalanx of reserve officers, all standing devotedly at the salute, I wondered what was in his mind and guessed that he was thinking, 'Ah, you, X, and you, Y, and you, Z, you look a model of soldierly discipline and loyalty, but I have got wind of your leanings for Veltcheff, of your membership of the Officers' League. I shall have to keep an eye on you'. That was before he had emerged triumphant from the tussle with the conspiratorial Officers' League by giving them something else to think about — re-armament. In the evening, with all Sofia, I walked through the gardens of the little palace, which is like a villa in Tooting, and saw him waving to the enthusiastic crowds that went by beneath, hour after hour. It was a great Sokol festival, a mass rally of those patriotic athletes who, in all the Slav countries, keep alive the spark of patriotism and of hatred of foreign oppressors, and the red shirts and feathered caps from Yugo-slavia were there in masses.

For fifteen years the Bulgars had been living inside an iron ring of enemies, all determined to hold territory which they had and to which Bulgaria laid claim — Yugoslavia, Greece, Rumania, Turkey. The Bulgars had had little cause for making whoopee in these post-war years. Now they had become reconciled with at least one of their neighbours, and that their kinsman, the Serb.

They let themselves go. In the park hard by the palace they joined hands, Serb and Bulgar, and danced the horo to a military band. A traversing searchlight lit the dancing figures and the clouds of dust rising into the air. An endless chain of dancers, a long step and two short steps, steps forward and steps backward, winding in and winding out, Sokol uniforms and peasant costumes, a festival of Slav music and song and dance and colour.

From his palace windows Boris, the scion of the Bourbons and Orleans and Coburgs and Koharys, looked down medi-tatively on his simple peasant people and their guests. Serb and Bulgar. Fraternization. A very good thing too, as far as it went. But it must not go too far, or you would have one of those two enemies creeping up behind it.

CHAPTER 35

GRECIAN DETOUR

It was cold that Sunday night on the little Greek destroyer, with its scrubby-chinned and lackadaisical crew, as she rattled and plunged from Athens to the Corinth Canal. Beyond, in the Adriatic, a gale had been blowing, and had left a gusty breeze and a sky ragged with scurrying clouds, and it had only abated just in time, or King George II of Greece would have had to put off his homecoming for forty-eight hours; his subjects would not have wished him to tempt Providence as Alexander of Yugoslavia had done and land on a Tuesday, that day on which the Turks had taken Constantinople nearly five hundred years before.

Up on the bridge a French girl journalist, who for all I know may have been a great writer but was certainly a mistress of the art of exploiting sex appeal and for some weeks kept all the interviewable people in Athens happy in the expectation of favours that never came, vamped the captain. On the wet iron decks we huddled together and sought shelter from the wind, G. E. R. Gedye and Pembroke Stephens and Harold Peters and the rest of us, the eyes and ears of the waiting world. In these days of dictatorships and censors we were coming to regard the three monkeys as the symbol of our craft, and 'See nothing, hear nothing, know nothing' as its motto, but still, from time to time, came some event, like the homecoming of a king, on which we could, without misgiving, lavish such gifts of description as we had.

Late at night we anchored before the dark and narrow canyon of the Corinth Canal and waited for the dawn. Beyond it lay Corinth, still half ruined from the earthquake, and the currant fields and the remains of those colonnaded streets where the golden youth of Greece had been wont to dally, and the blue gulf of Corinth, and the Temple of Apollo looking across at

Mount Parnassus, where for all I know the gods might still be shaking with homeric laughter at the comic antics of mankind in this nether world.

It was a long wait, but at last the old cruiser *Helle* emerged from the gloom of the Corinth Canal, little more than a black mass barely distinguishable from the surrounding darkness, and we fell into line behind and began the short voyage to Athens.

This restoration of a Balkan king was one of the loveliest things I have ever witnessed. Gradually the stars paled and the *Helle* took shape, with its double line of escorting destroyers and torpedo boats, and the water changed from black to grey and then to deepest blue, and suddenly the sun shot over the shoulder of historic Salamis and blazed a golden trail down the bay to show us the way to Athens, and from astern came fast coastal motor-boats that shot between the escorting vessels and the *Helle* on great curving wings of silver-spray, like flying fish, and overhead from Athens came seaplanes and aeroplanes that dipped to salute us and in the distance the vivid green of olive trees framed the blue water.

At last the little armada came to Athens, where the cliffs of the Piraeus and the waterfront of Phaleron were packed with people, and the sirens of the men-of-war and merchantmen and the horns of the motor cars incessantly tooted and hooted in a unison of three beats that meant 'Er-che-tai, er-che-tai' — 'Here he comes, here he comes'. It was the welcome that they had given King Constantine at his restoration, and now they gave it to King George at his.

While we watched, unshaven and still chilled from the night watch, a fast launch shot out from under the *Helle's* bows and a minute later the King of the Hellenes set foot on Greek soil and was greeted by General Kondylis, the King Maker, the soldier-politician who had expelled him and brought him back, a weird, paunchy figure in ill-fitting evening clothes. And King George, late of Brown's Hotel, London, drove up the long straight street from Phaleron to the capital, past the great monuments of Greek and Roman civilization, to the Parliament building, that had been his father's palace, and showed himself on the balcony to his wildly enthusiastic Athenians who cheered and cheered and would not disperse.

How Prussian he looks, I thought, as I watched him. His bottle-green uniform was on the French model, but his monocle, his features and bearing all reminded me strongly of a Prussian officer. Perhaps he had caught the trick from his service with his uncle's Prussian Guards in Berlin before the World War, for his uncle was that Kaiser Wilhelm who now was a squire in exile at Doorn, complaining of the world that had treated him so scurvily, and his mother was that Kaiser's sister.

He is the fifth king that Greece, after ousting the Turks, has had in a hundred years. He is the second King of Greece to have been King of Greece twice during the past twenty years.

Greece, like Rumania and Bulgaria, followed the earlier English example and looked to Germany for a king. They sent the first one, Otto of Bavaria, back after twenty years; they say he had queer ideas about castles, like his kinsman Ludwig, and at one time wanted to pull down the Acropolis and build a palace there. Then the Greeks put Prince George of Schleswig-Holstein on their throne, and he reigned happily for forty years until his assassination in 1913, and was succeeded by his son Constantine, him for whom the Athenians first cried 'Er-che-tai, er-che-tai'.

That was the beginning of twenty years of domestic strife that gave Greece no rest. For the accession of Constantine coincided with the rise of Venizelos, a politician of rare quality. Greece might be ruled well by a strong-willed king with a succession of compliant Prime Ministers, or by a strong-minded statesman with one or more compliant kings, but when the two come together the result is like mixing a Seidlitz powder, and Greece fizzed. Constantine and Venizelos both acquired great popularity from the Greek victories in the first Balkan War, with Serbia and Bulgaria against Turkey, and the second Balkan War, with Serbia against Bulgaria, and when the spoils were finally divided after the second one Greece had almost doubled her territory and population.

But then came the World War and the conflict of wills. Venizelos wanted to come in with the Allies, and had visions of further Greek expansion in Asia Minor. Constantine, by all good evidence, wanted to keep Greece out of the war altogether, but Venizelos and the Allies thought he was playing a pro-German game and suspected the influence of his Queen.

This led to the spectacle of Greece torn in two halves — Venizelos sitting at Salonica at the head of a Provisional Government and fighting with the Allies, Constantine beleaguered by the Allies in his Palace at Athens and even bombarded by them, so that King George II's memories of his early manhood include a vivid picture of a day when Allied shells fell in the courtyard of the palace and his mother, the Queen, had to put her children in the cellar. A few months before this the Allies had even sent a small landing party up that straight from Phaleron to Athens, along which King George came on his restoration, and they were driven back by Greek troops with the bayonet, and the Queen telegraphed triumphantly to her brother the Kaiser that the troops of four Great Powers had fled before the Greeks, 'and may the infamous swine receive the punishment they deserve'.

At last, on June 12th, 1917, the Allies expelled King Constantine by force, and would not have his eldest son, Prince George, who is now King, on the throne, but his supposedly more compliant younger brother Alexander. And thus Greece, under Venizelos and Alexander, came in with the Allies, and at the Sèvres Peace Conference in August 1920 Greece obtained further large slices of Turkish territory, on the edge of Europe and in Asia Minor, and Venizelos's policy seemed to have been triumphantly justified. But in October 1920 Alexander inopportunely died of a monkey's bite and the Greeks, who had never forgiven the Allies for their expulsion of Constantine, overwhelmingly voted for his return, so that Venizelos was

283

humiliated and Constantine came back, and Greece resounded with the three-beat greeting 'Er-che-tai!'

But then the Turks turned round and in 1922 drove the Greeks out of their newly acquired possessions in Asia Minor, and once more Venizelos seemed to have been vindicated and Constantine was discredited, so that the army, smarting under this military disaster, and the nation, weary from eight years of war conditions, dethroned Constantine again — he died in exile — and made George king. The Revolutionary Committee, which made him king, shot out of hand several generals supposed to be responsible for the defeat in Asia Minor. King George soon became unpopular with the Republicans; he did not recall Venizelos, as they wished, and General Metaxas, who is his Prime Minister to-day, launched a revolt against the Revolutionary Committee. And about this time General Kondylis, the King Maker of twelve years later, was wont to speak of Constantine as 'the king of perdition and shame' and the dynasty as one of 'cowards and traitors' and he played a chief part in bringing about George's expulsion.

Well, well, women have no monopoly of changing minds and twelve years later General Kondylis obsequiously bowed as King George II stepped on to the landing stage. Kondylis, for a brief while dictator of Greece, had brought him back. He had driven Venizelos, his old chief, out, and suppressed by arms his attempt to save the Republic. Kondylis interested me and I was glad to find myself sitting talking to him in his study.

Here was another dictator, and I was by way of collecting dictators. He was surrounded by lethal weapons; even his inkpots and spittoons were made in the shape of cannon and machine-guns, and the walls were covered with portraits of Corporal Kondylis (the rank of Corporal ought to be suppressed, Napoleon was a corporal, and Hitler, and Mussolini, there is obviously something dangerous about it) fighting the Bulgars and General Kondylis fighting the Turks. He was fantastically vain — and a dying man. He did not know it, any more than other dictatorial natures I have met. I could see it in his eyes and swollen neck. Here, I thought, is the secret of the new turn in Greek politics, that twilight period in a man's mind before darkness enshrouds him.

Kondylis had organized the plebiscite for the King's return. The plebiscite ran true to contemporary form and the result was almost 100 per cent for the King. As La Rochefoucauld said, that which is exaggerated is not true, and this result was an exaggeration of the state of Greek feeling. But by the time the King actually returned, helped by encouraging messages from his father's and his own old enemy Venizelos in Paris, he was really popular.

The King's first act was politely to dismiss the incalculable Kondylis, and to guarantee absolute equality and justice to all Greeks. Then death stepped in and within a few weeks cleared the board of all his main problems. Kondylis, Venizelos, his first Prime Minister Demerdjis, the leader of the Popular Party Tsaldaris, all died within a few weeks.

King George was left with a clear board and, within a few months of his restoration, was able to appoint as Prime Minister General Metaxas, who had led the unsuccessful anti-Revolutionary Committee revolt during his first kingship.

A few months later a bewildered Greece learned that it had been saved overnight from an impending Communist revolution by the suspension of the Constitution, the abolition of parties and parliament, and so on. This happened on August 4th, and the nation was only just saved, because 'bloodshed would have started throughout Greece on August 5th', if the Government hadn't acted. Greece had been rescued in the nick of time by Metaxas, as Germany by Hitler and Göring after the Reichstag fire, as Austria by Dollfuss and Starhemberg and Fey. Greece became another blank on the political map of Europe.

General Metaxas, a short, plump and bespectacled man, is an interesting figure. He never had more than five or six supporters in Parliament, so that he could have risen to power by no other means than the King's collaboration in the suppression of Parliament and the fortunate accident of the impending Communist revolution. I contemplated him with interest, because he was one of the men whom the Allies in the war had accused of belonging to the pro-German group around Constantine. He, like King George, had had a military education in Germany. He had a great reputation as a soldier. They called him 'the Little Moltke', and he was Greek chief-of-staff when the World War broke out.

Anyway, it was interesting that the first act of his collaboration with King George should be to abolish parliamentary government and introduce a dictatorial regime by methods which looked as if they had been taken from a primer of German National Socialism. As Germany was saved from Bolshevism, so was Greece saved from Bolshevism. The Bolshevism was not apparent, you have to have faith nowadays. As Germany became 'the new Germany' so Greece became 'the new Greece'. As Marxist books were burned by students outside Berlin University so were Marxist books burned by students outside Athens University. As in Germany, all domestic bickering ceased and a cathedral hush spread over the country, so long a pandemonium of political quarrels. As in Germany, opposition politicians disappeared quietly into captivity; Greece has many islands.

General Metaxas is a man who gives good advice. It has been proved. As he told me, he advised Lord Kitchener not to try and force the Dardanelles by the proverbial British strategy of battering at the front door, but to come down through the garden and force the back door. His advice was not taken, more's the pity, and this is said to have offended him.

They say that he also gave King Constantine a piece of advice in the matter of choosing between the Allies and Germany, and I am not sure whether this advice was so good. The advice was, if report is true, 'If Greece comes in with the Allies and Germany wins, Greece is finished. If Greece comes in with Germany and the Allies win, Greece will be let down lightly. Therefore Greece should come in with Germany'.

When King George came back to Athens his father's other adviser who was so much disliked by the Allies, M. Streit, King Constantine's Foreign Minister, was still living in his villa some miles outside the city. When I saw the German-descended M. Streit he was wearing a swastika tiepin and I thought for a moment that all that had been said in the war about his German sympathies must be true. But I learned that it was a present, twenty-years old, from Constantine himself.

Greece is one of the smaller sideshows in Insanity Fair, but not an unimportant one. Her harbours and strategical position are valuable. King George, as he looks out on the European line-up from Athens, finds an alignment of forces taking shape very much like that which so perplexed his father in 1914 — Germany seems in military might far superior to any other power on land, but Greece is surrounded by sea and England is still the strongest naval power. He has one complication less, in that he has no pestilent Venizelos; he has one complication more, in that Italy is the ally of Germany and the Greek shores lie within a few hours' or minutes' reach by Italian war vessels and aircraft.

How can we keep out of war if it comes, or if we can't keep out, how can we spot the winning side? The same question plagues rulers and politicians everywhere.

Consider King George's background. On the one hand, his youthful service with the Prussian Guards, his mother's relationship to the German Emperor, the Allied shells falling in the palace courtyard, the Allied humiliation of his father and himself.

On the other hand, twelve years of exile spent almost entirely in England, often as a guest at Court, at Balmoral, in the Royal Box at Ascot, at the weddings of the Dukes of Kent and Gloucester.

I thought over these things as I watched him that day on the balcony, acknowledging the plaudits, his tall brother, the Diadoch Paul, beside him; George has not remarried and is childless but the Diadoch is looking after the succession, having married Princess Friederike of Brunswick-Lüneberg, a grand-daughter of the Kaiser. I watched him driving away, escorted by his Evzones in their white fustanellas, embroidered jackets and tasselled fezzes — the Evzones, I ought to mention, are the handsomest soldiers in the world — to try and restore order in the palace, cobwebbed with long neglect. I watched him again as he shook hands with us of the world's newspapers, and found him self-possessed, wary, and without illusions.

Then I went back to the Grande Bretagne, where Herr Schmidt rules by day and Miss Smith by night, and where in the bar you will sooner or later meet everybody of account, coming in from the Imperial Airways flying boat or driving up in a motor car dusty from a Balkan tour or breaking the train journey to Constantinople for a night. Outer Athens is poverty stricken and drear; but here you will see white-shirted and top-hatted gentlemen who go about in bevies and partake amply of the fleshpots and are known generically as the Power and Traction, British brains that provide the Athenian masses with tramcar transport and electric light and apparently do very well from it, and since good General Metaxas came there have been no more of those annoying labour troubles. Outside in the poorer cafés you will still see old gentlemen smoking hookahs, that purr like cats as the water bubbles up, or telling their amber beads to keep themselves from drinking and smoking. Here in the bar of the Grande Bretagne is the Western World.

I ordered a drink and spent a quarter of an hour discussing with others of my kind a telegram that one of us had just received from his editor, one of those go-getters who earn big salaries for telling other men to go-get. This is how it read:

WELCOME FOR SUNDAY GOOD COLOURFUL STORY BASED ON INTERVIEW WITH KING GEORGE BUT NO POLITICAL STUFF ONLY HUMAN INTEREST WANTED SUGGESTED THEME LOOKING BACK ON LONDON DAYS COCKTAIL TIME WITH THOUGHT GOOD BYE ALL THAT

288

I am in a position to be able to reveal, as some of my fellow-craftsmen say, that King George had at least one good laugh during the first few difficult days of his restoration, and that was when he read this telegram.

I went out to Soulion, where Byron had carved his name on a column of a white temple on a headland overlooking islet-speckled sea. I swam, in December, in warm blue water and trod on spikey little creatures that hurt abominably, and I fled before shoals of dark blue jellyfish. Treasures worth millions are still lying beneath the ground along these coasts, and the peasants know better than the archaeologists where to look for them, they know just where the wealthy Greeks had their estates, but the law is stringent and priceless things will continue to moulder under the soil because the peasant has to surrender what he finds.

I wonder why a profit-sharing scheme of excavation is not introduced, which would make it worth the peasants' while to apply their knowledge. Sometimes a well-organized illicit expedition goes out under cover of night, digs up some marvellous piece of statuary, buries it in a stable while negotiations are carried on with the dealers in Athens, and then one dark night it is brought out to some quiet spot on the coast, put in a fishing boat, transferred at sea to a cargo steamer, and months later in Paris a wealthy American writes a six-figure cheque for it.

At night I came back to Athens. The Acropolis was floodlit, in honour of the King's return. Standing on its hill top, with the black mass of the hill beneath, and under that the myriad lights of Athens, it seemed to be suspended from the sky. The Turkish Pashas, the Byzantine Empire, the Vandal hordes, the Roman legions, the Republics of Ancient Greece, have all come and gone and Athens is a backward little capital, with a Germanic King, struggling to catch up with the great cities of the Mechanical Age. But the Acropolis outlasts them all, and it is good for another thousand years or more.

CHAPTER 36

GETTING THROUGH DARDENELLES

NAKED as on the day I was born, I drew my oars into the boat and looked around. The Lake of Geneva is just five miles across at the Montreux end, something over an hour's steady pull either way, and when you are half-way across you are clean out of sight from the land and can be a nudist without feeling that you are being depressingly conventional.

I have swum all over Europe, in the Seine, Marne, Rhine, Spree, Danube, Vistula, Save, Traun, Inn, North Sea, Baltic, Mediterranean, Adriatic, Wannsee, Lake Mirow, Lake Balaton, Lake Constance, Lake Lugano, but I know of no swimming that compares with that in Lake Geneva, at the Montreux end and far out in the middle.

The water is forget-me-not blue, and as clean as if it were taken out every day and washed and it sparkles and invigorates like champagne. It is nectar itself, it falls straight out of the heavens on to the mountains near at hand and comes straight down to you, little man, spluttering around, an infinitesimal speck somewhere in the middle. In the distance the snow-crusted fangs of the Dent du Midi, above you a burnished blue sky and a blazing sun, around a green and flowery lakeside. On the slopes grows a wine as friendly as the water itself, gay and cheering and without a hint of malice in it, and at Villeneuve a little hotel gives you meals of omelet and fish and chicken and *pommes frites* and cress and cheese and fruit that you never forget.

After a month of it I was for the first time in my life done really brown on both sides and *durchgefüttert*, and yet I hadn't an ounce of spare flesh, but more muscle than I had ever had before. Somehow I had in forty years never fed properly, and realized it now for the first time. In those office-boy days in London before the war you snatched meals of ham-rolls and chocolate, and during the war it was bully-beef hash and biscuits, and wounds pulled you down, and after the war as you bicycled about with your unwanted maps you inadequately stilled your hunger with bread and cheese or joint and two veg., and then you ate miserably in a *prix fixe* restaurant in Paris, and in those rackety nerve-absorbing years in Berlin you ate at all hours of the day and night, and often drank and smoked too much.

I had always had a vision of the day when I would get really fit, but my conception of the process was exercise, more exercise, and still more exercise, and I never thought about the dietary side of the question, thinking that the main thing was to eat as little as possible. I had always rather disliked eating, but now I suddenly realized the inward strength that good food gives, without it all your exercise is wasted, and I ate voraciously and felt my limbs responding obediently as I strove after the machine-like precision of the crawl and played tennis better than I ever had before, and in the evening sat down to write with a head as clear as the water of Lake Geneva itself.

So I stood up in the boat, soaped off the sunburn oil, said Bon Jour to the Dent du Midi, which answered politely, Bon Jour, Sir Reed, and plunged in and swam round in a circle and then chased after my boat and climbed in and frisked myself down with a rough towel, and thanked God for the Dardanelles.

The Dardanelles had been always with me, more or less; I could not describe them, but felt that I should know them, like the elephant, if I saw them. Far back in the war, when we were stuck in the mud in Flanders, we had for a time reposed great hopes in our distant comrades who were getting through the Dardanelles, until we realized that they were just as badly stuck as we were.

It was, it seemed, one of those typically British enterprises which only British pluck and British brains venture upon. Headlong you hurled yourself upon an enemy impregnably fortified, as on the Somme, as at Passchendaele, and after great loss of life you came to a standstill, and you then took great pride in this operation and wrote poems about it, like the Charge of the Light Brigade at Balaclava, which seems to have been the result of an inexcusable mistake of the most elementary kind in the transmission of orders between staff officers, so that a French general aghast said it was magnificent but not war, and for some incomprehensible reason you took that as a compliment, whereas I should have thought that the job of soldiers was to make war and not to be magnificent.

In no other trade are the experts told that their mistakes are magnificent. If a motor-bus driver were told to drive straight through the barrier at a level crossing and were in consequence demolished with his passengers, nobody would say that was magnificent, they would say it was madness. It is confusing and seems to have something to do with the Public School Spirit and the Playing Fields of Eton.

However, I agreed that the Dardanelles were magnificent. Nations had been fighting about them, without any particular gain to anybody, since the wars of Troy, but they had brought me this month on Lake Geneva, and that was far more important. Far away on the lakeside I could see a golden glint, the sun striking on the great sign of the Montreux Palace Hotel. Inside, in a vitiated atmosphere, the conference was sitting. I was out here on the lake. The conference would not rise until the late afternoon. Then I could return, learn what had happened, and write in the cool of the evening.

For away back at that League meeting at Geneva, when Germany was condemned for tearing up the peace treaty and proclaiming her rearmament, the Turkish delegate, that Tewfik whom we called Toothache for short, and who is now Rushdi Aras, the Turkish Foreign Minister, had intimated that while Turkey would join in the general condemnation of Germany, she would not indefinitely submit to discriminatory military penalties, imposed after a lost war, which other defeated countries had thrown off. She would require to refortify the Straits.

Next year the Turkish generals, seeing that Germany had got away with rearmament and was highly respected by the countries that had condemned her, had been urging their Government to reoccupy and refortify the Straits, and be hanged to the world. Ever-widening ripples were spreading from the stone that Germany had thrown into the European pond. But the Turkish Government, more consistent than many others, refrained, and asked the other signatories of the Straits Convention to meet in conference and agree by negotiation on her demand.

There were loud plaudits from the Western World, where French and British Prime and Foreign Ministers hardly dared at this time to go for their week-end fishing or golf for fear of one of Hitler's Saturday morning surprises. The Sick Man on the Bosphorus had become the Good Boy of Europe. There was eloquent French approbation. There was weighty British approval. There was Turkish delight.

A conference was called at Montreux. Switzerland, a country which realized long ago that the more wars you have the more lucrative peace conferences you will need, warned M. Motta and his liveried attendant to be ready to welcome the delegates. The pot plants were installed, the chairs arranged in rows. The conference began.

So far, so good. The thing seemed simple enough. Turkey had to be courteously conceded, in proper legal form, a right which could not be denied. The Mediterranean, at its eastern end, narrows into the Dardanelles, the Sea of Marmora and the Bosphorus, on the European shore of which Constantinople stands, and these Straits widen again into the great Black Sea, a gigantic lake, the southern shore of which is the Turkish coast. Give Turkey the right to close these Straits in wartime and no enemy could come through and stab her in her vast exposed flank; her only vulnerable coast would be the little strip on the Mediterranean, or Aegean Sea.

You might think it strange that England in 1936 should have been ready gracefully to concede something for which she

293

was ready to fight a new war in 1922, four years after the World War had finished. For after the World War Turkey had been pushed right out of Europe, in favour of the Greeks, save for a last tiny foothold right down in the bottom right-hand corner — Constantinople, that the Turks had held since that fateful Tuesday in 1453. Thus Turkey only held one side of the Straits, and England, mindful of her heavy losses in trying to force them during the World War and take Germany in flank, had made it a fundamental principle of her policy that nobody should ever be able again to close the Straits. They were to be 'Free in peace or war'. The only way to ensure that was to see that the opposite sides were held by different states.

But in 1922 the Turks drove the Greeks out of their gains on the Turkish side, in Asia Minor, and then turned towards the Allied armies with the evident intention of driving them out, crossing the Straits and pushing the Greeks out of their newly-acquired Turkish territory in Thrace, on the European side.

At that moment England, under Mr. Lloyd George, invited the Dominions and the Balkan States to share in the defence of the Straits. The British Empire was ready to go to war for this 'freedom of the Straits', and yet fourteen years later the British Empire, at Montreux, was ready to consent to the maximum restriction of the freedom of the Straits, through their re-fortification. Why? Because in 1922 Mr. Lloyd George was apparently bluffing, and a few days after sounding the call to arms announced that England was only concerned to defend 'the freedom of the Straits' and would not fight 'for Eastern Thrace'. That was like saying that you would fight for the freedom of the Panama Canal but not for the land on either side of it. And a few days later an armistice was signed which gave back Thrace, and therewith the European shore of the Straits, to Turkey and sent the Greeks scurrying out of it again.

So thus you had Turkey astraddle the Straits again, in 1922, and although at Lausanne in 1923 the Turks undertook not to fortify or garrison the shores of the Straits, Turkey, as the man in possession, was actually master of them and could at any moment have closed them by moving up heavy artillery to the shores and concentrating aircraft and mine-layers near or on its waters. The freedom of the Straits, in war, was a fiction, the principle for which you have been ready to go to war had been surrendered when you let Turkey step across into Europe again, and in formally conceding her right to refortify and garrison the Straits in 1936 you were only making a ninety-per-cent probability into a hundred-per-cent certainty.

So you might think that the task of those delegates, sitting round the table in the Montreux Palace Hotel while the sun shone outside, was quite straightforward — just to put a good face on a bad job and thank Turkey for making an honest man of Europe by negotiating instead of springing a new surprise on that oft-wronged continent.

Far from it. This was the least of the tasks of the Montreux Conference. The Straits widen, at either end, into the Mediterranean and the Black Sea, and the Conference widened into the Niagara of Great Power politics. For you had simultaneously to decide what warships should, in peace or war, claim legitimate right of way through the Straits and into the Black Sea, and the Black Sea meant Russia, for whom it was a pond just under the drawing-room window. For Russia the conference was dominated by Germany, who was not present at it, but whose hand she saw in every proposal. For Russia the Black Sea was the Round Pond, and for the other powers the Mediterranean was the Serpentine. Russia wanted the Round Pond for herself, but she also insisted on her right to come and play on the Serpentine. The others wanted her to stay out of the Serpentine unless they too were allowed to go and play on the Round Pond.

It was, in fact, a new stage in the European line-up. In the bedrooms of the Montreux Palace Hotel the Great Powers sparred for position. They met at the conference table, produced new proposals which immediately aroused violent suspicions from other interested parties, and returned to the bedrooms to telephone for instructions. Litvinoff, wary and sceptical, telephoned to Moscow. Lord Stanley telephoned to London. Paul-Boncour, that velvet-tongued lawyer, telephoned to Paris. I don't know who telephoned to Berlin, but a spectral though not a flesh and blood Germany was always present, scaring the delegates.

It was a strenuous tussle, that lasted a month. It turned almost entirely on two main issues: what foreign warships should be allowed into the Black Sea (1) in peace, (2) in war, Turkey being a neutral.

Now in wartime, if Turkey were neutral and not his ally, no admiral from the outer world would dare to pass through the Straits, because Turkey might join the other side while he was within and close the door, so that this whole discussion soared into clouds of unreality.

Soviet Russia, in the stout person of Litvinoff, thought England was playing Germany's hand at Montreux, and indeed it often looked like that. The discussion went something like this.

Russia and France said: 'Let's see, wartime, Turkey being neutral. I tell you what, let's close the Straits entirely to all war-vessels in wartime save for those sent by the League against an aggressor or, if the League should fail to reach agreement on action against an aggressor, for warships operating under pacts of mutual assistance concluded within the framework of the League Covenant, which allows for precisely that emergency. You, England, are all for the League.'

And England answered: 'Ah, you are thinking of your Franco-Soviet Pact. You want to close the Straits to all others than yourselves. No, no, that would never do. That would make Turkey an accessory after the Pact. It would place Turkey in a Most Invidious Position.'

To which France and Russia answered: 'Ah, now you are trying to sabotage our Franco-Soviet Pact, specifically designed by our best jurists to fill that gap which the League Covenant itself foresees — League failure to order joint action against an aggressor. But you specifically approved of our Franco-Soviet

Pact, you agreed that it was consonant with the League Covenant, you approved of a decision of The Hague Court being sought, at Geneva you have consistently supported the idea of regional and mutual assistance pacts dovetailed into the League Covenant by League States seeking to find joint security against an aggressor.'

And England: 'Ahem, we feel that Turkey should not be required to discriminate between belligerents under agreements to which she is not a party. This would place Turkey in An Extremely Difficult Position.'

France and Russia: 'Aw shucks, you know perfectly well what you are at, you don't want our Franco-Soviet Pact inter-locked with this new convention because Germany doesn't like it and would start yelping about being encircled again. Who is it that's always talking about having a go at Russia, after all? Who proclaims that slices ought to be carved off Russia for the settlement of Germany's surplus population — Hitler, Hugenberg, Schacht, Rosenberg, Germany.'

England: 'Er — I must maintain that your proposal would place Turkey in a Distinctly Embarrassing Position.'

Meanwhile, the impetuous Titulescu of Rumania, friend of France and the League and collective action against an aggressor, hears what is happening in his bedroom and comes rushing downstairs and flings into the conference room and bangs on the table, crying in faultless French: 'You, England, why do you support mutual assistance pacts at Geneva and oppose them here at Montreux scarcely twenty miles away? What is your little game? Give us a definite declaration of your policy, whether you are opposed to the operation of these pacts or not. I, Nicolai Titulescu, who for once in a long while am going in a few moments to the capital of my native country, I tell you that this is vital for Rumania.'

And Rumania flings out to catch the train, leaving Lord Stanley and Sir Alexander Cadogan to tell his disappearing coat-tails that this is a Most Discourteous Proceeding.

Then we all consult our Governments, Rendel goes to

London, and Litvinoff takes a trip to the mountains, and Paul-Boncour disappears to Paris, and after a few days we all re-assemble and England says: 'I tell you what, let's close the Straits in wartime, Turkey being neutral, to all warships except those exercising their Belligerent Rights.'

France and Russia: 'Did you say "belligerent rights"?'

England: 'Yes. A fleet that has fought an engagement with a Black Sea enemy in the Mediterranean should not be prevented from chasing that enemy if he flees through the Straits.'

France and Russia: 'Ah, so you would open the Straits to an aggressor, but close them to fleets operating against an aggressor condemned by the League or under mutual assistance pacts concluded within the Covenant of the League for the event that the League fails to order action? You are playing the German game, and why? Did not your Eden, in Moscow a year ago, declare that there was no conflict of interests on any major issue between England and Russia? Why do your proposals so clearly reveal the thought of hostilities against Russia, either by yourselves or by Germany? But we will meet you. Let's drop our proposal about the Franco-Soviet Pact. Let's close the Straits in wartime, Turkey being neutral, to all warships save those sent against an aggressor by the League or, if the League fails to act, operating under mutual assistance pacts "to which Turkey is a party".'

England, aside: 'Ah, you have a secret agreement with Turkey.' To France and Russia: 'Let's say, "Mutual assistance pacts *registered with the League* to which Turkey is a party.'

France and Russia: 'Done.'

And if you now know who is going to pass the Straits in wartime, Turkey being neutral, you know more than I do. But I know that Turkey is on very good terms with Russia, and that Russia would do her utmost to see that Turkey acted as armed door-keeper for her in case of war. England, however, carried her main point, which was to prevent the Franco-Soviet Pact, which England had formally blessed, from being appended to the new Convention as a golden key to the Straits.

The other great struggle fought at Montreux, with London, Paris, Berlin and Moscow all watching, was the question of the warships allowed to enter or leave the Black Sea in peace. This might seem unimportant. On the contrary, behind this issue loomed the shadow of a great Russian fleet, just as the shadow of German ships loomed, for Russia, behind the proposal about 'belligerent rights'.

England, with an air of bluff and hearty candour, said to Russia at the beginning: 'Well, I suppose it's equal rights all round. We accept certain restrictions on the amount of war tonnage we send in and you accept equivalent restrictions on the amount you send out. Cheerio!'

'Pardon me,' said Russia, 'I'm all for fair play and good fellowship, but reciprocity pre-supposes an equal basis of comparison. The British Empire, which alone surpasses in size the Soviet Union among the empires of the world, has the complete freedom of the Seven Seas. The Soviet Union, which covers a sixth of the world's surface, has a small stretch of Baltic coast, but the Baltic Sea is controlled by Germany and the Soviet ships are bottled up there. Also, our yards there are within easy distance of surprise attack in these days of wars begun without declaration. We also have a long stretch of Black Sea coastline. But the Black Sea is a closed sea, and leads nowhere. Why should you, or anybody for whom you have a brief — I hope you are not playing the German game again — wish to send large forces in there? On the other hand, why should the Soviet Union accept any restrictions on the forces she sends out? Is she to keep her ships floating round the Black Sea, denied all access to the oceans of the world?'

England: 'Oh, you want to make the Black Sea a Russian Lake, do you? And you want to upset the Balance of Power in the Mediterranean, do you? I must refer this to my Government.'

So it went on. In these days, when wars are made without declaration, Russia was determined not to have large naval forces assembling in the Black Sea, at her doorstep. Her case was irrefutable, and she gained her point. The outer world agreed not to send more than 30,000 to 45,000 tons of warships in at any one time, according to the strength of the Russian fleet. England tried to gain a further 15,000 tons for warships engaged on 'humanitarian missions'. 'Humanitarian missions?' said Russia darkly. 'Would you call "help for the poor Ukrainians" a humanitarian mission? Are these humanitarian battleships any kin to the civilizing aeroplanes that Mussolini has been using in Abyssinia? Still, if it will quieten you we will give you another 8000 tons.'

What was back of all this sparring and shadow-boxing? That Anglo-German naval agreement which England, after Simon's visit to Berlin, had sprung upon her beloved ally France. For right at the back of the Black Sea lies Odessa, and Russia, though she only has a few old warships now, might decide one day to begin building a large navy there, where she could not be reached by surprise attack. And if she built a large fleet the Germans would probably denounce our cherished Anglo-German naval agreement and begin a vast building programme to maintain the peace, and we should have to outbuild Germany to maintain the peace, and so on. If large foreign naval forces were allowed to assemble in the Black Sea at her doorstep, Russia would be discouraged from building.

But the Russians did not feel any call to sacrifice their own interests to the Anglo-German naval agreement, and they even managed to change the definition of the largest foreign war vessels allowed to enter the Black Sea in peace from '10,000 tons' to 'light surface vessel'. Now, the 'light surface vessel', as defined at London, is of 10,000 tons but must carry no guns heavier than 8 inch. And the German 'pocket battleships', the first of which we saw launched at Kiel so long ago, are of 10,000 tons but carry heavier armament, and the Black Sea is closed to them.

Under the Convention, as finally signed, sealed and delivered, the Black Sea States — and for the purposes of the European line-up this means Russia — may send out all the ships they have, a little at a time. At present this only opens the way for a few ancient Russian or Turkish battleships and heavy cruisers, but it keeps the door to the seven seas open if Russia ever decides to build a great fleet again, at Odessa.

While the Great Powers of Europe manœuvred and bluffed in the bedrooms of the Montreux Palace Hotel, I rowed and swam on the lake during the day and came back in the afternoon to write. In the evenings I lay, at peace with the world, and read *A Farewell to Arms*, for here in Montreux were played the last scenes of the tragedy that Ernest Hemingway told. The Château Chatelard, that he described, stood on the hillside above Montreux and supplied that excellent wine of which I told you earlier. And along the lakeside was the old Castle of Chillon, where Byron's prisoner spent seven years chained to his stake, and one day, when the sparring for position had exhausted the chanceries of half a dozen capitals, the whole conference went along there, drank the wine of Montreux and Villeneuve, ate sandwiches and cakes, and listened to the songs and watched the dances of a group of Vaudoises, in the costume of the district. The Vaudoises are renowned in Switzerland for their looks, and justly so. It was a marvellous afternoon. To see Litvinoff and Paul-Boncour and Sato of Japan and the agile Rushdi Aras and tall Lord Stanley, surrounded by their delegations and the world's newspapermen and Vaudoises, sitting all together in that magnificent banqueting hall, with wine flowing as wine should, and everybody in high spirits, was to see a vision of what conferences should be.

Sometimes I took leave of the lake for a day and travelled round the lake to Geneva, at the other end, where strange and historic things were happening.

An Empire had crashed; I saw the Negus, a figure of extraordinary dignity, and he made his eloquent plea that the world that had espoused his cause should not desert him. The same day the League pronounced the funeral oration on the first attempt in history to defeat aggression by the united action of the world against an aggressor. It was a cause that had stirred the enthusiasm of the world, and by leading it England had given new hope to millions of people in all countries, only to betray their trust within a fortnight. The League solemnly decided to abandon sanctions.

A Jew, Stephen Lux, shot himself during the League meeting, and in the League chamber, from despair at the failure of collective action against an aggressor, from fear of the future. 'I know Germany', he wrote, 'and because there is no other means of warning the men who rule the world, at the eleventh hour I have decided to sacrifice my life before the eyes of fifty foreign Ministers.' As he was dying he said to the doctors, 'Let me die. I must die, otherwise my deed has no point'. He died. It had no point. He was forgotten before the printing presses had stopped running.

A Nazi, one Greiser, the spokesman of Danzig, cocked a snook at the League Council in full session. It was a fitting end.

All too soon, for me, I had to leave Montreux. If ever I have the means to live where I want I shall have great difficulty in deciding between a little house at the Villeneuve end of Lake Geneva and one on the hills overlooking Vienna or Salzburg or Linz.

Switzerland remains, for me, one of the most inspiring countries in Europe, a citadel of neutrality, where men can only be roused to patriotic enthusiasm for that ideal. Every one of them will fight for neutrality and for nothing else. Every one of them is a citizen soldier and takes his gun home with him. Think of that, you dictatorship states. Would you trust your population with arms? In Switzerland, you feel at peace. Here no moron wants to 'make history'. I thought when I was there of my hard-faced Prussian acquaintance in Magdeburg, who contemptuously said, 'We Prussians have no use for a Swiss paradise of fat flocks and prosperity'. Well, it was good enough for me, and I wish myself a long, long sojourn, one of these days, at Montreux on Lake Geneva.

CHAPTER 37

'TRUTH PREVAILS'

I came into Prague by air, and that is an experience to be treasured. The approach to a great city from above is always thrilling, you see it gradually emerge from formless mass into plastic relief, a doll's town of cathedrals and towers and rivers.

Prague, one of the loveliest cities in Europe from any elevation, is particularly lovely from a few hundred feet up. The Moldau is a winding silver ribbon, the bridges tiny and toylike, the castle of the Kings of Bohemia on the hill, with St. Vitus's Cathedral within its courts, passes before you as if a dealer showed you for a moment a coloured print of Old Prague. Then the tigerish roar of the engines drops to a contented feline purr, you feel a slight pressure on your ears, Prague disappears behind a tree or two and your wheels are running smoothly across the green turf of Prague Airport, which in its situation and equipment is one of the finest I know in Europe, not excluding Germany.

Everywhere the black flags were flying, as we dropped down into the town in the airport bus. I had come to Prague for the funeral of the greatest man in Europe — Masaryk, a man who had never rattled a sabre nor made a swashbuckling speech, who had never advocated violence when he was fighting for his cause nor used it against his opponents when he had power, but had nevertheless liberated his people and built a free, solid, hard-working State. His mother a cook and his father a coachman, himself at first a locksmith's apprentice, his life is a monument to what can be achieved against tyranny and oppression by intellect, principle and faith in a cause.

As a University Professor at Prague, as a Czech deputy to the old Austrian Parliament at Vienna, he worked unceasingly for the liberation of the Czechs and Slovaks. When the World War began he was already sixty-four and might, like ageing politicians in other countries, have been tempted to relax his efforts for the sake of a cushioned old age in a comfortable job.

His goal seemed as distant as at the beginning, fifty years before. Not all his efforts had roused any particular interest abroad for the Czechs and Slovaks. Apart from a few unheeded specialists like Wickham Steed and Seton Watson, who had studied the subject races of the Austro-Hungarian Empire, nobody in the outer world knew or cared who the Czechs and Slovaks were, any more than anybody cares to-day about the Basques, and Masaryk, going into exile with a death sentence over him when he was already within reach of the allotted span, looked at the World War and gloomily foretold that 'nothing would be done for us in the case of an Allied victory'.

That, in the event, free Czechoslovakia rose from the ashes, was his work, and that of his companion and exile and successor Eduard Benes. Journeying all over the Allied and neutral world, to America and Russia and France and Italy, working busily in Geneva and at Hampstead, he gradually won Allied support for his cause until first France, then America, England and Italy officially recognized the Czechoslovaks as an Allied nation and their liberation from Austro-Hungarian rule as an Allied cause, so that at Washington on October 18th, Masaryk proclaimed Czechoslovakia an independent State and in Prague on November 14th the Revolutionary National Assembly, having taken over control from the collapsing Habsburg administration, unanimously elected him President of Czechoslovakia.

That was his diplomatic achievement. His other great achievement was the creation of a Czechoslovak Army. In their own country the Czechs were serving, many of them even loyally, as conscripts with the Imperial Austro-Hungarian army. Abroad, Czech emigrants or Czechs who had been taken prisoners of war by or deserted to the French, Italians and Russians were formed into Czechoslovak Legions, that fought with the Allies.

When Russia collapsed, and the Soviets turned hostile to

them, the Czechoslovak legionaries there had to march and fight their way clean across Siberia to the Pacific, an extraordinary military achievement of which the world has never been told enough. It was these Legions that came back and occupied the territory of the new state that had been proclaimed at Washington and still form the backbone of it. Their leaders were given the highest positions; the rank and file had first claim on other small livings in the public gift, such as the Trafik shops, the retail stores of the State tobacco monopoly.

Masaryk, sixty-eight years old, came back to Prague, as first President of Czechoslovakia, on December 21st, 1918, amid scenes of enthusiasm the like of which Prague had never seen.

He left it, eighty-seven years old, on September 21st, 1937, amid scenes of mourning the like of which I had never seen.

Two years before, true to his whole philosophy, he had laid down the Presidency when he felt that his powers were failing, and had seen that it passed into the hands of his lieutenant, Benes. Unlike the dictators, he had not clung to office until the bitter end, but had surrendered it when he felt his powers failing, as man should who was physically and mentally healthy. In the last nineteen years of his life he saw the state he had created grow out of post-war confusion into a free, prosperous, *bourgeois*, peace-loving Republic. He saw his life's work completed as few men have ever seen their labours completed, from the seed to the ripe fruit.

And when he died the shadow of a new menace hung heavy over the young State, and fear for their hardly-won freedom filled the hearts of the people as they watched the Liberator-President go.

I sat in the forecourt of the old castle on the hill, where the great black banners flapped lugubriously in the gusty wind, and listened as Benes spoke his funeral oration standing before Masaryk's coffin, draped in the Presidential standard with the legend, 'The truth prevails'. 'Does it?' I thought. 'You, Masaryk, may have thought so when you returned triumphant to Prague in 1918. Do you think so in 1937 if your shade is watching our contemporary Europe, our contemporary world? In Spain Germans and Italians and Moors are saving Spain from the Spaniards. The Basques have been crushed in their own country by Italian regiments and German air squadrons. The world is placidly watching while Japan carves slices off China for herself. What are the odds on or against the survival of your free Czechoslovakia for which you so nobly laboured? For how long will truth prevail? For twenty-five years between centuries of darkness? Is that truth?'

The democratic godparents of Czechoslovak independence had taken no great pains to show their sympathy in the passing of the founder of the last surviving democracy in Europe east of the Rhine. France had sent an ex-Prime Minister, England a little-known Peer.

I followed the coffin on its long journey down the hill, across the Moldau, through the winding streets of Old Prague and up the spacious Wenceslas Square to the President Wilson Station, a long, long trail that severely tested the older members of the Diplomatic Corps, and never have I seen such crowds, not even in Germany, and there I became accustomed to crowds on the gigantic scale.

Prague was like one great blackberry bush, so thickly did human beings throng the streets and windows and balconies and roofs and every possible vantage point, near and far, from which this funeral *cortège* could be seen. Czechoslovakia has fourteen million people, Prague itself a million inhabitants, and more than two million people were in Prague that day. The Czechoslovaks, sub-consciously, were proclaiming to the world their answer to the new threat to small nations. It was a gigantic parade of Czechoslovak unity, and it meant 'Desert us if you will, we shall fight to the end if we are attacked'.

At the President Wilson Station I watched as Benes took his stand by the coffin and the Legionaries marched past — 30,000 of them. Czechoslovaks who had fought with the Italian armies, in the feathered bonnet and grey-green uniform of the Italian mountain regiments, Czechoslovaks who had fought with the French in dark blue bonnets and powder-blue uniforms, Czechoslovaks who had fought with the Russians, every second man wearing the long-forgotten St. George's Cross. Behind them, though no British newspaper found this worth mentioning in 1937, came a little group of Czechoslovaks who had fought with the British armies. Khaki uniforms, the gleaming brass buttons and badges of British regiments, R.A.S.C., R.E., and the like.

The name of the station — President Wilson; the man in the coffin — Masaryk; and these Allied uniforms and decorations; for a moment the clock seemed to have been put back twenty years and I was back in the days of the World War, of the great struggle for freedom and democracy.

Then behind the Legionaries came the army of liberated Czechoslovakia, horse, gun and foot, tank and aeroplane. It was a panorama in little of the history of Czechoslovakia.

Two million Czechoslovaks watched in dead silence, many with reddened eyes, their thoughts divided between the past and the future.

The Czechoslovaks are a dour and gruff people. They do not cultivate the social graces nor seek to ingratiate themselves. They are not a comely race. They have not yet evolved an officer caste, bred to grace the drawing-rooms of the diplomatic corps. They should. The aristocracy, among which the foreign diplomats seek their society, is not Czechoslovak, but mainly German, and mainly Habsburg or Hitler; it has retired into a shell of dislike for the new State. Young British diplomats in Prague have been known openly to profess a testy impatience with Czechoslovakia. This would not be allowed them for an instant in a dictatorship State, and is curious in the representatives of a State whose Ministers constantly profess their inalienable love for the democratic ideal, for it connotes an open sympathy with a neighbouring anti-democratic country openly hostile to Czechoslovakia.

British agents are being allowed too openly to show their sympathy for military dictatorships.

A British official in beleaguered Republican Madrid one day sent triumphantly for British newspaper correspondents — one of my useful friends informed me of this — to tell them that at last he had discovered the Russian regiments. He directed them to a barracks in which they found many of many races and tongues, the men of the International Brigade, predominantly Poles and Germans and Austrians and Italians and Britishers and Frenchmen, with hardly any Russians, real volunteers who had been recruited in half a dozen different countries. The unfamiliar languages were enough for this British official, in his zeal to outwit the Bolshevists, to identify them as Soviet Russian troops, just like that British visitor to Spain who wrote to the home newspapers to say that he had inspected the dead in a Republican tank and 'could see at a glance that they were Slavs'.

Straws show the direction of the wind. There are Britishers in Czechoslovakia who hold that Czechoslovakia is not worth saving.

In Masaryk's chair in the Hradschin sits Benes. Around him are the painted Habsburgs, in the brilliant scarlet-and-white uniforms of Imperial Austria. If you ask him, he will profess complete optimism. He does not believe that Czechoslovakia will be attacked by anybody. She harms none, asks only to be left in peace and work.

The country is thriving, largely as the result of the armaments boom. She is arming herself, as far and as fast as she can, fortifying her impossibly long frontiers, supplying armaments to her Little Entente associates, Rumania and Yugoslavia. The more expensive hotels and cafés of Prague are filled with well-to-do Jews, prospering from an armaments race begun by anti-Semites.

The country, apart from overriding military control in the frontier districts and other things dictated by the growing menace of recent years, is a real democracy in a large degree. You may demonstrate against the Government or attack it in your press, and the Henlein Party, which is the Hitlerist branch concern in the German-speaking districts, makes full use of this freedom, being immediately supported by the brassy bellowings of Göbbels's gigantic propaganda machine if its freedom in this respect is in the least restricted.

On that day of Masaryk's funeral, as we passed between the silent crowds, I saw Socialist and Fascist and Catholic and Jewish and Communist organizations all lining the streets together, shoulder to shoulder.

Is Benes's unconcern optimism or ostrichism? I have looked out from his windows to the opposite hilltop and seen slender pencils pointing at the sky — anti-aircraft guns. They took my thoughts at a bound to that Berlin-Dresden-Prague road along which I once drove, only a few minutes distant by air from here, with its bee-like military preparations, its great aerodromes and encampments.

In Prague, and all over Central Europe, people have of late been reading a novel written by an Englishman, Fowler Wright's *Prelude to Prague*, which is enthralling to read and tells of a German ultimatum to Czechoslovakia in 1938, on some trumpery pretext, and of 'intervention' in the form of a gigantic air-attack, the destruction of Prague, the paralytic indecision of governments in Paris and London. It was written before Spain had shown the world that such a picture was no wild Piccardesque flight into the stratosphere of fancy.

Czechoslovakia at her birth took into her cradle over three million Germans, and whether she can digest them has yet to be seen. But those Bohemian frontiers have always been, and nobody then thought of changing them. Still, Benes is right in thinking that Czechoslovakia is not Germany's real enemy. The real enemy is England. But is he right in thinking, as he has repeatedly said, that an attack on Czechoslovakia would mean a world war, instantly? Who can believe that, after recent events? And Czechoslovakia, though in herself but a pawn in the European game, would be a very valuable power-unit for the great German war-machine.

Remember that German domination in pre-war Europe was

divided into two parts. Protestant Prussia ruled the present Third Reich, with some Frenchmen in Alsace, a few Belgians and Danes, and a large number of Poles in that part of Poland which Germany held. But the great German family ruled through Austria, and on a sharing basis with Hungary, over the Czechs and Slovaks and Croats and Slovenes and Ruthenians and the Bosnian and Herzegovinian Serbs and over all their lands and resources. When Germany took the field she had as ally Austria-Hungary, which really meant another Germany, under a Catholic Emperor, with a population of over 60 millions and vast resources in animal, vegetable, mineral and industrial wealth.

To-day that second Germany, that powerful military ally, has dwindled to a small state of 7,000,000 people. The Austrians, as far as I can see, would have to fight for Germany if she made war, if by that time they were not already part of Germany. You may permit yourself a roseate dream of Austrian neutrality, but I think it is only a dream. Austria's destiny is handcuffed to that of Germany.

Even Austria would mean a welcome increase in power and valuable raw materials, such as the iron ores of Styria.

Czechoslovakia was the workshop and gunsmith's shop of the old Austro-Hungarian Empire. Her industry, save for a regrettable leaning towards the manufacture of trashy goods, is on the level of the German, her armaments factories are equal to almost any in the world. Germany in possession of Czechoslovakia would have another great reservoir of man-power and munition-power, waiting to be turned into striking-power against the real enemy. True, you may say that the Czechoslovaks would be as indigestible to the Germans as the Germans to the Czechs; but the Czechs worked for and fought for the Germans for long enough, and why should they not do so again if the outer world deserts them?

So don't talk about 'fighting for Czechoslovakia'. If Czechoslovakia goes, that means more men and more munitions to be used against you, more aeroplanes one day over the south-east of England. If Czechoslovakia goes, Hungary, the kingdom without a king, cannot survive as anything more than a docile dependency of Germany. You would be well on the way to the reconstruction of that German domination over Central Europe, with its man-power, munition-power, metal-power, food-power and fuel-power, which enabled Germany to face the last world war.

But instead of a dual domination, with the weakness that division brings, it would be a united domination, under the exclusive leadership of the martial Hitlerist Reich, not under the part-leadership of the easy-going Habsburg Empire.

Czechoslovakia means, ultimately, you.

Neither Masaryk, nor Benes, nor Hodza, the present Czechoslovak Prime Minister, thought of complete Czechoslovak independence when they began their struggle. They detested rule from Vienna and particularly the promotion of Hungary to a privileged place among the peoples ruled by Habsburg. Either central rule for all from Vienna, or home-rule for all, was their cry. If the Kaiser is to be crowned King of Hungary in Budapest why cannot he be crowned King of Bohemia in Prague. Why should Prague be degraded to the status of a provincial town that never sees the Emperor? Why should not Prague have its Parliament?

Hodza, a Slovak who was a lonely deputy in the Budapest Parliament, himself loves Vienna, and was a good friend and collaborator of Franz Ferdinand, that Archduke whose murder at Serajevo led to the World War. For Franz Ferdinand himself saw that Austro-Hungarian dualism could not survive and wanted, when he should become Emperor, to improve the lot of the Czechs and Croats and others. And for that very reason there were people both in Vienna and Budapest who welcomed his death, for all that Austria sent an ultimatum to Serbia and bombarded Belgrade when it was not unconditionally accepted, and that began the World War.

Bear that in mind, and you will see that Benes's Czechoslovakia, if it were deserted by the outer world and too long subjected to intolerable pressure from Germany, would have no choice but to make terms with Germany. That would mean a nominal independence in exchange for submission to German aims. And that, in the long run, would mean that Czech hands would be forging weapons for Germany in peace and bearing those weapons for Germany in war.

Think back a moment to the beginnings of the European line-up in 1935. Germany left the League of Nations, left the Disarmament Conference, proclaimed rearmament. France, with the specific approval of England, answered, 'That means that you tear up treaties and base your policies on your armed strength. If you don't mean that, come with us into a collective pact for mutual resistance against an aggressor. You won't? Then we shall look for friends strong enough to help us overbear you if you attack us. We shall sign the mutual aid pact with Russia.'

Czechoslovakia, having no Great Power behind her which would automatically come to her aid if attacked because that Great Power's own safety would be threatened thereby, as in the case of Belgium and Great Britain, immediately signed a similar pact with Russia, providing for immediate mutual assistance against an aggressor, on condition that the victim of aggression were assisted by France.

This was an inevitable move in the line-up. Everybody understands it in Europe across the Channel; only in England, where all thinking is fogged by fear of the hook-nosed and bearded scoundrels far away who are designing to steal our two-seater, and by Hitler's talk about Germany being 'a bulwark against Bolshevism', is it misunderstood.

France had to nip in and make that treaty, and she did so only in the nick of time. On the European chessboard there are two king-pieces — Germany and Russia. Bismarck knew that nothing could stop Germany in Europe as long as she had her re-insurance with Russia. Kaiser Wilhelm, who put Bismarck overboard, forgot it and paid the penalty, for Germany lost the World War when the Russians came down on her rear in East

Prussia in 1914 and made her pause just as she was within reach of Paris.

If you have Russia dangling about in the air and liable to come down on either side at any moment, peace in Europe is as unstable as a blancmange.

If Germany and Russia come together, peace is finished, and I for one should take the first boat to the Bahamas.

France, once again, steadied the boat. Her treaty with Russia was a perfectly timed piece of interception. Its value is not in the military assistance that Russia would give her but in the barrier it erects between Germany and Russia, and that is precisely why Germany is so angry about it.

In the fourteen years between the Armistice and Hitler, Germany was on excellent terms with Russia. A German woman, two years before Hitler, committed suicide because her husband, a German officer, had been killed learning to fly — in Russia. The German Minister in Moscow, not long before Hitler, was assembled with his colleagues of the diplomatic corps on Moscow Station one morning to take leave of the departing Lithuanian Minister when he was embarrassed by the simultaneous appearance of a detachment of Reichswehr, fresh from a Bolshevist gas-course and bound for Germany by the only route which would save them from passing through Poland. These things were done by the Reichswehr, the State-within-a-State, not by the Marxist-Jewish Governments of Republican Germany.

The German 'abhorrence of Bolshevist Russia' is as unreal as the monster of Loch Ness. It is fragrant dust for English eyes, the gold brick that Hitler sells to confiding English visitors, worried about their two-seater.

From the greater European point of view the Franco-Soviet Pact was simply France's answer to the German rearmament move — checkmate. It kept the Russians out of the German camp. It does no harm to Germany if she starts no trouble because, as the map will show you, a German-Russian war is the one thing that can't happen in Europe. They can only

313

come to grips in some general European dog-fight when everybody is at it and you can't tell where one dog begins and the
other leaves off.

The one question that nobody has ever been able to answer
for me yet is, how could Russia give Czechoslovakia the help
she has promised her if she were attacked? They have no
common frontier and Russia is not stupid enough, for all the
mutual aid pacts in the world, to divest her own frontiers of
troops in order to defend other people's, even if that did not
mean marching them through intervening States and automatically making enemies of the Poles or Rumanians. Her
assistance, therefore, would be limited to a few aeroplanes, and
you can estimate how much that would help Czechoslovakia by
looking at the plight of the Madrid Government in Spain.

I wonder what would actually happen if Germany were
one day to intervene in Czechoslovakia, on the Spanish model.

England, by all the portents, would ward off the appeals of
France to join hands against aggression with the words 'For
God's sake, let's form a committee', and then some phrase
would be invented like 'non-intervention' or 'non-active disapprobation of aggression', and by one device or another the
committee would be kept going until Czechoslovakia was no
more and Germany was in possession, a moment for which the
committee would in private fervently pray, and then an English
statesman would get up and say it was unfortunately clear that
the policy of non-active disapprobation of aggression, though the
only possible and right and proper policy, had failed, and facts
are facts, and it is midsummer madness not to take account of
them, and the House rose at seven minutes after nine o'clock.

Meanwhile Czechoslovakia is a pleasant country to visit and
I commend it, particularly to you who took seriously all that
stuff during the war about fighting for democracy and the right
of small nations to live their own lives. The Czechoslovaks have
accomplished wonders in twenty years, to my mind. They had
to build a state out of a scrap-heap of old iron and they have
built a very creditable one. They are working hard, plodding

314

along country roads in bright peasant costume or along city streets in drab town clothes, all bent on some allotted task.

And Prague is a fine town for a holiday. I don't think I should care to live there, but I am always glad to go there. The Old Town, with its winding alleys and bawdy statuary, is a fascinating place, where you can wander for hours.

I particularly like that relief of the saint who emasculated himself in order to remove the temptations of the flesh and threw that which he no longer needed to a dog. There is the saint, primly self-righteous, like a boy scout who has done his day's good deed, and the dog near by looking faintly surprised, with the unexpected morsel in its mouth. I also like the little costume-piece of a good citizen of Prague engaged in amorous dalliance with a citizeness who is no better than she ought to be.

Go there in winter, perhaps. The Wenceslas Square, as the dusk falls, is limned in neon shades of mauve and pink and green. The Moldau is frozen over and, with crowds of dark figures skating about, looks like a painting by Breughel. Above and beyond is the Hradschin, with the tall cathedral topping it, that has taken six centuries to build, and is not finished yet. You may see a row of lighted windows. Benes, Masaryk's picture on the desk before him, is working in the castle of the Kings of Bohemia.

CHAPTER 38

RUMANIAN RUMINATION

STROLLING along the Calea Victoriei in Bucharest I thought I saw the Horse Marines, so strangely and yet so splendidly attired were the soldiers who came towards me. From the waist up they were heavy cavalrymen, with their great helmets and cuirasses, but from the waist down they were just ordinary panted infantrymen, and they carried the longest rifles, with the longest bayonets, that I had ever seen.

It was King Carol's guard, going to the Palace. At the funerals of Alexander of Yugoslavia and Masaryk and on other occasions I came to know the brilliant parade uniforms of the Rumanians, and a treasured memory is of a Rumanian General in Prague carefully removing a plume a foot long from his kepi and putting it in his pocket as he climbed into a taxicab with a low roof. The average Rumanian conscript, seen in his native habitat, makes a rather drab impression after all this splendour, and his boots often make your feet ache in sympathy with him.

Rumania is a little France on the Black Sea and Bucharest a little Paris, with its Arc de Triomphe, long straight boulevards that Haussmann might have planned, and a wood that clearly dreams of the Bois, and French stores in the main street. The Rumanians, tucked away down there in the far corner of Europe among Slavs and Magyars, are Latins by culture and inclination. A hundred years ago a French Consul in Bucharest told his Government that France had in Rumania, 'whether she accepts it or not, an inevitable clientele which attaches itself to her as the head of the Latin nations and as their political metropolis and which tries every day to assimilate her language, her legislation, her literature and even her most futile fashions'.

Bucharest is the best place to study Balkan contrasts. In the centre you find it, like all the Balkan capitals, striving after Berlin and Paris and London and New York. Great multi-storied buildings rise mushroom-like on all sides, pushing aside the pleasant and shady villas of the Turkish and post-Turkish periods. Lean and swarthy gipsies, who work for next to nothing, build them, and live on the scaffoldings with their wives and families. On one side is a ghetto like a human ant heap. Beyond is outer Bucharest, all confusion, hovels and modern flats, peasant costume and cheap mass-produced frocks, radio and barking dogs and noisy geese, rutted and pot-holed streets and asphalted thoroughfares.

In the Calea Victoriei on Sundays you will see long processions of expensive motor cars. Rumanians are getting married. The expensive motor cars are hired taxis. Fares are cheap and one of the mysteries of the Balkans is why Bucharest should have the most luxurious taxis of almost any city in Europe. Between the taxis, with their radio, you see fiacres drawn by well-tended horses and driven by fat, motherly looking men. These are the Russian coachmen, members of a strange religious sect that had to leave Russia in Tsarist days because of the offence its practices gave to the Church. The men, who lead an austere life and are model citizens, have themselves castrated after the first child and thereafter become corpulent and old-wifely in appearance.

Beyond this Bucharest lies Rumania, which means several millions of hard-working peasants who in good times enjoy a rude plenty and in bad ones count themselves lucky if they have enough to eat. Apart from the vast quantities of food which it produces Rumania has enormous deposits of oil. Rumania's wealth in matters animal, vegetable and mineral, indeed, is incalculable; it is a land where every prospectus pleases and lures the foreign financier as jam lures a fly.

That is precisely why Rumania is important in the European line-up. Rumania is a small country, though one wealthy in natural resources, and has everything to make it, soundly governed, an earthly paradise. It has the very things which others want. A great military dictatorship may have all the men and brains it needs, it may be in valour and organization unconquerable, but all these things do not suffice if it cannot grow enough food to withstand a siege nor produce enough oil fuel within its borders to drive its tanks and aeroplanes. Then it is liable to be starved into defeat, either starved in food or in fuel or in some other essential things.

That is why Rumania, a small country which can want nothing but to be left in peace, would be an ideal larder and fuel-tank for some predatory great power bent on war. Just as the man-power and munition-power of what is now Czechoslovakia helped the Central Powers to hold out for four years in the World War, and would similarly increase the wartime staying-power of any country that swallowed Czechoslovakia to-day, so would the food-power and fuel-power of Rumania vastly improve the chances of victory for any great power that could draw on the wheat and oil of Rumania, either because Rumania was her friend or her prisoner. That is one of the reasons for that long tussle at Montreux about the right to pass the Straits in wartime; France wanted to keep the pipeline open to her friend Rumania, and did for that matter succeed in having oil-tankers exempted from the class of vessel to which the Straits have to be closed in wartime, Turkey being neutral.

The resources of Rumania, like those of Czechoslovakia, did actually go to prolong the World War, for German armies occupied Rumania, and during the last year of the struggle Rumania was bled white to enable Germany to carry on the battle on the Western Front, against England, France and America. Sheep and cattle and grain and oil were seized and exported, forests cut down, factories dismantled.

Rumania, like Czechoslovakia, means, ultimately, you.

When you consider the Treaty of Versailles, think back to the Treaty of Bucharest of May 1918, under which Rumanians were reduced to serfs, who were to grow wheat and dig oil for the exclusive use of Germany and Austro-Hungary. To produce foodstuffs and motor-spirit, two essential things for further conquests, this was to have been the part of Rumania.

The collapse of the Central Powers six months later changed

all that and brought Rumania liberation far beyond the rosiest dreams of Averescu, her wartime commander. Her population and territory doubled, Greater Rumania arose.

There you have the background of King Carol, as he contemplates the European line-up from his palace in Bucharest, or, draped in the white cloak of St. Michael the Brave, takes a parade of the army he is trying hard to improve. A German Prince, he, like all the other rulers and politicians, is watching attentively the prowess of the quick-on-the-draw martial dictatorships, Germany and Italy and Japan, and the irresolution and weakness of England and France, to whom for all their faults men in the small countries still look with diminishing hopes as the guardians of reason and right and freedom, and he is trying to foresee which side will prevail when next war comes in Europe.

His own grandfather, Carol I, kept just such a watch from Bucharest and backed the wrong horse. After the quick German victories against Austria and France in 1866 and 1871, Carol I was convinced that Germany was unconquerable and made a secret alliance with Germany that crumbled to dust in his hands in 1914, for neither the Rumanian army nor the Rumanian people would have anything to do with it. And there was a strong pro-German party, the Conservative Party, in pre-war Rumania, a party that fell to pieces in 1918 because the result of the war seemed to prove conclusively that its policy and that of Carol I had been hopelessly wrong.

But now that Germany is again the mightiest military power in Europe and that Anglo-French opposition to militarist aggression has suffered such disastrous defeat, a new pro-German party is rising in Rumania, this time in the garb of anti-Semitic Fascism, and the problems of King Carol II are taking exactly the same shape as those of King Carol I.

As yet Rumania has kept firmly to her place in the European line-up, at the side of England, France, the Little Entente and the League, but there have been slight signs of wobbling, for instance the affair of Titulescu, that Titulescu whom we last saw at Montreux bitterly criticizing the two-tonguedness of British policy and flinging out of the conference room. Titulescu was the very incarnation of that traditional Rumanian policy. He was that rare thing, an absentee Foreign Minister with full authority. From time to time an admiring Rumania heard of his successes in Paris and Geneva; and at rare intervals he came to Bucharest, to see if his laurels were keeping fresh. He was feared and hated by the Germans and Hungarians; even the British resented the intolerable suggestion that British policy could ever be perfidious.

Titulescu began to find his authority weakening. One day at St. Moritz or Cannes, I forget where, he heard that the Rumanian Prime Minister, Tatarescu, had paid a visit to Belgrade. You might think that, with Rumanian foreign policy so often proclaimed to be immutable, it was only a matter of a few vowels and consonants whether Tatarescu or Titulescu went to Belgrade, merely Tat for Tit, but not so Titulescu, and he objected vigorously.

One day, in the most cavalier manner, he was dropped altogether by telegram, and they say that the reason was that he favoured the better relations with Russia which Rumania's friends, France and Czechoslovakia, had pursued after Germany's new entry, with lowered horns and steaming nostrils, into the European bull ring. This was a sensitive point with Rumanians because the only possibility for Russia to give Czechoslovakia that help she had promised in case of emergency seemed to be for her to send troops or aircraft across Rumanian territory and Rumanians did not want any foreign troops in Rumania again if they could help it, least of all Russian troops, for Russia had never clearly waived her claim to Bessarabia, Rumania's easternmost province.

We may never know just how far Titulescu wanted to go in this matter. At all events, the bogy of the Russian army, which has made its spectral appearances all over Europe in the last twenty years, though the only flesh and blood armies to have invaded foreign soil of late have been German and

Italian, enabled Titulescu's enemies in Bucharest to gain Carol's ear and have him dismissed.

Carol rules Rumania. His word is ultimately law, and he is now, in the contemporary fashion, suppressing parties and ruling without Parliament. With ripening age he has emancipated himself successively from all feminine influences in his rule, his mother Queen Marie, his divorced Queen Helen, his Lupescu, and he is becoming strict in matters of the heart; he has sent his own brother Nicolas into exile because he wanted his marriage with a divorced Rumanian lady, though formally annulled, to be recognized and his wife given the title of Princess.

Rumania is an attractive country and parts of it are lovely and its people appeal to me and life is pleasant there, but a little dangerous in these days for Gentiles because of the growth of the anti-Semitic movement. This was originally called the Iron Guard and its founder and leader was a young man, who is an excellent shot and violent anti-Semite, called Corneliu Codreanu. The Iron Guard was suppressed. A new movement was formed called 'All for the country' and led by a choleric and aged anti-Semite called General Cantacuzino. The real name of this movement is the Iron Guard and its leader is Corneliu Codreanu.

Some years ago he killed the Police Chief of Jassy, a Gentile who was not anti-Semitic enough for his liking. A little later he managed to send his men into a prison and kill another Gentile, one of his own lieutenants, in fact, whom he thought to have betrayed him. Then M. Duce, the Gentile and Liberal Prime Minister who had ordered the ban on the Iron Guard, was sentenced to death at an executive meeting of the Iron Guard and killed; fifty of fifty-three accused were acquitted. Then Corneliu Codreanu decided one day that he had been betrayed by another Gentile, this time his own right-hand man and chief collaborator, Michael Stelescu, and Michael Stelescu was sentenced to death by the executive of the non-existent Iron Guard and killed in the hospital where he was lying, receiving good measure, for he had thirty-eight bullet wounds and several knife thrusts.

Corneliu Codreanu and General Cantacuzino are both well and the anti-Jewish Iron Guard is going strong. Both they and it are passionately fond of Mussolini, Hitler and Franco. Since they are able to remove with impunity people they dislike, up to Prime Ministers, they must presumably have protection in high places, and echo answers why? The Iron Guard sent some volunteers to Franco and one or two of them were killed and were given a great all-Fascist funeral in Bucharest, with the German and Italian Ministers present. King Carol, it is said, privily watched the scene from a curtained window not far away.

As things are moving in Europe, the Iron Guard is worth watching.[1] In December 1937 it gained heavily at the elections, and King Carol did exactly what Hindenburg did in Germany in 1932: he tried to wear down the Iron Guard, as Hindenburg tried to wear down Hitler, by appointing as Prime Minister a politician of moderate pro-Italian, pro-German, anti-Jewish views, who would steal the Iron Guard's thunder by doing a few of the things it demanded. Octavian Goga, a poet-politician, was his Papen and within six weeks, the victim of half measures, he had withdrawn to the Riviera to recuperate. Papen at least had the satisfaction of overwhelming defeat at two elections; Goga didn't even get as far as his first one, since the protests of the American, British and French Governments against his anti-Jewish measures had shown Carol that a small country like Rumania cannot easily do even a tithe of the things that Germany did. And then Carol formed a Cabinet of National Union, comprising half a dozen Elder Statesmen who detested each other, headed by the venerable Patriarch Miron Cristea of the Rumanian Church. The end of the Rumanian experiment is still in the melting-pot.

[1] The Iron Guard has since been dissolved.

CHAPTER 39

LITTLE ENTENTE

I RAN out of Vienna on a mellow Saturday afternoon in September, drove for an hour at a comfortable forty miles with occasional glimpses of the Danube and a word of greeting to my friends the two Roman amphitheatres, passed quickly through the Austrian and Czechoslovak customs and was in Bratislava, or Pressburg as the tramcar from Vienna calls it, which started running in the Emperor's day and has not yet acknowledged the new frontiers drawn up by the Peace Treaty.

Danubia is pleasantly compact, in these days of swift travel, and all your favourite problems of race and language are near together. An hour from Vienna by road or air and you are in Czechoslovakia or Hungary or Yugoslavia, in Prague or Budapest or Zagreb.

Bratislava, a town where the population is so mixed that it is a wise Czechoslovak that knows if his father was a Magyar or a German or a Jew, is a particularly good lookout post for studying Danubian affairs. It lies on the Danube at the spot where Czechoslovakia touches that river, and just near here the Austrian, Czechoslovak and Hungarian frontiers all meet, so that from the old hilltop fortress in Bratislava you look into three men's land, with the Danube joining them all.

Once at this Three-State-Corner Austrian firemen put out a Hungarian fire with water from a Czechoslovak hydrant, thus giving the politicians a magnificent practical example of that Danubian co-operation of which they talk so much but never achieve. So you see that the solution for all these apparently insoluble Danubian problems is really quite simple — leave them to the firemen. The owner of the Hungarian farm didn't even say 'Nem, nem, soha', meaning, 'No, no, never', when the Czechoslovak water attacked the proud Hungarian flames.

Bratislava does not often find itself in the spotlight and was enjoying itself on this sunny Saturday afternoon for it was to be the home for a few days of the Little Entente, a curious phrase which means the Iron Ring around Hungary.

I had often watched the Little Entente at work in its home towns, Prague, Belgrade and Bucharest, and now had come to pass the time of day with it again at Bratislava.

Seldom have I seen such precautions as were taken at Bratislava to guard the Little Entente — the Foreign Ministers of Czechoslovakia, Rumania and Yugoslavia, Messieurs Krofta, Antonescu and Stoyadinovitch.

Once I thoughtlessly left the hotel where the Little Entente and myself were staying and was not allowed to re-enter it. Once I left my bedroom on the fifth floor to come down to the hotel lobby and was not allowed to return to the fifth floor. Once I left the hotel lobby to go to the lavatory and was not allowed — but why harrow your feelings further. The police of Bratislava that day seemed to think that the only hope of preserving the Little Entente intact was to stop me from going some place.

Meanwhile the Little Entente debated, as it debates twice a year, and a communiqué was issued full of the most original phrases, I can't think who invents them, to the effect that all current problems had been discussed and complete unity of views had been registered.

The Little Entente was, is and will be unanimous on one point — Hungary — for Hungary was the reason for its birth and is the reason for its continued existence. In all other questions, interests and views of the three partners tend to diverge.

For twenty years, ever since the war, Hungary has been crying that she refuses to recognize her frontiers, drastically foreshortened to make or enlarge liberated Czechoslovakia, greater Rumania, united Yugoslavia. For exactly so long these three countries have been leagued together jointly to resist any attempt by Hungary to recover territory from them.

It is an iron ring, for Hungary has about eight million inhabitants and the three allies between them fifty million. If Hungary were to attack either or all of them Budapest would become the capital of the Little Entente in about five minutes. That is why Hungary, alone, will never attack them.

But Hungary is the friend and protégé of Italy and Germany. There's the rub. In a general mix-up, with Great Powers involved, opportunities might offer for Hungary.

That is why the Little Entente listens alertly when the Great Powers begin talking about a New Locarno, the broad idea of which is that France and Germany should solemnly, as solemnly as usual, recognize each other's frontiers, and that England and Italy should guarantee them both against an attack by the other. Then you would have what they call, I believe, a Concert of Great Powers, all sweetly harmonious because everything in their own garden would be lovely and what happened elsewhere was elsewhere's business.

But elsewhere the small powers begin and the Little Entente pricks up suspicious ears when it hears talk of dividing Europe into a western sphere peopled by great powers where all should be quiet, and an eastern sphere peopled by smaller ones in which there should be a free hand. What if Germany were to attack Czechoslovakia or Italy Yugoslavia and if Hungary were to jump on our backs, thinks the Little Entente.

The Peace Treaty was a good treaty in its most essential part — the new frontiers. The reparations and armaments penalties were lunatic, because you couldn't enforce them, but the frontiers were good.

In new Europe you have, I should think, at the most five or six million people who could conceivably, by a redrawing of frontiers, be returned to the arms of their countrypeople. That is a pity, but a very much smaller pity than the 80,000,000 people who were entirely submerged under alien rule and within foreign states before the war. How trivial an irritation is the Polish corridor to Germany compared with the complete partition of Poland among three rapacious great powers. Thus, relatively, it is better to have three million Hungarians under foreign rule than six million non-Hungarians under Hungarian rule. The perfect frontier can never be drawn; if you want it you must sort out populations in the mixed areas and transplant part of them to their own country.

But within these limits it is true enough that a fault of the Peace Treaty frontiers — a minor fault in relation to the size of the problem, not a major fault — was committed with the Hungarian frontiers. They were foreshortened too much.

In pre-war Europe you had whole nations, several of them, with no state of their own but completely subject to alien rule. In new Europe you have only, in the overlapping districts, German-speaking minorities under Polish, Czechoslovak and Italian, Hungarian minorities under Rumanian, Yugoslav and Czechoslovak rule.

The lot of these minorities, often hard, is often exploited by politicians entirely for their own ends and without real feeling for their fellow-countrymen across the frontiers at all. For instance, the best-treated of all the German minorities is that in Czechoslovakia, where the Sudeten Germans have their own newspapers and parties and are strongly represented in Parliament and can attack the Government as much as they wish on the platform and in the Press. Yet the German attacks are concentrated on Czechoslovakia, for political reasons, because she is the ally of France and Russia.

The worst treated of the German-speaking minorities is that under Italian rule in South Tirol; but because Hitler and Mussolini need each other Germany ignores their existence and even makes difficulties for their emigrant publicists. The German minority in Poland has a far harder time than that in Czechoslovakia, but because Hitler needs a friendly Poland not a word is ever heard about them.

Hungary has kept up her curtain-fire of revisionist propaganda against all three of her neighbours without distinction until recently, when her friends Italy and Germany advised her to ease off in respect of Yugoslavia, whom they are both courting for the moment.

For all these reasons the Little Entente, noticing that England in particular tends to perceive the justice of Germany's revisionist claims against other countries more and more clearly in proportion as Germany grows stronger, keeps a wary eye on any Great Power moves tending to promote frontier revision at the expense of the smaller states.

Thus at Bratislava, with the police doing their bit by chivvying me around, Little Entente unity was once more proclaimed. There was the usual banquet. The deeper you get into Danubia and the Balkans the more tail coats and orders you see at these banquets. Evening dress is a religion in the Balkans. You are married and buried in it and if you weren't too small you would probably be born in it.

But this banquet had brighter moments, or perhaps I should say darker moments. Half-way through it the lights in the hotel failed, quite innocently as it proved, the powers of darkness had nothing to do with it on this occasion, there wasn't a Red for miles, and in the blackness the diners heard the sound of hastening feet and then the beams of pocket torches pierced the gloom and you saw plain men grouped behind Lucky Milan Stoyadinovitch's chair with torch in one hand and revolver in the other, looking for trouble.

A dramatic scene. Then the lights went on and after a minute they failed again and the plain men rematerialized, and that happened a third time, and at last the banquet came to an end, with the diners feigning devil-may-care and with worried mechanics in the basement working with might and main to get the lights going, but they wouldn't, and all the beautiful illuminations outside were wasted.

So I packed and fetched my car from the garage and set out for a night run to Budapest. I hoped for a good road and no punctures. Perhaps I could make it by midnight. Nadya was dancing there. I hadn't seen her for ages. I could appear suddenly and surprise her, have a drink and a talk. I trod on the starter. It was a great life.

CHAPTER 40

MAGYARLAND

THERE are many ways of seeing Hungary. One is to spend five days in Budapest, five evenings in the bars on the Margareten Island, and five nights in bed at the Duna Palota Hotel, and then to come away exclaiming 'Hungary is a marvellous country, I love Hungary'. This is the method adopted by most English visitors.

Another way by which you will see less but perceive more of Hungary is to drive to Budapest on a dark night in an ailing car. For Hungary is not the Váczi Utca, the Margareten Island and the Duna Palota, Hungary is Budapest and Lake Balaton entirely surrounded by miles and miles of damn-all. In case you do not know what damn-all is, it is *puszta* and *paprika* and *kukuruz*. Hundreds of kilometres of it, on a dark night in an ailing car.

I shall never forget that ride. First a puncture on a pitch dark road and a mislaid jack. Then on again, with no reserve wheel. Then a misfire, then more misfires, then incessant misfires, the engine misfiring like a machine-gun; no that's wrong, a misfiring machine-gun is presumably silent and my car was making a noise like a hysterical machine-gun. I don't know what was wrong with it that night. Everything. The needle sank and sank to thirty and twenty and fifteen kilometres an hour — ten miles an hour and forty miles to go and one o'clock in the morning and not a petrol pump or a repair station nearer than Budapest. There was no point in stopping in that black tunnel that was the road to Budapest. As long as she would move at all I must go on.

I spluttered and rattled and banged on, making enough noise to wake all Hungary but not a soul stirred. I exploded through dead villages, barely distinguishable from the enveloping night, with never a friendly light in any window, praying not to have to climb a hill and luckily there isn't one on all that road.

At long intervals the kilometre stones loomed up and mocked my progress — 60, 59, 58, 57 kilometres to Budapest, it was hopeless, I should never get there like that, I should have to wait for daylight and go in search of a farm-cart to tow me.

But I struggled on. I thought of the rides of John Gilpin, Paul Revere and Dick Turpin, and would gladly have changed places with any of them. A grey mass loomed up in front of my wheels and I swerved just in time to miss it; a dead cow lying in the road. Two red lamps flashed malevolently at me out of the darkness; a fox. Two green ones; a cat. I nearly ran into the back of a farm wagon, trailing through the night to Budapest. The driver was asleep, I saw, as I slowly overhauled him, and the horses too, I thought. They took no notice of me. More and more farm wagons loomed up ahead of me, dozens, scores of them, all jog, jog, jogging to Budapest. Three o'clock, four o'clock.

I came to houses, and more houses, and tramlines, even, at long last, a light or two. I crawled round a corner and suddenly found myself crossing the bridge over the Danube, pulling up outside the Alcazar. My car expired with a final explosion. I went in. They keep late hours in Budapest — in the foreigners' Budapest. Nadya was just going home. She was tired and unwell. We had a drink. We had a dance. All around were foreigners learning to love Hungary.

Budapest, with that magnificent river-front, is a great shop-window for Hungary, but the contents of the shop itself are somewhat monotonous. Out beyond the city, on that endless plain that you see from the heights of Buda, grim poverty dwells among the *kukuruz* fields, and life there is anything but one grand sweet song, with peasant lads and lasses in decorative costumes eternally dancing the czardas.

In Hungary, alone among the countries of continental Europe except for the big landlord areas of Germany, the peasant does not own his land, but is hired by the great landlord. The Magyar nobles and squires, about two thousand of them, own half the country. The landless peasant works for them and is often paid, not in cash, but in kind, and in winter, when the ground is too hard to work, he eats his wages, while they last.

Only in England do anything like similar conditions prevail and I imagine that this is the reason why so many English visitors fall in love with Hungary. They see themselves in a looking-glass and like it.

The enormous estates owned by a few men and employing farm labourers; the large farms owned by yeomen farmers and also employing farm labourers; the wealthy aristocratic families; the white-tie-and-tail-coat life of the little champagne-and-caviare circle in Budapest; their easy-mannered Hungarian hosts, who speak such delightful English and have been everywhere outside Hungary — it is all very much like England. If they don't notice this resemblance their attention is sure to be called to it.

Hungary is a Kingdom without a King, a very suitable arrangement in the circumstances, for you have all the means of inculcating respect for the existing order that monarchy offers, without the possibility that the occupant of the throne might develop ideas running counter to those of the Magyar aristocracy, as the ill-fated Franz Ferdinand of Serajevo, with his misguided notions of emancipating Czechs and Slovaks, seemed likely to do.

It is the Kingdom of St. Stephen's Crown. Everywhere in Budapest, on the great palace dominating the Danube, on the stamps, the money, the post boxes, the uniforms, everywhere you will see this crown, with a crooked cross atop of it. Nobody knows to-day just why that cross leans over at an angle of forty-five degrees. I always go about Budapest wanting to push it straight.

Hungarians have a mystic reverence for this crown which does not always extend to its wearer, for the last King of Hungary, that Karl who was also Emperor of Austria, was twice thrown out by the present rulers of Hungary when he tried to regain his Hungarian throne by *coup d'état*. I once found a Hungarian acquaintance writing an official summary of Hungarian post-war history and looked through it, being curious to see in what terms he had described these painful incidents. Under 'March 1921' he had merely written 'First visit of the King to Hungary', and under 'October 1921' 'Second visit of the King to Hungary'.

The point about the Holy Crown of St. Stephen, with its crooked cross, is that it is supposed, as distinct from its wearer, to carry with it certain territories, and among these are the lands lost by Hungary under the Peace Treaty.

Unless or until some radical change comes in Europe, the present Habsburg claimant to it, Otto, can never wear it, for Hungary is unlikely to restore a Habsburg unless Austria does so and opposition to a Habsburg restoration in Austria, which the Austrian Government would accomplish to-morrow if it could, comes both from the Little Entente, which is not necessarily conclusive, but also from Germany, for whom it would mean a major defeat in her aim of unifying the entire German family and the recommencement of the old rivalry between North Germany and South Germany for the leadership of that family.

Thus Hungary seems likely to remain indefinitely a kingdom without a king, for the present under the regency of Admiral Nicholas Horthy, who with General Julius Goemboes, now dead, led the White Terror in Hungary after the war. There was a brief Communist interregnum, ended when Rumanian troops expelled the Communists, and then the Fascists set about re-establishing the old order, killing large numbers of lower-class Hungarians and Jews with much gusto.

This was the first real Fascist experiment in Europe and the men who led it control Hungary to-day, although in the eighteen years that have elapsed the regime has quietened down to a benevolent and almost paternal one, based on a packed parliament, and a good deal of open public criticism in the Press and parliament is allowed.

But while in other large areas of Europe, where the land had been largely in the hands of the aristocracy and the peasants mainly in the position of feudal serfs, the immediate result of the war was to dispossess the big landowners and give the land to the peasants — for instance in Poland, Czechoslovakia and Rumania — in Hungary the Horthy counter-revolution quickly re-established the old order and left the nobles undisturbed in possession of the land and the peasants in a state of semi-serfdom.

At that time, when the universal feeling of the outer world was that the social and material lot of peasants and workers everywhere should be improved, Hungary seemed like a dark feudal island in an enlightened world. Since then, curious thought, the deprivation of the masses in one country after another of all voice in affairs has left Hungary, with its modicum of free speech, looking like a relatively democratic and liberal land.

But the real control of everything remains in the hands of the little group of Magyar noble families. Prince Bülow, one of Kaiser Wilhelm's Chancellors, in his day wrote of Hungary, 'At bottom all internal Hungarian politics, which made such a noise during recent decades, was nothing more than a fight among some noblemen and their satellites: Count Andrassy, Count Albert Apponyi, Count Banffy, Count Khuen-Hedervary, Count Michael Karolyi, and the greatest of them, Count Tisza.'

That stands for 1938. It needs much more than a world war to dislodge the Hungarian aristocracy. And they retain their contempt for the peoples they used to rule and would like to rule again; for the Magyar noble, a Slovak or a Croat is a creature only fitted to work for and wait on Magyars.

It is a country with many good points, good food, good liquor, good music if you like Hungarian gipsy music, and the best female figures in the world. If you wish to test this last statement you need only go one fine day to the St. Gellert baths. Hungary makes the best apricot brandy that you can get. I have often felt so good after drinking this *Barack* that I wanted to have two photographs taken, before and after *Barack*, and send them to the manufacturers.

332

The gipsy music — well, that is a matter of taste, and personally I like the Bulgarian and Rumanian and Serb gipsy music better. There is a Serb gipsy girl in Belgrade whom you should get to sing 'If the dawn knew whom I have in my bed it would never break' any time you go there. But the Budapest gipsy music pleases the Hungarians and plucks at their very heartstrings, no matter how happy they were, so that the tear unbidden trickles down and there was one song, 'Joyless Sunday', which they had to forbid for some time because of the number of suicides it caused, and if the picture it conjured up was anything like that which I have in my mind of a wet November Sunday afternoon in a back street in Brondesbury in the England of about 1910 I can well understand it.

The Hungarians have been bred to think day and night about frontier revision. They are given no rest about it. They are the most intensely patriotic people in the world, and dearly love Hungary. But when they go on holiday they put it behind them as quickly as possible.

CHAPTER 41

WINDSOR INTERLUDE

HE came out of the Western Station in Vienna, Sir Walford Selby after him, and stood for a moment at the head of the steps, bareheaded, blond and boyish in the glare of the lamps, the man under whose rule England might have ridden out the coming storm.

Forty-eight hours before he had been King of England. I looked at him, and thought of the other times and places I had seen him — the Coronation coach, running along the canal-side at St. Omer, on the Somme, here in Vienna. Around me a few curious Viennese waved a friendly greeting. He got into his car and was driven off to his Jewish host, Baron Rothschild, at Enzesfeld.

Forty-eight hours before, I had sat in my darkened room in Vienna, with the Charles Church bathed in green light on the opposite side of the square, and listened to Sir John Reith announcing, in sepulchral tones, 'This is Windsor Castle. His Royal Highness Prince Edward'. The hush that filled all English homes extended to my little room in this foreign capital. It seemed a solemn moment. Then the departing King took his leave of the nation. A good farewell speech. 'God Save the King' at the end — particularly effective.

A while later, I sat again in my little room and heard the new King speaking to the nation. A wonderful thing, radio. He carefully controlled his stutter, the new King, whom we had known as Prince Albert and who was now to be George VI. I wondered why. Because of Albert the Good? Albert the Good, Albert the Better — yes, yes, let's leave it at George.

So that chapter is closed, I thought, as he finished. It had been a well-managed change over, particularly Baldwin's Shakespearean passages with the King. England might have lost her grip on foreign affairs, but she could still handle abdications.

I had known what was coming for long enough, like most Englishmen who lived abroad and most foreigners. The great British public, with its Parliamentary Institutions and Free Press, had been told nothing, until the thing was decided; it had no word to say in a little matter like an abdication. The tact of the British press on this occasion was only outdone by the positively dinosauric *Takt* of the German press which at the command of Göbbels withheld all information about the case from its readers save for the actual news of the abdication, which was hurled at them like a bolt from the blue.

A Sense of Tact had moved the united newspaper proprietors of England to withhold from their readers what all the world knew. The same Sense of Tact ('no intervention whatever from any government quarter') subsequently moved the united picture theatre proprietors of England to withhold from their patrons pictures of the Windsor wedding, which all the world had seen. The same Sense of Tact had even torn pages about the affair from incoming American newspapers, had smashed a photographer's camera at Ipswich when the Simpson divorce action was heard.

Now the thing was finished, I felt that it had been done efficiently but not very creditably. Why this tone of awful righteous indignation from bishops and editorial writers? Why these reproofs of the King after he had been abdicated? Why the vindictive references to 'a woman who has failed to keep two husbands?'

The contrast between the tone of oleaginous adulation used by the ruling classes in England towards the King as long as he was the plastic instrument of their will and the venomous dislike of him which they showed when he wished to marry a woman they did not like was more than I and most of my acquaintances could stomach, although I personally had no strong feelings about the actual issue at all. But I could not understand people who changed their loyalties — which were not necessarily my loyalties — like their socks. I could not understand why a King who had been held up as a model of princely merit for twenty years should have to slink out of England at dead of night simply because he wanted to marry somebody who couldn't be Queen. It could all have been done without rancour. For the British ruling classes that jingle about the Prussian Junkers also seemed to hold good:

> Our unchallenged King and Lord
> As long as he obey our word.

With a few English friends I sat in a studio in Vienna discussing the statements of the Archbishop of Canterbury, and we jointly composed the sonnet, in the best contemporary English manner, which the Poet Laureate would have made about this affair if Poets Laureate were wont to write about such things:

> The hand that blew the sacred fire has failed,
> Laid down the burden in the hour of need,
> So brave begun but flinching in the deed.
> Nor Mary's prayer nor Baldwin's word availed
> To curb the beating heart by love assailed.
> Vainly did Delhi, Canberra, Capetown plead
> The Empire's ruler flouts the Empire's creed
> By Princes, prelates, people sore bewailed.
>
> The triple pillars of the Empire shake,
> A shock of horror passes o'er the land,
> The greatest throne in all the world forsake
> To take a favour from a woman's hand?
> The hallowed pleasures of a kingly life
> Abandoned for a transatlantic wife.

Discussing the thing objectively, we came to the conclusion, as we looked upon it from that Viennese attic, that the people in England who were being most indignant and vindictive about it were all the ones who would have liked to be divorced twice but hadn't.

One evening, while he was awaiting his wedding, I met the Duke of Windsor at the Beefsteaks Club in Vienna, an Anglo-

American dinner club which you will immediately recognize if you see it because beefsteak is never eaten by it and, as an American member once said, all the Englishmen try to behave like gentlemen and all the Americans like Englishmen. You put on a black tie, a thing nobody else in Vienna does, the Viennese don't wear mourning clothes in the evening, and fore-gather at the Grand Hotel, eat solemnly, drink the toasts of The King and the President of the United States, and go home.

On this evening the American Minister, Mr. Messersmith, proposed the King, and Sir Walford Selby the President, and then Sir Walford proposed a third toast, that of the guest of the evening, The Duke of Windsor. The Duke returned thanks by saying 'Thank you gentlemen. I will only answer that, as they say in German — *alle gute Dinge sind drei*'. Which I thought as neat a cap as you could wish.

Afterwards we gathered round him in a circle and he talked eagerly with many of us in turn, usually beginning with 'What was your school?' I thought of that foreign officer in the war, whose idol was the Public School Spirit and whose favourite question this was, and I waited with some inward amusement for this question to be put to me. An instinct must have guided him, for when my turn came the question was one which I could answer without any embarrassment to him — 'What newspaper do you represent?'

He complained of newspapers that evening, and again, some months later, at a press lunch in Paris, rather bitterly.

I thought, as I listened and read, of the thousands, the tens of thousands of journalists all over the world who had contributed to spread the fame of this Prince's charm and merit. I thought of the perfect tact and sympathy, the complete absence of *Schadenfreude*, with which hundreds of newspapers big and little all over Europe had written of his crisis and abdication. I had hardly read a niggardly or even a seriously critical word. No man ever had such selfless service from men of all nations completely unknown to him, who took him completely on trust. Through the press, he had become more popular, throughout the world, than any king in any history. And he complained of the press!

One summer's night, in Vienna, I heard the noise of faint cheering and looked out of my window. The Duke and Duchess of Windsor were leaving the Hotel Bristol. A few pedestrians recognized the car and gave them a friendly cheer as they drove away.

A little later I strolled into a bar. They were there, the Duke and Duchess, with Dudley Forwood, whose friends affectionately called him 'The Perfect Lady in Waiting' because of his admirably discreet and deferential manner in attendance on the great. He had just completed a term as honorary attaché in Vienna when the Duke arrived after the abdication, and had been appointed equerry.

It was rather a dull and dingy bar. In the summer most of the bars are closed in Vienna; the Duke's favourite bar — the Rotter Bar, where the proprietor has the signatures 'Edward P. September 1935' and 'Edward R.I. 1936' in his visitors' book, but asked in vain to have the collection completed by 'Windsor September 1937' — was closed.

The place was half empty.

It was hot and stuffy. A slightly convivial gentleman had the band play 'Ich schenk Dir Tausend Rosen', and sent the waiter across to the Duchess with a bunch of roses. He followed them up himself.

I went home.

CHAPTER 42

GADARENE GALLOP

ON a day I dined with Greeks in Athens. 'What is this news from Paris?' they asked me, 'that, with sanctions against Italy barely begun, your Foreign Minister Hoare and Laval between them have concocted a plan for the partitioning of Abyssinia.'

'It can't be true,' I said.

The next morning I flew over green islands in a blue Aegean to Salonica, and they asked me the same question. 'It's bunk,' I said.

I lunched at Belgrade and heard it again, and in the train to Budapest, where I dined with Hungarians who smiled ironically and said, 'We told ourselves so'.

I read it in the *Zagreb Morgenblatt*, which said that if this news were true the English call to the world to rally against the aggressor had been a lamentable farce. That was what they were thinking about England in the little capital of the Croats.

And the next day, when I lunched in Vienna, not only the whiskers and forepaws but the whole cat was out of the bag, and a mangy beast it was. 'Is that really your English cat?' asked the Viennese. 'God help us, but it is', said I.

That was the beginning of the European rot, and the responsibility for it was England's. Original sin began with Adam, but as far as anybody is ever guilty of anything responsibility for this was English. Everything that has happened in Europe since derives directly from the Abyssinian fiasco and from the failure or refusal of England to face up in time to what was coming. The final bill that England will have to pay for this has not yet been presented.

The mass of English people never gets a clear view of the sequence of events, of cause and effect, of the path along which it is being led. Too much information is withheld. Ministerial speeches in Parliament are often smoke clouds obscuring the facts. Within a few weeks or months Ministers of the Crown expound diametrically opposed theories in the same terms of sincere conviction and inflexible determination. His Majesty's Opposition is under present Parliamentary procedure completely ineffective, a foil for the Government.

That is the awful thing, that a Socialist Government would be even worse than the Conservative ones; the only thing to hope for is a better Conservative Government. The great British public, like a frustrated foxhound, casts vainly about for the scent of the truth among the welter of false trails and red herrings. It thinks to have found the true line one day, only to find the Government careering off on an entirely different line the next, and it gets giddy.

Only a few specialists at home and abroad, students, foreign office officials, diplomats, journalists, see and foresee the inevitable sequence of event leading to event, but as long as the British public is treated like an infirm old lady, who must not be told about anything for fear of heart failure, their knowledge must lie fallow. By this process of cloaking the wolf of truth in the sheepskin of blarney the little pig that is British public opinion was left to play blithely in its house of straw until the big bad wolf was at the door.

The truth about two things that were vital to it — German rearmament and Italian intentions in Abyssinia — was concealed from it until too late. The same process is continuing. The war in Spain, Guernica, the German guns covering the Straits of Gibraltar; in all these things a skin of illusion is drawn over the eyes of the British public.

The Abyssinian War began in October 1935. In April 1935, at Stresa, England, France and Italy had jointly condemned Germany as a treaty breaker, and not a word had been said about Abyssinia.

In 1927 — eight years earlier — one of my useful friends was told by Baron von Neurath, then German Ambassador in Rome and now German Foreign Minister, that Mussolini had told him, 'If I can't get colonies by fair means I shall take Abyssinia'.

All foreign Governments knew of Mussolini's intentions, so

there was plenty of time to prepare. Yet for years after this date British Governments claimed to believe that the cardinal tenet of Italian foreign policy was never to do anything that would antagonize England. Italy, the booted leg standing up to the knee in the Mediterranean, would never challenge the most powerful naval power in the world.

The vast armaments of Italy seem to have been similarly underestimated. Perhaps the gods had made England blind. In January 1935, three months before Stresa, Mussolini asked Simon to define England's attitude about Abyssinia and received no answer from that cautious attorney.

In June 1935, two months after Stresa and four months before the invasion of Abyssinia, Eden saw Mussolini and reported home that Mussolini, learning of inflexible British opposition, was deeply depressed. I believe he even expressed sympathy for 'the defeated Napoleon'.

In July one of my useful friends, who had been to Abyssinia, foretold to me the exact course of the Italian campaign.

In October 1935 Italy invaded and in May 1936 annexed Abyssinia. A triumph not of martial valour but of forethought, well-laid plans, well-weighed odds and superb organization.

I do not lie awake at nights worrying about the Abyssinians. I could never understand why British public opinion was so sensitive about Abyssinians being killed by Italians and Chinese by Japanese and so placidly indifferent about white men in Spain, whose fate affects themselves much more directly, being killed by Italians and Germans and Moors.

Italy took Abyssinia by exactly the same methods by which the Abyssinians once took Abyssinia, by which England took her colonies. The ruling clique in Abyssinia consisted of a group of families, rather like the *deux cent familles* in France, who were only concerned to keep a vice-like hold on the country and enrich themselves. The majority of the population, as my useful friend from Abyssinia tells me, is indifferent whether it is ruled by these men or by the Italians.

It is nonsense that black men all over Africa have been

moved by the Italian annexation to an undying hatred of the whites that will one day take a bloody revenge. The black men are not yet so far; perhaps they will be one day. At present they do not much care whether they are ruled by Britishers, Germans or Italians. In the British Colonies neighbouring Abyssinia, the Italian victory made so deep an impression that native traders advertise their wares as 'Mussolini goods'; they sell better so. Do not believe that Abyssinia is not conquered. Abyssinia is finished. The Italians are as firmly set in Abyssinia as the Japanese in Manchukuo.

I had only a personal sympathy for the Negus, who is a man of rare dignity and who had to sell his table silver at Christie's about the time that the Abyssinian issue was being buried beneath the Anglo-Italian gentlemen's agreement of January 1937, a gentlemen's agreement being one of those things that it takes two to make. He complained with justice that he would have made terms with Mussolini if he had not been encouraged to resist by the prospect of a British-led world rallying to his succour.

Abyssinia does not harass me on its own account, but on my account. Abyssinia is dead, but the ghost of Abyssinia will long stalk England. For that experience of triumphant escape, by the skin of his teeth, from a world mobilized against him by England drove Mussolini into the arms of Germany, and that partnership is an enormously strong military combination and has a very high nuisance value.

The fear of that isolation which he had felt during the Abyssinian war drove Mussolini, two months after its close, to force his protégé Austria to sign a truce with Germany, that Austria in support of whose independence he had at the murder of Dollfuss in 1934 mobilized an army on the Brenner. That means that if Mussolini gets into a war with England in the Mediterranean he will have Germany with him.

The Rome-Berlin partnership — I have the authority of one of my most useful friends for it — is 'solid for all emergencies'. If war comes Germany's price will be Austria and Czechoslovakia at the least; so much Mussolini will have to pay, and that is why as the Abyssinian war was drawing to a close he began strongly fortifying that Italo-Austrian frontier across which he had once been willing to throw troops. If he has to have Germany as a neighbour, he will take no chances. Austria and Czechoslovakia, if the thing temporarily ends there, mean, ultimately, you. They mean that Austrian and Czechoslovak man-power and munition-power will be converted into striking-power somewhere else, and that the German military machine will become even mightier than before.

Abyssinia was a cardinal blunder in British foreign policy. When you look back at it the thing becomes more and more inexplicable.

First there were the wasted years when Italy's military strength was either grotesquely miscalculated or the issue pigeon-holed from sheer inertia. Prime Minister in England was Ramsay MacDonald, who had given way to that form of self-indulgence which expresses itself in a desire to consort with film stars and had had a lunch invitation calmly ignored by Charlie Chaplin. Foreign Minister was John Simon, whose cronies in his Oxford Union days had remarked that he 'might have been a little more impassioned'.

Then came the furious burst of energy when Italy invaded Abyssinia, the British call to the world to combine in action against an aggressor.

This was the most inspiring moment in post-war history. At last that clear clarion call from England for which a trembling world had been waiting. Old England was not decadent, she had not forgotten how to lead a great cause. England rose like one man to the summons; a few weeks later, pricked by the Hoare-Laval plan, British public opinion collapsed like a deflated balloon into an inert and shapeless mass and I am not sure that this was not its last real effort.

The world responded with glad alacrity, happy to have found a leader. Fifty states agreed to apply sanctions against Italy, among them little states which had every reason to avoid incurring her hostility—Greece, whose shores were within jumping distance

343

of the Italian fleet, Bulgaria, though she was a revisionist country and her Queen a daughter of the King of Italy.

An inspiring speech by Sir Samuel Hoare at Geneva produced this world-wide acclamation. Yet behind the scenes, unknown to all, he was already in agreement with Laval, of France, that sanctions should in no event be extended to warlike measures — and how can you enforce sanctions if you are not prepared in the last resort to go to war?

What happened? Sanctions were agreed by an enthusiastic world, glad that England was again taking her place in the lead, in November. On November 14th the Baldwin government went to the country and gained an enormous majority, the tribute of England to its action against the aggressor, against that Italy which had brought Abyssinia into the League and was now invading Abyssinia.

Already in October the *Daily Herald* had reported the existence of a Franco-British plan for the partitioning of Abyssinia, and the report had been officially denied. On December 8th the Hoare-Laval plan, which was precisely that foretold by the *Daily Herald*, was made public.

Sanctions collapsed. A flabbergasted world shook its head. Sir Samuel Hoare resigned, for a brief while. Italy quickly conquered Abyssinia; among other absurdities England had forbidden the export of arms alike to the Italian Goliath, armed to the teeth, and to the Abyssinian David, armed almost only with teeth.

England had made an enemy; Italy had gained an African empire. The Italo-German alliance loomed ahead. The small states shook in their shoes. The prospects of stopping aggression in Europe dwindled to disappearing point.

When will the world know the whole truth of that fatal crisis? The cynics pointed to the victory of the Baldwin government at the polls and said the sanctions-against-Italy cry had only been raised to ensure another four or five years of office, that the intention was never sincere. It looked like that.

How is England ever to know what to think about foreign policy when you lead England for years to believe that Italy is

344

your friend, conceal from England the truth of what you knew to be Italy's intentions in Abyssinia, and then, when the truth is out, lead the world in sanctions against Italy when you have already made up your mind privately to condone the partitioning of Abyssinia?

How is England to know what to think about foreign policy when you tell her in May 1934, 'If you are going to adopt a sanction you must be prepared for war, if you adopt a sanction without being prepared for war you are not an honest trustee of the nation', when in November 1935 you lead the world in applying sanctions against Italy, when in June 1936, after opposing even the full application of economic sanctions, you tell England, 'There is only one way of altering the course of events . . . and that is to go to war . . . I am quite certain that I should not cast my vote to-day for that course of action'. Is that honest stewardry?

How is England to know what to think about foreign policy when you tell her in November 1934 that in a year's time she will still be twice as strong as Germany in the air and in March 1935 you have to learn from Hitler's own lips that Germany is already stronger in the air than the whole British Empire?

Apparently there is no public opinion in England. Apparently there is no blunder a politician can make so great that it will make him unpopular or jeopardize his job.

One motive for the British right-about-turn in the Abyssinian affair may have been the fear that, if war came with Italy, Germany might jump on our back. This was a real danger. German rearmament, concealed by tranquillizing assurances from the British public, was already immense. Three years were lost while a deaf ear was turned to all warnings from specialists who knew the facts. German rearmament began within five minutes of Hitler's advent to power in 1933. In the autumn of 1934 Baldwin was still soothing Parliament with reassuring statements about the British lead in the air. In the autumn of 1935 British rearmament at length cumbersomely got under way. The locusts had eaten three years, and that is the real explanation of everything that is happening in Europe.

To-day you hear that British rearmament will be completed in 1940 or 1942 or 1944, I don't know exactly which, and then, ah then, Britain will take her rightful place. I hope it's true. Perhaps the other heavyweights will wait until the British heavyweight has got his weight down and has had plenty of practice and is ready to think about a match. Blundering is not the monopoly of any one country.

I remember, however, that Farinacci, the former Secretary-General of the Fascist Party, in the summer of 1937 wrote an article in an official Fascist magazine urging that Italy and Germany should go for France and England without further ado, since they would have to fight them one day anyway, and why wait until they were ready? I don't think the great British public ever learned of this article.

But none of these things seems adequately to explain the fiasco of British policy in the Abyssinian issue. After all, England had the Suez Canal in her hands and a great Italian army bottled up, and all its supplies able to be cut off, and the Mediterranean then under English control. England could have given peacebreakers an unforgettable lesson, and never mind how we got our own Empire. We might very well give away some of the Empire once we have shown that we are able to trounce anybody who starts trouble.

The real weakness of British foreign policy may have been a private sympathy with military dictators. While the Abyssinian dispute was yet at fever heat British ministers and British diplomats were saying that, while we must stop aggression, we must not bring Mussolini down. The crowning absurdity. If you go into a boxing match determined not to knock the other man out you are liable to be knocked out yourself.

Grounds for this suspicion first became perceptible when British policy performed its acrobatic feats during the Abyssinian affair. They became clearer during the Spanish civil war, which began in July 1936 and has not yet ended in victory for the Fascist Generalissimo Franco.

The average British reader is probably completely fogged

346

by now about the Spanish war. All newspapers exaggerate one side or the other; actually this is not so much a case where there is much to be said on both sides as one in which there is little to be said for either. The Spaniards are caught between two groups.

Spain is one of the few sideshows in Insanity Fair that I have not visited; but my useful friends have, and I can vouch for the following facts. The war began, hard on the heels of the Abyssinian war, as a military and Fascist revolt against a Republican-Liberal Government, duly elected and without a Red in it.

Franco began by using large numbers of Moors — it took several centuries, I believe, to get the Moors out of Spain in the name of civilization and now they are back in the name of civilization — and Spanish Foreign Legionaries, who are largely foreigners, and later Mussolini sent him an Italian army and Hitler large numbers of German-manned aeroplanes and heavy guns. Franco also had some Spaniards, how many you can imagine for yourselves, since with this help, he has been trying for nearly two years to conquer Spain.

The spectacle of this foreign invasion of Spain so offended foreign eyes that a Non-Intervention Committee of all the intervening powers and some non-intervening ones was formed in London. A British contribution was again to forbid the export of arms to both parties, and France followed suit. The Franco insurgents had all the arms they wanted from Italy and Germany. The Madrid forces could get none from France and England. With the wickedness of the animal that defends itself when attacked they got some from Russia.

Even without this export ban, the British public was told, the Madrid Government could not have obtained supplies from England or France, which were busy with their own rearmament. Remember that Italy and Germany were able to send vast quantities of men and arms and munitions and yet face with equanimity the possibility of a major European war. This will give you some idea of the real state of armaments in Europe.

When the insurgents were approaching Bilbao, the capital of the Basques, British shipping was warned not to try and go to Bilbao on account of Francist mines. The Bilbaons were being starved out. One or two British skippers ran their ships nevertheless to Bilbao and showed that the alleged mine blockade was a myth. Nevertheless Bilbao fell to Italian troops and German aeroplanes and the victory was officially celebrated in Italy as an Italian one.

All this time the Non-Intervention Committee was sitting, and discussing the withdrawal of the volunteers. The real object of this ghastly comedy was apparently to keep up a pretence of international efforts at mediation until Franco won, when Non-Intervention could be quietly interred alongside sanctions.

What are the facts about foreign intervention on both sides? By October 1937 Italy, which had at first angrily denied that she had any troops in Spain, had officially stated that she had 40,000 there, this in refutation of the Madrid assertion that 100,000 Italians were fighting for Franco. Casualty lists of Italians killed in Spain 'in the cause of Fascist civilization' were being published regularly in the Italian press.

Germany had by the air bombardment of Guernica, which was completely obliterated, given the first example of 'totalitarian' warfare — the extermination of every living thing you see. The facts of this exploit, the most terrible thing that has happened in Europe since the war, were given in detail by a British newspaper correspondent at Guernica in a fully documented dispatch containing the types of the German machines used, an eye-witness account, survivors' stories, and the like. Several attempts in the House of Commons to bring the matter of Guernica to debate were defeated by pigeon-hole methods. England suggested an international investigation to several other intervening and non-intervening countries, some did not reply, and there the matter dropped. Basque was Catholic and peasant and peaceful, not in the war zone, and a Basque priest set off for Rome to tell the Holy Father, who is an Italian patriot, about it, but nothing more was ever heard of his mission.

No proof has ever been given that Russian troops were sent

to Spain. In fact, none were sent. A British official in Madrid who saw some Austrian and German and Polish anti-Fascists of the International Brigade went about saying he had seen the Russian army; a political pilgrim saw some dead in tanks and 'was sure they were Slavs'. Russia did send tanks and quite a lot of Russian-manned aeroplanes.

In the circumstances non-intervention seemed to be a device for hushing-up intervention until Franco should win and Mr. Lloyd George, finding his form again in his old age, said in the House of Commons on October 28th, 1937, that 'the history of non-intervention was discreditable in many respects and in most respects dishonourable ... if its aim was to prevent the intervention of foreign powers it had been an utter failure and a boasted failure, but if its object was to give a definite and what might be a decisive advantage to the insurgents over the legitimate government of Spain then it had been a triumphant success'. Mr. Lloyd George's figures about foreign intervention — 80,000 Italians and 10,000 Germans fighting for Franco and 20,000 mixed foreigners fighting for the Government were also about right, according to my useful friends. But the Italians and Germans were sent by their governments; the others were real volunteers.

The position in Spain is as if Sir Oswald Mosley, with the help of Italian and German troops and aircraft and artillery and a large number of Gurkhas, were to save England for the English.

By the end of 1937 the victory of Franco seemed in sight and Eden in the House of Commons was only able to say that he did not believe a Franco government would be unfriendly to Great Britain, that 'there are countries which hold Communist propaganda to be more culpable of the Spanish civil war than any other body', that 'opinion in the democratic countries on this question is deeply and completely divided'.

Well, I still have to learn how Communist propaganda starts a military revolt led by Fascist officers, and by what devilish devices it coaxes a reluctant Mussolini and an unwilling Hitler to invade Spain.

349

Is another government based on the people's vote to be destroyed? Another military despotism to be set up in Europe twenty years after a world war fought to overthrow military despots and make the world safe for democracy?

> To you from failing hands we throw
> The torch; be yours to hold it high.
> If ye break faith with us who die
> We shall not sleep, though poppies blow
> In Flanders fields.

In 1938 all this talk about poppies seems to me just poppycock.

For some reason Franco is popular in England. Madrid is an execrably bad propagandist, and the word 'Red' is coming to have such hypnotic force that it blinds people to all reason; and produces such oddities as the letter written to an English newspaper by a rabbit-trapping reader who said, 'All this talk about the inhumanity of spring-traps is nonsense and in my opinion Bolshevik money is behind it'.

The naive calculation now apparently is that a generalissimo who would owe his victory entirely to Italian and German arms, fighting men and money, would after his victory be friendly to England, and not in any way encroach on our right of way through the Mediterranean to our overseas Empire.

Another painful awakening is in store for England. When Japan attacked China, Germany and Italy openly showed their sympathy for her by signing with her the Triple Alliance against Bolshevism at Rome, the wording of which claims for these countries the right to intervene anywhere — in England, Iceland Yugoslavia, where you will — in any place they consider 'Red'. Are these Powers going to let Franco out of their grasp, when he has Spain in his?

The thing was most succinctly put by Captain Liddell Hart, the Military Correspondent of *The Times*, when he wrote:

> The danger to English interests through the Spanish War is so obvious that it is difficult to understand the eagerness

with which some of the avowedly patriotic sections of the British public have desired the rebels' success. Class prejudice and property sense would seem to have blinded their strategical sight.

In 1850 the Austrian General Haynau, who had fired on a Hungarian crowd, was beaten up when he came to London by Barclay and Perkins's indignant draymen, and Lord Palmerston withstood Queen Victoria's demand to apologize to Vienna by saying that Vienna should have known better than send Haynau to England, since it perfectly well knew what England thought of his cruelties in Italy and Hungary. In 1938 Franco, Hitler and Mussolini could count on a courteous welcome in England and if the draymen of Barclay and Perkins started any nonsense they would soon find themselves in the place where Reds ought to be.

In 1914, I think, opinion throughout the world rose in angry remonstrance against a savage display of Prussian militarism somewhere in Alsace, when a Prussian officer cut down with his sword a crippled cobbler who did not get out of his way quickly enough. In 1938 crippled cobblers might be mowed down in swathes with machine-guns in Andalusia and a complacent outer world would only be invited to applaud the exploits of the anti-Reds, who had nipped some new Bolshevist devilry in the bud.

But the first victims of Hitler's New Army have not been Reds or Marxists or Jews or Bolshevists, but Spanish fisherfolk and peasants and good Catholics at that, and this means, ultimately, you.

This obsession with the word Red causes many people in England to toy with the pleasant delusion that you can use Germany, Germany who wants your colonies, as a Bulwark against Bolshevism. Germany, who covets your backyard, is to be your armed doorkeeper.

The returned burglar turned moralist yourself, you want to buy off the new burglar by giving him the spoons — but not your own spoons, somebody else's spoons. Give Germany Tanganyika? Oh no.

If this chapter has not already depressed you enough, buy a copy of the 'Memorandum on the Present State of British Relations with Germany' which is published, as No. 16 in their series, by the Friends of Europe. It costs you 2d., and you could not spend twopence better.

The memorandum gives you an exact picture of the present state of British relations with Germany and of what you have to expect. But you will need to change the dates and names, because it was written in 1907, by Eyre Crowe, who was then a Foreign Office Official, became head of the Foreign Office after the war and, unfortunately for England, died far too young. He had German blood, he was married to a German lady, and he knew Germany perfectly. In fact, he even had his windows smashed when the war broke out and anything more ludicrous than that I can't imagine, because if his advice had been taken there might well have been no war.

Thirty years have passed. A World War has been fought. A million British lives have been laid down. The graves of your dead girdle the world, as King George V said. And in 1938 you are back exactly where you were in 1907 when Sir Eyre Crowe wrote his memorandum, hoping to open people's eyes. Germany is mightier than ever. She wants just the same things. England is as irresolute as ever. We are drifting to war.

Here are some of the things Eyre Crowe said. Change a few names and you have a photograph of Europe to-day.

'Prince Bismarck had also succeeded by all sorts of devices, including the famous reinsurance treaty with Russia, in keeping France and Russia apart so long as he remained in office. The conclusion of the Franco-Russian alliance some time after Bismarck's fall filled Germany with concern and anxiety and she never ceased in her efforts at least to neutralize it by establishing the closest possible relations with Russia herself.'

'Germany is bound to be as strongly opposed to a possible Anglo-Russian understanding and indeed there is already conclusive evidence of German activity to prevent any such contingency happening in the near future.'

'Germany's foreign policy always has been and will be to try and frustrate any coalition between two states which might result in damaging Germany's interests and prestige and Germany will . . . not hesitate to take such steps as she thinks proper to break up the coalition.' (Quotation from a German statesman.)

'England, as a tiny island power with vast overseas colonies and dependencies whose existence and survival is inseparably bound up with the possession of preponderant seapower, has a greater interest than any other country in the independence of nations . . . England's traditional policy has been to maintain the balance of power by throwing her weight now in this scale and now in that, but ever on the side opposed to the political dictatorship of the strongest single state or group at a given time. The opposition into which England must inevitably be driven to any country aspiring to such a dictatorship assumes almost the form of a law of nature.'

'Is it right or even prudent for England to incur any sacrifices or see other friendly nations sacrificed merely in order to assist Germany in building up step by step the fabric of a universal preponderance?'

'Between England and Germany there has never been any real clashing of material interests, no unsettled controversies over out-standing questions. Yet for the last twenty years German Govern-ments have never ceased reproaching British Governments with want of friendliness and with persistent opposition to German political plans . . . From 1884 onward, when Bismarck first launched his country into colonial and maritime enterprise, numerous quarrels arose between the two countries. They all have in common this feature — that they were opened by acts of direct and unmis-takable hostility to England on the part of the German Govern-ment.'

'But in spite of their indignation successive British Governments agreed to make concessions and accept compromises which not only appeared to satisfy all German demands but were by the avowal of both parties calculated and designed to re-establish if possible on a firmer basis the fabric of Anglo-German friendship.'

(After Kaiser Wilhelm's congratulatory telegram to President Kruger anent the Jameson raid.) 'The hostile character of Germany's foreign policy was for the first time thoroughly understood by the British public who up to then, owing to the anxious care of their Government to minimize the results of the perpetual friction with

Germany and to prevent any aggravation of that friction by concealing as far as possible the unpleasant details of Germany's aggressive behaviour, had been practically unaware of the persistently contemptuous treatment of their country by their Teutonic cousins.'

'It might be deduced that the antagonism is too deeply rooted in the relative position of the two countries to allow of its being bridged over by the kind of temporary expedients to which England has so long and so patiently resorted. On this view of the case it would have to be assumed that Germany is deliberately following a policy which is essentially opposed to vital British interests and that an armed conflict cannot in the long run be avoided, except by England either sacrificing those interests, with the result that she would lose her position as an independent Great Power, or making herself too strong to give Germany the chance of succeeding in a war. This is the opinion of those who see in the whole trend of Germany's policy conclusive evidence that she is consciously aiming at the establishment of a German hegemony, first in Europe, eventually in the World.'

'Bismarck suffered from the nightmare of coalitions. He particularly dreaded the hostile combination against his country of France and Russia and, as one certain means of counteracting that danger, he desired to bring England into the Triple Alliance, or at least to force her into independent collision with France and Russia, which would inevitably have placed her by Germany's side. He knew England's aversion to the entanglement of alliances and to any policy of determined assertion of national rights, such as would have made her a power to be seriously reckoned with by France and Russia. But Bismarck had also a poor opinion of the power of English Ministers to resist determined pressure. He apparently believed he could compel them to choose between Germany and a universal opposition to England. When the colonial agitation in Germany gave him an opening, he most probably determined to bring it home to England that meekness and want of determination in foreign affairs do not constitute a policy; that it was wisest and certainly least disagreeable for her to shape a decided course in a direction which would secure her Germany's friendship; and that in co-operation with Germany lay freedom from international troubles as well as safety, whilst a refusal to co-operate brought inglorious conflicts, and the prospect of finding Germany ranged with France and Russia for the specific purpose of damaging British interests.'

'The action of Germany towards this country since 1890 might be

354

likened not inappropriately to that of a professional blackmailer whose extortions are wrung from his victim by the threat of some vague and dreadful consequences in case of refusal. To give way to the blackmailer's menaces enriches him; but it has long been proved by uniform experience that, although this may secure for the victim temporary peace, it is certain to lead to renewed molestation and higher demands after ever-shortening periods of amicable forbearance. The blackmailer is usually ruined by the first resolute stand made against his exactions and the determination to face all risks of a possible disagreeable situation rather than to continue in the path of endless concessions. But, failing such determination, it is probable that the relations between the two parties will grow steadily worse.'

'There is one road which, if past experience is any guide to the future, will most certainly not lead to any permanent improvement of relations with any power, least of all Germany, and which must therefore be abandoned: that is the road paved with graceful British concessions — concessions made without any conviction either of their justice or of their being set off by equivalent counter-services. The vain hopes that in this manner Germany can be "conciliated" and made more friendly, must be definitely given up. It may be that such hopes are still cherished by irresponsible people, ignorant, perhaps necessarily ignorant, of the history of Anglo-German relations during the last twenty years, which cannot be better described than as the history of a systematic policy of gratuitous concessions, a policy which has led to the highly disappointing result disclosed by the almost perpetual state of tension existing between the two countries. Men in responsible positions, whose business it is to inform themselves, and to see things as they really are, cannot conceivably retain any illusion on this subject.'

'Germany will be encouraged to think twice before she gives rise to any fresh disagreement if she meets on England's part with unvarying courtesy and consideration in all matters of common concern, but also with a prompt and firm refusal to enter into any one-sided bargains or arrangements and the most unbending determination to uphold British rights and interests in every part of the globe. There will be no surer or quicker way to win the respect of the German Government and of the German nation.'

When you have read that you can see how far we have progressed since 1907. The position now is exactly as Eyre Crowe saw it then, with one added complication, and that a very grave one.

In those days each country thought only of its own national interests — 'What we have we hold.' To-day the whole question is fogged by the smoke cloud that the dictators give out — 'Come in with us and save the world from Bolshevism.' They do not intend to save the world from anything. They are after exactly the same things as their predecessors — territory and power. At the end they will have destroyed neither Bolshevism nor Russia, and most of their victims will be peaceable citizens, workmen and peasants who are conscripted into the respective armies, inhabitants of some town that suddenly finds itself destroyed for no reason at all, like Guernica. But they put out their smoke cloud — and when smoke gets in your eyes . . .

It is all part of a much bigger process, which has nothing at all to do with the patriotism and everything to do with greed. Up to the beginning of the nineteenth century the peasants were mainly serfs, whose labour and daughters were the property of the lord of the manor. During the nineteenth century they gradually cast off the bonds of slavery and began to acquire possession of the land. At the same time the mechanical age brought a new race of slaves, the slaves of the machine. Their conditions of life were at first also little better than those of serfs. All through the nineteenth century there was a gradual movement towards improving the lot of the peasants and workers, and this process reached its climax in the world war. This not only set nations free — in Europe 80,000,000 people who had lived under alien rule. It also gave a wider measure of freedom to the workers and peasants in the defeated and liberated countries. The peasants in liberated Czechoslovakia and in Rumania were given their land. The workers in Germany and Austria gained greater freedom of speech and organization than ever before, and this led to improved housing and health conditions and higher wages.

What you are really seeing in Europe to-day is the reaction to this process, which met with general acceptance in the nineteenth century, a century of enlightenment, and humane

356

thought, but is being more and more widely challenged in the twentieth century, which is a century of darkness and retrogression.

In many respects you are already back in the dark ages. In many countries you have no individual rights at all, only the right to be a member of one big mutual admiration society, one of millions of men all pulling on the Hitler or Mussolini rope and singing, like sailors the old sea chanty, 'Oh, what a wonderful man, oh, what a wonderful man'.

You are not allowed to know what is happening either in your own or other countries. You have to be seen and not heard. You have to do what you are told, and die when you are told.

The new feature in Spain is that for the first time the parent Fascist Powers have intervened to ensure the success of the home Fascist movement. ('As Signor Mussolini has said, with characteristic terseness, Fascism is not an article of export.' — Colonel Blimp, writing to the newspapers.)

Spain has shown once again that, at the moment when the masses in any country are within grasp of real emancipation and freedom, the army and church and royalists and aristocrats and white-collar classes will turn on them with cannon, and if necessary call in foreigners or even black troops to help suppress them. You remember the German plaints about 'black troops in the Ruhr'; Germans are fighting shoulder to shoulder with Moors in Spain against Spaniards.

If there were a republican labour movement in England, and it seemed likely to get a majority at an election, the same thing might happen there. Don't believe the cliché about 'it can't happen in England'. It can. The revolver argument is universally convincing and Englishmen are no more bullet-proof than foreigners. You already have in England some of the stigmata of a Fascist regime — a parliament with an enormous majority returned on a false issue and a dummy opposition, a press that in part is already subordinated to German and Italian wishes — and the rest of the change-over might be

357

quickly made if the working-class masses became really restless.

I don't want to give an exaggerated picture. Human life goes on everywhere much the same, whether a dictator is ruling a country with a rod of iron, or a paternal prince governing by kindness, or Socialists republicanizing the land; the bakers bake their bread, the milkman delivers the milk, the boys and girls stroll under the trees in the dusk. Only the relatively few who are cast into concentration camps in peace or the much larger number who suffer in war directly feel the consequences of these things. In their day-to-day lives they may not even notice whether their country is moving upwards to the stars of humanity and enlightenment and toleration or downward to the gloomy valley of tyranny and ignorance.

But if man is to become a dignified human being and not just a stupid forked radish there is only one choice for him. Are you going to shape your own thought, your own work, your own life? Or are you going to have these things decided for you by other people from the day you are born to the day you die, like sheep in a pen?

Possibly all these things are less important than they seem. Mr. Wells says that if the world were the size of a ping-pong ball the sun would be a globe nine feet thick nearly a quarter of a mile away, and the moon a small pea two and a half feet from the world, and all around there would be practically nothing at all, and I am not prepared to challenge him. In that vast emptiness beyond human understanding we are all the most infinitesimal maggots scratching at the rind of an insignificant cheese, and Lord Maggot, and Old School Tie Maggot, and King Maggot, and Führer Maggot and Duce Maggot and Henry Ford Maggot and Oil Trust Maggot are all rather ridiculous with their self-important clamour about this piece of the cheese being better than any other part of the cheese and Black Maggots being better than Red Maggots, and the League of Maggots being nothing but the instrument of the Jew Maggots. For my part, I am for the cheese, the whole cheese and nothing but the cheese.

CHAPTER 43

ENGLAND GROPING IN THE DARK

I CAME to England at the end of 1937. An Austrian friend of mine in Vienna, who knows England very well, had been across and returned depressed. He said it reminded him of Austria before the war which destroyed that great Empire. Times were good but there was a defeatist spirit abroad that ill accorded with them. I wanted to form my own opinions.

I saw what he meant. I found abundant, hectic prosperity, but an undertone of fear and incomprehension of the future. The country was afraid of the future because it could not understand the present. I could feel the universal, almost religious horror of war, the inarticulate question, 'How is it possible that we have come to this plight again so soon?' the desperate endeavour to understand what was going on in Europe from the tangle of contradictory statements, misleading declarations, smoke-cloud debates and right-about-turn politics.

What is the use of a religious horror of war in a world where you have encouraged the rout of moderate men and the rise of belligerent martial dictatorships?

I reached England on the eve of Armistice Day. After nineteen years the ceremony of remembrance at the Cenotaph was as thronged as ever, and had remained the same in every detail but one — a man ran out of the crowd shouting, 'Cease this hypocrisy. You are conniving in a new war'.

Sir Samuel Hoare stated in the House that he suffered from delusions.

In the evening I went to a cinema and saw the ceremony, and the interruption, on the screen. Afterwards an organist played wartime songs, songs to which I had marched and danced for four years, songs which for years after the war had reawakened in me the emotions of the war — 'It's a long way to Tipperary', 'There's a long, long trail a-winding', 'Who were you with last night?', 'Land of hope and glory', 'Everybody ought to know how to dance the tickletoe', 'Pack up your troubles in your old kit-bag'.

As I watched the ceremony about the Cenotaph and listened to those songs, with the picture of Insanity Fair in my mind, I found myself empty of any emotion but cynicism. Not yet twenty years, and out there in Insanity Fair 'pacifist' is a shameful name, men who never knew and never will know war are preaching its glories while they amass their bank balances in neutral countries, men who learned the lesson of the last war and preached peace are lying in perpetuity in concentration camps and prisons, in England rich old men and women are the apostles of the martial dictatorships.

In Flanders Fields the poppies blow!

The first newspaper I took up in England contained a quotation from a new official textbook for the Hitler Youth. Some old German professor had written what Papen, Banse, Göbbels and others who will die in their beds had previously said:

'It is repugnant to the heroic man that death on the battlefield should be made the occasion for lamentations and sentimentality. Such a death sets the seal on life and is an inspiration to those who come after. Death on the battlefield should be regarded as a longed-for conclusion of life.' A religious horror of war won't help you much against that.

The next newspaper I picked up told me that Lord Halifax was going to Berlin to see Hitler. In thirty years, with a world war in between, the position has changed by four letters — from the Haldane Mission to the Halifax Mission. Haldane in 1906 and 1912 achieved nothing, unless he misled the Germans about England's feeling. Simon and Eden in 1935 achieved nothing. England, uncomprehending, looks on. Are we with Germany or against her? Is she against us or not? Are we going to give her back her colonies or not? What is our policy to be? Questions never answered.

'The English are a decadent people.' Do you remember

360

who said that? Bismarck, when England ceded the Ionian Islands to Greece.

I found in England a growing feeling that Germany had not had a fair deal and that France and Czechoslovakia ought to give her one. I found that, as Germany grew stronger, wealthy English people in increasing numbers were coming to perceive the justice of her claims against Austria and Czechoslovakia. I found a certain body of opinion that was for flinging Austria and Czechoslovakia to the German wolves. And I found these people convinced that God and his angels shared their ideas and that anybody who challenged them and thought that England ought to begin by giving away Tanganyika before she gave away other people's land was a saboteur and Red, or had lived too long abroad and gone native.

I shall be curious to see if Halifax subdues Hitler, as he subdued Gandhi. It is a far cry from India to Berlin.

Largely responsible for his visit was that Sir Nevile Henderson whom you last saw walking behind the coffin of his murdered friend Alexander of Yugoslavia. In Belgrade they used to call Sir Nevile, bachelor and martinet, the uncrowned King of Yugoslavia. He believes in strong-hand politics. He was Alexander's greatest friend, approved of the King's dictatorship. His friendship was a great asset to Alexander, for the Balkan mind attaches extraordinary importance to Great Power opinions, seldom distinguishes between Great Powers and their Ambassadors, and saw in this friendship a sign that England was behind Alexander.

Alexander's death disclosed the weak point in all dictatorships — the void, so difficult to fill, that follows the death of the dictator. It showed that dictatorship solves no problems. Most Serbs now feel that the dictatorship was a mistake.

Sir Nevile, on his arrival at the British Embassy in Berlin, made a speech calling for England to discard her critical attitude towards National Socialist Germany and show more understanding for 'this great social experiment'. He is said to correspond directly with members of the British Cabinet,

361

and he persuaded it to make a big show at Hitler's Hunting Exhibition in Berlin, after its meagre display at the World Exhibition in Paris. This enabled him to invite Halifax over 'for the Hunting Exhibition'.

Will Henderson's method achieve anything? Low drew an immortal cartoon which showed Hitler conducting a nervous Halifax and an apprehensive British lion round the Hunting Exhibition, on the walls of which were fine trophies labelled 'Weimar', 'Versailles', 'Locarno', and a number of vacant spaces marked 'Reserved'. Dotted lines from the eyes of the apprehensive British lion to the largest of these reserved spaces.

I found in London that most of the snobs had gone Fascist. They no longer asked 'What was his school?' or 'Is he quite out of the top drawer?' They had invented a new question — 'Isn't he rather far to the Left?' They meant the same thing.

I marvelled at London. Rolls-Royces as thick as black-berries. Deification of the white tie. New restaurants opening on every hand, all foreign-owned and foreign-staffed — ' 'Ow many breads you 'ave, please?' In the Café Royal, English people were in a minority. In many of the restaurants I visited the majority of the guests were foreigners or Jews. I saw many German immigrants. I found half a dozen Jews I had known in Berlin in pre-Hitler times occupying highly paid posts in British firms — newspapers, chemicals, television.

I hardly dared venture into Piccadilly or Bond Street at night — my French was too rusty, through disuse. When I struggle with it nowadays it reminds me of a notice I once saw in an Italian hotel: 'Avec le garçon on tire un coup, avec la femme de chambre on tire deux coups.'

The traffic-light system was the best I had ever seen, from the point of view of the pedestrian and of general safety. A Jew, they told me, was responsible for it, and he was now Minister of War. That meant that he would be in charge of one branch of British rearmament, and I was glad to hear it, because he seemed to be a man who would get on with his job.

Between Park Lane, Piccadilly, St. James's Street and Pall Mall I found that Little England which, to judge from the British newspapers, you would think to be England itself. Sometimes a newspaper sends a special correspondent to the derelict areas, as you might send Stanley to Africa to look for Livingstone, and he writes them up and for a moment the British newspaper reader is able to see what prosperity looks like from Durham. But for the most part the British Press lives on the activities of a few thousand people in London's West End. 'Garter Ceremony at Windsor — two pages of pictures'; 'Ascot — two pages of pictures'; 'Eton v. Harrow at Lord's'. I should like to see Eton v. Jarrow at Jarrow.

In Parliament, as I judged from my newspapers, there was a shadow Labour opposition, led by shadow leaders, Attlee, Sir Stafford Cripps — how circumstances alter K.C.s — Dalton, Greenwood, Thurtle.

The newspapers still printed selected but succulent divorce cases, with the inevitable British paraphernalia of worst man, bribesmaids and decree obsolete.

The same insufferable things were being patiently borne in the London I returned to, as if it were beyond the power of God or man to alter them — railings round the gloomy squares, imbecile licensing laws that led the less well-to-do to order two drinks together at five minutes to twelve so that they might get a little more alcohol into them before they were turned out, pubs with first, second and third class compartments, queues for the cheaper theatre seats that could just as easily be booked.

My Serb friend whom I met in London, after contemplating with baffled incomprehension the private-bar-saloon-bar-public-bar-jug-and-bottle-department system, said, 'In my country you'd have riots if you tried to introduce the first, second and third class systems into drinking'. I tried to get a drink for him after midnight, paid five shillings each to become members of a bottle-party in a mildewed cellar where the band consisted of a trapdrummer accompanying a gramophone and the lavatory was more squalid than anything you could find

363

in the Balkans, was offered a choice between non-alcoholic near-beer or whisky at twenty-five shillings a bottle, and fled. 'In this country', he said, 'you seem to do everything you can to make a man feel small if he hasn't much money.'

The girls were prettier and better-dressed than I ever remembered them and were growing straighter, discarding that adenoidal manner of speech, very self-possessed, most intelligent. You felt you could cut diamonds with them. They seemed to have been changed beyond recognition by the talking films, from which they had taken their appearance, mannerisms and speech. They smoked in the streets and that's a matter of indifference to me, but it would cause a riot from Berlin to Athens.

I found everybody uneasy about Europe, ignorant about Europe, uncomprehending. Too little is told the public, too much concealed. Parliamentary debates often curtain the truth instead of revealing it. Parliamentary procedure often acts as a gag. Government answers to questions are often red herrings. A fierce law of libel hampers public discussion and criticism. It may cost you £25,000 to call a man a Jew, or £7500 to call a variety artists' organization a racket. The living are thus adequately protected. You are a Red if you criticize the Government. You are a bounder if you criticize a permanent official. You are a cad if you speak ill of the dead.

Thus I discovered some of the many reasons for the feeling my Austrian friend had noticed.

But I rediscovered England on this trip. The people, I found, were better than their leaders. Class and caste were still paramount, like useless but indestructible Norman fortresses, but the masses were gradually becoming enlightened, and this process will continue unless it is forcibly repressed by some development akin to that of Fascism abroad.

On the bookstalls you could for a shilling buy a little book, *This England*, that in simple quotations from the words and writings of England's leaders gave an amusing but startling picture of Anglo-Saxon attitudes towards burning problems of the day. 'Sir Francis Fremantle (Conservative, St. Albans), referring to the physical condition of the people, said hunger in some cases was a good thing. Considerable trouble was caused to-day by over-eating, bad eating or by bad choice of food.'

The newspapers still gave unquestioning adulation to British Institutions, but were beginning to pillory and lampoon snobbery and ignorance when these became too blatant, and the fact that nearly all newspapers read by the masses carried these debunking columns and cartoons showed that they were reflecting a widespread popular feeling of impatience and cynicism. But where a world war has failed to shake these things debunking is unlikely quickly to dislodge them. The old school tie has been jollied to death in England but lives on, as virile, ignorant and arrogant as ever. The most powerful trade union in the world is that of the old school tie in England.

But it was refreshing to be in England. Except in Parliament and the daily press, which were being progressively muzzled, there was still much freedom of thought and speech, and that is a thing beyond price. You have to live in a dictatorship country to know how your brain shrivels up in course of time from disuse, from keeping your tongue and your thoughts constantly in check. When you come to England and go to lunch with two or three cronies who freely but undogmatically air their views about this and that, without fear or favour, you actually begin to feel your grey matter awaking to life from that long-forgotten stimulant, good conversation.

And I loved the manners of porters, newspaper-men, taxi-drivers, bus-drivers and conductors, their quiet and unenvious but emphatic cynicism about the class-ridden world in which they worked hard for a meagre livelihood. I liked the tranquil, but succinct remarks about the powers that rule London that I heard from a bus-conductor who was going to be two hours late reaching his home and a cold dinner after a long day's work because King Leopold of the Belgians was being driven to the Mansion House.

I went and renewed the acquaintance of men with whom I had worked nearly twenty years earlier at a typist's desk. They were still sitting at their desk; they had been catching the 9.15 to town every morning and 6.30 from town every evening for all those years; I had in the meantime been all over Europe and had a grand life and earned enough to support myself in a manner to which I had not been accustomed. They were glad to see me and entirely without envy and were as pleased as I was that I had had a break, and in my heart I humbly made obeisance to them.

And in my heart, and almost against my will, I felt some feeling stirring in me for that London where I was born, the biggest — I would not say the greatest — city in the world, to which I had crept back, a frustrated runaway, so many years ago, that London which has more acres of dingy squalor to the square mile than the capital of a great empire has any right to. True, when I walked through Leicester Square one night and heard a girl behind me say, in that extraordinary adenoidal accent, 'I love Luddud at dight, I thig id's a marvellous spod, dode chew?', I wanted to turn on her and say, 'No, I don't, I think it's lousy, with its lunatic electric signs all over Piccadilly Circus and its imbecile drinking laws and its hole-and-corner bottle parties and its French tarts all over Piccadilly and anyway have you seen Praed Street at night?'

But after a few weeks I had to be honest with myself and admit that, if you have to have modern cities, London at present has more merits than most. For in London you have wealth and opportunity. Both the wealth and the opportunity are closely guarded by little cliques and cabals sitting in the clubs of Pall Mall and St. James's Street, but there are inlets, and if you have a brain or an idea to sell you are more likely to find a buyer for them in London than most places. Wit can still find a market there.

366

Imagine the problem of an author of genius, for instance, if he happens to be born a Bulgar or Greek, knowing no language but his own, his struggles to find a publisher even for his tiny home market, the almost impossibility of ever finding the narrow channel of translation into the great markets of the English, French or German-speaking worlds.

In London, that London that I strove so hard to escape as an office-boy, the pavements are still paved with gold, if you can find it.

That is one thing that gives London a magnetic attraction to men of talent from all lands. It accounts for the high standard of your books, of many of your popular newspapers, which you criticize for their sensationalism but which are often very well written, of your satirical journals and weeklies — other than those dreary hebdomadal collations of pictures of titled people blinking blearily over their cocktail glasses at the photographer's flashlight.

I liked the cheapness of good clothes, and wondered why so many of my countrymen were so incurably ill-dressed. I liked the cheapness of other things, less essential but desirable, which are quite beyond the reach of the average man in most of the efficient dictatorship countries I know, immolated behind their patriotic tariff walls. I liked the high standard of the plays and revues, the zest of the players and the dance girls, the pace of the numbers and the music. Above all, after many years abroad, I recovered a deep respect for the quality of the wares sold in many — not all — shops, for the general standard of business morality, the desire to satisfy, the readiness to exchange, the punctuality of delivery.

I even enjoyed London, and England. In Insanity Fair as I have seen it, it is one of the biggest, most solid, most prosperous booths. I don't know how long that can last. I came away unconvinced that 'the English are a decadent people'. I didn't think they were decadent. I wondered about their leaders, and whither they were being led. The finest troops cannot avail without good generalship.

CHAPTER 44

FIRST MAKE MAD

In Vienna, on a Sunday, at midday, and particularly on a sunny Sunday, the whole population is abroad. The streets are full and the coffee houses are full. But on this Sunday the streets were empty, save for an occasional pedestrian, and in the coffee houses the waiters stood about in unaccustomed idleness. Hitler was speaking. For the first time his voice was being heard in Austria, his native land. Everybody was indoors, at the loudspeaker.

I sat in a little room overlooking the deserted Karlsplatz, with a Viennese family, father, mother, son, daughter. We sat in a hushed semi-circle, expectantly watching the box as if we thought Hitler himself might jump out of it. I heard the sounds, that I remembered so well, of the assembling Reichstag, Göring's opening address, and then The Voice burst upon us.

'Give us four years' he had said that day of the Potsdam pilgrimage. Now five years had passed, and he was presenting his accounts to the German people, not only in Germany, but already beyond the Reich frontiers.

I thought of all that had happened between. The Voice had changed, and so had the accent; it was no longer broad Austrian it was almost Prussian. But its message was the same — hatred, war. I looked at my Viennese friends. The parents were Austrians of the old school, good Catholics with a longing for the Kaiser. The son was a Nazi. The daughter, who had spent many years in Germany, detested the Nazis. They all sat spell-bound.

A few weeks before, on February 4th, 1938, there had been a half-sequel to the great clean-up of June 30th, 1934. In 1934 the army, and the classes traditionally associated with it, had won hands down; Hitler, at their bidding, had had his Party extremists shot. This time the Party got a little of its own back.

The men who counted as the 'go-slow' group were relegated and some of their places were taken by fierier spirits. Foreign Minister Constantin von Neurath, the old-school diplomat, was shelved and Joachim von Ribbentrop, the man of the German-Japanese-Italian anti-Comintern Pact, became Foreign Minister. That meant full-steam-ahead on such adventures as intervention in Spain, threats to Austria and Czechoslovakia, and — who knows what? Hjalmar Schacht, the go-slow Minister of Economics had already been shelved, and Hermann Göring, now promoted Field-Marshal, was in charge of the four-years-plan for making Germany, militarily and economically, ready for war. Reichswehr Minister Blomberg was retired, not so much because he was a go-slow man as because he married a young lady of lowly birth and thus offended the officers' corps; this was an irrelevant incident in the reshuffle of February 1938.

But Commander-in-Chief Baron von Fritsch, the head of the go-slow group in the army, who had tried to restrain Hitler from seizing the Rhineland, was dropped. Hitler appointed himself Supreme War Lord. A dozen other generals were dismissed. Their places, however, were taken by other orthodox soldiers, men with whom strategical considerations came first.

On the whole the February reshuffle seemed to be the second round of the contest between the full-steam-ahead group, headed by Party extremists, and the go-slow group, headed by the senior generals. This round ended, perhaps, as a draw, or as a slight win on points for the Party. The third round has yet to come.

And, as part of the reshuffle, Franz von Papen was cavalierly dismissed. Sitting in his Legation in Vienna he read that he had been retired, and took the first train to Berlin to see what had happened. I saw him go.

At last, after six years, this man seemed about to disappear finally from the European scene in which he had wrought such stupendous changes.

Not a bit of it. He, the instrument of destiny, who had

narrowly escaped with his life in June 1934, who had now been brusquely dismissed in 1938, was yet to play a decisive part in another great event. He, the Papal Chamberlain who had made the anti-Papist Hitler dictator of Germany, was about to bring Catholic Austria under the shadow of the same thrall.

An extraordinary episode. Diverted by a telegram, he left the train at Linz and rushed to that chalet in the Bavarian mountains where Hitler was waiting to see him, surrounded by his new generals and by his new full-steam-ahead adviser, Ribbentrop. Hitler, who had postponed his great speech from January 30th, the fifth anniversary, to February 20th, now had his reshuffle behind him and wanted something showy to offer Germany.

The same evening Papen was back in Vienna, and during the next four days I saw him busily coming and going between his Legation and the Chancery. The dismissed Envoy was deep in negotiation with Chancellor Kurt von Schuschnigg and his Assistant Foreign Minister Guido Schmidt, and I racked my brains to think what was afoot. On Thursday he made another lightning trip to the waiting Hitler at Berchtesgaden and again returned the same evening, and on Saturday the world learned that Schuschnigg, successor of the murdered Dollfuss, had gone to see Hitler at Berchtesgaden.

'Will you walk into my parlour?' said the spider to the fly. Who knows by what arguments Papen, the discredited minister, achieved this success a few days after his dismissal? Apparently he combined persuasion with dark hints. The present situation was intolerable, the Austrian Nazis had no more liberty than they had had before the Austro-German truce of July 1936, if disturbances occurred in Austria Hitler would certainly march in and support his followers; why not avert this catastrophe and go and arrange matters in a friendly talk with Hitler?

So Schuschnigg went and found Hitler surrounded by generals, and a good many troops in the offing, and for nine hours a storm of impassioned words, threats and reproaches, beat about him. Hitler demanded that he should release all his imprisoned Nazis, including men who had helped to murder his predecessor Doll-fuss, who had plotted his own death, who had schemed to provoke incidents that would bring about armed German intervention. He must give his Nazis liberty to demonstrate their political sympathies. As a pledge of his good faith he must appoint Arthur von Seyss-Inquart Police Minister.

And if he didn't? Then, said Hitler, he would frame his speech a week later accordingly, in its references to Austria, and the first time he saw good German Austrians being ill-treated by the Austrian Police simply for demonstrating their Germanic sympathies, he would march in. Schuschnigg need not think that France or England or Italy would support him. He stood alone. Germany could seize Austria with far less danger to herself than when she had occupied the Rhineland in 1936.

And Lord Halifax, added Hitler, was in full agreement with everything he, Hitler, might do about Austria or Czecho-slovakia.

Was it true? I doubt it. I was not present when Lord Halifax saw Hitler. But this gives you a good example of the sort of thing that ultimately springs from these British do-let's-try-and-get-together trips to dictators. Eden and Simon achieved nothing in 1935; but at least the British public was told the awful things that Hitler's tirade to them contained. The British Government has never dared to tell its public what Hitler said to Halifax. The 'conciliate Germany' group in England which brought about this visit had no programme, no idea of any particular thing that might result from it. They just thought it might do good, at any rate it couldn't do any harm, if Halifax went and talked to Hitler — who has a burning contempt for this kind of tactics and has repeatedly said that he will not allow himself to be trapped into time-saving conversations, to be ushered gently into a chair at a conference table and kept there.

The 'conciliate Germany' group possibly did not foresee the use to which this Halifax visit might be put, a few weeks later, in compelling the submission of Austria. But I don't think they would have cared, anyway. Up to now this is the only fruit of the meeting between Hitler and the kindly, courteous, god-fearing Halifax, who tamed Gandhi. Gandhi is a civilized human being with the instincts of a gentleman.

Schuschnigg yielded to relentless and overwhelming force. Three and a half years earlier Italy, the self-proclaimed protector of Austrian independence, mobilized an army on the frontier to warn Germany not to move. Now no Italian army was mobilized to deter Hitler, good friend Mussolini was away ski-ing and could not possibly be reached, the deadly foes Italy and Germany were bosom friends.

I saw Schuschnigg return from Berchtesgaden, his face set and grim. He had saved all he could. For three days — Hitler had given him a time-limit of four — Vienna buzzed with rumour. Guido Schmidt gave a great ball, the finest since the war, in the old Imperial Palace, where Maria Theresa and Francis Joseph had held sway, where the glasses from which the guests drank champagne still bore the eagles of Imperial Austria. The Envoys talked together in low voices, and from the corners of their eyes watched Schuschnigg and Schmidt and Seyss-Inquart. 'The Congress Dances.' They reminded each other of that night, long ago, when Napoleon landed from Elba, and all Europe trembled, and in Vienna the congress danced.

Next day the tall, blond, athletic Arthur von Seyss-Inquart, Hitler's nominee, was Police Minister. I had often talked about Austria with him over cups of coffee and he had told me how he had for years longed and worked for a better relationship with Germany, on the basis of an independent Austrian State, and had even had an appointment to discuss these matters with Dollfuss, who had cancelled it at the last moment, on the morning of the very day he was killed.

The prison doors opened to release all the imprisoned Nazis. I saw Anton Rintelen, aged and ill from the effects of his attempt at suicide, leave the hospital where he had been detained; he was the man whose name the Nazi raiders in the Radio Building shouted into the microphone as the new Chancellor

372

of Austria, while their fellows in the Chancery were killing Dollfuss.

And the Nazis came into the streets and shouted for Hitler and sang Nazi songs.

It was all over. The co-ordination of Austria with the Hitlerist Reich may proceed fast or slowly, but Austria has now come under the wing of the Reich, and her future, whether the name 'Austria' remains on the map or not, is inseparably linked with that of Germany.

I thought of these things as I listened to Hitler and watched my Viennese friends. Their faces showed respect as he recapitulated the deeds of National Socialism in the Reich, rising trade, falling unemployment, 'rearmament without its like in history'. They smiled involuntarily as he repeatedly poured derision and contempt on England.

I smiled too, ruefully, and wondered whether this speech would at last open England's eyes. True, it needed to be heard, the bitter satire, the volleys of laughter, cold print could never convey the full effect. He derided the well-fed incompetency of England, English cant in moralizing about the wickedness of war when England had obtained her empire by war and grab. He lavished contempt on people who thought that Germany's good behaviour or Germany's renunciation of her aims could be bought by credits, on people who thought of enticing Germany back into the League, and particularly on people who thought they could get him to the conference table.

What he said was absolutely candid and, from his angle, right. He was kicking the 'conciliate Germany' group in England in the pants, as hard as he could, over and over again.

Inwardly I prayed 'Let them hear this in England, and let it bring them to their senses'. But inwardly I knew that England would neither hear nor understand.

That evening the British radio announced that Hitler had made 'a friendly gesture to England'.

That same evening, before going to bed, I picked up a book that contained by chance Ernst Lissauer's Hymn of Hate.

Consider Ernst Lissauer for a moment. Like most people who preach war, he never knew and never could have known war. He was grotesquely fat, a figure of fun. For writing that poem, which all Germany was forced to learn, in the schoolroom and in the trenches, with which German soldiers were goaded on to the barbed wire, he was decorated by the Kaiser, became a national hero. After the war, when hating England was bad for trade, he was abused and pilloried until he left Germany and went to Vienna. He told me that he regretted writing the poem, and I believe it, for it ruined his livelihood. When war and hating England became popular again in Germany he did not profit, for his works were banned in Germany — not because of this warlike poem, but because he was a Jew.

But that poem, at the time it was written, perfectly depicted the German mind.

> We will never forgo our hate
> We have all but a single hate
> We love as one, we hate as one,
> We have one foe, and one alone —
> ENGLAND!

That was precisely the undernote of Hitler's speech that Sunday. I put it to my Viennese friends, and they agreed. A hundred million people heard the speech and smiled at the jibes. The next day all my Viennese acquaintances were asking me, 'Is England going to stand that?'

And the British Radio announced that Hitler had made 'a friendly gesture to England'.

But that was not the worst. He made two bitterly sarcastic references to Anthony Eden by name. That was between noon and three o'clock. At five I sat down and wrote to a friend in England saying I was sure that Berlin had heard that Eden's resignation was likely, and that the references to him had been included so that this, too, could appear as a success for Hitler.

At midnight I walked down the Kärntnerstrasse. Nazis had been marching about all over the town, cheering Hitler, celebrating their regained liberty, and I had watched them. Outside St. Stephen's I met Robert Best of the American United Press. 'Hey,' he said, 'have you heard that Eden's resigned?'

It was incredible. It looked as if the whole British Cabinet had been sitting round the loudspeaker that Sunday afternoon and, when Hitler had finished, had turned to Eden and said, 'Well Anthony, you hear what the Führer says?'

England seems to have lost the instinct for the effect of these things upon millions of people all over Europe who still, hoping against hope, look to England for leadership. On the one hand they see a triumphant Hitler, imparting in hoarse accents his lesson of hatred and war, proclaiming his success in Austria, making sinister hints about the future, deriding England and jibing at England's Foreign Minister. On the other hand they see, a few hours later, the resignation of that Minister and the grateful acknowledgment of Hitler's 'friendly gesture to England'.

Masochism is the only word that fits it.

Eden resigned rather than go cap-in-hand to Italy. Hitler's methods about Austria had possibly at last opened the eyes of British Ministers. At all events a school of thought formed which was for bringing Italy back at all costs into the company of resisters against large-scale aggression in Europe. It was, these people thought, the last hope of forming a solid front strong enough to daunt and deter Germany. To reach it they seemed ready to recognize Abyssinia, to close an eye to the great Italian army in Spain, probably to give Italy a loan.

Eden resigned, saying that this Gadarene policy was hopeless. It only took you farther and quicker down the slope. The time had come to resist blackmail, for England to stand fast. He was right, a thousand times right. He was overborne by the company of black-coated, elderly gentlemen about him, who were still convinced of the value of those methods on which Hitler had poured such derision a few hours before — negotiation, conference, conciliation.

375

The tragic thing is that at the time Eden made his stand it was probably irrelevant which policy England pursued. The course of coming events is clear and obvious; the tragedy moves like a Greek drama, with every new event — Austria, Hitler's speech, Eden's resignation — falling into its allotted place with dreary inevitability. The English policy of hoping that the avalanche will stop in the middle of its path and go off at right angles, or recede, is vain. Still, it would have been better for the spirit of England in coming ordeals if England had been staunch and unyielding this time, at long last.

But all that happened was that, the day after Hitler had jeered at Eden and England and particularly at those good people who thought they could tie him up in negotiations or immobilize him at a conference table, Neville Chamberlain got up and disinterred from the dead past the Halifax-Hitler meeting, saying he hoped it had been the starting point to negotiations which would one day be usefully renewed.

Well, well. I walked to my rooms, and as I passed through the Kärntnerstrasse, where the Nazis had been uproariously celebrating Hitler's speech a few hours before, I looked back along the long long trail of dangers ignored and opportunities missed. I thought of Armistice Night in France and my misgivings then, and of my years in Republican Germany when I found them confirmed, and then of my trip to England and of my influential friend who warmed his behind at an empty grate and said, 'I think you are wrong. I think Hitler will prove a force for peace in Europe, like Mussolini'. And then I thought of Stresa, Geneva, Abyssinia, Spain, Austria, and looked ahead to the morrow — Czechoslovakia . . .

In his speech after the Black Sunday of Hitler's oration and Eden's resignation, Chamberlain rang the death knell of the League and of collective action against an aggressor. The ghost of Abyssinia had risen to haunt England, which fled before it from Geneva. The great Conservative majority, elected by an enthusiastic England on the promise that

England would lead the nations ranked in the League against the Italian aggressor in Abyssinia, voted solidly for the abandonment of the League. Thanks to the inspiring effect of that cry in the late autumn of 1935, it was impregnable in Parliament and had another three years to run. England, which had put it there to lead the League of Nations against the aggressor, had no word to say· in the complete reversal of that policy. Public opinion seemed still to be numbed and apathetic from the shock of the Hoare-Laval plan for the partitioning of Abyssinia, sprung on it immediately after that election.

Now England was embarked on the course of negotiation with the predatory martial dictatorships, which had pocketed Abyssinia, which had fastened their fangs in Spain, which had declared their support for the Japanese in China, which had browbeaten Austria and now menaced Czechoslovakia, which poured derision on the decadence of democracies, which jeered at attempts to lure them into conference. Italy, who was determined to break the British stranglehold on the Suez Canal and the British supremacy in the Mediterranean; Germany, who wanted the British colonies; Mussolini and Hitler, who had worked incessantly to bring about the downfall of Eden; England was to get together with them and, by some magic formula, to induce them to leave her in peace and acquiesce in that 'general settlement in Europe' which Hitler had repeatedly refused to consider.

It is in the nature of great empires to decline and fall. Apparently men do not fight to defend wealth and prosperity and great possessions. They fight when they haven't got these things. To hold such a great empire, in your hands, I should have thought ought to be the greatest inducement to fight for it, providing that you use it well. But if you let it lie fallow and unpeopled, and leave your unemployed to vegetate in Special Areas, and fill your papers with pictures of a few wealthy people playing golf and tennis and hunting and drinking cocktails, you must expect other people, who run their own countries better and are avid for more territory, to take it from you. Perhaps you will make a fight for it; perhaps you will hand it to them on a salver; but the result will be the same.

The morning after that Black Sunday a Jewish acquaintance, a man I had known rich and powerful in pre-Hitler Berlin and who now lived in Vienna and was wondering whether he would have to pack again and move on somewhere else, telephoned to me in great agitation. 'I must see you and have a talk about these events in England,' he said. 'I still cannot believe that England is going to pursue this policy of poltroonery to the end, to abandon one position after another, to let herself be insulted and abused with impunity.'

'Can't you,' I asked, 'can't you believe your eyes?'

'No, I can't,' he answered, 'in spite of everything — not yet.'

CHAPTER 45

FADE OUT

I HAVE taken you a long way round Insanity Fair and kept you waiting far too long at some of the sideshows, which interested me, and have megaphoned my opinions about them at you until you must be nearly deaf, and most irritable, and longing for your cup of tea. Let's go, taking a last look back as we pass.

Look at the strong men, feeling their biceps, throwing shadows so much bigger than themselves. Look at the funny men, little gesticulating figures. Look at the people on the Foreign Policy Roundabouts, going round and round in vicious circles. Look at the man on the moving platform at the Westminster Sideshow; he marches and marches but stays always where he is. Hark to the shrieks coming from League House, with its collapsing stairway paved with good resolutions. Hark to those brazen organs all playing against each other. Look at the lights. Look at the crowds, shuffling, shoving, watching the three-card-trick man bemusedly, listening with sheepish grins to the cocksure showman, following him sheep-like when he turns and leads the way into the tent.

It's a great life.

INDEX

ALBRECHT, DR., 134 f.
ALEXANDER I, (OBRENOVITCH) 255, 257, 258, 259, 273
—— II, (KARAGEORGEVITCH) 221, 257, 260, 276, 361
—— OF GREECE, 283
ALOISI, BARON, 228
ANDRASSY, COUNT, 238, 332
ANTONESCU, 324
APPONYI, COUNT, 332
ARAS, RUSHDI, 301
ASQUITH, LORD, 59

BALDWIN, EARL, 186, 187, 191
BANFFY, COUNT, 332
BARTHOU, LOUIS, 221
BARTLETT, VERNON, 208
BENES, PRESIDENT, 211, 304-6, 308, 311, 315
BEST, ROBERT, 375
BETHMANN-HOLWEG, THEOBALD VON, 73
BIRCHALL, FREDERICK, 224
BISMARCK, 71, 101, 270, 312, 352, 353, 361
BLOMBERG, GENERAL VON, 173, 179, 369
BORIS, KING, 270 f.
BOURNE, SIR ROLAND, 64
BRAUN, OTTO, 120
BRIAND, ARISTIDE, 73, 274
BRÜNING, HEINRICH, 90, 92, 100, 109, 110, 112-13, 149
BÜLOW, PRINCE VON, 332
BÜNGER, LORD CHIEF JUSTICE, 136
BURROWS, ARTHUR, 236
BUTLER, NEVILLE, 224

CADOGAN, SIR ALEXANDER, 297
CAMPBELL, SIR RONALD, 266
CANTACUZINO, GENERAL, 322
CAROL I, KING, 319
CAROL II, KING, 316 f.
CHAMBERLAIN, AUSTEN, 71, 72
—— JOSEPH, 71
—— NEVILLE, 71, 376
CHRISTIANSEN, AIRMAN-GENERAL, 141
CIANO, COUNT, 250

CODREANU, CORNELIU, 321
CONSTANTINE, KING, 281 f.
CRIPPS, SIR STAFFORD, 363
CROWE, SIR EYRE, 352, 355
CUMMINGS, A. J., 197

DALTON, DR., 363
DELMER, SEFTON, 97, 131, 209
'DEUTSCHLAND', THE, 90-1
DIMIETRIEVITCH, COLONEL (APIS), 256, 257, 268, 273, 277
DIMITROFF, 132 f.
DOLLFUSS, DR., 221, 246, 249, 250, 252, 342, 370, 372-3
THE DO.X, 69, 141
DRAGA, QUEEN, 255, 258
DURANTY, WALTER, 224

EBBUTT, NORMAN, 208, 209
EDEN, ANTHONY, 188, 189, 191, 192, 194, 199, 200, 201, 202, 203, 204, 210, 212, 213, 214, 298, 341, 360, 371, 374-7
EDWARD VII, 18
EINSTEIN, ALBERT, 157
ERNST, KARL, 166-7

FARINACCI, 346
FEY, MAJOR, 249
FITZGERALD, MAJOR, 26
FLANDIN, 221, 222
FORWOOD, DUDLEY, 338
FOWLER WRIGHT, 5, 309
FRANCE, ANATOLE, 256
FRANCIS JOSEPH, EMPEROR, 237, 238, 239, 240, 372
FRANCO, GENERAL, 346, 347
FRANZ FERDINAND, 256, 270, 271, 275, 330
FRENCH, SIR JOHN, 26

GANDHI, 372
GEDYE, G. E. R., 280
GEMPP (BERLIN FIRE CHIEF), 133
GEORGE II OF GREECE, 280 f.
GEORGE V, 254, 273, 352
GEORGE VI, 335
GHEORGHIEFF, VLADA, 262, 263, 276, 278

GILBERT, PARKER, 68
GLADSTONE, W. E., 63
GLOUCESTER, DUKE OF, 287
GÖBBELS, DR., 87, 119, 120, 144-5, 158, 164, 168, 177, 179, 309, 335
GOEMBOES, GENERAL, 331
GOGA, OCTAVIAN, 322
GORDON-LENNOX, V., 197, 211, 214
GÖRING, HERMANN, 126, 132, 136, 138, 144, 148, 165, 179, 189, 252-3, 259, 368-9
GREENWOOD, ARTHUR, 363
GREISER, HERR, 302
GUNTHER, JOHN, 208

HAILE SELASSIE, 301, 342
HALIFAX, LORD, 251, 360, 361, 371-2, 376
HAYNAU, GENERAL, 351
HEINE, HEINRICH, 181-2
HEINES, 87, 89, 98, 160-73
HENDERSON, SIR NEVILE, 254, 259, 361, 362
HILTON, JOHN, 43
HINDENBURG, PRESIDENT, 73-80, 90, 100, 105, 108, 110-13, 114, 115, 120, 121, 122, 126, 128, 132, 143, 144, 146, 147, 168, 171, 177, 178, 179, 180, 181, 182, 322
HITLER, ADOLF, 72, 78, 82, 89, 92, 94, 96-99, 101, 105, 109, 118, 119, 128, 131, 132, 134, 143, 144, 146, 147, 148, 149, 153, 154, 164, 165, 166, 170, 171, 173, 177, 178, 179, 182, 188, 191, 192, 198, 204, 209, 210, 213, 214, 230, 233, 234, 236, 237, 244, 246, 247, 248, 249, 250, 251, 252-3, 273, 284, 293, 296, 307, 313, 326, 349, 351, 360, 361, 368-9, 371-7
HOARE, SIR SAMUEL, 343, 344, 359, 377
HODZA, DR., 236, 311
HORTHY, ADMIRAL, 331

JAGOW, VON, 141
JEWS IN GERMANY, 151-9

KAAS, PRELATE, 150
KARL, EMPEROR, 330
KAROLYI, COUNT, 332
KENT, DUKE OF, 287
KHUEN-HEDERVARY, COUNT, 332
KITCHENER, LORD, 26, 27, 286

KNICKERBOCKER, H. R., 208, 224
KONDYLIS, GENERAL, 281
KRUGER, PRESIDENT, 354
KRUPPS, 92

LANDRU, 55
LANGHOFF, WOLFGANG, 87, 88
LANSING, ROBERT, 115
LANSBURY, GEORGE, 189
LAVAL, PIERRE, 221, 222, 230, 344, 377
LEBRUN, PRESIDENT, 273
LEOPOLD II, KING, 366
LIDDELL HART, 350
LIEBKNECHT, KARL, 82
LISSAUER, ERNST, 373-4
LITVINOFF, 198, 199, 202, 228, 229, 236, 296, 301
LLOYD GEORGE, 59, 191, 294, 349
LONDONDERRY, LORD, 192
LOW, DAVID, 166, 216, 362
LUBBE, MARIUS VAN DER, 132 f.
LUDENDORFF, GENERAL, 44, 75, 106
LUPESCU, MME., 321
LUX, STEPHEN, 302
LUXEMBOURG, ROSA, 82

MACDONALD, RAMSAY, 110, 220, 221, 222, 223, 224, 225, 343
MACFADDENS, BERNARR, 69
MASARYK, JAN, 303 f.
MEMORY, F. W., 205, 206, 211
MESTROVIC, IVAN, 258, 267, 268
METAXAS, GENERAL, 284 f.
MICHAILOFF, IVANTCHO, 262, 263
MOSLEY, SIR OSWALD, 349
MOWRER, EDGAR, 208
MUSSOLINI, 207, 220, 221, 223, 236, 248, 250, 251, 253, 265, 284, 300, 340, 342, 349, 357, 372, 376-7

NEURATH, BARON VON, 185, 340, 369
NORTHCLIFFE, LORD, 57-61

OCHS, ADOLF, 65
OLDENBURG-JANUSCHAU, 120, 125
OSSIETZKY, KARL VON, 131, 177
OTTO, GRAND DUKE, 331

PALMERSTON, LORD, 351
PAPEN, FRANZ VON, 111, 114-27, 146, 163, 168, 171, 252-3, 322, 360, 369-70
PAUL OF YUGOSLAVIA, PRINCE, 264, 265

PAUL-BONCOUR, 296, 298, 301
PETER, KING, 259, 260, 262, 264, 265
PETERS, HAROLD, 280
PILSUDSKI, MARSHAL, 211
POPOFF, 132 f.
PRIESTLEY, J. B., 219
PRINCIP, GABRIEL, 258

RADITCH, STEFAN, 261
REICHSTAG FIRE, 131-42, 148, 190
REINHARDT, MAX, 157, 247
REITH, SIR JOHN, 334
RIBBENTROP, JOACHIM VON, 125, 367-70
RINTELEN, ANTON, 372
ROCHEFOUCAULD, LA, 285
RÖHM, ERNST, 87, 97, 98, 160-73
ROTHSCHILD, BARON, 334

SAMUEL, SIR HERBERT, 190
SCHACHT, HJALMAR, 369
SCHLEICHER, KURT VON, 100, 111, 120, 122, 123, 125-7, 161, 167, 172, 174
SCHMIDT, GUIDO, 370, 372
SCHRATT, KATHERINA, 240
SCHUSCHNIGG, KURT VON, 252-3, 370-2
SELBY, SIR WALFORD, 334, 337
SEYSS-INQUART, ARTUR VON, 253, 371-2
SIMON, SIR JOHN, 188, 189, 191, 192, 204, 212, 222, 228, 229, 230, 300, 341, 343, 360, 371
SNOWDEN, VISCOUNTESS, 209
STALIN, 166, 200, 202, 213, 214
STAMBULISKY, 275, 276
STANLEY, LORD, 296, 297, 301
STARHEMBERG, PRINCE, 182, 249
STEED, WICKHAM, 304
STELESCU, MICHAEL, 321

STOYADINOVITCH, MILAN, 264, 266, 324, 326
STRASSER, GREGOR, 123, 124, 174
STREICHER, JULIUS, 87, 153
STEPHENS, PEMBROKE, 280
STREIT, 287
STRESEMANN, GUSTAV, 70, 72, 73
SUVICH, 221, 248

TANEFF, 132 f.
TATERESCU, 320
THÄLMANN, 94
THURTLE, ERNEST, 363
TISZA, COUNT, 332
TITULESCU, 228, 236, 297, 319
TORGLER, 117, 132, 139
TOSCANINI, ARTURO, 247
TZANKOFF, PROFESSOR, 276, 278

VANSITTART, SIR ROBERT, 230
VELTCHEFF, COLONEL, 276, 177
VENIZELOS, 282 f.
VICTORIA, QUEEN, 351
VOLTAIRE, 236

WALTER, BRUNO, 157, 247
WATSON, SETON, 304
WEBER, WALTER, 133
WELLS, H. G., 359
WELS, OTTO, 149, 150
WENDT, ALBERT, 134 f.
WHEELER-BENNETT, JOHN, 111
WILHELM II, KAISER, 92, 173, 284, 288, 312, 332, 353, 368
WINDSOR, DUKE OF, 207, 236, 247, 334 f.

ZETKIN, CLARA, 117, 118
ZHIVKOVITCH, 255, 257
ZINOVIEFF LETTER, 190